Gottfried Keller

STORIES

The German Library : Volume 44

Volkmar Sander, General Editor

Gottfried Keller

STORIES

Edited by Frank G. Ryder
Foreword by Max Frisch

CONTINUUM · NEW YORK

1982

The Continuum Publishing Company
575 Lexington Avenue, New York, NY 10022

Copyright © 1982 by The Continuum Publishing Company

Foreword © 1982 by Max Frisch
Introduction © 1982 by Frank G. Ryder

Printed in the United States of America

Library of Congress Cataloging in Publication Data

Keller, Gottfried, 1819–1890.
Stories.

(The German library; v. 44)
Contents: The three righteous combmakers / translated
by Robert M. Browning—A village Romeo and Juliet /
translated by Paul Bernard Thomas and adapted by Frank
G. Ryder—Mirror, the cat / translated by Robert M.
Browning—[etc.]
I. Ryder, Frank Glessner, 1916–   II. Title.
PT2374.A2   1982   833'.8   81-22067
ISBN 0-8264-0256-9   AACR2
ISBN 0-8264-0266-6 pbk

For acknowledgments of previously published material, see page 369,
which constitutes an extension of the copyright page.

Contents

From SEVEN LEGENDS:

Foreword

How an American reader will feel as he turns the pages of this volume I can only guess. The world of these stories is so foreign to him. More foreign perhaps than Latin America. And these people— what is he supposed to find interesting about them? The assurance that Gottfried Keller is one of the greatest writers of fiction in the German language is not going to make any difference. This isn't the way we feel today; it isn't the way we live today. A bygone world, then. . . .

An idyll?

Assuming that the American reader still has this volume in his hands, I would like to point out to him that Gottfried Keller fought for liberalism but was not naive; he soon grew bitterly apprehensive that middle-class liberalism, the great social achievement of his century, might disintegrate into a profit society pure and simple, without utopias, without transcendent values. And that is what we have today. Or so I fear. If you read further you will find there is something strangely disturbing about these stories: One life after another ends in quiet failure. You won't notice it immediately because the man who tells these tales has a sense of humor. He likes people even though he sees through them. He is kind. He knows a lot about the relationship between money and morals, for example, and he doesn't cover it up; because he still has hope.

His country, Switzerland, is proud of him.

He would be horrified at his country—as he would be at other "democracies" as well.

And in those days storytelling was slow and leisurely—not for readers in the subway, but for readers in their armchairs at home, with nothing planned for whole evenings but reading; with no interruptions for listening to the TV news. This relaxed narrative style, something that Keller shares with other great storytellers of the nineteenth century, makes us nervous. The only time we have that much patience is when we're in the hospital. I must also confess: The country and the city (my own native city) and the villages that are the setting of his stories are as remote from me as Tolstoi's Russia. Why do we read Tolstoi or Balzac or Melville? Insight into human nature is, I believe, impossible unless human nature is seen in the light of its historically determined context, and this historical context becomes that much clearer when it differs from our own. Distance makes for sharper insight. Naturally it is more comfortable—and comfort is something one has a right to, after all—to read stories set in our own lifetime, in our own surroundings; everything seems so obvious. The fact that human behavior is historically determined scarcely enters our minds; we can, as the expression goes, immediately identify with the characters. What we are really doing is luxuriating in self-delusion.

Literature as Polaroid snapshots?

That's not what the classics are for.

Seldwyla:

There's no place in Switzerland by that name; there never was. Keller invented it. *Switzerland* is a geographical historical political administrative term, a handy label for use in tourism and patriotism; *Seldwyla* is a term for a place where the *condition humaine* becomes visible. *Swissair,* yes; but there's no *Seldwyla Air;* the only way to get there is by reading.

I feel strange, acting as a press agent for Gottfried Keller. If he could hear me it would make him grumpy. He would drain his glass, without a word, without looking at me, and then in all modesty he would get up, this man with the short legs, and leave his tavern; and out in the street, in the night air, he would shake his head over so much busy-ness.

MAX FRISCH

Introduction

He was a remarkably small man, not well-proportioned, but aggressive and surprisingly strong. He was quick-tempered and quick to fall in love. In fights, inevitably with larger men, he fared well. He was drawn to women who were young, tall, and attractive—at least one of them a renowned beauty. Here his luck was uniformly bad. As a youth he was aimless, quarrelsome, and notably disinclined to support himself. Even as a grown man he remained gruff and socially ill at ease, suffered from long bouts of indolence and depression, drank (and fought) too much to suit most people—indeed the scandalous news of one of his escapades seems to have triggered his fiancée's suicide. He was painfully aware of all his shortcomings but never able fully to overcome them. This is *one* Gottfried Keller and the portrait is not exaggerated.

The other Keller is a giant: in the literature of his own country, Switzerland, and in the entire canon of German writing. Despite his misspent youth and the vagaries of his early career, he was to become one of the highest civil servants of his native Zurich. And despite his quirks of personality, he was gifted with unsparing but sensitive insight into human nature, his own and others', and with bristling integrity. Those qualities are the twin sources of his mastery as a writer and the determinants of a humor which ranges from the gently ironic to what would be grotesque if it were not so painfully sad.

Almost everything he wrote is strongly autobiographical: "I have never produced anything which did not have its impetus in my outer and inner life." His vision of the principal foibles and occasional virtues of ordinary people was established by observation, but even more by introspection, in the main during his youth in Zurich and in two years of seemingly fruitless study in Munich. It matured as Keller matured, slowly, painfully, and with frequent remissions. Only after six more years at home and seven years of another, more propitious venture into the larger world (Heidelberg and Berlin) was his vision strong enough to sustain literary creativity. The great narrative works began to appear in 1855 and 1856, when Keller, born in 1819, was over thirty-five. He is not among the precocious writers.

Indeed by age twenty he had still never left home. He had not finished school and had no training. "I have nothing I can do," he said. "I see no way I can get ahead." An unhappy, almost disabling pattern of dependence on his mother (later, on his sister) was well established. Keller's failure to develop a sense of purpose and independence was not simply a failure of will. But it was not all a matter of bad luck either. One of the recurring figures of his narrative world is the young man who, out of petulance or inertia, or simple passivity, refuses to take initiative in the determining of his own fate and is rescued from this paralysis—if at all—only by crisis.

Still, the bad luck was almost unremitting. He had to grow up without a father, and the loss was substantial. Johann Rudolf Keller had not merely been a skilled artisan (a cabinetmaker); he was a man of broad and active interests, particularly in education and literature, and a writer of poetry. His death in his early thirties, when Keller was five, deprived the family not only of guidance and resources but of happiness and domestic stability. His mother remarried—her chief journeyman in the business she inherited from her husband—but not happily. Divorce ended a relationship which clouded rather than illumined Keller's life and her own. The boy cherished an idealized memory of his father and never forgave his mother for remarrying.

The course of Keller's schooling and professional training is largely a history of frustration and waste—although it started well enough. His father had been a kind of trustee of what was somewhat uncompromisingly called the Poor School, a private establishment designed to make up for the absence of good public instruction for children of needy families. Keller was enrolled in this school and he enjoyed it, learning easily and rapidly. In 1831, however, his mother transferred him to the *Landknabeninstitut,* essentially a trade school, and one which precluded thoughts of university study. Here Keller felt inferior and excluded. He was referring to these and the immediately succeeding years when he said that the record of his "encounter with the rest of the world" was one of "uninterrupted failure."

Keller's fate in his next school was doubly traumatic. Despite his continuing sense of alienation he remained, academically, a good student; he was prepared to work and do well. But he did not have the opportunity. Fellow students talked him into joining a demonstration against a radical and unpopular mathematics teacher. Almost inadvertently, Keller ended up leading a sort of protest parade. He was identified (wrongly) as the ringleader, and promptly expelled. "To exclude a child from public education," he wrote later, "is tantamount to choking off his inner development, his intellectual life."

His expulsion meant that Keller had to choose *some* occupation without having finished training for *any*. He had written plays and poetry, had tried his hand at art and been apprenticed to one painter, tutored by another. Although literature was his first interest, Keller had made substantial progress in his painting, especially with his second teacher (who unfortunately decamped). He decided—a bold choice for one of his background—to become a landscape artist.

After two more years spent largely in idling about at home, he insisted upon his share of a small inheritance and went to Munich to study. His life there was pleasant enough, if erratic, but the training he received was unproductive. He got none in his chosen field of landscape, and he literally could not afford trips into the countryside. So he resorted to painting from memory and from his own portfolio of Swiss sketches. All this brought him no income, of course. He was paid for painting flagpoles for a royal Bavarian wedding. And the Munich Art Society offered to buy one of his oils, but Keller, having decided to make a few minor changes, set the canvas out to dry by a fire, where it burned. During this entire time he was living off his tiny inheritance—and his mother. At one point, in order to continue his studies, he persuaded her to mortgage her house and send him the proceeds. He associated mostly with the Swiss colony in Munich, wrote for their little weekly, became seriously ill (with typhus), indulged his proclivities for fighting, and finally, no longer able to pay for his room, was evicted and went home. It was November, 1842. Keller was twenty-three.

The bleak diagnosis of three years before was seemingly still in force: "nothing I can do . . . no way I can get ahead." And all the first winter back in Zurich—it is his own word—he "vegetated." But from his feelings of anger and misery over wasted time and of guilt toward his mother, came the resolve to write a sort of confessional novel. The end result is one of the greatest works in a great and strongly German genre, the *Bildungsroman* or developmental novel. The first version of *Green Henry* [*Der grüne Heinrich*] was not published until 1855, but it is the main source for our knowledge, not of the precise facts of Keller's early life, but of the state of his mind and spirit. It is a record of frustration and guilt. The young painter Heinrich Lee comes to doubt his mission in life, the value of art, and the order of the world. He despairs and fails, and in failing drags down his friends, his mother, and himself. (The second version is less somber.)

During the next years in Zurich, before the renewal of his studies at Heidelberg in 1848, Keller turned increasingly to literature, at first imitatively, then independently, even aggressively. His anticonservative political poetry was matched by his participation in two questionable, putsch-like marches on Lucerne, where the conservative government was in open strife with the radical opposition. Keller went along; he was armed.

The marchers never reached Lucerne, but the entire abortive operation helps to explain Keller's concern, in *The Lost Smile,* with political agitation and conflict—by that time with a quite different bias. In 1845 and 1846, when many of his poems were published in a journal of German liberal emigrés, Keller received his first honorarium. Those years before 1848 were formative ones. His career was decided; he made some of his most lasting friendships; he met one of his most serious loves (to whom he never declared himself)—and he compensated for continuing depression with bouts of drinking and fighting. He fell hopelessly in love once more, this time with a tall, beautiful, and much younger woman, who roundly rejected him. The frank confession of love, the admission of hurt, the defense of love itself, despite the hurt, the recognition of the maturing effect of rejection—all remind one of his stories and of characters such as Strapinski, Jocundus, Karl.

It is a curious coincidence that this emotional maturing came at a time of increasing political sophistication, and that the year 1848, when Keller began to gain real public recognition, also brought revolution to Europe, revolution which Keller compared unfavorably with the political ferment that led at the same time to the establishment of the Swiss Confederation. Keller had already served on a volunteer basis in the cantonal offices where he would later be first secretary. Now, through the intervention of government officials, professors, and friends he was given a government fellowship to study in Heidelberg.

Obviously there is much left to tell of Keller's life, but all the foundations were now laid for his career, and he rightly identified this period as a "turning point in my destiny." The foundations were likewise laid for all of the later works—not for their execution or even their specific outlines, but for the characters and themes that mark them and the attitude toward the human condition that informs them.

To concentrate on Keller's early life risks detracting from the picture of his accomplishment, by showing only its genesis and not its fruition. In Heidelberg he associated, almost for the first time, with his intellectual equals: the anthropologist Henle, the literary and cultural historian Hettner, the philosopher Feuerbach. It was Feuerbach who supervised Keller's "conversion," not perhaps to atheism, but to a thorough and urgent secularism: "The world has become infinitely more beautiful and deeper to me, life more precious and intense, death more serious and sobering, now and for the first time challenging me with all its force to fulfill my mission in life, to cleanse and satisfy my conscience, since I have no prospect, anywhere at all, of making up for lost opportunities."

In Berlin from 1850 to 1855 he sustained his greatest burst of writing: *Green Henry, The People of Seldwyla I,* plans for *Seven Legends* and other works. But he was still poor, even hungry. He was still combative—one fight got him a police record. He was still alienated—two years without a letter home. He was still carried away by unattainable feminine beauty. But he was working, and his fellowship was renewed. He was even offered a professorship of literature and art history at the new Zurich Polytechnic. As he had once advised Luise Rieter not to marry him (even if she were so inclined), so now he refused the professorship, saying he was not qualified. It went to the eminent critic and writer, Friedrich Theodor Vischer, later his friend.

His return to Zurich, however, was in some ways like a relapse into earlier miseries. Before he could leave Berlin, friends had to save him from debtor's prison, and his mother had to send her last money to pay for his trip home. For the next six years he was still basically dependent on her and on his sister, though he was increasingly respected as a writer and increasingly well acquainted in literary and musical circles.

In 1861, when Keller was 42, he was, to his apparent surprise, elected First Secretary of the Canton of Zurich (and later member of the Cantonal Council), an office in which he served with distinction—but also with frequent lapses and consequent scandal, most prominently connected with his two old vices: fighting and drinking. Of one noteworthy excursion, Keller reports that he and a friend consumed (besides considerable food): "eight glasses of beer, two mugs of wine, two bottles of wine, two glasses of grog."

Keller's position was a responsible one. It kept him productively busy—somewhat impeding his literary career in the process—and encouraged in the former liberal-radical the unfolding of a broadly conservative philosophy of constitutional government, traditional values, and individual self-reliance. This view is implicit in *The Lost Smile*.

In 1876 Keller retired with sufficient income from his books to permit a life of independent writing. He rejected the trappings of fame. In his fiftieth year, however, he accepted an honorary doctorate from the University of Zurich. His seventieth birthday was widely—to him, embarrassingly—celebrated. Keller died in 1890. His heirs were the Zurich University Foundation, the City Library, and the Winkelried Foundation.

Perhaps because his work is so autobiographical, Keller's view of the human condition is largely consistent and cohesive. He is an observer of the life around him; but he is not a detached observer. Keller looks first inside himself, seeing his own flaws and foibles, and then outside, observing, usually with regret, the effect of his own character upon the lives of others. The consistency of this view is rendered eloquent by the immediacy and contemporaneity of Keller's work.

His characters are for the most part ordinary people in ordinary situations. His great contemporary Meyer wrote of famous men and portentous times: Beckett, Pescara, the Renaissance, the Reformation. Keller never did. Even the Naturalists, soon in the ascendancy, could scarcely claim greater verisimilitude.

Interestingly, Keller thought little of Naturalism. One suspects this is because he is, in a way, strongly didactic or hortatory—not a mere "reporter." What he hoped to attain, the heart of his message, is best summed up in his reaction to Feuerbach's teaching: a fully secularized view of this world as our only one, and the effective elimination of a personal god and of any thought of an afterlife. Keller believed that, armed with these insights and freed of delusion, one could actively pursue a useful and happy life.

It is a question whether Keller himself ever really attained this goal. His characters rarely do. When and where in his fictive work does it in fact happen? Where cats talk and wise owls help them overcome witches! Or when the Virgin Mary intercedes and does what the feckless "hero" can't! A few women seem by their better natures to possess the gift: Bertrade in *Seven Legends,* Hermine in *The Upright Seven,* Nettie in *Clothes Make the Man.* A very few men make it, on tortuous paths and at great cost. The surpassing integrity Keller sought, the happiness of independence and a clear conscience, exists, in pure form, in the transplanted world of fairy tales and myths.

Elsewhere, Keller records the inexhaustible capacity of human beings to avoid decisive action, undermine their own happiness, frustrate what might be their good fortune and delude themselves by hiatuses of logic and action:

> Bertrade . . . was famous in German lands for her wealth as well as her beauty. Since she also exhibited great modesty and friendliness toward everyone, [she] seemed to all noblemen . . . easy to win, and many a one, when he had once seen her, asked himself why she was not already his wife.

> Zendelwald was . . . indolent in deed and word. When his mind and heart had become set on something . . . he could not make himself take the first step to bring about its reali-

zation, for the matter seemed to him settled when he was inwardly certain about it.

The humor with which Keller portrays such shortcomings of mind and character exhibits a startling range. The gentle irony of poor Zendelwald's divinely sponsored emergence from fecklessness is almost matched by Strapinski's progress from grateful passivity to mercantile success-cum-revenge. But the latter, being more like Keller, has to pass through existential crisis, to the edge of despair, before Nettie helps him to pull himself together. Karl in *The Upright Seven* is one of the few males who seem to travel a relatively short and painless road from comparative indolence to active self-assurance. At the other end of the spectrum the humor is almost savage—but never black. The picture of man's folly is devastating. The three combmakers are not so much portrayed as stripped and pilloried: mindlessly intent on a stupid and trivial goal of material gain, they fall victim to one of Keller's most terrifyingly shallow, remorselessly dominating females. Their mad descent to virtual subhumanity is no less cruelly funny for being largely self-inflicted.

In general it may be said that the typical history of Keller's male protagonist begins with spoiled indolence, self-delusion, disabling passivity; from there it runs straight downhill, like the combmakers, to crisis and despair—from which he either expires or, with desperate effort and considerable assistance, recovers. In effect there is no salvation until the last crutch of dependence is removed—or replaced by the love and support of a woman. If he is lucky, Keller's "hero" at long last abandons illusion and asserts independence, initiative, and responsibility, moving from passive guilt to a kind of altruism or at least to a recognition of his obligations.

Keller's portrayal of women is on balance more favorable than his depiction of men. Apparently his own unhappy love life did not embitter him. But the gallery is not homogeneous, nor uniformly flattering. Züs is a bizarre monument to *libido dominandi,* clutter-headed, parched, and vain.

Justine's mother in *The Lost Smile* has an equally unsinkable spirit of dominion and is in her way as repressive, but she is more nearly civilized. It is, in Keller's world, a curious reversal of roles when Eugenia's silly venture into women's rule is set sharply to rights by an uncomplicatedly stalwart man; or when Justine yields to her husband's insistence upon self-reliance. Most of his women, in fact, are relatively strong and independent, ready to devote themselves to the less sturdy male of the species, essentially compassionate: Nettie, Hermine, Bertrade. No woman has to be roused from the torpor of passivity. None has to or does "reform" except Manz's wife.

It is a tribute to Keller's lack of sentimentality that even in these good—or better—women the glint of steel remains. Of Hermine he says: "Something stern and tyrannical gleamed amid the laughing sweetness of her glance and two spirits spoke eloquently in the gleam: one was the commanding will, but with it was fused the promise of a reward, and out of that fusion arose something new and mysterious. 'Do my will. I have more to give than you dream,' said those eyes." This could have been written of Nettie. It is one of Keller's most mature perceptions of the eternal feminine.

Verena as Juliet is a special case, just as *A Village Romeo and Juliet* is itself a special work. For if we accept the irreconcilability of their dilemma, she and Sali live out the tragedy—or rather the ultimate pathos—of love without hope or prospect in this world, but a love that cannot be denied. Verena's very passion is itself exceptional. Keller's narrative world contains no slave of love, no *femme fatale*, no betrayer; no Phaedra, no Carmen, no Delilah.

Keller describes people as they (too often) are and as they should be (but often aren't); he also describes society as it is and speculates on what made it that way and what (if anything) can be done about it.

Like many fictions grounded in a highly specific environment—Balzac's in Paris, Joyce's in Dublin, Hesiod's in Boeotia—Keller's fictions, though set in his native Switzerland, reflect more general concerns. Swiss absorption in things and money may be legendary, but it stands, *pars pro toto,* for materialism everywhere. The hope for gain moves Frymann in *The Upright Seven,* the Glors and the Pastor in *The Lost Smile,* Gebizo in *Seven Legends.* It is not automatically condemned, but unalloyed it leads to temporary disaster or downfall. Savagely parodied in *The Three Righteous Combmakers,* the hope for gain totally supplants common sense and all proportion; ruin is inevitable. Nettie and Strapinski prosper, deservedly. Dietrich the combmaker will prosper by guile—and be sorry. Karl and Hermine in *The Upright Seven* presumably "have it made" and it is foolish to suggest that they will abuse their prosperity. It is hard to see Keller as a disciple of any school of unrelieved economic determinism or as the horseman of an economic apocalypse.

Things as things are meaningless or worse. But the same applies to words for words' sake. The accumulation of inanities is one of the butts of Keller's satire: Züs is no less ridiculous for her temple of worthless mementos than for her flood of worthless scraps of knowledge. The misguided avarice of the Pastor is reproduced in his bombast of empty religious sonorities. Gentler irony touches the whole crew of *The Upright Seven*, who fuss about prizes, try *almost* ingenuously to outwit one another, and fall from the extreme of tongue-tied embarrassment into amiably pointless loquacity.

It used to be said that Keller bathed the world of small town Switzerland in sunny humor—and that he castigated it for its folly. But both judgments cannot be true. And both are dated. If anything, Keller's judgment of society leans to the negative, its expression to the satiric. So does his judgment of individual men—men, not women. Society in the broader sense is no better than its component individuals. It fares neither better nor worse in Keller's portraiture. In his frequent depiction of the "generation gap" Keller may show a kind of bias, but it does not always favor the young.

His view of politics is a different matter. Here we can discern specific preferences, and they are strong. Interestingly, his early radicalism has no substantial precipitate in the prose works, which pursue, except in the nostalgia of *The Upright Seven*, their "memories of bitterly passionate days." Perhaps only as a function of time of composition, his stories show a curious blend of sturdy individualism and staunch loyalty to tradition—very Swiss, some will say. There can be little doubt of authorial intent in the praise of the old *Ehgaumers* in *The Lost Smile*. The story contains a virtually topographical hierarchy of merit: modern affluence and emptiness on the lakeshore; greater stability (still vulnerable) in the family home above the lake; true domestic and social virtue on the old mountain farm—all in the same family. Jocundus' progress toward decent independence and integrity cannot continue until he conquers the temptation of political turmoil for turmoil's sake.

Most Swiss of all, perhaps, is Keller's vision of the festival, the ritual of celebration and the collective expression of love for land. His view of it is almost wholly positive. Whether it functions as an idyllic state from which separates fallible man has indeed fallen, as in *The Smile,* or as the heartfelt goal toward which the seven upright old "activists" make their unsteady way, carrying their banner, it is the common good epitomized. Any irony in gentle. The festival is Keller's image of a cohesive and happy society. Only a gentle irony attaches to Karl's encomium in *The Upright Seven:* the youth almost rejected as not good enough has to be the one who praises the unbroken heritage of the old in the collective world of the new, the dependence of the latter on the former. Like most men of true humor and irony since Aristophanes, Keller is, or becomes, an upholder of tradition.

The length of *Green Henry* [*Der grüne Heinrich*], Keller's great "developmental novel," precludes its appearance in this collection. Many of its themes and much of its autobiographical insight will be found in briefer but still revealing form in such stories as "The Lost Smile" and "Clothes Make the Man," at least some of its commentary on society in "The Banner of the Upright Seven." It is also separately available in a modern translation, by A. M. Holt (London and New York, 1960).

Apart from the *Green Henry,* the body of work that justifies Keller's claim to a position of prominence in European literature is his shorter fiction: his novellas, stories, tales, "legends." Some of the best of these are presented here, many in new translations. The "Banner of the Upright Seven" is given (with very slight revisions) in the version of one of our most prolific scholar-translators, the late B. Q. Morgan of Stanford University. Harry Steinhauer, Professor Emeritus at the University of California, Santa Barbara, translated "Clothes Make the Man" for his *Twelve German Novellas.* We are happy to include it here. The "Seven Legends" are represented in part by Martin Wyness's lively English versions of two of them. The others have been done for this volume by Professor Emeritus Robert Browning of Hamilton College, reveals his gifts as translator and stylist in "The Three Righteous Combmakers" and "Mirror the Cat." The Editor has done an extensive revision, mostly in the interest of more natural language, of an old standard translation of "Romeo and Juliet" (by Paul Thomas, from Kuno Francke's *German Classics*), along with a new translation of "The Lost Smile."

This volume also carries a foreword by a man who occupies, among Swiss authors of the present day, a place of distinction not unlike that of Keller in the previous century: the writer Max Frisch, well known to English and American readers for such plays as *The Firebugs* and *Andorra,* and for his many stories and novels, among the latter *I'm Not Stiller* and *Homo Faber.*

F.G.R.

From
THE
PEOPLE OF
SELDWYLA

The Three Righteous Combmakers

The citizens of Seldwyla have proven that a whole town full of unrighteous or frivolous persons can, in a pinch, continue to survive despite the vicissitude of time and trade; the three combmakers, on the other hand, that three righteous men cannot live for long under the same roof without getting in each other's hair. We are not speaking here, however, of divine righteousness or of the natural sense of righteousness ingrained in the human conscience but of that anemic righteousness that has stricken from the Lord's Prayer the petition: "And forgive us our debts, as we also have forgiven our debtors!" because such righteousness incurs no debts and has none outstanding. It offends no one, but it also gives no one pleasure; it is, to be sure, willing to work and earn money, but not to spend any and finds in devotion to work only profit, but no joy. Righteous men of this stamp don't throw stones at street lamps, but neither do they light any, and no light proceeds from them. They pursue all kinds of trades and like one as well as the other, provided there is no danger connected with it. They prefer to settle where there are many unrighteous (in their sense of the word), for if they had only their own company, with no unrighteous among them, they would soon grind each other to dust, like millstones with no grain between them. When misfortune befalls such people, they are mightily astounded and wail loudly, as though stuck on a spit, because they have harmed no one. They regard the world as a great, well-ordered institution run by police, where no one need fear a fine for contravening the law, as long as he diligently sweeps before his own doorstep, places no unguarded flowerpots in his upper window and pours no slops out of it.

In Seldwyla there existed a combmaking establishment whose owner usually changed every five to six years, even though it was a profitable business when well run; for the tradesmen who visited the surrounding market fairs were in the habit of buying their combs there. Besides indispensable coarse horn combs of every variety, the establishment also produced wonderful decorative combs for the village belles and servant girls. These were made of beautiful translucent oxhorn, in which the artful journeymen (for the masters never worked) etched large brownish-red tortoiseshell cloud banks, each according to his fantasy, so that when one held the combs against the light, one seemed to see the most glorious sunrises and sunsets, red mottled skies, storm clouds and other speckled natural phenomena. In summer, when the journeymen liked to take to the road and were hard to find, they were treated with politeness and received a good wage and good food, but in winter, when they were looking for a roof over their heads and were easy to come by, they had to humble themselves and make combs with a vengeance for poor pay. One day after another the master's wife would put a dish of sauerkraut on the table and say: "That's fish!" and if a journeyman dared say: "Beg pardon, that's sauerkraut!" he was dismissed on the spot and had to take to the road in the middle of winter. But as soon as the fields turned green and the roads were passable, they said: "Oh yes, it is sauerkraut!" and packed their knapsack. For even if the master's wife immediately threw a big chunk of ham on the kraut and the master said: "My word, I thought it was fish! But I guess it must be ham!" they still longed to be off, because all three of the journeymen employed there had to sleep in a bed made for two and got heartily sick of each other in the course of the winter on account of all the jabs in the ribs and frozen sides.

One day, however, an orderly and meek-mannered journeyman from some part of Saxony turned up. He submitted to everything, worked like a dog and couldn't be driven away, so that he finally became a fixture in the business and saw masters change several times, things being at that time somewhat more unsettled than usual. Jobst stretched out in the bed as stiff as a board and maintained his place next to the wall winter and summer; he willingly admitted that the sauerkraut was fish and in the spring helped himself with modest thanks to a little piece of ham. He laid aside his smaller wage in the winter as well as his larger one in the summer; he spent nothing and saved everything. He did not live like other journeymen, never drank a drop, associated with none of his countrymen or with other young journeymen, but stood beside the front steps in the evening and joked with the old women, lifted their water buckets onto their heads for them, if he was in a particularly gracious mood, and went to bed with the chickens; that is, unless there was so much work to do that he could work all night and earn an extra penny. On Sundays, he also worked until afternoon, even in the finest weather, but let it not be thought that he did so cheerfully and willingly, like John the Merry Soapmaker; on the contrary, he had a downcast air when he undertook this voluntary extra labor and complained constantly about his hard lot.

When Sunday afternoon arrived, he went across the street to his laundress in his dirty workclothes and flappy slippers and fetched a fresh shirt and ironed shirtfront, a high starched collar or his better kerchief and bore these splendors home with an elegant journeyman's tread, holding them in front of him on the palm of his hand. For when they wear their apron and slippers some journeymen assume a singularly affected gait, as though hovering in a higher sphere, especially the cultivated bookbinders, the jolly shoemakers and the rare, unusual combmakers. In his room, Jobst took careful thought whether he ought actually to put on the fresh shirt or the shirtfront, for with all his meekness and righteousness he was a regular pig, or if he should stay home and work a bit and make the shirt he had on do for another week. In the latter case, he would sit down again with a sigh at the difficulties and hardships of this world and sullenly cut teeth in combs or transform oxhorn into tortoise shell, performing this task, however, so soberly and with such lack of imagination that he always smeared the same three wretched spots on the horn; for if it wasn't absolutely demanded, he took not the slightest pains with his work.

But if he did decide to take a walk, he first spent an hour or two fussing with his toilet, then took his walking cane and strode stiffly out before the city gate. Here he stood around, humble and bored, and conducted boring conversations with others who were lounging about and likewise had nothing better to do: poor old Seldwylers for the most part, who could no longer afford to go to the tavern. With them he liked to take up his post before a house that was just going up, before a field of young grain, a weather-beaten apple tree or before a new yarn factory and expound endlessly on the utility of these things, their cost, yearly prospects, the state of the crops, about all of which he hadn't the vaguest idea. But that was not the point; in this way he could pass the time in the cheapest and, to his way of thinking, most interesting fashion, and the older people always spoke of him as that polite, sensible Saxon; for they also didn't have the vaguest idea. When the Seldwylers decided to found a big incorporated brewery, promising themselves fat profits from such an enterprise, and the extensive foundations were already rising from the ground, Jobst would poke around there on Sunday evenings, investigating the progress of the building with a knowledgeable eye and apparently the liveliest interest, as though he were an architectural expert and the heaviest beer drinker. "Don't tell me!" he would exclaim time after time, "that's a building for you! that'll be a fine establishment! But it'll cost some money. Ah well, what's money! Too bad though, this vault ought to be a bit deeper and that wall a shade thicker!" And all the while he had no other thought in his head but to get home to supper before dark, for the only injustice he did his landlady was never to miss Sunday supper, as the other journeymen often did, so that she had to stay home just on his account or make some sort of arrangement for him. Once he had gotten himself a piece of roast or a sausage, he would fool around in the bedroom for a while, then go to bed. This was what he called spending a pleasurable Sunday.

For all his modest, meek and honorable ways, Jobst did not lack a slight touch of inward irony, as though he were secretly making fun of the frivolity and vanity of the world. He seemed to doubt the greatness and importance of things in no uncertain way and to be aware of a much profounder concept. In fact, he assumed now and then such a wise look, especially when he was holding forth as an expert in his Sunday speeches, that one could readily see that he actually had much weightier things on his mind, things in comparison to which everything that others were undertaking, building, erecting was only child's play. The great plan he cherished day and night and which had been his guiding star all the years he had been a journeyman in Seldwyla was none other than this: to save up his wages until one fine morning they would be sufficient to buy out the business when it again came up for sale and thus to make himself the owner and master. This was at the bottom of all his deeds and endeavors; for he had seen how a diligent and thrifty man was bound to prosper here, a man who went his own quiet way and was smart enough to benefit from the carelessness of others without suffering its disadvantages. But once he was master, then he would soon earn enough to become a naturalized citizen and *then* he planned to live in a wiser and more practical way than any citizen of Seldwyla had ever lived, to bother about nothing that did not contribute to his wealth, to spend not a cent, but to attract as many as possible into his own pocket in the frivolous whirl of this town! This plan was as simple as it was correct and understandable, especially since he was already tenaciously carrying it out and had already laid aside a nice little sum, which he kept carefully concealed, and according to all calculations this was bound in time to become large enough for the attainment of his goal.

But the inhuman thing about this plan, so secret and so peaceable, was that Jobst had conceived it in the first place; for nothing in his heart forced him to stay precisely in Seldwyla—neither love for the region or the people, nor a preference for their political institutions and customs. To all these he was as indifferent as to his own country, for which he had absolutely no longing. There were a hundred places in the world where he could gain as firm a foothold with his diligence and his righteousness as here, but he had no free choice and in his dreary mind seized the first accidental wisp of hope that offered itself, attaching himself to it and sucking on it like a leech. *Ubi bene, ibi patria,* wherever I'm well off is home, sweet home to me! as the saying goes, and we will not dispute its validity for those who can show a better and more necessary reason for their well-being in their new homeland than Jobst; for those who of their own free will left their country to gain by vigorous effort some advantage abroad and return well-to-do, or those who flee in droves from intolerable conditions at home and, obeying the call of the age, join the new migrations of peoples across the seas. Nor will we dispute it for those who have found elsewhere dearer friends than at home or conditions more in keeping with their personal inclinations or who are bound by some happier human bond. But wherever they are, all these persons must love the new land of their prosperity and there too, if need be, stand up for humanity. But Jobst hardly knew where he was; Swiss institutions and customs were Greek to him. He only said now and then, "Oh yes, the Swiss are a political people! I'm sure politics is a fine thing, if one is fond of it. For my part, I'm no judge; where I come from, it wasn't customary." The ways of the Seldwylers repelled and upset him, and whenever there was some demonstration or parade, he cowered in the back of the workshop, afraid for his life. And yet the sole theme of his thought and his great secret was to remain here till the end of his days. Such righteous characters are found throughout the world. They have squatted down where they are for no other reason than that they happened upon a pipette that secretes a good living and so they quietly suck at it, feeling no homesickness for their native land nor love for their adopted one, looking neither backward nor forward; thus they less resemble free human beings than those lower organisms, strange plants and animals, that have been carried by air or water to the spot where they chance to prosper.

Thus he lived for one self-satisfied year after another in Seldwyla, increasing his secret hoard, which he kept hidden under a flagstone in the floor of the bedroom. No tailor could yet boast that he had ever made a cent on him, for the Sunday coat he had worn upon his arrival was still in the same condition as then. Nor had any shoemaker taken in a penny from him, for not even the soles of the shoes that had adorned the back of his knapsack when he came yet had holes in them, seeing that the year has only fifty-two Sundays and only half of these were devoted to a stroll. No one could claim ever to have seen either a large or a small piece of money in his hand; for when he got his pay, it immediately disappeared in the most mysterious fashion, and even when he took a walk before the city gate, he never put a cent in his pocket, so that it was impossible for him to spend anything. When women came into the shop selling cherries, plums or pears and the other workmen satisfied their appetites, his mouth also watered, but he was able to calm his desire by attentively joining in the bargaining, petting and gently squeezing the juicy cherries and plums, and then finally letting the women, who had taken him for their most eager customer, leave the shop nonplused, while he rejoiced in his abstinence. With great self-satisfaction he would watch his fellow workmen eat, offering detailed advice as to how they should bake or peel the apples they had bought. But just as no one had ever glimpsed a coin in his possession, so too had no one ever heard from him a harsh word or an unfair demand or received a disapproving look. He avoided any semblance of a quarrel and never took a joke in bad part, and as eager as he was to hear all kinds of gossip and to observe and pass judgment on a controversy, because these things provided him with free entertainment while the other journeymen were wasting their money getting drunk, still he was careful never to interfere in the affairs of others or to let himself be caught in an imprudent act. In short, he was the most remarkable combination of truly heroic wisdom and endurance and of meek, base heartlessness and lack of feeling.

At one time he had been the only journeyman in the shop, and during this undisturbed period he felt as happy as a fish in water. At night, he especially enjoyed the broad expanse of bed and made very economic use of this time to indemnify himself for the days to come and, as it were, to triple his person by constantly changing his position and imagining that three were lying in bed together, two of which were entreating the third not to feel embarrassed but to go ahead and make himself comfortable. This third person was himself, and thus encouraged he would voluptuously wrap himself in the whole blanket or spread his legs wide apart, lie crosswise over the bed or, with innocent pleasure, turn somersaults in it. One day, however, when he was already lying in bed at sundown, another journeyman came to apply for work and was shown into the bedroom by the master's wife. Jobst was just lying in Epicurean comfort with his head at the foot of the bed and his feet on the pillows when the stranger entered, took off his heavy knapsack and at once began to undress with the air of one fatigued. Jobst whirled about like a flash and stretched out stiffly in his old place next to the wall, thinking to himself: "He'll soon be off again; it's summer and fine weather for walking!" In hope of this, he resigned himself to his fate with a suppressed sigh, expecting the usual nocturnal jabs in the ribs and the struggle for covers. Imagine then his astonishment when the new arrival, although he was a Bavarian, lay down in the bed with a polite greeting, keeping to the other edge just as peaceably and as mannerly as Jobst himself, and did not bother him the whole night long. This unheard-of event so disturbed his rest that, although the Bavarian slept blissfully, he did not get a wink all night. In the morning, he observed his strange bedfellow with a curious eye and saw that, like himself, he was no longer young and that he politely inquired about the circumstances and the life in Seldwyla, just as he himself would have done. As soon as he noticed this, he restrained himself and held his peace about even the simplest matters, as though they were a great secret, striving on the other hand to fathom the Bavarian's secret; for that he had one was obvious from a mile away. For what other reason should he be such a sensible, meek and shrewd customer, if he didn't have something mysterious and very advantageous to himself up his sleeve? Now the pair of them sought to worm information out of each other, all very cautiously and peaceably, by means of hints and insinuations. Neither was willing to give a clear, reasonable answer, but after a few hours each knew that the other was nothing more or less than his perfect double. When, in the course of the day, Fridolin, the Bavarian, ran to the bedroom a number of times and busied himself there, Jobst took advantage of the opportunity to steal in there himself and hastily make an inventory of Fridolin's possessions, when the latter was sitting at the workbench. He found nothing more, however, than almost exactly the same things he owned himself, even down to a wooden needle-box, which in this case, however, was in the shape of a fish, whereas Jobst's wittily represented an infant in swaddling clothes, and instead of a dog-eared French grammar for popular use, which Jobst sometimes thumbed through, the Bavarian possessed a well-bound little volume entitled *The Cold and Hot Vat: An Indispensable Manual for Dyers*. But inscribed on the flyleaf were the words "Security for the 3 coppers I lent the Hessian." From this he inferred that the Bavarian was a man who didn't throw away his money, and involuntarily surveying the floor, he discovered a flagstone that seemed to him as though it had recently been lifted, and, sure enough, beneath it he found a hoard wrapped up in an old torn handkerchief and tied with a string, almost as heavy as his own, which, by way of distinction, was stuck in an old tied-up sock. Trembling, he replaced the floor tile, trembling from excitement and admiration for foreign greatness and deep concern for his own secret. Straightway he ran down to the shop and began to work as though the whole earth must be provided with combs, and the Bavarian worked as though heaven too was in need of combing.

The next week provided full confirmation of their opinion of each other; for if Jobst was hardworking and modest, Fridolin was active and abstemious and sighed as dubiously as Jobst at the difficulties of such virtue; if Jobst was serene and wise, Fridolin was jocose and clever; if the former was modest, the latter was humble, the former sly and ironic, the latter cunning and almost satiric, and if Jobst assumed a contented, stupid mien about something that distressed him, Fridolin looked the very picture of a jackass. It was both rivalry and the exercise of self-conscious mastery that animated them, and neither disdained to take the other as his model and to imitate such minute traits of perfect conduct as he might lack himself. They looked so much of one heart and mind that they seemed to be doing something for their common good and thus resembled two bold heroes who mutually steel each other by their chivalrous behavior before commencing a duel. But hardly a week had gone by when another journeyman came applying for work, a Swabian by the name of Dietrich; at this the pair felt a secret joy, as though they now had an amusing yardstick by which to measure their calm grandeur, and they planned to place the poor Swabian, who was certainly a regular good-for-nothing, betwixt and between their own virtues, like a monkey between two playful lions.

But who can depict their astonishment when they saw that the Swabian conducted himself exactly as they did, and the recognition that had taken place between them was now repeated in triplicate, thus placing them in an unexpected position not only to the third but also completely changing their situation in regard to each other.

As soon as they assigned him a place in the bed between them, the Swabian proved himself their perfect equal and lay as straight and quiet as a matchstick, so that there still remained a bit of space between each of them and the cover lay on top of them like packing paper on three herring. The situation now became more serious, and since all three faced each other on equal footing, like the angles of an equilateral triangle, and no confidential relationship was any longer possible between two of them, no treaty or friendly rivalry, all three were doggedly determined to outlast each other both in bed and in their place of employment. When the master saw that these three oddities would put up with anything, merely in order to stay, he reduced their pay and shortened their rations, but they only worked all the harder and forced him to throw large supplies of cheap goods on the market and to fill larger orders, so that he earned an inordinate amount of money on his three modest journeymen and possessed in them a veritable gold mine. He loosened his belt a couple of notches and played a big role in the town, while his foolish employees strained day and night in the dark shop and tried to work each other out of a job.

Dietrich, the Swabian, who was the youngest, proved to be made of the very same stuff as the two others, but as yet he had no savings, not having been on the road for long. This would have constituted a serious drawback for him, seeing that Jobst and Fridolin had such a head start, had he not as an inventive Swabian conjured up a novel magical power to even the score. Since he was by nature free of all passion, just as free as his fellows, except the passion to settle here and no place else and take advantage of the situation, he invented the scheme of falling in love and suing for the hand of some person who possessed approximately as much as the Saxon and the Bavarian had lying under the flagstones. It was one of the more likable peculiarities of the Seldwylers that they did not marry ill-favored or unpleasant women for the sake of their means. The temptation was not great in any case, since in their town there were no wealthy heiresses, either beautiful or ugly, but they at least had the backbone to disdain even smaller crumbs and preferred to marry jolly, good-looking women whom they could show off in public for a few years. For this reason it was not difficult for the watchful Swabian to find a virtuous miss who lived in the same street and who, as he had ascertained through shrewd conversation with older women, owned a mortgage worth seven hundred gulden. This was Züs Bünzlin, a young lady of twenty-eight years, who lived with her mother, the laundress, but was sole mistress of her paternal inheritance. She had the mortgage lying in a small lacquered chest, in which she also kept the accrued interest, her baptismal certificate, her certificate of confirmation and a painted and gilded Easter egg; further, a half-dozen silver teaspoons, a Lord's Prayer printed in gold letters on a tenuous, red, translucent glassy substance she called "human skin," a cherry pit, in which a Crucifixion was engraved, and an ivory box covered with perforated red taffeta, in which there was a little mirror and a silver thimble; further, another cherry pit, wherein there rattled a tiny game of ninepins, a nut with a little image of the Virgin behind glass, which, when opened, was seen to hold a silver heart, in which was inserted a small perfumed sponge, and a bonbon box made of lemon peel, on whose lid a strawberry was painted and in which lay a golden pin on a piece of cotton in the shape of a forget-me-not, and a medallion with a monument of hair; further, a bundle of yellowed papers with recipes and secrets, a bottle of Hoffmann's drops for fainting spells, another of eau de cologne and a box with musk; another box with a bit of licorice, and a little basket plaited of fragrant grasses as well as one made of glass beads and cloves; finally, a little book with silver edges bound in sky-blue ribbed paper and entitled *Golden Rules of Life for a Young Woman as Bride, Wife and Mother;* and a small dream-expounder, a guide to letter-writing, five or six love letters and scarificator for letting blood; for once she had cultivated a relationship with a journeyman barber or surgeon's helper, whom she thought to marry, and, since she was a skillful and very sensible person, she had learned from her suitor how to let blood, apply leeches and cupping glasses and so on, and could even shave him herself. However, he had proved unworthy, a man with whom she might well have risked all her happiness, and so with sad but wise determination she had dissolved their relationship. They returned each other's presents with the exception of the scarificator; this she kept as security for one gulden and forty-eight kreuzers, which she had once lent him in cash, though the unworthy fellow maintained that he owed nothing since she had put the money in his hand at a dance to pay for their expenses and she had eaten twice as much as he. So he kept the gulden and forty-eight kreuzers and she the scarificator, with which she clandestinely let blood for all the women of her acquaintance and so earned many a pretty penny. But every time she used the instrument she was painfully reminded of the base character of the man who had been so close to her and who had almost become her husband!

All this was contained in the lacquered chest, well locked up, and the chest itself was shut up in an old walnut cabinet, the key to which Züs Bünzlin always carried in her pocket. She herself had thin reddish hair and watery blue eyes, which were not without charm and were sometimes capable of looking gentle and wise. She owned a great many clothes, of which she wore only a few and always the oldest, but she was always carefully and neatly dressed, and just as neat and clean was her room. She was extremely diligent and helped her mother in the laundry by ironing the finer things and washing the caps and cuffs of the women of Seldwyla, earning in this way a nice sum. Perhaps it was due to this activity that every week on wash-days she maintained that severe and measured air that always comes over women when they are doing the laundry and that this mood took such firm hold of her on these days. Only when the ironing began, did she become gayer, and in Züsi's case such gaiety was always seasoned with wisdom. This spirit of measure and moderation was also evident in the main decorative feature of the house, a wreath of square, precisely measured pieces of soap, which were laid around the cornice of the pine wainscoting to harden. These bars Züs herself always measured and cut off from the soft blocks of freshly made soap with a copper wire. The wire had a wooden handle at either end to make it easier to grasp and cut with; the handsome pair of compasses for measuring off the pieces had been made and presented to her by a journeyman tool-maker, with whom she had once been as good as engaged. From him also came a small shiny spice-mortar, which adorned the top of her cupboard between the blue teapot and the painted flower vase. She had long wished for just such a nice little mortar, and the attentive tool-maker was therefore most welcome when he appeared with it on her name day and also brought something to grind in it: a box full of cinnamon, sugar, cloves and pepper. He had hung the mortar by one handle from his little finger before entering the room and struck it with the pestle, so that it rang like a bell. That had been a gay morning. But shortly afterward the deceitful fellow had fled the region and was never heard from again. His master had had the nerve to demand the return of the mortar, claiming that the journeyman had taken it from his shop without paying for it. But Züs Bünzlin would not surrender her treasured memento; she waged a valiant and vehement minor lawsuit for it, even defending her action in court on the basis of a bill for washing shirts for the fugitive. The days when she had had to defend her mortar were the most significant and painful days of her life, since she, with her deep understanding, comprehended and felt such things, especially an appearance in court in such a delicate matter, much more vividly than other, more frivolous, people. But she won her suit and kept the mortar.

If the decorative soap-gallery bore witness to her industry and exactitude, a stack of books that lay neatly ordered on her window sill—and which she diligently perused on Sundays—were no fainter praise of her pious, well-schooled mind. She had kept all her school books from years past and hadn't lost a single one, just as she still kept in memory all her small store of learning: she still knew the catechism by heart, as well as her book of declensions, her arithmetic, geography, Biblical history and secular readers. She also owned some of Christoph Schmid's storybooks and his little tales with their well-turned proverbs in verse at the end, at least a half-dozen various *Treasure Troves* and *Gardens of Roses* for reference, a collection of almanacs chock-full of proven wisdom and experience, several remarkable prophecies, an introduction to fortune-telling with cards, a devotional manual for every day of the year for thoughtful young women and an old copy of Schiller's *Robbers,* which she reread as often as she thought she had forgotten it sufficiently, and was moved at each reading, though she made very sensible and critical remarks about it. Everything to be found in these books was also to be found in her head and she could talk about it and much more besides, in the most elegant fashion. When she was in a good mood and not too busy, incessant speeches resounded from her mouth and she knew how to assign all things their proper place and how to judge all things, so that young and old, high and low, learned and unlearned had to submit to her judgment when she had smilingly or pensively turned her mind to the matter in hand for a few moments. Sometimes she talked as much and as unctuously as a learned blind woman, who sees nothing of the world and finds her only pleasure in hearing herself talk. From school and from her catechismal instruction she still retained the skill of writing essays and composing edifying passages for memorization and for inditing all kinds of apothegmatic schemata, and sometimes on a quiet Sunday she would compose weird essays by attaching to some euphonious title she had heard or read a string of the strangest and oddest sentences, whole pages full, just as they sprang from her singular brain, as, for example, on the usefulness of sickness, on death, on the wholesomeness of renunciation, on the enormousness of the visible world and the mysteriousness of the invisible, on life in the country and its pleasures, on nature, on dreams, on love, something on salvation through Christ, three points concerning self-righteousness, thoughts on immortality. She would read these compositions to her friends and admirers and, if she was particularly well-disposed toward someone, would give him one or two such essays, and he had to lay them in the Bible, if he owned one.

This spiritual side of her nature had once gained her the deep and upright affection of a journeyman bookbinder, who read every book he bound and who was an ambitious, emotional and inexperienced young man. When he brought his bundle of laundry to Züsi's mother, he thought himself in heaven, so much did he delight in hearing her daughter's wonderful idealistic speeches, such as he had often thought of himself but never dared to utter. Shyly and reverently, he approached this alternately severe and eloquent virgin, and she granted him her company and attached him to herself for the course of a year, but not without keeping him within the bounds of complete hopelessness, bounds she marked out herself with unrelenting hand. For since he was nine years younger than she, poor as a churchmouse and inept at his trade, for which there were in any case hardly fair prospects in Seldwyla, seeing that the people there did not read and had few books bound, she did not conceal from him for a minute the impossibility of their union and only sought to raise his spirit to the height of her own ability for renunciation and to embalm him in a cloud of motley phrases.

He would listen to her devoutly, occasionally venturing some beautiful saying himself, which she, however, hardly had it left his mouth, would cap with one still more beautiful. This was the most spiritual and noblest year of her life, undimmed by any breath of coarseness. The young man rebound all her books for her during that year and built besides, working many nights and holidays, an artistic and precious monument to his veneration. This was a large Chinese temple made of pasteboard with innumerable containers and secret drawers, the whole of which could be taken apart in many pieces. Colored patches of fine pressed paper were pasted on it and all the edges were adorned with a gold stripe. Mirrored walls alternated with columns, and if one lifted out a section or opened a chamber, one saw other mirrors and tiny hidden pictures, bouquets of flowers and pairs of lovers. Everywhere on the scalloped points of the roof hung little bells. A casing for a woman's watch was also mounted on the columns, together with pretty hooks on which to hang the golden chain and wreathe it about the structure; but up to now no watchmaker had put in his appearance to lay a watch, and no goldsmith to lay a chain on this altar. Endless patience and skill had been expended on this ingenious temple, whose geometric plan was no less laborious than the careful, exact workmanship. When this monument to a year passed in beauty was completed, Züs Bünzlin, suppressing her own desires, encouraged the good bookbinder to tear himself away and move on: the world, she said, lay before him, and now that he had ennobled his heart in her society, in her school, good fortune would be sure to smile on him; meanwhile she would never forget him, though she must resign herself to loneliness. He wept real tears upon allowing himself to be thus dismissed, then he left town. His work, on the other hand, covered with a veil of seagreen gauze, to protect it from dust and unworthy glances, commanded since his departure a place on Züsi's chest of drawers. She held it so holy that she kept it new and unused and put nothing in its multitudinous containers; in addition, she remembered its maker by the name of Emanuel, whereas he was actually called Veit, and told everyone that only Emanuel had ever understood her and fathomed her nature. To him himself, however, she was loathe to admit as much but kept him strictly in check, and to spur him on to higher things had often shown him that he understood her least when he imagined he understood her best. In return, he also played a trick on her by placing in a double bottom in the very middle of the temple a ravishingly beautiful letter, dampened with tears, in which he expressed his unutterable sadness, love, devotion and eternal fidelity in such appealing and innocent language as only true feeling caught in a labyrinth can find. Such lovely things he had never said, because she never let him get a word in edgewise. But since she had no inkling of this hidden treasure, it happened in this instance that fate was just and a deceitful beauty did not get to see what she was undeserving to behold. It was also symbolic that it was she who did not understand the foolish but cordial and sincere nature of the young bookbinder.

She had long praised the way of life of the three combmakers, calling them three righteous and sensible men; for she had observed them well. Therefore when Dietrich the Swabian began to linger about when he brought his shirts or when he fetched them and to pay court to her, she received him kindly and detained him for an hour at a time, while Dietrich flattered her in the strongest terms he could think of, and she was well able to bear strong praise. In fact, she loved it all the more the stronger it was, and when one praised her wisdom, she would keep as still as a mouse until the eulogist had poured his heart out, whereupon she would take up the thread of his discourse with heightened unction, adding extra touches to the portrait he had sketched. Dietrich had not been seeing Züs very long before she showed him the deed of mortgage. Now he was full of hope and acted as mysteriously toward his fellow journeymen as though he had invented perpetual motion. Jobst and Fridolin soon penetrated his secret, however, and were astounded at his deep and ingenious mentality. Jobst especially fairly beat his head, since for years he had been frequenting the house and it had never occurred to him to look for anything there but his laundry. The fact was, he almost hated the laundress and her daughter, because they were the only ones for whom he was forced to pry loose a bit of cash every week. He was not accustomed to think of marriage, because he could conceive of a wife only as a person who wanted something from him that he did not owe her, and to want something from her that might be to his advantage did not occur to him, since he trusted only himself, and his shallow ideas did not reach beyond the depth of his intimate and strictly kept secret. But it was now a question of besting the Swabian, for he could make plenty of trouble with Miss Züsi's seven hundred gulden, if he got hold of them, and the seven hundred gulden themselves now assumed a transfigured glory in the eyes of both the Saxon and the Bavarian. Thus it was that Dietrich, so richly inventive, had now discovered a land which at once became common property and so shared the fate of all discoverers; for the other two at once followed his trail and sought out Züs Bünzlin, so that she found herself surrounded by a whole court of sensible and honorable combmakers. With this she was extremely pleased; she had never possessed more than one admirer at a time, so that it became for her a new intellectual exercise to treat these three with prudence and impartiality, to keep them in check and encourage them with her marvelous speeches to renunciation and selflessness until heaven should decide the inevitable. For since each had secretly confided to her his plan, she at once decided to reward the one who should first reach his goal and make himself owner of the comb factory. The Swabian, who could attain his end only through her, she eliminated and determined not to marry in any event, but since he was the youngest, cleverest and most amiable of the three, it was he to whom through quiet hints she gave most grounds for hope and spurred the others on to greater zeal by the solicitude with which she seemed to watch over him and guide him, so that our poor Columbus, who had discovered this lovely land, was chosen to play the fool in this game. All three tried to outdo each other in devotion, modesty and prudence, in the gracious art of selfless admiration and in allowing themselves to be ruled by their strict mistress, so that when the whole company was together it resembled some strange prayer meeting where the most peculiar witness is borne. In spite of all piety and humility, however, it constantly happened that one or the other, jumping the track of praise for their common mistress, sought to blow his own horn and saw himself gently reprimanded by Züsi or was forced to listen to her reminding him of the virtues of the others, which he was then quick to recognize and confirm.

But it was a hard life for the poor combmakers. As unfeeling as they were by nature, now that a woman was in question they felt quite unaccustomed stirrings of jealousy, concern, fear and hope. They wore themselves to a frazzle with work and frugality and grew visibly thinner; they became melancholy, and although they were anxiously eloquent in the presence of others and especially in the presence of Züs, when they were alone together at work or sitting in their bedroom, they scarcely exchanged a word and lay down with a sigh in their common bed, as silent and compatible as three lead pencils. One and the same dream hovered nightly over this trio, until one night it became so vivid that Jobst flung himself back from beside the wall and shoved Fridolin, whereupon there broke out in the hearts of the sleep-drunk journeymen wild resentment and in their bed a terrible struggle, so that for three minutes they kicked, stomped and struck out at each other so violently that all six legs got entangled in one another and the whole coil tumbled out of bed with a fearful yell. They thought, when fully awake, that the devil had come to fetch them or that burglars had broken into their room. They sprang up with a scream, Jobst took up a position on his floor tile, Fridolin hastened to his and Dietrich to the one beneath which he had already collected a little nest egg, and thus they stood in a triangle, trembling and striking out into the empty air, yelling bloody murder and crying: "Go away! Go away!" until the startled master came in and calmed his crazed journeymen. Trembling with fright, anger and shame, they finally crept back into bed and lay silently beside each other until morning.

But the nocturnal hubbub had been only a prelude to a still greater fright which now awaited them when the master announced to them at breakfast that he could no longer use three workmen and that two of them would have to go. They had, it seemed, done their work only too well and in their zeal produced such a stock of goods that part of them could not be sold, while the master had meanwhile expended his increased income on ruining the business just when it was at its height by leading such a riotous life that he soon owed twice as much as he earned. For this reason, the journeymen, as industrious and provident as they were, had suddenly become a burden to him. To comfort them, he said that he esteemed them all equally and would leave it up to them to decide which one should stay and which ones should go. But they refused to make such a decision. They only stood there pale as death and smiled at each other. Then they grew fearfully excited, for they suddenly realized that the master's announcement was a sure sign that the fatal hour had struck, that he would soon have to give up the business and the comb factory would at last again be for sale. Thus the goal for which they had all striven was near and shone like a heavenly Jerusalem, and two of them were supposed to turn back before its gates and never see it again! Without further hesitation, each of them declared that he wanted to stay, even if he had to work for nothing. But the master would not hear of this and assured them that two would have to leave in any case. They fell at his feet, wrung their hands, implored him, and each begged that he might at least keep *him,* for only two more months, only four more weeks. However the master was well aware of what they were speculating on; this vexed him and he made fun of them by suddenly suggesting a jocose solution to the matter. "If you absolutely can't make up your minds," he said, "which two must leave, I'll tell you how the matter can be settled and that will be the way it is! Tomorrow is Sunday; I'll give you your pay, you pack your knapsacks, take your staffs and all three of you walk peaceably out of the city gate for a good half hour, in any direction you choose. Then you can rest a bit and drink a pint if you're thirsty, and when you've done that, you head back into town and the first one who then applies here for work I'll take; the other two have to leave without argument and go wherever they please." They again fell on their knees before him and begged him to abandon this cruel scheme, but in vain: he remained firm and immovable. Unexpectedly, the Swabian jumped up and ran out of the house as though possessed and straight across the street to Züs Bünzlin. As soon as Jobst and the Bavarian realized what was happening, they ceased their lamentations and ran out after him, and so the desperate scene was immediately transferred to the house of the startled virgin.

She was much moved and disconcerted by this unexpected event, but she was still the first to regain her composure and, surveying the situation, determined at once to make her own fate dependent upon the master's singular idea and to look upon it as a higher inspiration. Touched, she took out her *Treasure Trove* and stuck a pin between the leaves; the passage she hit upon concerned perseverance in following a worthy goal. Then she let the excited journeymen try their luck and everything they lit upon concerned zealous pursuance of the straight and narrow, going forward without a backward glance, a career of some kind; in short, it all had to do with walking and running, so that it was evident that tomorrow's race was ordained by heaven. But since she feared that Dietrich, being the youngest, would run fastest and easily win the prize, she decided to go with her three suitors herself and see if something might not be arranged to her advantage; for she wanted one of the older men to be the victor, which one made not a particle of difference to her. She therefore enjoined silence upon the lamenting and squabbling journeymen and resignation to their fate, saying, "Know, my friends, that nothing comes to pass without significance and that as remarkable and unusual as the proposition made by your master may be, we must look upon it as decreed by heaven and submit to this sudden decision with a higher wisdom, quite unknown to this wanton fellow. Our peaceful and reasonable life together was too beautiful to last for long in such an edifying manner; for alas! all that is beautiful and useful is transitory and passing, and nothing endures but evil, stubbornness and the lonely heart, which we then observe and consider in our piety and reasonableness. Therefore, before some base demon of dissension shall raise its head amongst us, let us rather separate beforehand of our own free will and depart from one another like the gentle spring breezes hastening across the heavens, ere we must violently disperse like the storm winds of autumn. I myself will accompany you on your hard path; I shall be present when you begin the race that shall test you, so that you may be of good cheer and have at your backs a beautiful stimulus, while before you beckons the meed of victory. But, just as the victor shall not exult in his victory, so shall those who are defeated not despair and depart in sadness or anger, but rather be assured of our fond remembrance and go out into the wide world as cheerful young pilgrims; for men have built many cities that are as beautiful, or even more beautiful, than Seldwyla; Rome is a great and remarkable city, wherein the Holy Father dwells, and Paris is a mighty city, with many souls and splendid palaces, and in Constantinople the Sultan reigns, Turkish by religion, and Lisbon, which was once destroyed by earthquake, has been rebuilt in even greater beauty. Vienna is the capital of Austria and is called the imperial city, and London is the wealthiest city in the world, situated in England, on a river called the Thames. Two million souls live there! Petersburg is the capital of Russia and the residence of the czar, just as Naples is the capital of the kingdom by the same name, with its fire-

spewing mountain Vesuvius, where once a damned soul appeared
to an English sea captain, as I have read in a remarkable book of
travel, this same soul having belonged to a certain John Smidt,
who a hundred and fifty years before had been a godless man and
now came to give the above-mentioned sea captain a message for
his progeny in England, so that he might be redeemed; for the
whole volcano is a sojourn of the damned, as one can also read in
Peter Hasler's learned treatise *On the Probable Location of Hell.*
There are also many other cities, of which I will mention only
Milan, Venice, which is built entirely in the water, Lyon, Marsei-
lingen, Strassburg, Cologne and Amsterdam. Paris I already named,
but not Nuremberg, Augsburg and Frankfurt, Basel, Berne and
Geneva, all beautiful cities, as is also Zurich, and furthermore a
greater number than I can here recount. For everything has its
limits except the inventiveness of men, who spread out everywhere
and undertake anything that seems to them useful. If they are
righteous, they will succeed; the unrighteous wither like the grass
of the field and are dispersed like smoke. Many are chosen, but
few are called. For all these reasons, and in many other respects
besides, which duty and the virtue of our clear conscience impose
upon us, let us submit to the call of fate. Therefore go and prepare
yourselves for your journey, but go as righteous and meek men,
who bear their worth within them wherever they may wend, and
whose staff takes root everywhere, and who, whatever may befall
them, can say: 'I have chosen the better part!' "

But the combmakers wanted to hear none of this: they vehemently importuned their prudent mistress to choose one of them
and command him to remain with her, and by "one" each meant
himself. But she refused to make such a choice, announcing in a
serious and authoritative tone that they must obey her or she would
withdraw her friendship forever. Now Jobst, the eldest, ran out
again and across the way into the master's house. The others followed him like a flash, fearing that he would undertake something
to their disadvantage, and so they continued the whole day, shooting about like falling stars and becoming as hateful to each other
as three spiders in one web. Half the town saw this spectacle of
the deranged combmakers, who had up to now been so calm and
peaceful, and the older people grew anxious, regarding this phenomenon as a mysterious omen of coming evil. Towards evening

they had grown weary and exhausted, but without having thought of anything better or come to any decision, and they went to their old bed with chattering teeth. One after the other they crawled under the blanket and lay there in confused thought, stretched out as though axed, until sleep mercifully overcame them. Jobst woke up first, very early, and saw that a fine spring morning was shining into the room where he had now slept for six years. As poverty-stricken as it looked, it seemed to him a paradise that he now must leave—and so unjustly! He let his glance wander about the walls and noted all the traces of the many journeymen who had lived here for a shorter or longer time. Here was where that one used to rub his head and had left a dark spot, there that one had driven a nail to hang his pipe on and the red cord was still hanging from it. What good chaps they had been to leave again so peaceably, while these who were lying there beside him wouldn't budge an inch. Then he fixed his gaze on the place beside his face and observed the small objects he had already looked at a thousand times, when in the morning or in the evening when it was still light he would lie in bed and rejoice in his blessed, expense-free existence. There was a damaged spot on the plaster that looked like a country with cities and lakes, some grains of sand represented the Islands of the Blest; a bit farther on there extended a long hog bristle that had come out of the paint brush and remained stuck in the blue coating; for last fall Jobst had found a half-empty can of this coating and, so that it wouldn't be wasted, had painted a quarter of a wall with it, as far as it would go, and in fact he had painted the part next to where he lay in bed. Beyond the hog bristle there projected a slight unevenness, like a small blue mountain, which threw a delicate shadow over the bristle towards the Islands of the Blest. He had pondered about this mountain the whole winter, since it seemed to him that it hadn't been there earlier. He now sought this projection with sad, sleepy eyes and suddenly couldn't find it, and he could hardly believe his senses when instead of it he found a small bare spot, while a bit farther on the blue mountain seemed to be moving. Astounded, Jobst abruptly sat up, as though he beheld a miracle, and saw that it was a louse which he had inattentively painted over last fall when it was already benumbed with cold. But now the warmth of spring had reanimated it, and it had set out again and was just at this moment climbing up the wall, blue-backed and undaunted. He gazed after it, touched and full of admiration; as long as it stayed on the blue paint, one could scarcely distinguish it from the wall, but when it left the painted area and the last scattered splashes were behind it, the brave little sky-blue creature trod its path through the darker regions, highly visible. Jobst sadly sank back in the pillows; as little as such things ordinarily concerned him, the apparition of the louse now stirred in him a feeling as though he too must after all finally take to the road again, and he thought it a good sign that he had resigned himself to the inevitable and would at least depart willingly. These calmer thoughts brought the return of his natural discretion and wisdom, and when he considered the matter more closely, he felt that if he assumed a resigned and modest attitude, submitted to the difficult task before him and at the same time pulled himself together and acted prudently, he would after all have the best chance of winning out over his rivals.

Softly, he climbed out of bed and began to put his things in order and above all to retrieve his trove and pack it in the bottom of his old knapsack. At this, his companions immediately awakened. When they saw that he was calmly tying up his pack, they were much amazed and their amazement grew when Jobst addressed them with conciliatory words and wished them good morning. He offered no explanation but went on quietly and peaceably about his business. Although they did not know what he was up to, they surmised some strategic maneuver and immediately began to imitate him, watching carefully to see what he would do next. The strange thing was that all three for the first time openly took their treasures out from under their tiles and stowed them in their packs without counting them. For they had long known each others' secret and in old-fashioned honesty did not suspect each other of trespass on personal property: each knew that the others would not steal from him, and it is only right that in the sleeping quarters of journeymen, soldiers and so on there should be no locks and no mistrust.

Now they were all unexpectedly ready to set out. The master had paid them their wages and returned their books of credentials, in which the handsomest testimonies from the city and the master himself concerning their blameless conduct and excellent work-

manship were inscribed. Now they stood in a melancholy row before Züs Bünzlin's door, dressed in long brown coats covered with
old washed-out dust jackets and their hats, though they were ancient and brushed bare of nap, carefully protected with oiled linen.
Each had fastened onto his knapsack a little cart to pull his pack
in, if the way was long, but since they did not think they would
need these wheels, they projected high above their backs. Jobst
was leaning on a stout bamboo cane, Fridolin on an ash staff,
flamed and painted red and black, while Dietrich had a fantastic
giant of a staff, twined about with an untrimmed network of
branches. He was almost ashamed of this ostentatious accoutre-
ment, which was a relic of his early days on the road, when he
had been by no means as settled and sensible as he was now.
Many neighbors and children were standing about the three earnest men, wishing them luck on their way. Then Züs appeared
before her door with a solemn air and proceeded at the head of
the journeymen resolutely out of the city gate. She had donned an
unusual costume in their honor. She was wearing a wide hat with
big yellow ribbons, a rose-colored chintz dress with out-of-style
flounces and furbelows, a broad black velvet belt with a copper
clasp and red fringed shoes of Moroccan leather. In her hand she
carried a big green silk reticule filled with dried pears and prunes
and over her head she held an opened umbrella topped by a large
lyre made of ivory. She had hung her medallion with the monument of blond hair about her neck and stuck the golden forget-
me-not on her breast. She was wearing white knitted gloves. She
looked appealing and tender in all this finery; her face was slightly
flushed and her bosom seemed to heave higher than usual, and the
departing rivals knew not how to contain themselves for sadness
and melancholy; for the critical state of affairs, the beautiful spring
day that shone on their departure, and Züsi's fine attire lent their
tense feelings an emotion almost akin to love. Before the city gate,
the kindly virgin admonished her suitors to put their packs on the
carts and pull them, in order not to tire themselves unnecessarily.
They did so, and as they proceeded beyond the town towards the
mountains it almost looked like a small detachment of artillery
laboring upward to a gun emplacement. When they had marched
for a good half-hour, they halted in a semicircle beneath a linden
tree, where there was a wide view over the woods, lakes and vil-

lages. Züs opened her reticule and gave each one a handful of dried pears and prunes for refreshment, and thus they sat, earnest and silent, for some while, making only a gentle smacking sound as they chewed the sweet fruit.

Then Züs, tossing away a prune pit and wiping her discolored fingertips on the fresh grass, began to speak. "Dear friends! Behold how beautiful and extensive the world is, everywhere full of splendid things and full of the dwellings of men! And yet I would wager that in this solemn hour there are nowhere in this wide world four such just and well-disposed souls as we are collected and sitting together, persons so ingenious and discreet, so given to every laborious exercise and virtue, to seclusion, frugality, peaceableness and ardent friendship. How many flowers grow here about us, of all kinds, brought forth by spring, especially yellow cowslips, which make such an appetizing and healthful tea; but are they righteous or diligent? are they thrifty, cautious and endowed with prudent and instructive ideas? No, they are unconscious beings deprived of soul; without the use of reason they waste their time, and, as beautiful as they are, they only end up as dry hay, whereas we in our virtue are far superior to them, nor do we yield to them in grace of form; for God has created us in His own image and blown His breath into our nostrils. Oh, if we could only sit here forever in this paradise and in such innocence; indeed, my friends, it seems to me that we are in a state of innocence, but ennobled by sinless knowledge; for we can all, thank God, read and write and have all learned a trade. I would have the skill and talent for many things and could venture upon undertakings such as are beyond the powers of the best educated noblewoman, if I wanted to exceed the bounds of my class, but modesty and humility are the most precious virtues of an honest woman of my condition, and it is enough for me to know that my mind is not deemed worthless and not despised by a higher intelligence. Many have already desired me in marriage who were not worthy of me, and now I suddenly see three dignified bachelors gathered about me, each of whom would be worthy of possessing me! Judge by this how my heart must languish in this wonderful superabundance, and take, each of you, an example from me and imagine that you are each surrounded by three blooming maidens of equal worth who want you for a husband and that you cannot for that reason incline to any of them! Picture to yourselves in all detail that three Miss Bünzlins are suing for each of you and sitting here around you, dressed as I am and looking just like me, so that I am, as it were, here present in ninefold form, gazing at you with longing from every side! Are you doing that?"

In surprise, the stouthearted journeymen ceased chewing and sought to solve this strange problem, a stupid expression on their faces. The young Swabian was the first to come up with a solution and cried out lasciviously, "Yes, my dearest Miss Züs! If you will kindly allow me, I see you hovering about me, not merely three-fold but hundredfold, looking at me with beckoning glances and offering me a thousand kisses!"

"Not that!" said Züs with a gesture of indignation, "not in such an indecent and exaggerated way! What on earth are you thinking of, you immodest man? I did not permit you to imagine me a hundredfold and offering kisses, but only threefold for each and with a reserved and modest manner, so that I am subjected to no familiarity!"

"Yes," Jobst now finally exclaimed, pointing about him with a nibbled pear stem, "only threefold and with the most modest air do I see our dear Miss Bünzlin walking about me and kindly beckoning to me as she lays her hand on her heart! I thank you very much, thank you, thank you!" he said, smirking and bowing in three directions, as though he really saw three figures. "That's the way," Züs said with a smile. "If there is any difference at all among you, then you, my dear Jobst, are the most talented, or at least the most sensible!"

Fridolin, the Bavarian, was still not finished composing his mental picture, but when he heard Jobst praised, he grew anxious and hastily cried out, "I also see our dear Miss Bünzlin walking about me in threefold form with the greatest modesty and volup-tuously beckoning to me as she lays her hand—"

"For shame, you Bavarian!" screamed Züs, averting her face, "not one word more! Where do you get the nerve to talk about me in such dissolute terms and to imagine such degrading impro-prieties? Shame, shame!" The poor Bavarian was thunderstruck and turned red as a beet, without knowing why; for he had imag-ined nothing at all, but merely repeated what it sounded to him that Jobst had said, having heard him praised for it. Züs turned again to Dietrich and said, "Well, my dear Dietrich, haven't you managed to think of something a bit more modest?" "Yes, with your permission," he replied, happy to be spoken to again, "I now see you hovering about me only three times, looking at me with reserve and offering me three white hands to kiss!"

"Very well, then!" said Züs. "And you, Fridolin? Have you returned from your aberration? Can't your raging blood still not calm itself enough to conjure up a more decent image?" "Forgive me," said Fridolin meekly. "I now think I see three maidens who are offering me dried pears and who don't appear to dislike me. One is no more beautiful than the other and to choose among them would be bitter."

"Well then," said Züs, "since in your imagination you three are surrounded by nine such maidens of fully equal worth and still your hearts suffer want in this charming superabundance, judge thereby my own condition; and as you saw that I am able to control my emotions wisely and modestly, let my strength serve as an example, and promise me and each other to continue to bear with each other and, as I depart affectionately from you, to part just as affectionately from one another, however the fate that awaits you may decide! Lay your hands in mine and promise!"

"Yes indeed!" cried Jobst, "at least I will; you can't say I lack good will!" And the other two immediately chimed in, "Neither do I, neither do I!" and all laid their hands together, each determining in his heart to run as fast as he could in any event. "I certainly don't lack good will!" Jobst repeated. "From my youngest days I've been of a merciful and peaceable nature. I never had a fight and could never bear to see any creature suffer. Wherever I've been, I've always behaved myself properly and gained praise for my peaceful conduct; for although I know a bit about a lot of things and am a knowledgeable young man, you never saw me interfering in anything that didn't concern me, and I've always done my duty in a circumspect fashion. I can work as hard as I will and it doesn't hurt me, because I'm young and healthy and in the prime of life! All my masters' wives have always said I was a man in a thousand, a very model, and that it was easy to get along with me. Yes, I really think I could live with you as though in heaven, my lovely Miss Züs."

"Oh-hoh!" exclaimed the Bavarian, "I think so too, it would be no trick to live with Miss Züs as though in heaven! I could do that too, I'm not so stupid. I know my trade from the ground up and know how to keep things in order, without wasting a word. I never got into fights, though I've worked in the largest cities, and I never struck a cat or killed a spider. I am moderate and temperate and satisfied with whatever food is set before me, I'm happy and content with the slightest things. But I'm also healthy and cheerful and can take punishment, a clear conscience is the elixir of life, all animals love me and follow me around because they scent my clear conscience—it's common knowledge they don't like an unrighteous man. A poodle followed me once for three days when I was leaving the city of Ulm, and I finally had to entrust it to a peasant, since a lowly journeyman can't afford to feed such an animal, and when I was walking through the Bohemian Forest, stags and does would stop twenty paces from me and not be afraid. It's strange thing the way even wild animals can fathom the human heart!"

"Aye, that's a fact!" cried the Swabian, "don't you see how this finch has been flying around in front of me and trying to light on my shoulder? And that squirrel up there in the pine treee keeps looking around at me, and here's a little beetle crawling about on my leg and won't let me brush it off. It must like it with me, the good little creature!"

Züs now became jealous and said rather vehemently: "All animals like to be around me! I had a bird for eight years and it was most reluctant to die on account of me; our cat follows me wherever I go, and the neighbors' pigeons push and shove at my window, when I strew crumbs for them! Marvelous are the characteristics of animals, each according to its kind! The lion likes to follow kings and heroes, and the elephant accompanies princes and brave warriors; the camel bears the merchant through the desert and stores fresh water for him in its stomach, and the dog sticks by its master through every danger and plunges into the sea to rescue him! The dolphin loves music and follows ships, and the eagle follows armies. The monkey is a creature similar to man and does everything it sees men do, and the parrot understands our language and chats with us like an old man! Even snakes can be tamed and taught to dance on the tips of their tails; the crocodile weeps human tears and is respected and spared by the citizens of

Egypt; the ostrich can be saddled and ridden like a horse; the wild buffalo pulls man's carts and the horned reindeer his sled. The rhinoceros furnishes him with gleaming ivory and the tortoise gives him its translucent bones—"

"Excuse me," all three combmakers interrupted at once, "you are certainly mistaken in this. Ivory comes from elephant tusks and tortoiseshell combs are made from the shell and not the bones of the tortoise!"

Züs became red as fire and said, "That question isn't settled. You've never seen where it comes from but only worked with pieces of it. I'm not usually wrong, but be that as it may, let me finish what I was saying: not only animals have their singular, divinely ordained peculiarities but even inanimate rocks dug from the mountains. Crystal is as transparent as glass; marble, on the other hand, hard and veined, now white, now black; amber has electrical properties and attracts lightning, then it burns and smells like incense. The magnet attracts iron, you can write on a piece of slate, but not on a diamond, because it is small and pointed. You see, dear friends, I also know how to talk a bit about animals! So far as my relationship to them is concerned, the following should be noted: The cat is sly and cunning and therefore attached only to sly and cunning people; the pigeon, however, is an emblem of innocence and feels attracted only to simple, innocent souls. Now, since both cats and pigeons are attached to me, it follows that I am wise and simple, sly and innocent at the same time, just as we read in the Scriptures: 'Be ye therefore wise as serpents, and harmless as pigeons.' In this way, we can appreciate animals and estimate their relationship to ourselves, if we know how to view the matter aright."

The poor journeymen did not dare say another word; Züs had snowed them under, and she continued to expound confusedly on many high-flown matters until they were blind and deaf. They admired her intellect and her eloquence, and in his admiration none thought himself too lowly to possess such a jewel, especially since this ornament of any household was so cheap and consisted solely of a non-stop tongue. Whether they themselves are worthy of that which they esteem so highly and would know what to do with it is a question such weak brains ask themselves last or not at all, for they are like children who reach out for anything that glitters, try to lick the colors off of gaily-painted objects and stick a rattle in their mouths, instead of holding it to their ear. And so their eagerness to win this paragon grew all the more heated, the more they imagined such an eventuality, and the meaner, the more heartless and vain Züsi's senseless tirade became, the more touched and pitiable were the poor combmakers. At the same time, they were beginning to feel a desperate thirst after having eaten the dried fruit. Jobst and the Bavarian went into the woods to look for water and, finding a spring, drank their fill of the cold water. The Swabian, on the other hand, had cunningly brought a flask with him, in which he had mixed cherry brandy with water and sugar; this appetizing drink was to strengthen him and give him an advantage in the race; for he knew that the others were too stingy to take anything along or to stop at a tavern. While the others were filling themselves with spring water, he hastily pulled out his flask and offered it to Miss Züs; she drank it half empty; it tasted delicious to her and refreshing, and she looked at Dietrich out of the corner of her eye as she drank in such an encouraging way that the rest, which he drank himself, tasted better to him than Cyprian wine and strengthened him mightily. He could not restrain himself from grasping Züsi's hand and delicately kissing her fingertips. She rapped him gently on the lips with her index finger, and he acted as though he meant to bite it, making a mouth like a smiling carp. Züs smirked falsely and invitingly, Dietrich smirked slyly and coyly; they sat down on the ground opposite each other, occasionally tapping their shoe soles against one another, as though they wanted to shake hands with their feet. Züs bent forward a little and laid her hand on his shoulder, and Dietrich was just about to return this loving gesture and continue the game when the Saxon and the Bavarian returned and stood looking at them, pale and groaning. For all the water they had drunk on top of the dried pears had suddenly made them miserable, and the anguish they felt at the sight of this playful pair, combined with the awful sensation in their stomach, caused a cold sweat to break out on their brow. Züs did not lose her composure but beckoned to them in a very friendly way and called out, "Come here, my dears, and sit down a bit with me, so that we may enjoy for yet a little while and for the last time our concord and friendship!" Jobst and Fridolin hastened to comply and stretched out their legs; Züs gave the Swabian one hand, Jobst the other and touched the soles of Fridolin's boots with her feet, meanwhile showing her smiling face to each in turn. There are, we know, virtuosos who can play a number of instruments at once: on their head they shake a glockenspiel, with their mouth they blow a harmonica, with their hands they strum a guitar, with their knees they beat a cymbal, with their foot a triangle and with their elbows a drum that hangs down their back.

Then she rose from the ground, smoothed out her dress, which she had carefully hoisted up, and said, "Now it is time, dear friends, for us to set out and for you to prepare yourselves for that earnest trial which your master in his folly has imposed upon you, but which we regard as the decree of a higher fate! Enter upon this trial full of fine zeal, but without enmity or envy toward each other, and willingly yield the victor the crown!"

The journeymen sprang to their feet as though stung by a wasp. There they stood on their legs and were supposed to use them to outrun each other, those same good legs that up to now had only moved with a cautious, dignified gait! None of them could recollect that he had ever run, much less run a race. The Swabian seemed the most confident and even seemed to paw the ground a bit and impatiently lift his feet. They gave each other strange, mistrusting looks, pale and sweating, as though already engaged in strenuous running.

"Shake hands with each other once more!" Züs said. They did so, but laxly and irresolutely, so that their hands coldly slipped apart and fell away as though made of lead. "Are we really going through with this idiotic business?" said Jobst, wiping his eyes, which were beginning to drip tears. "Yes," said the Bavarian, "are we really going to run a race?" and he too began to weep. "And you, Miss Bünzlin," wailed Jobst, "what part are you going to play?" "It befits me," she answered, holding a handkerchief to her eyes, "it befits me to hold my peace, to suffer and look on!" "And afterwards, Miss Züsi?" said the Swabian slyly and amicably . "O Dietrich!" she replied gently, "don't you know the saying 'the impulse of fate is the voice of the heart'?" And she looked at him so meaningfully that he again raised his legs and felt a desire to break into a trot at once. While his two rivals prepared their little go-carts with their knapsacks and Dietrich followed suit, Züs emphatically brushed against his elbow several times and stepped on his foot; she also wiped the dust from his hat, at the same time, however, smiling at the others as though making fun of the Swabian, though taking care that he didn't see her smile. All three now puffed out their cheeks mightily and expelled great sighs. They looked about them on all sides, took off their hats, wiped the sweat from their brows, ran their hand through their sticky hair and put on their hats again. Once more they looked in all directions and gasped for air. Züs took pity on them and was so moved that she even wept herself. "Here are still three prunes," she said. "Let each put one in his mouth and hold it there—it will refresh you! And so depart and convert the folly of the scorners into the wisdom of the righteous! What they have conceived as a wanton jest, you shall transform into an edifying work of testing and self-control, into a conscious, intelligent act of enduring good conduct and a race in the name of virtue!" She stuck a prune in the mouth of each and they sucked on them. Jobst pressed his hand to his stomach and cried, "If it must be, then let it be, in heaven's name!" and raising his cane and deeply bending his knees, he suddenly began to stride forth, pulling his knapsack behind him. Hardly did Fridolin see this than he followed with long strides, and, without looking around again, they hastened fairly rapidly down the road.

The Swabian was the last to set out. With a slyly amused look, apparently quite nonchalant, he walked along beside Züs, as though sure of his superiority and magnanimously willing to grant his companions a head start. Züs praised his friendly serenity and familiarly linked her arm in his. "How wonderful it is," she said with a sigh, "to have a firm support in life! Even if one is sufficiently gifted with wisdom and insight and follows the path of virtue, still it's much pleasanter walking on this path on the arm of a trusted friend!" "Bless me, yes, I'll say it is!" replied Dietrich and gave her a good punch in the ribs with his elbow, at the same time casting a weather eye at his rivals to see whether they were getting too far ahead. "Now you see, my dear Miss Züs! Finally it's dawning on you, now you know which side your bread's buttered on!" "O Dietrich, dear Dietrich," she said with a much deeper sigh, "I often feel so lonely!" "Hoops-a-daisy, that's the way it ought to be!" he cried, and his heart hopped like a rabbit in the cabbage patch. "O Dietrich!" she cried and snuggled up against him more firmly. A mist clouded his sight and his heart almost burst with sly joy, but at the same moment he discovered that his forerunners were no longer visible: they had disappeared around a corner. Immediately he tried to tear himself away from Züsi's arm and run after them, but she held him so fast he was unable to, clinging to him as though about to faint. "Dietrich!" she whispered, rolling her eyes, "don't leave me alone now, I trust you, support me!" "The deuce you say, miss, let me go!" he cried anxiously, "or I'll get there too late and then good-bye Easy Street!" "No, no! You mustn't leave me, I think I'm going to be sick!" she wailed. "Sick or not!" he shouted, violently tore himself loose, ran to the top of a rise and looked about him; he could see the contenders already in full gallop far down the mountain. He made ready to head off, but when he looked about for Züs he saw her sitting at the entrance of a narrow shady path into the woods, sweetly motioning to him to join her. This sight was too much for him, and instead of hastening down the mountain he hastened back to her. When she saw him coming, she stood up and went deeper into the woods, glancing back at him, for she meant to keep him from joining the race at all costs and to hoax him until he arrived at his master's door too late and would not be able to remain in Seldwyla.

But at this juncture the inventive Swabian changed his plan and determined to gain his salvation up here on the mountain, and so things fell out quite differently than sly Züsi had hoped. As soon as he caught up to her and was alone with her in a secluded spot, he fell at her feet and stormily importuned her with the fieriest declarations of love ever made by a combmaker. First, she imperiously tried to calm him and, without frightening him away, to admonish him to better manners, summoning up all her words of wisdom and all the expectations she had of him. But when he brought forth every argument on heaven and earth, his aroused spirit of enterprise lending him magical words in this effort, when he overwhelmed her with tendernesses of every kind, seeking now to grasp her hands, now her feet, and praised to the skies her body and her spirit and everything about her, till heaven almost turned green with envy, when, to cap it all, the forest was so still and the weather so mild, Züs, as a person whose thoughts were after all as shallow as her senses, at last lost control—her heart kicked about in her breast, as fearful and as helpless as a beetle turned on its back, and Dietrich became its master in every respect. She had tempted him into the thicket to betray him and had in a wink been conquered by the cunning Swabian; this did not come about because she was really in love, but because, being of a shallow nature, she could not, in spite of all her imagined wisdom, see beyond the end of her nose. They tarried for perhaps an hour in their entertaining solitude, embracing each other again and again and exchanging a thousand kisses. In all sincerity, they swore eternal fidelity and agreed to get married, come what might.

Meanwhile, the news of the strange adventure on which the three journeymen had embarked had spread about the town, the master himself having made it public for his own amusement. The Seldwylers were therefore looking forward to the unexpected spectacle and were curious to see the three righteous and honorable combmakers running in full career and arriving at their destination. A big crowd marched out before the city gate and lined both sides of the road, as when a racer is expected. The boys climbed up in the trees, the elderly and retired sat in the grass and smoked their pipes, happy to be afforded such cheap amusement. Even men of quality had joined the throng to view this great joke and were sitting gayly conversing in the beer gardens and arbors of the inns and laying many bets. In the streets through which the runners had to pass all the windows were open; the housewives had laid red and white pillows in the sills of the windows facing the street to rest one's arms on and were receiving their neighbors, so that jolly coffee parties sprang up on the spur of the moment and the servant girls had plenty of running to do, fetching *kuchen* and zwieback. Before the city gate the boys in the highest trees now saw a little cloud of dust drawing near and began to shout, "They're coming! They're coming!" Nor was it long before Jobst and Fridolin came rushing along like a whirlwind down the middle of the street, stirring up a thick cloud of dust. With one hand they were pulling their carts with the knapsacks, which bounced crazily over the paving stones; with the other they were holding fast to their hats, which had slipped down onto their necks, while their long coats were flying and waving for all they were worth. Both men were bathed in sweat and covered with dust; their mouths were gaping and gasping for breath; they neither heard nor saw anything of what was going on around them; great tears, which the poor devils had no time to wipe away, were streaming down their cheeks. One was running on the heels of the other, but the Bavarian was leading by a length. A fearful outcry and volley of laughter arose and reechoed along the way. Everyone sprang up and pressed closer to the road, and cries were heard on all sides: "That's the way to go! "Run, Saxon, run! Beat him! Keep up the good work, Bavarian! One's already dropped out, there are only two left!" The gentlemen in the beer gardens were standing on the tables and holding their sides with laughter. The laughter echoed and thundered over the confused noise of the crowd along the street and gave the signal for an unheard-of celebration. The boys and the mob streamed together behind the two poor journeymen and a wild rout, raising a terrible cloud of dust, rolled along with the contenders toward the city gate. Even women and little girls playing in the streets mixed their high-pitched voices with the shouts of the young men. They were already near the city gate, whose towers were occupied by curious onlookers waving their caps; the Saxon and the Bavarian were running like frightened horses, their hearts full of torment and anxiety; at this moment a street urchin knelt like a goblin on Jobst's cart and let himself be pulled along to the cheers of the bystanders. Jobst turned around and entreated him to get off, even striking at him with his cane, but the boy only ducked and grinned at him. Through this, Fridolin gained a still greater lead, and when Jobst noticed it, he threw his cane between his legs, bringing him to a fall. But as he was about to jump over him, the Bavarian grabbed him by the coattail and pulled himself up on it; Jobst struck his hands and yelled, "Let go ! Let go!" When Fridolin wouldn't let go, Jobst in turn grabbed him by the coattail, so that now they were both holding each other fast, and in this state they slowly wheeled in through the city gate, trying only now and then to escape from each other by a sudden jerk. They wept, sobbed and wailed like children and cried out in their inexpressible anguish, "O God! let go! Dear Jesus, let go! Jobst, let go! Fridolin, you Satan, let go!" At intervals they would strike each other on the hand, making all the while very slight progress. They had lost their hats and canes; two boys were carrying them on ahead, the hats stuck on the canes, while the unruly mob streamed along behind them. All the windows were occupied by the ladies, who tossed their silvery laughter down into the roaring surf below; it had been a long time since the city had been in such a gay mood. This riotous entertainment was so much to the taste of the Seldwylers that not a soul pointed out their goal, the master's house, to the two struggling men when they finally reached it. And so the mad procession rolled on through the whole town and out again through the other gate. The master had been leaning in his window, laughing, and, after waiting a short hour for the final victor, was just about to go out and reap the praise of his fellow townspeople for his capital joke, when Dietrich and Züs quietly and unexpectedly entered the room.

These two had put their heads together and figured out that the master combmaker, since he wouldn't be able to hang onto his business for long anyway, might be interested in selling it for cash. Züs was willing to contribute her deed of mortgage and the Swabian to add his small savings; then they would be masters of the situation and could laugh at the other two. They explained their plan to the surprised master, and he immediately saw the advantage of closing the deal at once behind the backs of his creditors, before the business had failed, and thus, which was more than he had hoped for, get hold of the selling price in hard cash. All was quickly arranged and before the sun had set Miss Bünzlin was the lawful owner of the combmaking business and her fiancé the renter of the building in which it was situated, and thus was Züs, without having had an inkling of such an eventuality when she woke up that morning, finally won and contractually bound by the dexterity of the wily Swabian.

Half dead with shame, fatigue and disappointment, Jobst and Fridolin were lying at the inn they had been brought to after having finally fallen down from exhaustion, still obstinately clinging to each other, in an open field. The whole town, since it was now in an excited mood, though it had already forgotten why, went on celebrating merrily late into the night. There was dancing in many of the houses and in the taverns drinking and singing, as on days of greatest festival in Seldwyla, for the Seldwylers didn't need much of an excuse to organize a celebration in a masterful fashion. When the two poor devils saw how their valiant efforts, by means of which they had thought to outwit the folly of the world, had only served to make this folly triumphant, their hearts almost broke, for they had not only failed in their plan of many years and ruined it wholly, they had also forfeited their reputations as prudent, calm and law-abiding men.

Jobst, who was the oldest and had been here for seven years, was completely confused and could not get his bearings again. Overcome with melancholy, he left town before dawn and hanged himself on a tree at the spot where they had all rested the day before.

When the Bavarian came by an hour later and saw him, he was seized by such terror that he took to his heels as though possessed; his whole nature changed and, according to later reports, he became dissolute and never advanced to the rank of master, an old journeyman who was no one's friend.

Only Dietrich the Swabian remained a righteous man and kept up his head in Seldwyla, but he had little joy from it, for Züs gave him no credit for anything; she ruled the roost and kept him strictly under her thumb, regarding herself as the sole source of all that is good.

Translated by Robert M. Browning

A Village
Romeo and Juliet

To tell this story would be a pointless imitation, were it not founded upon an actual occurrence, showing how deeply rooted in human life are those plots on which the great works of the past are based. Such plots are relatively few in number, but they are constantly reappearing in new forms and when they do the writer's hand is compelled to preserve them.

Near the beautiful river which flows by Seldwyla at half a league's distance rises an extensive ridge of well-cultivated land, which merges into the fertile plain. Far off at its foot lies a village, comprising several large farmhouses; some years ago there were three splendid long fields here, side by side, stretching far over the gentle slope, like three gigantic ribbons. One sunny morning in September two farmers were out plowing in two of these fields—that is, in the two outside ones. The middle field had apparently been lying there untilled and desolate for years, for it was covered with stones and high weeds, and a world of little winged creatures buzzed about in it undisturbed.

The farmers following their plows on either side were tall, rugged men of about forty years, whose appearance marked them at first glance as self-reliant, well-to-do landowners. They wore short knee breeches of strong twill, in which each fold had its own unchangeable place and looked as if it were chiseled out of stone. Whenever their plows struck an obstacle, causing them to grip the handles tighter, the light shock made the sleeves of their coarse shirts quiver. Their well-shaven faces, calm and alert, but squinting a little in the glare of the sun, looked steadily ahead and measured the furrow, except that now and then they would turn around when some far-off noise interrupted the stillness of the countryside. Slowly and with a certain natural grace they moved forward step by step, and neither said a word, except to give directions to the hired man who was driving the magnificent horses.

Thus from a little distance they looked exactly alike, for they represented the original type of the region; and at first sight one could have distinguished them only by the fact that the one wore his white cap with the peak tipping forward over his brow, while the other's fell back on his neck. But even that distinction alternated between them, depending upon the direction in which they were plowing; for when they met and passed each other on the crest of the ridge, where there was a fresh east wind blowing, the one who was facing it had the peak of his cap thrown back, while that of the other, with the wind behind him, stuck out in front. Each time they passed there was a brief moment when the gleaming caps stood upright, fluttering in the breeze and shooting skyward like two tongues of white flame.

And so the two men plowed calmly on, and it was a beautiful sight in that quiet, golden September landscape to watch them move past each other on the ridge slowly and silently, and gradually draw apart, farther and farther, until they both sank, like two setting constellations, behind the brow of the hill and finally vanished from view, to reappear again after some time. Whenever they came across a stone in the furrow, they would hurl it with an easy, powerful fling into the waste field; this, however, happened only rarely, for it was already nearly covered with all the stones that had ever been found on the two adjoining fields.

Thus the long morning had partly passed, when a pretty little vehicle, hardly visible as it started up the gentle slope, drew near from the direction of the village. It was a child's cart, painted green, in which the children of the two plowmen, a boy and a little wisp of a girl, were bringing out their fathers' lunch. In the cart there was, for each man, a fine loaf of bread wrapped in a napkin, a jug of wine with glasses, and some extra little delicacy which the fond housewife had sent along for her hard-working husband. Also packed in it were all sorts of strangely shaped apples and pears, which the children had gathered on the way and bitten into; likewise a doll, absolutely naked and with only one leg and a dirty face, sitting like a young lady between the two loaves and enjoying the ride. After many a jolt and halt, the vehicle finally came to a stop on the crest of the ridge in the shade of a linden grove that stood on the border of the field.

It was now possible to obtain a closer view of the two wagoners. One was a boy of seven years, the other a little girl of five, and both were healthy and bright. Otherwise there was nothing remarkable about them, except that both had very pretty eyes, and the little girl a brownish complexion and very curly dark hair, which gave her an open-hearted and fiery appearance.

The plowmen, who had once more arrived at the top, put some clover before their horses, left their plows in the half-finished furrows, and went like good neighbors to their joint repast, greeting each other now for the first time; for as yet they had not exchanged a word that day. The two men ate their lunch in comfort, sharing it contentedly and benevolently with the children, who did not leave the spot as long as the eating and drinking continued. As they ate they cast sweeping glances over the landscape far and near, and saw the little city among the mountains in its smoky, sunlit haze; for the abundant meal which the people of Seldwyla prepared every noon would often send up over their roofs a cloud of far-gleaming, silvery smoke, which floated cheerily along their mountains.

"Those rascals in Seldwyla are hard at work cooking again!" said Manz, one of the farmers.

And Marti, the other, answered; "One of them came around yesterday to see me about the field."

"From the District Council? He came to me too," said Manz.

"So? And I suppose he told you too that you ought to use the land and pay the gentlemen rent for it?"

"Yes—until it's decided who owns the field, and what to do with it. But I had no mind to fix that wasteland up for somebody else. I told them they ought to sell the land and set aside the proceeds until the owner has been found—which will probably never happen, because anything that's brought to court in Seldwyla lies there a good while, and besides the matter is a hard one to settle.

But the rascals would be only too glad to get a rake-off from the rent, though of course they could do that with the money they'd get by selling it. But we'd take care not to bid too high for it, and then at least we'd know what we had and who owned the land."

"That's what I think too, and I gave the loafer the same kind of answer!"

They were silent for a moment, and then Manz began again: "But just the same it's too bad for the good land to lie there this way and be an eyesore. It's been like that for at least twenty years, and not a soul bothers to ask about it! There's nobody here in the village who has any claim at all to the field, and no one knows what ever became of the lost trumpeter's children."

"Hm!" said Marti, "it's a queer business! When I look at the black fiddler, living among the vagrants one day, and the next playing for the village dances, I could swear he's a descendant of the trumpeter, though of course he doesn't know he still has a field. But what would he do with it?—drink it up for a month, and then go on as before! Besides, who has any right to talk when we can't know anything for sure?"

"That might start a lot of trouble!" answered Manz. "We have enough to do disputing this fiddler's right to make his home in our community, now that they're forever trying to unload the tramp on us. His parents took up with the vagrants, so let him stay there too, and saw his fiddle for them. How in the world are we supposed to know that he's the trumpeter's grandson? As far as I'm concerned, even when I'm sure I recognize the old trumpeter in the fiddler's black face, I say: To err is human; the least piece of paper, a tiny scrap of a baptismal certificate, would satisfy my conscience better than some sinner's face, ten times over."

"Why, naturally!" said Marti. "Of course he says that it was not his fault he wasn't baptized. But what are we supposed to do, make our baptismal font portable and carry it around in the woods with us? No, it's in the church permanently, and what's portable is the bier we have hanging outside on the wall! We're already overpopulated in the village; we'll soon have to have two school-masters!"

With this the meal and the conversation of the two farmers came to an end, and they rose to finish their morning's work. But the two children, who had already made plans to return home with their fathers, pulled their cart under the shelter of the young lindens, and went off on an excursion into the waste field, which to them, with its weeds, bushes and heaps of stones, represented an unfamiliar and fascinating wilderness. After they had wandered hand in hand for a little while in the midst of this green waste, and had amused themselves by swinging their joined hands above the high thistles, they finally sat down in the shade of one of these, and the little girl began to dress her doll with long plantain leaves, so that it soon had a beautiful, green, scalloped skirt. A solitary red poppy, still blooming, was drawn over its head as a hood and fastened on with a blade of grass; all of this made the little figure look like a sorceress, especially after it had acquired in addition a necklace and belt of little red berries. Then it was placed high up on the stalk of a thistle, and the two children joined in contemplating it for a while, until the boy had looked at it long enough and knocked it down with a stone. This completely disarranged the doll's clothing, and the girl speedily disrobed it in order to dress it again. But the moment the doll was naked once more, retaining possession only of its red hood, the wild youngster grabbed the plaything away from his companion and threw it high into the air. The girl ran after it with a cry, but the boy got it first and gave it another toss. He continued to tease her in this way for a long time; the little girl kept struggling in vain to get hold of the flying doll, which suffered considerable damage at his hands, especially to the knee of its one leg, where a small hole appeared, allowing some bran stuffing to trickle out. As soon as the tormenter noticed this hole, he stopped still as a mouse and, with his mouth open, started busily enlarging the hole with his fingernails, in order to ascertain the source of the bran. His silence seemed highly suspicious to the poor little girl; she crowded up close to him and was horrified to see what a wicked thing he was doing.

"Look!" he cried, and jerked the leg around in front of her nose, so that the bran flew into her face. When she made a grab for the doll and screamed and begged, he ran away again and did not stop until the whole leg was empty and hung down limp, like a pitiful husk. Then he flung down the much-abused toy once more and assumed an extremely impudent and indifferent air, as the little girl, crying, threw herself upon the doll and covered it with her apron. Presently she drew it out again and sadly contemplated the poor thing. When she saw the leg she began to cry all over again, for it hung down from the body like the tail of a salamander. The evil-doer, seeing her crying so violently, finally began to feel bad and stood before the wailing child, anxious and repentant. When she became aware of this, she suddenly stopped crying and struck him several times with the doll. He made believe that it hurt him and cried ouch! so naturally that she was satisfied, and they now joined forces in resuming the dissection and destruction. They bored hole after hole into the little martyr's body and let the stuffing run out from all sides. Then they carefully gathered it into a little pile on a flat stone, stirred it around, and looked at it intently.

The one intact member which the doll still retained was its head, and of course this now attracted their chief attention. They severed it carefully from the eviscerated body and peeped with amazement into the hollow interior. When they saw the ominous hole and also the bran, their next and most natural idea was to fill the head with the bran. And so the children's small fingers began to vie with one another in putting the bran into the head, which now, for the first time in its existence, had something in it. The boy, however, must still have regarded it as lifeless knowledge, for he suddenly caught a large blue fly, and holding it, buzzing, in the hollow of his hands, he ordered the girl to empty the head of bran. The fly was then imprisoned in it and the hole stopped up with grass, and after both the children had held the head to their ears, they solemnly put it down on a stone. As it still had on the red poppy hood, the resonant object now resembled the head of a prophet, and the children with their arms around each other listened in profound silence to its oracles and tales.

But prophets always awaken terror and ingratitude; the bit of life in the poorly formed image aroused the children's human propensity to be cruel, and it was decided to bury the head. Without asking the imprisoned fly's opinion, they dug a grave, laid the head in it, and erected over the spot an imposing monument of fieldstones. Then they began to feel apprehensive, because they had buried something with life and form, and they went some distance away from the eerie place. On a little spot completely overgrown with green weeds the girl, who was now very tired, lay down on her back and began to sing, monotonously repeating the same words over and over again, while the little boy, who was feeling so drowsy and lazy that he did not know whether to lie down or not, squatted beside her and joined in. The sun shone into the singing girl's open mouth, lighting up her dazzlingly white teeth, and suffusing her round, red lips. The boy saw the teeth, and, holding the girl's head, examined them curiously.

"Guess," he cried, "how many teeth we have?"

The girl thought for a moment, as if counting up carefully, and then said at random, "A hundred!"

"No, thirty-two!" he exclaimed. "Wait, I'll count them."

Then he counted the little girl's teeth, and as the number did not come out to thirty-two, he kept beginning all over again. The girl held still a long time, but as the eager counter did not seem about to stop, she got up hurriedly, exclaiming; "Now let me count yours!"

The boy then lay down among the weeds, and the girl leaned over him, putting her arms around his head. He opened his mouth and she began to count; "One, two, seven, five, two, one,"—for the pretty child had not yet learned to count.

The boy corrected and prompted her, however, and she too began all over again a great many times. This game seemed to amuse them more than any they had tried that day.

Finally, however, the girl sank down completely on the youthful mathematician, and the two children fell asleep in the bright midday sun.

In the meantime their fathers had finished plowing their fields, having converted the surface into brown, fresh-smelling loam. But when they reached the end of the last furrow and one of the farm hands started to quit for the day, his master called out, "What are you stopping for? Turn around again!"

"But I thought we were through," said the man.

"Shut up and do as I say!" cried the master.

And they turned around and plowed a deep furrow in the middle, ownerless field, making the weeds and stones fly. These latter, however, the farmer did not stop to throw aside; he very likely thought there would be time enough for that later, and for the present was content to do the work in a very rough way.

And so the man plowed swiftly up in a gentle curve, and when he reached the crest and the fresh wind again blew back the tip of

his cap, whom should he pass on the opposite side but the other
farmer, who, with the tip of his cap forward, was likewise plowing a deep furrow in the middle field and throwing the clods of
earth aside. Each doubtless saw what the other was doing, but
neither seemed to see it, and they disappeared from each other's
sight, each constellation silently passing the other and sinking below this round world. Thus the shuttles of fate pass one another,
and "what he is weaving, no weaver knoweth."

Harvest followed harvest, and with each one the children had
grown taller and handsomer, and the ownerless field narrower between its widened neighbors. With every plowing it had lost on
either side the width of one furrow, and not a word had been said
about it, and it seemed that no human eye had noticed the crime.
Each year the stones had been thrown in closer together, so that
they now formed a regular backbone up and down the entire length
of the field; the wild weeds on it were so high that the children,
although they too had grown, could no longer see each other when
they walked on opposite sides. For they no longer went out to the
field together, since the ten-year-old Salomon, or Sali, as he was
called, was now old enough to be with the larger boys and men;
while brown Verena, though a fiery little girl, had to go around in
the watchful company of her own sex, in order to avoid being
teased by the other girls as a tomboy. Nevertheless, once during
each harvest, when everybody was in the fields, they would use
this occasion to climb up the wild stone barrier that separated
them and push each other down from it. Although it was the only
contact they ever had with each other, this annual ceremony seemed
to be all the more carefully cherished, as their fathers' fields came
together nowhere else.

It was finally announced, however, that the field was to be sold
and the proceeds held in escrow by the authorities. The auction
took place on the field itself, but with the exception of Manz and
Marti only a few idlers showed up, since nobody had any desire
to buy and till the odd piece of land between the two neighbors.
For, although the latter were among the best farmers of the village
and had only done what two-thirds of the others would have done
under the same circumstances, people still eyed them with some
suspicion, and nobody wanted to be hemmed in between them in

the diminished and orphaned field. Most men are able and ready to commit a wrong when the opportunity presents itself and when they poke their nose right into it; but as soon as one of them has done so, the others are glad it was not they who did it or were tempted to do it, and they look upon the chosen one as an index of the wickedness in their own characters, and treat him with timid awe as the divinely marked scapegoat, while all the time their own mouths are watering for the advantages he enjoys from his crime.

Manz and Marti, therefore, were the only ones who bid for the field in earnest, and after some rather obstinate overbidding it was knocked down to Manz. The officials and onlookers left the field and the two farmers finished their day's work. On their way home they met and Marti said, "I suppose now you'll put your new land and your old land together and divide it into two equal strips. At any rate that's what I'd have done if I'd got it."

"And that's what I'm going to do too," answered Manz. "In one piece the field would be too large for me. But, as I was going to say, I've noticed that recently you've plowed diagonally across the lower end of this field, which now belongs to me, and that you've cut a big triangle off it. Perhaps you did so because you thought that sooner or later you'd own the whole field anyway. But now it belongs to me, so of course you understand that any such improper jog in the line is of no use to me and I won't stand for it; surely you'll have no objection to my making the strip straight again. That shouldn't cause any quarrel between us!"

Marti replied just as coldbloodedly as Manz had addressed him, "Nor do I see why we should quarrel about it! As I understand it, you bought the field just as it is. We looked it over, all of us, and in the course of an hour it hasn't changed by a hair!"

"Nonsense!" said Manz. "We won't rake up the past, but too much is too much, and before we're through everything will have to be properly straightened out. These three fields always lay there side by side, as if they were marked off by a ruler. You've got a strange sense of humor, trying to run such a ridiculous curlicue between them. People would make fun of us if we let that crooked piece stay there—it has to go, I tell you!"

Marti laughed and said, "It's remarkable, the way you're suddenly afraid of ridicule! But we can fix it. The fact that it's crooked doesn't bother me at all, but if it annoys you, all right—we'll straighten it. But not on my side! You can have that in writing if you like!"

"Don't be funny!" said Manz. "We'll make it straight—on your side; and you can count on that!"

"We'll see whether we will!" said Marti, and the two men separated without looking at each other again. They preferred to gaze off into the blue in various directions, as if they saw something remarkable and had to look at it with all their might.

The very next day Manz sent a farm hand, a hired girl, and his own little son Sali out to the field to clear away the wild weeds and underbrush and stack it into piles in order to facilitate the subsequent work of carting off the stones. This was something of a change for him to send the boy out despite his mother's protests, for Sali was not quite eleven years old and had never been required to do any work. Since Manz used earnest and soothing words in imposing this hard labor upon his own flesh and blood it seemed as if his severity were intended to stifle his own consciousness of wrong-doing, which was now quietly beginning to show its effects.

Meanwhile the little group he sent out worked happily at clearing away the weeds, and hacked with gusto at the curious bushes and plants of all kinds that had been luxuriating there for years. For, being an unusual and in a sense disorderly task, and requiring no rule and no care, it was regarded as a pleasure. The wild stuff, dried by the sun, was piled up with great glee and burned, so that the smoke spread far and wide, and the young people ran about as if possessed. This was the last joyous occasion on the unlucky field, and little Verena, Marti's daughter, stole away and came out to help. The unusual nature of the event and all the joyful excitement offered her a good opportunity to join her young playmate once more, and the children were happy and lively around their fire. Other children came too, and a cheerful group assembled. But whenever Sali got separated from Verena he would immediately try to rejoin her, and she likewise, smiling happily all the time, would contrive to slip up to him. To both children it seemed as if this glorious day must not and could not end.

Toward evening, however, old Manz came out to see what had been accomplished, and, although they were all through with the work, he scolded them for their jollity and broke up the company.

At the same time Marti appeared on his own land, and, seeing his daughter, whistled so shrilly and imperiously to her through his fingers that she ran to him in alarm. Without knowing why, he slapped her several times. And so both children went home crying and in great misery—really knowing just as little why they were now so sad as why they had been so happy before. For severity on the part of their fathers, in itself rather new, was something the innocent young things could not understand, and so it could not make a very deep impression upon them.

On the following days, when Manz was having the stones picked up and carried away, the work became more strenuous and required grown men. It looked as if there would be no end to it; all the stones in the world seemed to be gathered there. Manz, however, did not have them carted away from the field, but had each load dumped on the contested triangle, which Marti had neatly plowed. He had previously drawn a straight line as a boundary, and now covered this little plot with all the stones which both men from time immemorial had thrown into the middle field, so that an enormous pyramid arose, which he felt sure his rival would be slow to remove.

Marti had expected anything but this; he supposed that Manz would go to work with his plow in the same old way, and had therefore waited to see him setting out as a plowman. Not until it was almost completed did he hear about the beautiful monument Manz had erected. He ran out in a rage, took a look at the mess, and then ran back to fetch the magistrate, in order to get a preliminary injunction against the pile of stones and to have the plot attached. And from this day forth the two farmers were in litigation with each other, and did not rest until they were both ruined.

The thoughts of these hitherto sensible men were now cut as fine as chopped straw, each being filled with the strictest sense of justice in the world. Neither one of them could or would understand how the other, with such manifest and arbitrary injustice, could claim for himself the insignificant corner in question. Manz also developed a remarkable sense for symmetry and parallel lines, and felt himself deeply wronged by the foolish obstinacy with which Marti insisted on preserving that most ridiculous and arbitrary curlicue. But each held to the conviction that the other, in trying with such open insolence to defraud him, must necessarily take him for a contemptible fool; one might try that sort of thing on some poor, helpless devil, but never on the kind of shrewd and sensible man who was able to take care of himself. Each felt that the other was injuring his precious honor, and each gave himself over without restraint to the passion of strife and the decay that resulted.

From then on their lives were like the torturing nightmare of two condemned souls, who, floating down a dark stream on a narrow board, fall to quarrelling, thrash the air, and seize and destroy each other, each thinking he has hold of the cause of his misfortune. Since neither's cause was just, they both fell into the hands of the worst sort of shysters and swindlers, who inflated their distorted fancies into enormous bubbles filled with worthless ideas. These men were chiefly speculators from the city of Seldwyla, to whom this affair meant easy money. It was consequently not long before each of the rivals had behind him a following of go-betweens, informers, and advisers, who contrived in a hundred ways to get away with all the cash. For the little piece of land with its stone pile, on which a forest of nettles and thistles was again blooming, was merely the germ, or the foundation, of a complicated story, a new mode of life, in which the two men of fifty acquired habits and manners, principles and hopes, that were alien to their former experience. The more money they lost, the more passionately they longed to have some; and the less they had, the more obstinate they were in hoping to get rich and gain an advantage over each other. They allowed themselves to be seduced into all sorts of swindles, and every year they put money into all the foreign lotteries, tickets for which circulated abundantly in Seldwyla. Never once, however, did they set eyes on a penny of winnings, although they were always hearing about what other people had won and how they themselves had almost done so. Meanwhile this obsession was a constant drain on their money. Occasionally the people of Seldwyla amused themselves by inducing the two farmers, without their knowing it, to buy shares in the same ticket, so that each would base his hope for the other's ruin and downfall upon one and the same chance.

They spent half their time in town. Here each had his headquarters in a miserable dive, where he would let people stir him up, and tempt him into the most absurd expenditures and a life of wretched and heavy-handed carousing, which secretly made his heart ache. In keeping up the quarrel only to avoid being considered fools, both of them were as a matter of fact excellent representatives of the species and were so regarded by everybody. The other half of their time they spent sullenly lounging around home, or, when they went back to work, seeking to make up for lost time by mad, ill-advised rushing and goading, which frightened away every decent, trustworthy workman.

And so their lives went downhill at an alarming rate; before ten years had elapsed they were both head over heels in debt, and stood like storks, on one leg, at the threshold of their possessions, in danger of being blown over by the slightest breath of air. But whatever happened, their hatred for each other increased daily, each regarding the other as the originator of his misfortune, his hereditary enemy, his absolutely unreasonable antagonist, whom the devil had sent to earth on purpose to ruin him. They would spit at the mere sight of each other; no member of either household was permitted, under penalty of the grossest maltreatment, to say a single word to the wife, child, or servants of the other.

Their wives behaved quite differently during this impoverishment and debasement of their very existence. Marti's wife, who was a decent person, was unable to endure their ruin; she pined away and died before her daughter was fourteen years old. Manz's wife, on the other hand, adapted herself to the changed mode of life. All she had to do in order to become a partner in this bad business was to give free rein to a few feminine faults she had always had, and let them grow into vices. Her fondness for delicacies developed into inordinate greed; her volubility into a radically false and deceitful habit of flattery and slander, so that every moment she said the exact opposite of what she thought, kept everything in turmoil, and hoodwinked her own husband. The candor she originally displayed in more or less innocent gossip developed now into the hardened shamelessness of her new way of life. So instead of suffering at the hands of her husband, she thumbed her nose at him. If he acted badly, she put on airs, denying herself nothing; and thus she sprang into full bloom as the mistress of this decadent house.

All of this was very hard on the poor children. With nothing but quarreling and anxiety everywhere, they could neither cherish any hope for their future nor rejoice in a pleasant and happy youth. Little Verena was apparently in an even worse position than Sali, since her mother was dead and she was left alone in a dreary house under the tyranny of a debased father. At the age of sixteen she had already developed into a slender and graceful girl; her dark-brown curls hung down almost to her lustrous brown eyes; the dark red blood shone in her brownish cheeks and gleamed, a deep scarlet, on her fresh lips; it was something one rarely sees, and it gave the dark child a special and marked appearance. Joy and fiery love of life quivered in every fibre of her being; she laughed and was ready for joking and playing whenever the weather was the least bit pleasant, that is, if she was not too greatly tormented or harassed by her many worries. These bothered her often enough, however, for she had not only to bear the grief and the increasing misery of her home, but she had to look out for herself as well. She liked to dress halfway decently and neatly, but her father would not give her the money to do so. The lovely girl had the greatest difficulty getting herself even modestly dressed up, in providing herself with the simplest Sunday outfit, and in saving a few colorful, almost worthless scarves. So the cheerful young thing was hemmed in and humiliated in every way, and there was little or no chance of her falling victim to pride. Besides, at an age of awakening intelligence, she had seen her mother's suffering and death, and the memory placed a further restraint upon her joyous and fiery nature. With all this it was very sweet, innocent, and touching to see the good child cheered by every ray of sunlight and ready to smile in spite of all her trouble.

At first sight Sali did not seem to fare so badly, for he was now a strong, handsome young fellow, who knew how to look out for himself, and whose very bearing precluded mistreatment. He saw, of course, the bad management of his parents in domestic matters and thought he could remember a time when things were different; yes, the earlier picture of his father still lingered vividly in his memory—the strong, wise, calm farmer, the same man whom he now saw before him as a gray-haired fool, a quarreler and an idler, roaring and swaggering down a hundred absurd and deceitful paths and going backward every moment like a crab. All this displeased Sali and often filled him with shame and sorrow, it not being clear to him in his inexperience how matters had got into such a state, but his anxiety about it was quieted by his mother's flattering treatment. For, in order to be freer to lead her slovenly existence, and to have someone on her side, and also in order to gratify her vanity, she let him have whatever he wanted, dressed him neatly and even showily, and supported him in everything that he undertook for his own pleasure. He accepted all this without much gratitude, since his mother gossiped and lied to him far too much for that. Finding very little pleasure in it, he did in a sluggish and thoughtless way whatever he pleased, but never anything really bad. For as yet he was unharmed by the example of his parents and still felt the youthful necessity of being, on the whole, simple, calm, and fairly capable.

So he was very much the way his father had been at the same age, and this fact imbued the latter with an involuntary respect for his son, in whom, with his confused conscience and painful memories, he respected his own youth. But in spite of this freedom which Sali enjoyed, his life was still not happy; he realized that there was nothing worthwhile in store for him, that he was not learning anything worthwhile—for there had been no such thing as systematic and serious work in Manz's house for a long time. His greatest comfort, therefore, was to take pride in his independence and temporary good name, and in this pride he defiantly idled away the days and turned his eyes from the future.

The only constraint to which he was subjected was his father's enmity toward everybody and everything that bore the name of Marti or called him to mind. All he knew was that Marti had done his father some injury, and that everyone in Marti's house was equally malevolent; thus he did not find it difficult to avoid looking at Marti or at his daughter, or to assume on his own the role of an incipient, but still rather mild enemy. Little Verena, on the other hand, who had more to contend with than Sali and was much more neglected at home, felt less disposed to open enmity, and thought herself despised by the well-dressed and apparently happier Sali. For this reason she kept out of his sight, and whenever he was anywhere near her she would hurry away, and he would not even bother to look at her. The result was that several years passed without his having seen Verena up close, and he had no idea how she looked, now that she was grown up. Yet sometimes he wondered about it exceedingly, and whenever anything was said about the Martis, he involuntarily thought only of the daughter, of whose present appearance he had no clear mental picture, and whose memory was far from disagreeable to him.

His father, Manz, however, was the first of the two enemies forced to give up and leave home. He owed this headstart to having a wife who helped him along, and a son who also made demands on him, whereas Marti had been the only consumer in his shaky kingdom, his daughter having been allowed to work like a dog, but not to use up anything. Manz could think of nothing else to do but to move into town, on the advice of his "sponsors" in Seldwyla, and set up there as an innkeeper. It is always a pathetic sight when a one-time farmer who has grown old in the fields moves with the remnants of his property into town and opens a tavern or saloon, in order, as a last hope, to play the part of the friendly and clever landlord, when as a matter of fact he feels anything but friendly.

When the Manzes moved away from their farm people saw for the first time how poor they had become; for they loaded on the wagon nothing but old, dilapidated furniture, which obviously had not been renovated or replenished for years. Nonetheless, the wife was decked out in her best finery as she took her seat upon the cartload of junk, wearing a hopeful expression, and already, as the future town-lady, looking down with contempt upon the villagers, who peeked compassionately out from behind hedges at this odd procession. For she proposed to charm the whole town with her amiability and shrewdness, and whatever her stupid husband could not do, she herself was going to do, just as soon as she occupied the dignified position of Hostess in an imposing tavern.

This tavern, however, in which another man had already failed, was a miserable hole in a narrow, out-of-the-way alley, which the people of Seldwyla leased to Manz, knowing that he still had a few hundred thalers coming to him. They also sold him a few little casks of adulterated wine and the furnishings of the establishment, consisting of a dozen poor bottles, an equal number of glasses and some fir tables and benches which had once been covered with red paint, but were now bare in spots as the result of scouring. In front of the window an iron ring creaked on a hook, and in the ring a tin hand was pouring red wine out of a mug into a glass.

Hanging over the door there was also a dried-up sprig of holly. All of this was included in Manz's lease.

In consequence, Manz did not feel as cheerful as his wife, but was filled with wrath and evil forebodings as he urged along the skinny horses he had hired from the new farmer. His last shabby little farmhand had left him several weeks before. As he drove off in this way he could not fail to see that Marti, full of scorn and malicious joy, was pretending to be at work not far from the road; Manz cursed him, regarding him as the sole cause of his misfortune. As soon as the wagon was under way, however, Sali quickened his steps, hurried on ahead, and went into town alone, by side roads.

"Here we are!" said Manz, as the wagon drew up in front of the dingy hole. His wife was horrified, for it was indeed a sorry looking tavern. The people hurried to their windows and out in front of their houses to see the new farmer-landlord, and, with their Seldwyla superiority, assumed an air of mock sympathy. Angry and tearful, madame climbed down from the wagon and, sharpening her tongue in advance, ran into the house to keep out of sight for the rest of the day, like a fine lady; for she was ashamed of the dilapidated furniture and worn-out beds that were now unloaded. Sali too was ashamed, but he was obliged to help, and he and his father set up a strange showroom in the alley, in which the children of all the bankrupt Seldwylers were presently running about and making fun of the ragged yokels. The house looked even more dismal inside, and resembled a regular thieves' den. The walls were of badly whitewashed, damp masonry, and aside from the dark, uninviting bar with its once blood-red tables, there were only a few dingy little rooms; and the departed predecessor had left behind him everywhere the most discouraging dirt and trash.

So it began and so it continued. In the course of the first couple of weeks an occasional tableful of guests would drop by in the evening, curious to see the rustic landlord, and to find out whether there was any fun to be had. They did not find their host of much interest, for Manz was awkward, silent, unfriendly, and melancholy, and neither knew, nor cared to know, how to conduct himself. He would fill the mugs slowly and clumsily, set them down sullenly before his guests, and try to say something, but without success. His wife threw herself all the more zealously into the

breach, and for a few days she really held the people together—
but in a sense other than she herself thought. The rather stout
woman had put together a peculiar outfit, in which she thought
herself irresistible; in addition to an undyed country skirt of linen,
she wore an old, green silk jacket, a cotton apron, and a shabby
white collar. Over her temples she had curled her hair—no longer
thick—into funny-looking spirals and had stuck a high comb into
the knot at the back. Thus she pranced and danced about in an
effort to be graceful, puckered up her mouth comically to make it
look sweet, tripped elastically to the table, laid down the glass or
plate of salted cheese, and said with a smile:

"How about that? Isn't that nice? Fine, gentlemen, fine!" and
more such nonsense. For although she generally had a glib tongue,
she was now unable to say anything clever, being a stranger and
not knowing her guests. The Seldwylers, those of the worst kind
who hung about there, held their hands over their mouths and
nearly choked with laughter; they would kick one another under
the table and say, "God o' mercy! what a peach!"

"An angel!" said another. "By thunder! It's worth the trouble
to come here—it's a long time since we've seen one like that."

Her husband observed it all with a frown, gave her a poke in
the ribs, and whispered, "You old cow! What are you doing?"

"Don't bother me!" she replied indignantly. "You old block-
head! Don't you see the trouble I'm going to, and how I understand dealing with people? But these are just your worthless
hangers-on. You let me run things and I'll soon have more respectable customers here!"

This scene was illuminated by one or two small tallow candles.
But Sali, the son, went out into the dark kitchen, sat down on the
hearth, and wept over his father and mother.

The guests, however, soon grew tired of the spectacle which the
good Mrs. Manz afforded them, and went where they were more
at ease and could laugh at this bizarre innkeeping. Only now and
then a single customer appeared, who drank a glass and yawned
at the walls; or, by way of exception, there came a whole crowd
to deceive the poor people with a short-lived, noisy carousal. They
grew anxious and uneasy in this narrow hole in the wall where
they hardly saw the sun, and Manz, who had become accustomed
to lounging in town for days on end, now found it intolerable to

stay inside. When he thought of the free expanse of the fields he would brood and stare gloomily at the ceiling or at the floor, or run out the narrow front door and back in again, while the neighbors gaped in amazement at the grouchy landlord, as they were already calling him.

It was not very long before the Manzes were reduced to poverty and had absolutely nothing left. In order to get anything to eat they had to wait until somebody came and paid a little money for some of the wine they still had on hand; and if he asked for something like a sausage, they often had the greatest trouble procuring it. Before long they had no wine except what was kept in a large bottle which they secretly filled in another saloon, so that they were now called upon to play the host without wine or bread, and to be genial on an empty stomach. They were almost glad when nobody came in. So they crouched in their little tavern, able neither to live nor to die.

The effect of these sad experiences upon Mrs. Manz was to make her take off the green jacket, and again set about making a change in herself; instead of the faults, as before, she brought some of the virtues of womankind to the surface and cultivated them, now that there was an emergency. She exercised patience, sought to keep the old man on his feet and direct the boy into good ways, denying herself many things in so doing. In short, she exerted in her way a kind of beneficent influence, which, to be sure, did not reach far or improve things much, but was nevertheless better than nothing, or the opposite, and at any rate helped to pass the time, which otherwise would have run out a great deal sooner for these people. She was able, by her standards, to offer considerable advice in their miserable plight, and if the advice seemed worthless and did no good, she willingly bore the anger of the men. In short, now that she was old she did a great many things which would have been of more use had she done them earlier in life.

To have a little something to chew on, and a means of passing the time, father and son resorted to fishing, that is, with the rod, wherever the river was free to all for angling. This was, in fact, the chief occupation of the Seldwyla bankrupts. In fair weather, when the fish were biting well, one would see them strolling out by the dozen with rod and pail; walking along the riverbank, one would find a squatting fisherman at every step; here, a man in a long, brown town coat, his bare feet in the water; there another, standing on an old willow, in a blue swallowtail, his old felt hat cocked over one ear; over there still another, fishing away in a ragged, flowered dressing gown, since it was all he had, his long pipe in one hand, his rod in the other. If one followed a bend in the river, there, standing on a stone, fishing without a stitch of clothing on, would be an old bald-headed potbelly, whose feet, in spite of his being near the water, were so black one would think he had his boots on. They all had beside them a can or a box of squirming angleworms, which they used to dig up at odd times. Especially when the sky was overcast and the weather was murky and sultry, foretelling rain, these figures would be standing there by the meandering river in great numbers, motionless, like a gallery of saints and prophets. The country people passed by them with their wagons and cattle without taking notice of them; even the boatmen on the river paid no attention to them, while the fishermen would grumble quietly about the troublesome boats.

Had anybody prophesied to Manz twelve years before, as he was plowing with a fine span of horses on the hill above the river-bank, that some day he would join these curious fellows and, like them, take to fishing, he would have been more than a little annoyed. Even now he hurried past behind their backs and hastened up the river like a single-minded shade of the underworld, seeking as the place for his punishment a comfortable, lonely spot beside the dark waters. Meanwhile neither he nor his son had the patience to stand still with their rods; they recalled the many other ways in which peasants catch fish when they are feeling sporty, especially that of taking them by hand in the brooks. So they took along their rods merely for the sake of appearance, and walked up along the banks of the brooks where they knew there were particularly fine trout.

Meanwhile Marti, who had remained in the country, fared worse and worse and was also extremely bored, so that, instead of working in his neglected field, he likewise resorted to fishing and spent entire days splashing around in the water. Little Verena, who was not allowed to leave his side, had to carry his pail and tackle after him through wet meadows, over all manner of streams and marshes, in rain or sunshine, and was therefore compelled to neglect the most urgent matters at home. There was not another soul there, nor did they need anyone, since Marti had already lost the most of his land and now owned only a few acres, which he and his daughter cultivated either in a slovenly way or not at all.

So it happened one evening as he was walking along the bank of a rather deep and rapid stream, in which, under a sky overcast with storm clouds, the trout were busily jumping, that he unexpectedly met his enemy Manz, coming along the opposite shore. The moment he saw him a terrible feeling of anger and contempt came over him; for years they had not been so close to each other except in court, where they were not allowed to abuse one another. In fury Marti called out, "What are you doing here, you dog? Can't you stay in your dirty hole, you mangy Seldwyla cur?"

"You'll be there yourself pretty soon, you crook!" cried Manz. "I see you've taken to fishing too, so you won't have to wait much longer!"

"Shut up, you lousy dog!" Marti yelled, for here the current of the stream roared louder. "You got me into this trouble."

Now, as the willows by the stream began to rustle noisily in the rising wind, Manz was obliged to shout still louder, "I wish I had, you stupid fool!"

"You mongrel!" Marti called over, and Manz yelled back, "You ass!—what a fool you are!"

And Marti ran like a tiger along the bank, seeking a place to cross. The reason he was the more furious of the two was that he supposed Manz, being an innkeeper, had at least enough to eat and drink, and was leading a fairly pleasant existence, while life was tiresome for him on his dilapidated farm, and that was unfair. Meanwhile Manz too was furiously striding along on his side of the stream. Behind him followed his son, who, instead of listening to the angry quarrel, stared in curiosity and surprise at Verena, who was following her father and looking down at the ground in shame, so that her brown curly hair fell over her face. She was carrying a wooden fish-pail in one hand, her shoes and stockings in the other, and had pinned up her dress to keep it from getting wet. Since Sali was walking on the opposite side, however, she had modestly let it drop again, and was now encumbered and bothered three times over, with all the fishing paraphernalia to carry, her dress to hold up, and the quarrel to worry about. Had she glanced up at Sali, she would have discovered that he no longer looked very refined or very proud, and that he himself was deeply troubled.

While Verena, embarrassed and confused, was gazing down at the ground, and while Sali had his eyes fixed on her slender figure, charming in all its wretchedness, struggling along in meek bewilderment, they failed to notice that their fathers had fallen silent, and with increased anger were heading for a wooden footbridge which led across the stream a short distance away and was just coming into sight. Lightning began to flash, strangely illuminating the dark, melancholy waterscape; there was also a muffled roar of thunder in the gray-black clouds, and large raindrops began to fall. The two savage men rushed simultaneously onto the narrow bridge, which shook beneath their weight. They seized one another and lashed out with their fists at each other's faces, which were pale and trembling with wrath and bursting resentment.

It is not a pretty sight, and anything but pleasant, when two ordinarily sedate men, through arrogance or indiscretion or in self-defense, come to blows among a crowd of people who are of no particular concern to them. But this is innocent child's play in comparison with the profound misery that overwhelms two old men who know each other well and have known each other for years, when, in fierce hostility growing out of a lifetime together, they grab each other with their bare hands and engage in a fist-fight, which is just what these two gray-haired men were doing. Fifty years before, as boys, they had perhaps had their last fight; but since then neither of them, in the course of those fifty years, had laid hand on the other, except perhaps in good times, when they had greeted each other with a handshake—and even this they had done rarely, being naturally gruff and independent.

After they had exchanged blows they stopped, and, quivering with rage, silently wrestled with each other, now and then groaning aloud and ferociously gritting their teeth, while each one tried to throw the other over the creaking rail into the water. The children now came up and saw the pitiful scene. Sali made a leap toward them to assist his father and help him finish off his hated enemy, who seemed to be the weaker anyway and on the point of succumbing. But Verena, too, throwing down everything and uttering a long scream, sprang up and threw her arms around her father, thinking to protect him, but really only hindering and encumbering him. The tears were streaming from her eyes; she looked imploringly at Sali, who was also on the point of grabbing her father and completely overpowering him. But involuntarily he laid his hand on his own father instead and, taking firm hold of him, tried to separate him from his opponent and to calm him. So for a moment the fight stopped, or rather the entire group strained restlessly back and forth without separating.

Meanwhile the young people, pushing farther in between their fathers, had come into close contact with each other. At that moment a break in the clouds let the bright evening sunshine through, illuminating the girl's face, and Sali looked into this face, so familiar to him, yet now so different, so much more beautiful. In this moment, too, Verena noticed how surprised he was, and in the midst of her terror and tears she gave him a short, quick smile. But Sali, aroused by his father's efforts to shake him off, got himself under control, and finally, by urging and imploring, and by remaining firm, succeeded in separating him completely from his enemy. The two old fellows drew a deep breath and began to curse and shout at each other as they turned away. The children, however, were as quiet as death, scarcely breathing; they turned to leave and, unseen by the old men, quickly clasped each other's hands, still damp and cold from the water and the fish.

By the time the two angry men went their way, the clouds had again closed in; it grew darker and darker, and the rain poured down in streams. Manz jogged ahead on the dark, wet paths, with both hands in his pockets, ducking his head under the downpour. His face was still twitching and his teeth chattering; unseen tears trickled into his bristly beard and he let them flow rather than betray himself by wiping them off. His son, however, noticed nothing; he walked along, lost in visions of happiness. He was aware of neither rain nor storm, darkness nor misery. Everything within him and without him was light, bright, and warm, and he felt as rich and secure as a prince. He kept seeing the fleeting smile on that beautiful face so near his own, and now for the first time, a good half hour later, responded to it. Filled with love, he laughed and smiled through night and storm at her sweet face, which seemed to appear out of the darkness on every side, causing him to believe that Verena must of course see him as she walked along, and be aware of his laughter.

The next day his father looked crushed and would not leave the house. The whole quarrel and the long years of misery had assumed a new and more definite shape, spreading darkly in the oppressive air of the tavern, so that both Manz and his wife slunk in pale and timid circles about the ghostly apparition, dragging themselves from the barroom into the little dark bedrooms, from there into the kitchen, and from this back again into the public room, in which no guest ever appeared. Finally both of them sank down in a corner and spent the day in weary, lifeless bickering and contention with each other. Sometimes they would fall asleep and be tormented by restless daydreams, which would rise from their consciences and wake them again.

But of this Sali neither saw nor heard anything; he thought only of Verena. He still felt not only as if he were inexpressibly rich, but also as if he had learned something very important and knew infinitely many good and beautiful things, since he was now so definitely and distinctly aware of what he had seen the day before. This knowledge seemed to him as if it had fallen from heaven, and his mind was in a state of endless and happy amazement over it. Yet it seemed as if he had in fact always known and realized those things which now filled him with such wonderful sweetness. There is nothing like the wealth and the unfathomable depth of that happiness which comes to a man in such a clear and distinct form, baptized by a parson and fully provided with a name of its own, one which does not sound like other names.

On this day Sali felt neither idle nor unhappy, neither poor nor hopeless. On the contrary he was busily engaged in picturing to himself Verena's face and figure, which he did incessantly, hour after hour. But in all this excited activity the object itself vanished before him almost completely; that is, he finally imagined that he did not after all know exactly how Verena looked; that he had of course a general picture of her in his memory, but that if he were called upon to describe her he would be unable to do so. This picture was constantly before his eyes, as if it were actually standing there, and he felt the pleasant impression it made on him. And yet he only saw it as something seen but once, something one has come under the power of, but without really knowing what it is. He remembered exactly the way she looked as a girl, but not what he had seen of her the day before. Had he never caught sight of

Verena again, his memory would of course have managed some-
how cleverly to reconstruct her beloved face so that not a single
feature would be missing. Now, however, it cunningly and obstinately refused to serve him, because his eyes demanded their own
rights and their own pleasure.

In the afternoon, when the sun was shining warm and bright on
the upper floors of the black houses, Sali strolled out of the gate
toward his old home, which now seemed to him like a heavenly
Jerusalem with twelve shining gates, and it made his heart throb
as he drew near to it. On the way he met Verena's father, who
was apparently going to town. His appearance was wild and slovenly, his beard, now grown gray, had not been trimmed for weeks,
and he looked exactly like an angry, bankrupt farmer who has
lost his land through folly and is now out to make trouble for
others. Nevertheless as they passed each other Sali no longer looked
at him with hatred, but with fear and awe, as if his life were in
Marti's hands and he would rather defend it by entreaty than by
defiance. Marti only measured him from head to foot with an ugly
glance and went his way. That, however, was agreeable to Sali,
for the sight of the old man leaving the village gave him a clearer
vision of his own purpose. He stole around the village on old,
familiar paths and through hidden alleys, until he finally found
himself in front of Marti's house.

For several years he had not seen their place close up; for even
while they were still living here the two enemies took care not to
trespass on each other's property. He was now astonished at what
he saw, though he had seen the same in his own home, and he
stared with amazement at the desolate scene before him.

One piece after another of Marti's arable land had been mortgaged away, so that he now owned nothing but the house, the
yard in front of it, a bit of garden, and the field on the height
above the river, which he tenaciously persisted in keeping longest
of all. There was no longer any thought of systematic farming,
however, and on the field, where uniform crops of grain had once
waved so beautifully at harvest time, all sorts of poor, left-over
seed had been sown—turnips, cabbages, a few potatoes, and things
of that kind, swept up out of old boxes and torn bags—and all
this had sprouted up, so that the field now looked like a badly
kept vegetable garden. It was like a curious sample sheet, made

for living from hand to mouth, where, if one were hungry and knew of nothing better, one could pull up a handful of turnips here, a mess of potatoes or cabbages there, and let the rest grow on or rot, as the case might be. Furthermore, everybody ran about on it at will, and the beautiful broad strip of land now looked almost like the old, ownerless field, the origin of all the trouble.

There was in fact not a trace of orderly farming to be seen around the house. The stable was empty, the door hung on one hinge, and innumerable spiders, grown to half their full size during the summer, had spun their shining webs in the sunlight before the dark entrance. Beside the open barn door, through which the fruits of the sturdy earth had once been carried in, hung worthless fishing tackle, witness to Marti's bungling aquatic operations. In the yard there was not a hen or a dove to be seen, not a cat or dog. The spring was the only living thing left, and even that no longer flowed through the pipe, but gushed out through a crack, over the ground, and formed little pools all about the place, thus constituting the very symbol of laziness; for although it would not have been much trouble for her father to stop up the hole and replace the pipe, Verena was now hard put even to find clear water in all this devastation, and had to do her washing in the shallow pools on the ground, instead of in the trough, which was dried up and full of cracks.

The house itself was just as pitiful to behold. The windows were broken in many places and had paper pasted over them, but they were still the most pleasant feature in all the dilapidation. For even the broken panes were washed bright and clean, yes, actually polished, and they shone as bright as Verena's eyes—just as those eyes were the poor girl's only substitute for finery in all this poverty. And just as Verena's curly hair and orange cotton scarves went well with her eyes, so did the wild green vegetation, growing in rank confusion about the house, the small, waving forest of beans, and a fragrant wilderness of orange wallflower go well with these shining windows. The beans clung as best they could, some to a rake handle or the stub of a broom stuck in the ground upside down, others to a rusty halberd, or sponton, as it was called when Verena's grandfather as sergeant had carried it. This she had now, from necessity, planted among the beans; and over there others were merrily climbing up a weather-beaten ladder, which had been leaning against the house since time immemorial, and now hung down from it over the bright windows, as Verena's curly hair hung over her eyes.

This more picturesque than prosperous farmhouse stood somewhat apart and had no near neighbors; at this particular moment, moreover, there was not a living soul to be seen anywhere about. Sali, therefore, feeling perfectly safe, leaned against an old shed some thirty paces away and gazed fixedly across at the quiet, desolate house. He had been leaning and gazing in this way for some time when Verena came to the door and stood there looking out, her thoughts seemingly concentrated on one object. Sali did not move or turn his eyes away from her. Finally, chancing to look in his direction, she caught sight of him. They stared at each other for a moment, as if observing a phantom in the air, until finally Sali straightened up and walked slowly across the road and across the yard, toward Verena. When he was near her, she stretched out her hands to him and said, "Sali!" He seized her hands and gazed steadfastly into her face; tears gushed from her eyes, and she turned crimson under his glance.

"What do you want here?" she said.

"I just want to see you," he replied. "Can't you and I be friends again?"

"What about our parents?" she asked, turning her face to hide the tears, since her hands were not free to cover it.

"Are we to blame for what they've done and what they've become?" said Sali. "Maybe the only way to repair the damage is for the two of us to stick together and be very kind to each other."

"It won't ever turn out well," answered Verena with a deep sigh. "God be with you, Sali, but go away now."

"Are you alone?" he asked. "May I come in for a moment?"

"Father has gone to town to make trouble for your father; he said so. But you can't come in, because later you may not be able to get away without being seen, as you can now. Everything is still quiet and there's nobody around. Please, please, go now!"

"No, I won't go like that. I haven't been able to stop thinking about you since yesterday. I've had to think about you all the time, and I won't leave this way. We must have a talk together, at least half an hour or an hour—it'll do us good."

Verena thought a moment and said, "Toward evening I go out

to our field—you know which, we have only the one—to get some vegetables. I know nobody else will be there then, because the people are harvesting somewhere else. If you wish, meet me there. But go now, and make sure that no one sees you; nobody associates with us here any more, but people still talk so much that my father would certainly hear about it."

They now let go each other's hands, but immediately joined them again, and both said simultaneously, "How are you anyway?"

But instead of answering they both asked the same question over again, and the answer lay only in their eloquent eyes, since, as is the way with lovers, they were no longer able to manage words. Without saying anything more they finally separated, half happy and half sad.

"I'll be out there soon—you go right now," she called out after him.

Sali went directly out to the quiet, beautiful hillside over which the two fields extended. The magnificent, quiet July sun, the passing white clouds floating above the ripe, waving grain, the blue shimmering river flowing below—all this filled him once more, for the first time in years, with happiness and contentment instead of pain, and he stretched out full length in the transparent half-shade of the grain, on the border of Marti's desolate field, and gazed blissfully toward heaven.

Although it was scarcely a quarter of an hour before Verena joined him, and he had thought of nothing but his happiness and the name it bore, still it was with unexpected suddenness that he saw her standing before him and smiling down at him. Happily startled, he jumped up.

"Verena," he cried, as with a quiet smile she gave him both her hands. Hand in hand they walked along beside the whispering grain down to the river and back again, without saying much. They walked back and forth the same way two or three times, quiet, joyful, and calm; so now this happy pair also resembled a constellation passing up over the sunny crest of the hill and disappearing behind it, as their fathers once used to do in their sure-footed plowing.

But then, looking up from the blue cornflowers on which their eyes lingered, they suddenly saw another dark star, a swarthy fellow, walking along ahead of them. Where he had come from so unexpectedly, they did not know; he must have been lying in the grain field. Verena was startled, and Sali said in alarm, "The black fiddler!"

In fact the fellow strolling along before them was carrying a bow and fiddle under his arm, and he did, moreover, look very black. Not only the little black felt hat and the black sooty smock he wore, but his hair too was black as pitch, and so was his untrimmed beard, while his face and hands were likewise blackened; for he did all sorts of handiwork, chiefly kettle mending, and he also helped the charcoal-burners and pitch-boilers in the forests. He took his fiddle with him only if he saw a chance to make a little money when the country folk were having a good time somewhere or celebrating a festival.

Sali and Verena walked along behind him, as quiet as mice, thinking he would turn away from the field and disappear without looking around. And this indeed seemed to be his intention, for he acted as if he had not noticed them. Furthermore they were under a strange spell—they did not dare leave the narrow path but involuntarily followed the mysterious fellow until they reached the end of the field, where that iniquitous pile of stones covered the still disputed corner. Vast numbers of poppies had established themselves on it, so that the little mountain looked for the moment as red as fire.

Suddenly the black fiddler sprang up with a single bound onto the red pile of stones, turned, and looked around. The young couple stopped and gazed up in confusion at the dark figure; they could not pass him, for the road led into the village, and they did not want to turn around before his very eyes. He looked at them sharply, and called out, "I know you—you're the children of the men who stole my land here! I'm glad to see how well you're getting along—I'll certainly live to see you go the way of all flesh. Look at me, you two sparrows! Do you like my nose, eh?"

He had, in fact, a terrible nose. It stuck out from his withered, black face like a big square; or rather it looked more like a stout cudgel or club which had been thrown there. Under it a small, round hole of a mouth, through which he was all the time puffing and blowing and hissing, puckered itself up and contracted in a strange way. The little felt hat, moreover, looked very odd, being neither round nor square, but of such a peculiar shape that, although it lay motionless, it seemed at every moment to be chang-ing its shape. Of the fellow's eyes there was almost nothing to be seen but the whites, since the pupils were constantly making light-ning-like movements and running around zigzag, like two rabbits.

"Just look at me," he went on. "Your fathers know me well, and every man in this place knows who I am, if he just looks at my nose. Years ago they advertised that some money was set aside for the heir to this field; I've applied for it twenty times, but I don't have any certificate of baptism or papers of citizenship, and the testimony of my friends, the homeless folk who witnessed my birth, has no legal validity. And so the time expired long ago and I lost the miserable pittance I could have emigrated with. I begged your fathers to bear witness for me—their consciences must tell them I'm the lawful heir. But they chased me out of their houses, and now they have gone to the devil themselves. Oh well, that's the way of the world, and it's all the same to me. I'll fiddle for you if you want to dance."

With that he scrambled down on the other side of the stone pile and made off in the direction of the village, where toward evening the harvest was to be brought in and the people would be having a good time. When he had disappeared the couple sat down on the stones, dispirited and sad. They rested their heads dejectedly on their hands, which they had now freed from each other's em-brace, for the fiddler's appearance and his words had roused them from the happy forgetfulness in which they had been wandering back and forth like two children. And when they sat down on the hard ground of their misery, the bright light of life grew dim and their spirits became as heavy as stones.

Then Verena, happening to recall the fiddler's remarkable figure and nose, suddenly burst out laughing and cried,

"The poor fellow looks too funny for anything! What a nose!" And a charming, sunny merriment spread over the girl's face, as if she had waited for the fiddler's nose to drive away the gloomy clouds.

Sali looked at Verena and saw how happy she was. She had already forgotten the reason, however, and now looked at him and laughed only because she felt like it. Puzzled and surprised, Sali stared into her eyes, laughing involuntarily, like a hungry man who has caught sight of a delicious loaf of bread.

"My Lord, Verena," he cried, "how beautiful you are!"

Verena only smiled at him more, and at the same time there escaped from her resonant throat a few short mischievous notes of laughter, which to poor Sali seemed exactly like the song of the nightingale.

"Oh you little witch!" he cried. "Where did you learn to do that? What devilish tricks are you playing now?"

"Oh, goodness gracious!" said Verena in an endearing tone, as she took Sali's hand. "That isn't witchcraft. How long I've wanted to laugh! Now and then, when I was all alone I've had to laugh at something, but it wasn't real laughter. But now I want to smile at you for ever and ever, as often as I see you, and I'd like to see you all the time. Do you love me just a little bit?"

"Oh, Verena," he exclaimed, gazing into her eyes with candor and devotion, "I've never looked at a girl; I've always felt that I must love you some day, and without my wishing it or realizing it, you've always been in my mind."

"And you in mine even more," replied Verena, "because you never looked at me, and you didn't know what I had grown to be like; but now and then I took a good look at you from far away and secretly even from close by, so that I knew all along how you looked. Do you remember how often we used to come out here as children? And the little cart? How small we were then, and how long ago it was! You'd think we were very old."

"How old are you now?" asked Sali, filled with happiness and contentment. "You must be about seventeen."

"I'm seventeen and a half," she replied. "And how old are you? But I already know—you'll soon be twenty."

"How did you know that?" Sali asked.

"Oh, but that's telling!"

"Then you won't tell me?"

"No!"

"Positively not?"

"No, no!"

"You must tell me!"

"Do you think you're going to make me?"

"We'll see about that."

Sali carried on this foolish talk to have an excuse to keep his hands busy, pestering the beautiful girl with awkward caresses intended to look like punishment. Defending himself, she too drew out with great patience this silly exchange, which in spite of its emptiness seemed quite witty and sweet to both of them. Finally Sali became vexed and bold enough to seize Verena's hands and force her down among the poppies. There she lay, her eyes blinking in the sunlight; her cheeks shone crimson, and her mouth was half open, permitting two rows of white teeth to gleam through. Delicate and beautiful, her dark eyebrows met, and her young breasts rose and fell capriciously under all these four hands caressing and struggling, helter-skelter. Sali was beside himself with joy to see the slender, beautiful young thing before him, and to feel that she was his own; it seemed to him he possessed a kingdom.

"You still have all your white teeth," he laughed. "Do you remember how often we counted them once? Can you count now?"

"These are not the same ones, you child," said Verena. "Those came out long ago."

In his simplicity Sali now wanted to play the old game again, and count the shining, pearly teeth. But Verena suddenly closed her red mouth, straightened up, and began to twine a wreath of poppies, which she placed on her head. The wreath was thick and broad and gave the brown-skinned girl a look of charm and magic; poor Sali held in his arms something rich people would have paid a great deal for, if they could have had it as a painting on their walls.

Now, however, she sprang up and cried, "Heavens, how hot it is! Here we sit like two fools, getting scorched! Come, my darling—let's sit in the tall grain."

They glided in with such a light and nimble step that they scarcely left a footprint behind them, and built themselves a little prison in the golden grain, which towered up so high above their heads when they sat down that they could see nothing in the world but the azure sky above. They embraced and kissed each other incessantly, until they finally became tired, or whatever one chooses to call it when the kissing of two lovers outlives itself for a moment or two, and, in the very intoxication of the season of flowering, ominously suggests the transitoriness of all life. They heard the larks singing high above them and watched for them with their sharp eyes. When they thought they had caught a momentary glimpse of one, gleaming in the sun like a star that suddenly flashes in the blue sky or shoots out of sight, they kissed again as a reward and tried to get ahead of each other and cheat as much as they could.

"See, there's one!" whispered Sali, and Verena replied just as softly, "Yes, I hear it, but I don't see it."

"Yes you do. Look sharp, there by that white cloud—a little to the right of it."

And they both looked eagerly in that direction, and, like two young quails in a nest, opened their bills wide with expectation, to touch them together as soon as they imagined they had seen the larks.

Suddenly Verena paused and said, "And so it's all decided, then, that we've each got a sweetheart? Doesn't it seem that way to you?"

"Yes," said Sali, "I think so too."

"Then how do you like your little sweetheart?" asked Verena. "What kind of person is she? What can you tell about her?"

"She's a sweet little thing," said Sali. "She has two brown eyes, and red lips, and walks on two feet; but I know less about what she thinks than I do about the Pope in Rome. And what do you have to say about your sweetheart?"

"He has two blue eyes, a good-for-nothing mouth, and he can use his two strong, saucy arms; but his thoughts are stranger to me than the Emperor of Turkey's!"

"It's really true," said Sali, "that we don't know each other any better than if we'd never met—the long time since we've grown up has made us such strangers. What's been going through your little head, dear child?"

"Oh, not much. I've felt a thousand silly ideas stirring, but my life has always been so miserable that they couldn't amount to anything."

"My poor sweetheart!" said Sali. "But I bet you're pretty smart—aren't you?"

"You can find that out sometime—if you love me very much!"

"Once you're my wife?"

Verena trembled slightly at this last word; nestling deeper into Sali's arms, she gave him another long and tender kiss. Tears came into her eyes as she did so, and both of them suddenly grew sad when they thought of the hopelessness of their future and of the enmity of their fathers. Verena sighed and said, "Come, I must go now."

And so they rose, and were walking out of the grain field hand in hand, when they saw Verena's father spying around in front of them. With the petty shrewdness of idle misery he had been brooding about meeting Sali alone, wondering what he was looking for in the village. Finally, as he was trudging toward the city, he remembered what happened the previous day and so got on the right track from sheer ill-will and idle malice. When his suspicions began to assume definite form, he turned around in the very alleys of Seldwyla and strolled out again into the village, where he looked in vain for his daughter, in the house and yard and among the hedges. With growing curiosity he ran out to the field, and seeing on the ground Verena's basket, which she used to carry vegetables, but failing to catch sight of the girl herself, he went spying around in his neighbor's field just as the frightened children were coming out of it.

They stood as if petrified, and at first Marti also stood still and looked at them with a wicked stare, as pale as lead. Then he began to rave terribly, making wild gestures and calling them names; at the same time he reached out in fury to seize the young lad, intending to strangle him. Sali, terrified by the wild man, dodged and retreated a few steps, but he rushed up again when he saw the old man seize the trembling girl instead of him, give her such a slap that the red wreath fell off, and twist her hair around his hand in order to drag her away and mistreat her further. Without thinking what he was doing, he picked up a stone, and, half in fear for Verena and half in anger, struck the old man on the head. Marti first staggered a bit and then sank down unconscious on the stone pile, dragging with him his daughter who was screaming pitifully. Sali freed her hair from the unconscious man's hand and lifted her up; then he stood there like a statue, helpless, his mind empty.

When the girl saw her father lying there as if dead, she passed her hands over her pale face, shook herself, and said, "Have you killed him?"

Sali nodded mutely and Verena cried out, "Oh, God! It's my father! The poor man!" Out of her mind, she threw herself on him and raised his head, from which, however, no blood was flowing. She let it sink back again. Sali knelt on the other side of the man, and both of them, silent as the grave, their hands lame and motionless, gazed into his lifeless face.

Merely to break the silence, Sali at length said, "It can't be that he's dead already? That isn't necessarily true."

Verena tore off the petal of a poppy and laid it on his pale lips—it moved feebly.

"He is still breathing!" she cried. "Run to the village and bring help!"

When Sali jumped up and started to go, she held her hand out toward him and called him back.

"But don't come back yourself, or say anything about how it happened. I'll keep quiet too—they won't find out anything from me," she said, and her face, which she turned toward the poor, helpless boy, was suffused with painful tears. "Come, kiss me once more! No, go, go away! It's all over, all over for ever—we can never be together!"

She pushed him away, and he ran mechanically toward the village. He met a little boy who did not know him, and told him to go get the first people he could find, describing to him the exact place where help was needed. Then he set off in despair and wandered about in the woods all night.

In the morning he crept out to the fields to see what had happened. He heard from early risers, who were discussing the affair, that Marti was still alive, but unconscious, and what a remarkable thing it was, since nobody knew what had happened to him. Now at last he returned to town and hid himself in the dark misery of the house.

Verena kept her word; they could get nothing out of her except that she herself had found her father in that condition. And since on the following day he was moving and breathing again quite freely, though, to be sure, without consciousness, and since furthermore no accuser appeared, people took it for granted that he had been drunk and had fallen on the stones; so they let the matter drop. Verena nursed him, never leaving his side, except to get medicine from the doctor or perhaps to cook some thin soup for herself; for she lived on almost nothing, although she was obliged to stay awake day and night and had nobody to help her.

It was almost six weeks before the sick man gradually recovered consciousness, although he began to eat again long before that and was quite cheerful in his bed. It was not, however, his old consciousness that he now regained. On the contrary, the more he talked, the more evident it became that his mind was affected, and what is more, in a most remarkable manner. He could recall only dimly what had happened, and then it seemed to strike him as something jolly which did not particularly concern him; he was continually laughing foolishly, and in good spirits. While he was still lying in bed he would deliver himself of a hundred foolish, senseless, capricious phrases and whimsies, make faces, and draw his peaked cap of black wool down over his eyes and nose, so that the latter looked like a coffin under a pall.

Verena, pale and careworn, would listen to him patiently, weeping over this silly behavior, which worried her even more than his former evil ways. Occasionally, when the old man did something extremely funny, she had to laugh aloud in the midst of her grief; for her suppressed nature, like a drawn bow, was ever ready to spring for pleasure, whereupon a sadness all the more profound would follow. But when the old man was able to get up, there was absolutely no way to manage him. He did one silly thing after another; he would laugh and rummage about the house, sit down in the sun and stick out his tongue, or deliver long speeches to the beans.

By this time, moreover, the few remnants of his former possessions were gone, and the general disorder had reached such a point that even his house and the last field, which had been mortgaged for some time, were now sold by court order. For the farmer who had bought Manz's two fields took advantage of Marti's sickness and his complete demoralization, and made a swift, decisive end of the old lawsuit involving the contested stone field. Thus the loss of the case completely knocked the bottom out of Marti's barrel, while he, in his imbecility, no longer knew what was happening.

The auction took place; Marti was provided for by the community in an institution run for such poor wretches at public expense. This institution was located in the capital city of the region.

The healthy and voracious lunatic was first well fed, then loaded on a small wagon drawn by oxen, and driven to the city by a poor farmer who was at the same time going to sell one or two sacks of potatoes. Verena took a seat in the wagon beside her father to accompany him on this final trip to a living burial. It was a sad and bitter ride, but Verena watched over her father carefully and saw to it that he lacked nothing; nor did she look around or become impatient when the poor man's antics attracted the attention of people, causing them to run after the wagon as it bumped along.

Finally they reached a rambling structure in the city, where the long passages, the courts, and a pleasant garden were enlivened by a throng of similar wretches, all of whom were dressed in white blouses and wore durable leather caps on their thick heads. Marti was also dressed in this attire before Verena's very eyes; he enjoyed it like a child, and began to sing and dance.

"God bless you, worthy gentlemen!" he cried out to his new companions. "You have a beautiful house here. Go home, Verena, and tell your mother I'm not coming back again, for I like it here, by Jove! Hey? 'A hedgehog's creeping o'er the way, I'm sure I heard him bellow; O girlie, kiss no gray-haired jay, But kiss some nice young fellow!' 'All the brooks flow into the Rhine; The girl with the blue eyes, She must be mine.' Are you going already, Verena? You look like death warmed over, and I'm so happy. 'The she-fox yelps on the plain-y-o, heigho, She must be in terrible pain-y-o, ho ho!' "

An attendant told him to be quiet and gave him some light work to do, while Verena returned to find the wagon. She sat down in the vehicle, took out a little piece of bread and ate it; then she slept until the farmer came and drove her back to the village.

They did not arrive until night. Verena went to the house in which she was born—she could remain there only two days. For the first time in her life she was entirely alone in it. She made a fire to boil the last coffee she had left, and sat down on the hearth, for she felt wretched. She yearned painfully to see Sali just once more, and thought of him passionately. But cares and grief embittered her longing, and this in turn made her cares much heavier.

She was sitting there and resting her head in her hands, when somebody entered through the open door.

"Sali!" cried Verena, looking up, and she threw her arms around his neck. Then they stared at each other in alarm and cried, "How miserable you look!" For Sali, no less than Verena, was pale and drawn.

Forgetting everything, she drew him down to her on the hearth, and said, "Have you been sick, or have you had such a hard time too?"

Sali answered, "No, I am not exactly sick, only homesick for you. We're having a grand time at our place these days. My father's running a resort and a retreat for rabble from other parts, and from what I see I think that he's become a receiver of stolen goods. So there's enough and to spare in our tavern now, until they're caught and it all comes to a terrible end. My mother helps things along from desperate eagerness just to have something in the house; she thinks she can make a bad situation acceptable and useful by keeping a certain amount of order. They don't ask me about it, and I couldn't bother with it much anyway, because day and night I can think of nothing but you. All sorts of vagabonds come into our place, so we've heard about what's been happening here, and it makes my father happy as a child. We also heard about your father being taken to the asylum today. I thought you'd be alone, so I've come to see you!"

Verena now poured out to him all her troubles and sufferings, but with a tongue as easy and confidential as if she were describing some great happiness—for she was indeed happy to see Sali beside her. Meanwhile she got together a meager bowlful of warm coffee, which she constrained her lover to share with her.

"So you've got to leave here the day after tomorrow?" said Sali. "What in heaven's name is going to become of you then?"

"I don't know," answered Verena, "I'll have to get a job as a maid somewhere. But I won't be able to stand it without you, and yet I can never have you, even if there were nothing else in the way—simply because you struck my father and took away his reason. That would be a bad start for our marriage, and neither of us would ever have any peace of mind, ever!"

Sali sighed and said, "A hundred times I've thought of enlisting as a soldier, or else hiring out as a farm-hand in some strange place. But I can't go away as long as you're here, and after what's happened it'll destroy me. I believe my misery makes my love for you stronger and more painful, so now it's a matter of life and death. I had no idea anything could be like that!"

Verena looked at him with a loving smile. They leaned back against the wall and said nothing more; but they each gave themselves up in silence to the blissful feeling, which rose above all their sorrow, of being very deeply in love and knowing that the love was returned. With that thought they fell asleep on the uncomfortable hearth, without pillow or bolster, and slept as peacefully and quietly as two children in a cradle.

Morning was already dawning when Sali awoke first; he tried as gently as he could to rouse Verena, but she kept falling back against him drowsily and would not wake up. Then he kissed her hard on the mouth, and she started up, opened her eyes wide, and seeing Sali, cried, "Heavens! I was just dreaming about you! I dreamt that we were dancing together at our wedding for long, long hours, and were so very happy and neatly dressed and had everything we needed. Finally we wanted very much to kiss each other, but something kept pulling us apart, and now it turns out that you yourself were the one who got in the way and stopped us. But, oh, how nice it is that you're right here!"

Eagerly she threw her arms about his neck and kissed him as if she would never stop.

"And what did you dream?" she asked, stroking his cheeks and chin.

"I dreamt that I was wandering through the woods on an endlessly long road, with you in the distance ahead of me. Now and then you would look around, motion to me and laugh, and then I was in heaven. That's all."

They stepped to the unclosed kitchen door which led directly into the open air, and had to laugh when they saw each other's faces. For Verena's right cheek and Sali's left, which had been resting against each other in their sleep, were bright red from the pressure, while the other two were paler than usual because of the cool night air. They gently rubbed each other's faces on the cold, pale sides in order to make them red too. The fresh morning air, the dewy, quiet peace that lay over the landscape, and the early morning glow made them happy and they were lost to the world.

Verena, especially, seemed possessed by a cheerful spirit of uncon-
cern.

"And so tomorrow night I must get out of this house and look
for another place to stay," she said. "But first I want to be really
happy once more, just once, and with you. I'd like to dance with
you somewhere, for a long, long time. I can't stop thinking of the
dance in my dream."

"Anyway I'll be on hand to see that you find a place to stay,"
said Sali, "and I'd gladly dance with you, my darling—but where?"

"Tomorrow there's a church fair in two places not very far from
here," replied Verena, "where people won't be likely to know us
or notice us. I'll wait for you out by the river, and then we can go
wherever we like and have a good time, once, just once. But, oh
dear me, we don't have any money!" she added sadly. "So it's
hopeless after all!"

"Just leave that to me," said Sali, "I'll bring some money!"

"Surely not from your father's—from the—the stolen goods?"

"No! Don't worry! I've kept my silver watch, and I'll sell that."

"I won't urge you not to," said Verena blushing, "I think I'd
die if I couldn't dance with you tomorrow!"

"It would be best if we could both die!" said Sali.

They embraced in a sad and painful farewell, but as they separated they smiled happily at each other in the assurance of hope
for the next day.

"But when will you come?" cried Verena.

"By eleven o'clock in the morning at the latest," he replied.
"We'll have a really nice lunch together."

"Good, good! But come earlier—come at half-past ten!"

After Sali had started to go, she once more called him back, her
face suddenly taking on an expression of despair.

"Nothing will come of this after all," she said, crying bitterly.
"I have no Sunday shoes any more—I even had to put on these
clumsy ones yesterday to go to town. I don't know where to get
any shoes!"

Sali stood helpless and puzzled.

"No shoes?" he said. "Then you'll just have to go in these."

"No, no, I can't dance in these."

"Well then—we'll have to buy some!"

"Where? With what?"

"Oh, there are plenty of shoe stores in Seldwyla, and I'll have money in less than two hours."

"But I can't go around with you in Seldwyla, and you won't have money enough to buy shoes too."

"There'll have to be enough! I'll buy the shoes and bring them with me tomorrow!"

"Oh, you silly! The shoes you buy won't fit me."

"Then give me one of your old shoes, or wait—better still, I'll measure you. It won't take any magic to do that."

"Measure me? Why, of course! I hadn't thought of that! Come, I'll find you a string."

She sat down on the hearth again, drew back her skirt a little and slipped a shoe from her foot, on which she still wore the white stocking she had put on for yesterday's journey. Sali knelt down and took her measure as well as he knew how, spanning the length and breadth of her dainty foot with the string, in which he carefully tied knots.

"What a shoemaker!" cried Verena, blushing and laughing down at him fondly.

Sali blushed, too, and held her foot firmly in his hands, longer than was necessary, so that Verena drew it back with a still deeper blush. Then, however, she once more passionately embraced and kissed the embarrassed Sali before sending him away.

As soon as he reached the city he took his watch to a watchmaker, who gave him six or seven gulden for it; for the silver chain he also got a few gulden. He now thought himself rich indeed, for never once since he had grown up had he possessed so much money all at once. If only this day were over and Sunday were here, he thought, so that he could use the money to buy the happiness he promised himself. Even if the day after tomorrow loomed all the darker and more uncertain, the longed-for pleasures of tomorrow took on a strangely enhanced splendor and brilliance.

Meanwhile he spent the time to advantage, looking for a pair of shoes for Verena; it was the most pleasant business he had ever undertaken. He went from one shoemaker to another, made them show him all the women's shoes they had, and finally bought a light, elegant pair, prettier than any Verena had ever worn. He hid the shoes under his vest, and did not take them out the rest of the day; he even took them to bed with him and laid them under his pillow.

As he had already seen the girl early that morning, and was going to see her again the following day, he slept soundly and peacefully. He was awake bright and early and began to get his meager Sunday attire in order and to freshen it up as best he could. This attracted the attention of his mother, and she asked him in astonishment what he was going to do, for he had not dressed with such care for a long time. He was going to take a little walk and look around a bit, he replied—otherwise he would get sick, staying in the house.

"He's been leading a strange life lately," muttered his father. "This gadding about—"

"Oh let him go," said the mother. "Perhaps it'll do him good—he looks miserable!"

"Got any money for your trip? Where did you get it?" asked his father.

"I don't need any," said Sali.

"There's a gulden for you," replied the old man, throwing one over to him. "You can go into the village tavern and spend it, so they won't think we're so badly off here."

"I'm not going to the village, and I don't need your gulden—keep it yourself."

"Well, you've had it! It'd be too bad if you had to keep it, you pighead!" cried Manz, shoving the gulden back into his pocket.

But his wife, who did not know why she was so touched with sadness today on her son's account, brought him a large black Milanese scarf with a red border, which she herself had seldom worn, and which he had long coveted. He tied it around his neck, leaving the long ends loose. Moreover, in a burst of rustic pride he now for the first time put up over his ears, as grown men do, the shirt collar he always used to wear turned down.

Shortly after seven o'clock, with the shoes in the breast pocket of his coat, he set out. As he left the room a strange feeling impelled him to offer his hand to his father and mother, and on the street he turned around and looked at the house once more.

"I do believe," said Manz, "The boy is running after some woman. That's the last thing we need!"

His wife said, "Oh, I wish to heaven he'd have a bit of luck! That would be nice for the poor lad!"

"Right!" said the husband. "It'll happen! That'll be a heavenly piece of luck if he runs afoul of another such loudmouth as you. That would be nice for the poor lad, oh yes!"

Sali first directed his steps toward the river, where he intended to wait for Verena; but on the way he changed his mind and went directly to the village to call for her in her own house. It was too long to wait until half past ten.

"What do we care about people?" he thought. "Nobody helps us, and I am honest and fear nobody!"

And so he stepped into Verena's room before she expected him, and was himself no less surprised to find her completely dressed. She was sitting there all pretty, waiting until it was time to leave—only her shoes were still missing. But Sali stopped, with his mouth open, in the middle of the room, when he saw the girl—she looked so beautiful!

She wore only a simple dress of blue linen, which, however, was fresh and clean, and fitted her slender figure perfectly; over that she had a snow-white muslin scarf, and this was her whole outfit. Her curly brown hair was carefully arranged; her locks, usually so unruly, now lay neatly and prettily about her head. As she had hardly been out of the house for weeks, her complexion had become delicate and transparent, but this was also a result of grief and worry. Into this transparency, however, love and joy poured one flash of crimson after another; on her breast she had a lovely bouquet of rosemary, roses, and splendid asters. She was sitting by the open window, and breathing in sweet silence the fresh, sunny morning air, but when she saw Sali appear, she held out both of her pretty arms, which were bare to the elbows, and cried, "You were right to come so early, and to come here. But did you bring me some shoes? Really? Then I won't stand up until I have them on!"

He took from his pocket the shoes she had longed for and gave them to the beautiful, eager girl; she cast the old ones aside and slipped into the new ones, which fitted her nicely. Now she rose from her chair, balanced herself in the new shoes, and excitedly walked back and forth a few times. She pulled up her long blue skirt a little, and contemplated with satisfaction the red wool bows which decorated the shoes, while Sali gazed uninterruptedly at the lovely, delicate figure moving with such joy, charm, and excitement before him.

"You're looking at my bouquet?" asked Verena. "Didn't I pick a pretty one? You know, these are the last flowers I could find in this desolation. There was still a little rose here, an aster there, and to look at them all in a bunch you would never think that they were gathered from the ruins. But now it's time for me to go—not a flower left in the garden, and the house empty as well."

Sali looked around and observed for the first time that all the movable property that had been there was gone.

"You poor girl," he said, "Have they taken everything away from you already?"

"Yesterday," she replied, "they took what could be moved and hardly left me my bed. But I sold it right away, and now I've got some money too, see!" She drew some new shining silver pieces from the pocket of her dress and showed them to him. "The probate judge," she continued, "has been here too and he told me to take this money and leave at once to look for a position in the city."

"But there's absolutely nothing more left," said Sali, after he had glanced into the kitchen. "I see no wood, no pan, no knife! Haven't you had any breakfast yet?"

"Nothing!" said Verena. "I could have got myself something, but I thought I'd rather stay hungry so that I could eat a lot with you; it makes me so happy to look forward to that, you can't imagine how happy it makes me!"

"If I could only touch you," said Sali, "I'd show you how I feel, you beautiful, beautiful creature!"

"You mustn't—you'd ruin all my nice clothes, and if we spare the flowers, perhaps it will be a good thing for my poor head too, which you tend to treat pretty badly."

"Come on then, let's be off!"

"We must wait until the bed is taken away; after that I'm going to close up this empty house and never come back here! I'll give my little bundle of things to the woman to keep for me—the woman who bought the bed."

Accordingly, they sat down opposite each other and waited. The woman came soon; she was a robust farmer's wife with a loud mouth, and had a boy with her to carry the bedstead. When she saw Verena's lover and the girl herself so dressed up, she opened her mouth and eyes wide, set her arms akimbo, and cried, "Well, just look at you, Verena! You're getting on fine, I see. You've got a caller and you're decked out like a princess!"

"Well, of course!" replied Verena with a friendly laugh. "Do you know who he is?"

"Oh, I imagine it's Sali Manz. Mountains and valleys, they say, don't come together, but people—. But take care, child—remember what happened to your parents."

"Oh, that's all changed now; everything's all right," replied Verena, with a friendly and confiding smile, yes, even condescendingly. "You see, Sali is going to be my husband!"

"Your husband? You don't say!"

"Yes, and he's a rich man. He won a hundred thousand gulden in the lottery! Just think of that!"

The woman gave a jump, clapped her hands together in utter amazement, and screamed.

"A hun—a hundred thousand gulden!"

"A hundred thousand gulden!" repeated Verena with solemn assurance.

"Bless my soul! But it isn't true—you're lying to me, child!"

"Well, believe what you like!"

"But if it's true and you marry him, what are you going to do with the money? Are you really going to be a fine lady?"

"Of course! The wedding will take place in three weeks!"

"Get out! You're a wicked story-teller!"

"He's already bought the most beautiful house in Seldwyla, with a large garden and a vineyard; you must come and call on me when we're settled. I'm counting on it."

"Of course I will—you're a little witch, that's what you are!"

"You'll see how beautiful it is! I'll make a splendid cup of coffee and serve you fine bread and butter and honey!"

"Oh, you little rogue! You can count on my coming!" cried the woman with an eager face and a watering mouth.

"But if you come at noon, when you're tired after marketing, there'll always be strong broth and a glass of wine ready for you."

"That'll suit me fine!"

"And there'll be plenty of candies and white rolls for your dear children at home, too."

"I'm beginning to feel quite famished!"

"And a dainty little scarf, or a remnant of silk, or a pretty old ribbon for your dresses, or a piece of cloth for a new apron—we'll surely find all that when we rummage through my boxes and chests, some friendly hour!"

The woman turned on her heel and shook her skirts, exulting.

"And if your husband should have a chance to make a good deal in real estate or cattle, and should need some ready money, you know where to knock. My dear Sali will always be happy to invest a bit of cash safely and profitably; and I myself expect to have a spare penny now and then to help an intimate friend!"

By this time the woman was completely out of her mind. She said with emotion, "I've always said that you were a fine, good, beautiful girl! May the Lord make you prosper always, and bless you for what you do for me!"

"In return, however, I demand that you do the fair thing by me!"

"You may ask that—most assuredly you may!"

"And promise that you'll always bring your wares and offer them to me before you take them to market—I mean your fruit, potatoes, or vegetables—so that I may be sure of having a real farmer's wife around, one I can rely on. I'll certainly give whatever anybody else offers you for your wares, and with the greatest of pleasure. You know me! Oh, there's nothing finer than when a well-to-do city woman, sitting so helpless within her walls, needing so many things, and an honest, upright country woman, who knows about everything that's important and useful, form a good and lasting friendship! It helps in a hundred ways, in joy and sorrow, at christenings and weddings, when the children are instructed and confirmed, when they're apprenticed, and when they must go out into the world, and at times of poor harvests and floods, fires and hailstorms—from which God save us!"

"From which God save us!" said the good woman, sobbing and drying her eyes with her apron. "What a sensible and thoughtful little bride you'll be! Yes, things will go well with you, or else there can't be any justice in the world! Handsome, tidy, clever, and wise you are, industrious and skillful at all things! There isn't a finer or better girl than you in the village or out of it, and the man who has you must think he's in heaven—or else he's a scoundrel and will have to answer to me. Listen, Sali! See that you treat my Verena right, or I'll show you who's in charge! What a lucky boy you are, to pick such a rose!"

"Now take my little bundle along, as you promised me, and keep it until I send for it. But perhaps I'll come for it in the carriage myself, if you've no objection. I suppose you won't refuse me a little mug of milk, and I'll be sure to bring along a nice almond cake or something to go with it!"

"You little witch! Give me the bundle!"

On top of the bedding, which was tied together, and which the woman was already carrying on her head, Verena now loaded a long sack, into which she had stuffed her knickknacks and belongings, so that the poor woman stood there with a swaying tower on her head.

"It is almost too heavy for me to carry all at once," she said. "Couldn't I make two loads of it?"

"No, no, we must go immediately, for we have a long journey ahead of us, to visit some aristocratic relatives who have turned up since we became rich. You know, of course, how it is."

"Oh, I understand. Well then, God bless you, and think of me in all your splendor!"

The woman went away with her towering bundle, which she had difficulty in keeping balanced, and behind her followed her little farm boy, who placed himself under Verena's once gaily-painted bedstead, bracing his head like a second Samson against its canopy, which was covered with faded stars, and grasping the two ornamentally carved posts which supported the canopy in front.

As Verena, leaning against Sali, gazed after this procession, and watched the moving temple as it passed between the garden plots, she said, "That would make a nice little summer house or an arbor, if one were to plant it in a garden, set a little table and a bench inside it, and sow some morning glories around it. Would you like to sit in it with me, Sali?"

"Yes, Verena, especially if the morning glories had grown up!"

"But what are we waiting for?" said Verena. "There's nothing to keep us here any longer!"

"Then come along, and close up the house. Who are you going to give the key to?"

Verena looked around.

"We'll have to hang it here on the halberd. I've often heard father say it's been in this house for more than a hundred years, and now there it stands, the last watchman!"

They hung the rusty house key on a rusty scroll of the old weapon, on which the beans were climbing, and started off. Verena, however, turned paler, and for a while hid her eyes, so that Sali was obliged to lead her until they were a dozen paces away. But she did not look back.

"Where are we going first?" she asked.

"We'll take a regular country walk," replied Sali, "where we can enjoy ourselves all day long, without hurrying, and toward evening I'm sure we'll find a good place to dance."

"Fine," said Verena. "All day long we'll be together, and go wherever we please. But I feel miserable now—let's go and have a cup of coffee in the next village."

"Of course," said Sali. "Hurry up and let's get out of this village."

Presently they were out in the open country and walking in silence across the fields, side by side. It was a beautiful Sunday morning in September; there was not a cloud in the sky, the hills and woods were clothed in a delicate gossamer haze, which made the landscape more mysterious and solemn. On all sides the church bells were ringing, here the deep, harmonious peal of a rich town, there the chatter of two little tinkling bells in a poor village. The loving couple forgot what the end of the day had in store for them, and with a sense of relief gave themselves up completely to the unspoken joy of wandering, nicely dressed and free, like two happy people who rightfully belong to each other, out into the glorious Sunday. Every sound or distant call that died away in the Sabbath stillness sent a thrill through their souls; for love is a bell which echoes back anything, however remote or insignificant, converting it into a peculiar music.

Although they were both hungry, the half hour's walk to the

nearest village seemed to them a stone's throw; hesitantly they entered the tavern at the entrance to the town. Sali ordered a good breakfast, and while it was being prepared they sat as still as mice and observed the orderly and pleasant proceedings in the large, tidy dining room. The landlord was also a baker, and the last batch of baking filled the entire house with a pleasant odor. Bread of all kinds was being brought in, heaped up in baskets; for the people got their bread or drank their morning glass here after church. The hostess, a genial, neat-looking woman, was calmly and good-naturedly getting her children dressed up, and as soon as one of them was dismissed it would run up trustingly to Verena to display its finery and tell her all about the things it was so happy and proud of.

When the strong, fragrant coffee came, the young couple sat down modestly at the table, as if they were invited guests. Presently, however, they grew more lively and whispered quietly, but blissfully, to each other. Oh, how the blossoming Verena enjoyed the good coffee, the rich cream, the fresh warm rolls, the delicious butter and honey, the pancakes, and all the other delicacies! They tasted good to her beause she could look at Sali while she ate, and she ate with as much relish as if she had been fasting for a year. She was also delighted with the fine dishes and the little silver coffee spoons; for the hostess seemed to take them for honest young folks who were to be respectably served. Now and then she would sit down by them to chat, and they talked sensibly, which pleased her.

The good Verena was so undecided that she did not know whether she would rather go out into the open air again and wander alone with her sweetheart through meadows and woods, or remain there in the tavern, to dream of being, at least for a few hours, in an elegant home. But Sali made the choice easy for her by gravely and busily preparing for departure, as if they had a definite, important destination to reach. The landlord and landlady accompanied them to the door and took leave of them in a most benevolent manner, because of their good behavior, and in spite of their obvious poverty; and the poor young people said good-bye with the best manners in the world, and departed with propriety and decorum.

Even when they were out in the open again and had entered an oak forest, an hour's walk in length, they continued to stroll along dreamily side by side in this same manner, not as if they came from wretched, quarreling, ruined homes, but as if they were children of well-to-do people and were walking about, happy and full of hope. Verena lowered her head pensively on her breast, which was covered with flowers, and with her hands carefully laid on her dress, walked along on the smooth, damp ground of the forest; Sali, on on the other hand, strode swiftly and thoughtfully, his slender form erect, his eyes fixed on the strong oak trunks, as if he were a farmer considering which trees he could fell to the best advantage.

They finally awoke from these futile dreams, looked at each other, and discovered that they were still walking in the same dignified manner as when they left the inn. They blushed and hung their heads in sadness. But youth is youth; the forest was green, the sky blue, they were alone in the wide world, and they soon returned to their former mood.

But they did not continue to be alone much longer; for the beautiful forest road presently came alive with pleasure-seeking groups of young people, as well as with individual couples who were passing the time after church joking and singing. For country folk, no less than city people, have their favorite walks and parks, the only difference being that theirs cost nothing for maintenance, and are even more beautiful. Not only do they have a special feeling for Sunday walks through their blossoming and ripening fields, but they also have choice promenades through the woods and along the green hillsides; they sit down on a pleasant eminence offering a wide view, or at the edge of a forest, where they sing their songs and take comfort and pleasure in the beauty of the wilderness. And, as they obviously do this not for penance but for pleasure, it may be inferred that they have a feeling for nature—quite apart from its utilitarian aspect. They are forever breaking off green twigs, young boys as well as old women seeking out the familiar paths of their youth. Even stiff countrymen in the best years of their busy lives, when they walk out in the country and pass through a forest, like to cut a slender switch and trim off the leaves, leaving only a green tuft at the end. Such a switch they carry before them like a scepter, and when they enter an office or a court, they respectfully stand the switch up in a corner, but never forget, even after the most serious business, carefully to pick it up again and take it home intact, where it is turned over to the littlest boy, who has the privilege of finishing it off.

When Sali and Verena saw the numerous pleasure seekers, they laughed secretly and rejoiced that they too were a couple; but they slipped aside into narrower forest paths and lost themselves in the deep solitude. They stopped at the pretty spots, hurried on, and rested again and, just as there was not a cloud in the clear sky, so for now not a care troubled their spirits. They forgot where they had come from and where they were going, and in all behaved themselves so nicely and properly, in spite of all their glad emotion and commotion, that Verena's neat, simple adornment remained as fresh and tidy as it had been in the morning. Sali conducted himself on this walk, not like an almost twenty-year-old country lad or the son of a ruined innkeeper, but as if he were some years younger and had been very well brought up; it was almost comical, the way he kept looking, all tenderness, solicitude and respect, at his dear, happy Verena. For on this one day which had been granted to them, the poor young people had to experience all the moods and phases of love, to make up for the lost time of its tender beginnings, as well as to anticipate its passionate ending in the surrender of their lives.

Thus they walked until they were hungry again, and were glad to see shining before them, from the top of a shady hill, a village where they could have dinner. They descended rapidly, but entered this place as decorously as they had left the other. There was nobody around to recognize them; for Verena in particular had not been out among people during the past few years, and still less had she been in other villages. For that reason they were taken for a pleasant, respectable couple out on some important errand. They entered the first tavern in the village, where Sali ordered a substantial meal. A separate table was set for them in Sunday style, and again they sat down with quiet modesty and gazed at the beautifully wainscoted walls of polished walnut, the rustic, but gleaming and well-appointed sideboard of the same wood, and the clean, white curtains.

The landlady came up with an obliging air and put a vase of fresh flowers on the table.

"Until your soup comes," she said, "you can feast your eyes on the bouquet, if you wish. I'd say it's very likely—if you don't mind my asking—that you're a young couple, engaged, and on your way to town to be married tomorrow!"

Verena blushed and did not dare to look up; Sali too said nothing, and the landlady continued, "Well, of course, you're both still young, but it's a common saying that early marriage means long life. At any rate you look nice and pretty and don't need to hide yourselves. Decent folk can get somewhere when they marry so young, if they're industrious and loyal. But they do have to be that, for the time is short in a way and yet long, too, and there are many, many days to come! Ah, well, they're fine enough and entertaining too, if one makes good use of them. Pardon my saying so, but it does me good to look at you—you are such a nice little couple!"

The waitress brought the soup, and as she had heard part of these words, and would have preferred to be married herself, she looked askance at Verena, who seemed to her to be getting on so well in the world. In the adjoining room the disagreeable girl gave vent to her ill-humor, saying to the landlady, who was busy there, in a voice loud enough to be overheard, "There you have another couple of fools running off to town to get married, just as they are, without a penny, without friends, without a dowry, and without any prospects but begging and poverty. What's the world coming to when such worthless young things get married, and they can't even put on their own jackets or cook up a soup? I'm so sorry for that handsome young fellow—he's certainly stuck with that silly little hussy!"

"Hush! Will you keep still, you spiteful thing!" said the landlady. "I won't have anything bad said of them. I'm sure they're two decent folk from the mountains, where the factories are. They're dressed poorly but neatly, and if they just love each other and work hard, they'll get along better than you with your vicious tongue. You'll wait a long time before anybody comes and takes you, unless you're more pleasant, you vinegar jug!"

And so Verena enjoyed all the delights of a girl on the way to her wedding, the kind and encouraging words of a very sensible woman, the envy of a spiteful person who wished she were married and who from sheer vexation praised and pitied her lover, and an appetizing midday meal beside this same lover. Her face shone like a red carnation, and her heart throbbed. Nevertheless she ate and drank with a good appetite, and treated the waitress all the more civilly, although at the same time she could not refrain from looking tenderly at Sali and whispering to him so that his own head began to whirl.

So they sat comfortably at the table for a long time, as if they hesitated and feared to leave this charming illusion. The landlady brought some sweet pastry for dessert, and Sali ordered with it some choicer, stronger wine, which flowed through Verena's veins like fire when she drank a little of it. But she was careful and merely took an occasional sip as she sat there, modest and bashful, like a real bride. She played this rôle partly out of roguery and a desire to see how it felt, and partly because she was actually in that mood. Her heart was almost breaking with anxiety and ardent love, so that she felt oppressed within these four walls and wished to leave.

It seemed as if they were afraid to be off and alone on the path again; for they tacitly took the highway and went on through the midst of the people, looking neither to the right nor to the left. But when they were out of the village, and heading for the next one, where the church fair was, Verena took Sali's arm and whispered, trembling; "Sali, why shouldn't we belong to each other and be happy?"

"I don't know why, either!" he replied, fixing his eyes on the mild autumn sunshine which glinted over the meadows, and making a strange face in an effort to control himself. They stopped to kiss each other, but some people appeared, so they refrained and went on.

The large village where the church fair was being held was already alive with merry people. From the imposing hotel sounded pompous dance music—for the young villagers had started to dance at noon already—and in the open space before the hotel a small fair had been set up, consisting of a few tables loaded with candies and cakes, and a couple of booths covered with cheap finery, around which gathered a crowd of children and of such people as were for the present satisfied to be spectators.

Sali and Verena also went up and took a good look at the splendid things; for they both had their hands in their pockets, each wanting to give the other some little present, now that for the first and only time in their lives they were at a fair together. Sali bought a large house of gingerbread, which had a nice white icing and a green roof with white doves perching on it; and out of the chimney peeked a little Cupid representing a chimney sweep. At its open windows chubby-cheeked little people with tiny red mouths were hugging and in fact kissing each other; for the hasty practical painter had with a single daub made two little mouths, causing them to flow together. Black dots represented bright little eyes.

On the pink house door were these verses:

> "Walk in, my dear, but mark you:
>   That in my house today,
> We reckon and pay with kisses;
>   There is no other way."

> She answered, "Oh, my dearest,
>   I'm not the least afraid,
> I've thought the whole thing over,
>   In you my fortune's made."

> "And if my memory serves me,
>   That's why I came this way!"
> "Come in then with my blessing,
>   And be prepared to pay!"

In conformity with these verses a gentleman in a blue coat and a lady with a high bosom, painted at the left and right on the wall, were bowing each other into the house.

Verena, in turn, gave Sali a heart, on one side of which was pasted a piece of paper with the words:

> "An almond sweet is hidden
>   in this heart, you'll see,
> But sweeter than the almond
>   is my true love for thee!"

and on the other side:

> "When once this heart is eaten,
>   remember this from me,

> That my brown eyes shall fade
> before my love for thee."

They eagerly read the verses, and never has anything printed and rhymed been more highly appreciated or more deeply felt than were these gingerbread mottoes; for they regarded what they read as something written especially for them, so appropriate did it seem.

"Oh!" sighed Verena, "you're giving me a house! I've given you one too, and our only real one; because our hearts are now the houses we live in, and so we carry our homes around with us, like two snails. We have no other!"

"But then we're two snails, each carrying the other's house," said Sali.

And Verena replied, "Then there's all the more reason why we should stick together, so that each of us may be near home!"

They did not realize they were saying just such witty things as were to be read on the variously shaped cookies, and they went on studying this sweet and simple literature of love which lay spread out there, stuck for the most part on differently decorated hearts of all sizes. They found everything beautiful and uniquely applicable. When Verena read on a gilded heart, which was covered with strings like a lyre:

> "My heart is like a lyre string,
> Just touch the thing,
> It starts to sing,"

she herself began to feel so musical she thought she could hear her own heart singing. There was also a picture of Napoleon, which was likewise called upon to bear an amorous motto; under it was written:

> "A hero great was Bonaparte,
> Of steel his sword, of clay his heart;
> But roses on *your* breast conceal
> A heart within as true as steel."

While they seemed to be absorbed in reading, each took occasion to make a secret purchase. Sali bought for Verena a gilded ring with a green glass stone, and Verena for Sali a ring of black chamois horn with a golden forget-me-not inlaid on it. It is very likely they had the same idea: to give each other these poor tokens when they parted. With their minds concentrated on these things and oblivious of all else, they did not notice that a wide ring of people had gradually formed around them, and that they were being intently and curiously watched. For, since there were many young lads and girls from their village there, they had been recognized; now these people were all standing around the well-dressed couple and looking at them in amazement, while they in turn were so devoted and absorbed that they seemed utterly oblivious to the world around them.

"Oh, look!" somebody said. "That's really Verena Marti and Sali from town. They've found each other and joined up in fine style! And just look at that, will you—what tenderness and friendship! I wonder what they're up to?"

The astonishment of these spectators was due to a strange combination of sympathy for their misfortune, contempt for the demoralization and depravity of their parents, and envy of the happiness and unity of the couple, who in a singular, almost aristocratic way were so excited and in love and whose unrestrained devotion and self-forgetfulness seemed as strange to the rough crowd as did their loneliness and poverty.

So when they finally woke up and looked around, they saw nothing but gaping faces on all sides. Nobody spoke to them, and they did not know whether or not to speak to anyone else. But this estrangement and unfriendliness was due on both sides more to embarrassment than to intent. Verena felt anxious and hot; she turned pale and blushed; but Sali took her hand and led the poor girl away, and she following willingly, with her house in her hand, although the trumpets in the hotel were already blaring merrily and she was so eager to dance.

"We can't dance here," said Sali, when they had withdrawn some distance. "It doesn't seem that we'd find much pleasure here."

"I suppose," said Verena sadly, "we'd better give up the idea entirely, and I'll try to find a place to stay."

"No!" cried Sali. "You shall dance! That's why I bought you the shoes. We'll go where the poor people have their parties; that's where we belong now. They won't look down on us there. Whenever there's a church fair here they always dance in Paradise Garden, because it belongs to the parish. We'll go there and you can spend the night too, if necessary."

Verena shuddered at the thought of sleeping in a strange place for the first time in her life; but she unresistingly followed her escort, who was now all that she had in the world.

Paradise Garden was a tavern, beautifully situated on a lonely mountain slope, commanding a wide view of the country, but frequented on such days of pleasure only by the poorer people, the children of the smallest farmers and day laborers, and even by all sorts of vagrants. It had been built a hundred years before by an eccentric rich man as a small vacation house. Nobody had cared to live there after him, and since it was good for nothing else, the strange country house fell into disrepair and then into the hands of a innkeeper, who ran it as a business.

But the name and its corresponding architecture had clung to the house. It consisted of only a single story, above which was an open platform, the roof being supported at the four corners by sandstone figures representing the four archangels, now badly weatherbeaten. All around the corners sat small, music-making angels, likewise of sandstone, with thick heads and bellies, playing the triangle, the violin, the flute, the cymbal, and the tambourine. These instruments had originally been gilded. The ceiling, the parapet of the platform and the remaining walls of the house were covered with faded frescoes, representing merry bands of angels, and singing and dancing saints. But everything was now blurred and indistinct, like a dream, and furthermore profusely covered with grapevines, while blue grapes were ripening everywhere in the foliage. All around the house were neglected chestnut trees; here and there strong, gnarled rose bushes grew without being cared for, as wild as elders grow elsewhere.

The platform served as the dance hall. As Sali approached with Verena they saw from afar couples whirling under the open roof, and a throng of merry guests carousing boisterously around the house. Verena, who was devoutly and sadly carrying her love-house, resembled one of those old paintings of a saintly patron of the church holding in her hand the model of a cathedral or cloister which she has established; but what was so piously established in Verena's mind could come to nothing. As soon as she heard the wild music coming from the platform, however, she forgot her grief, and her only desire was to dance with Sali. They pushed their way through the guests who were sitting in front of the house and in the barroom—ragged people from Seldwyla enjoying a cheap outing, and poor folks from all over—ascended the stairs and immediately began to whirl about in a waltz, not once taking their eyes from each other.

Only when the waltz was over did they look around. Verena had crushed and broken her house, and was ready to cry when the sight of the black fiddler close beside them gave her an even more violent shock. He was sitting on a bench, which had been placed on a table, and he looked as black as ever; only today he had stuck a sprig of green fir into his little hat. At his feet he had set down a bottle of red wine and a glass, which he never upset, although he kept working his legs as he fiddled, thus executing a sort of an egg-dance. Beside him sat a handsome but sad-looking young man with a French horn; and a hunchback was playing a bass viol.

Sali was also startled when he saw the fiddler. The latter, however, greeted them amiably, and cried out, "I knew I'd play for you some day! So have a really good time, you two sweethearts, and drink my health!"

He offered Sali a full glass, and Sali drank his health.

When the fiddler saw how frightened Verena was, he tried to talk to her pleasantly, making a few jokes that were almost charming, and causing her to laugh. She cheered up, and now they were both glad to have an acquaintance here and to be, in a certain sense, under the special protection of the fiddler. They danced without interruption, forgetting themselves and the world in the whirling and singing and reveling that was going on inside and outside the house and echoing noisily from the mountain far out into the countryside, which had gradually become veiled in the silvery haze of the autumn evening. They danced until it grew dark and the majority of the merry guests went off, staggering and shouting, in all directions.

Those that still remained were the rabble proper, who had no homes, and proposed to follow up their pleasant day with a jolly night. Among these were some who seemed to be well acquainted with the fiddler, and who looked strange in their motley costumes.

Particularly striking was a young fellow who wore a green cor-
duroy jacket and a crumpled straw hat, around which he had tied
a wreath of mountain-ash berries. He was dancing with a wild girl
who wore a skirt of cherry-colored calico, dotted with white, and
had a garland of grapevine wound around her head with a cluster
hanging down over each temple. This couple was the most exu-
berant of all; they danced and sang untiringly and were everywhere at once.

Then there was also a slender, pretty girl in a faded black silk
dress, who had tied around her head a white cloth, the ends of
which fell down her back. The cloth had red stripes woven into it
and was a good linen towel or napkin. Beneath it shone a pair of
violet-blue eyes. Around her neck and on her breast hung a chain
of six strands made of mountain-ash berries strung on a thread,
like the most beautiful coral necklace. This girl danced all the time
alone, obstinately refusing to dance with any of the men. Nonetheless she moved about lightly and gracefully, and smiled every
time she passed the melancholy horn player, who turned his head
away each time she did so. Several other lighthearted women were
there, with their escorts, looking very poor, but all the more gay
and congenial.

When it was totally dark the landlord refused to light any candles, asserting that the wind would blow them out; besides, the
full moon would soon be up, he said, and moonlight was good
enough, considering what they paid. This announcement was received with great glee; the entire company gathered near the parapet of the open hall and watched for the rising moon, whose
glow was already visible on the horizon. As soon as it appeared
and cast its light obliquely across the platform of Paradise Garden,
they went on dancing by moonlight, and did it as quietly and
properly and happily as if they had been dancing in the brilliant
glow of a hundred wax candles.

The strange light made everybody more friendly, so that Sali
and Verena could not help taking part in the general merriment,
and dancing with others. But every time they were separated for a
little while, they flew together again and were as glad to be reunited as if they had been looking for each other for a year and
had finally met. Sali made a sad and ill-natured face whenever he
danced with anybody else, and kept turning his head toward Ver-

ena, who did not look at him when she floated by, but glowed like a red rose and seemed to be supremely happy, whoever her partner might be.

"Are you jealous, Sali?" she asked him, when the musicians grew tired and stopped playing.

"Not a bit!" he said. "I wouldn't know how to be!"

"Then why are you so cross when I dance with others?"

"That isn't what makes me cross—it's because I have to dance with someone else myself. I can't stand any other girl—when it isn't you I feel as if I were holding a piece of wood in my arms. And you? How about you?"

"Oh, I'm in heaven whenever I'm dancing and know that you are there! But I think I should drop dead if you were to go away and leave me here."

They had gone downstairs and were standing in front of the house. Verena threw both arms about him, nestled her slender, quivering form close to him, pressed her burning cheek, wet with hot tears, against his face, and said, sobbing, "We can't stay together, and yet I can't leave you, not for a minute, not an instant!"

Sali caught the girl in his arms and hugged her passionately, covering her face with kisses. His confused thoughts were struggling to find a way out, but he could see none. Even if he could overcome the misery and hopelessness of his origin, his youth and inexperience did not fit him to undertake and endure a long period of trial and renunciation; and then there was Verena's father, whom he had made miserable for life. The feeling that happiness could be had in the middle-class world only in an honorable and irreproachable marriage was just as strong in him as it was in Verena. In both of the forlorn souls it was the last flicker of that honor which had formerly shone in their houses, and which their fathers, each feeling himself secure, had blown out and destroyed by a trifling mistake, when they so thoughtlessly appropriated the land of a missing man, thinking to magnify this honor by increasing their property, and believing themselves safe in so doing. That sort of thing happens every day; but now and then fate makes an example of two such magnifiers of their family honor and property, by bringing them into collision, whereupon they infallibly ruin and consume each other, like two wild beasts. For it is not only on thrones that "defenders of the realm" miscalculate, but also at times in the lowliest huts; and when they do, they reach an end the exact opposite of that which they were trying to attain, and the obverse of honor's shield is a tablet of disgrace.

Sali and Verena, however, had seen the honor of their houses in the tender years of their childhood, and recalled what well-brought-up children they had been, and that their fathers had looked like other men, respected and self-reliant. Then they had been separated for a long time, and when they met again they at once saw in each other the vanished happiness of their homes, and their affections were all the more tenaciously intertwined. They were so eager to be gay and happy, but only on a sound and respectable basis, and this seemed to them unattainable; while their surging blood would have preferred to flow together at once.

"It's night now," said Verena, "and we must part!"

"And you mean I should go home and leave you alone?" cried Sali. "No, I can't do that!"

"Then day will come and we'll be no better off!"

"Let me give you a piece of advice, you silly people!" cried a shrill voice behind them, and the fiddler stepped up to them. "There you stand," he said, "not knowing what to do, and wanting each other. I advise you to take each other as you are, without delay. Come with me and my good friends into the mountains; you need no pastor there, no money, no papers, no honor, no bed—all you need is your own good will. It isn't so bad with us—healthy air and enough to eat, if you keep busy. The green forest is our house; we love each other there in our own way, and in the winter we make ourselves nice warm little nests, or else we crawl into a farmer's warm hay. So make up your minds quickly: get married here right now and come with us; then you'll be free of worry and have each other forever and ever—at any rate, as long as you please. Because you'll grow old living our free life—you can count on that. Don't think I'll take out on you what your fathers did to me. Not at all! It gives me pleasure, of course, to see you where you are—but I'm satisfied with that and I'm ready to be of help and service to you, if you'll follow me."

He said this in a really sincere and kindly tone.

"Well, think it over a bit—but if you'll take my advice, follow me! Let the world go, marry each other, and ask nothing of anybody. Think of a jolly bridal bed in the depths of the forest, or on a haymow, if it's too cold for you!"

With that he went into the house. Verena was trembling in Sali's arms, and he said, "What do you think? It seems to me it wouldn't be a bad idea to let the whole world go and just love each other, no matter what anyone says or does!" But he said this more as a despairing jest than in earnest.

Verena, however, kissed him and replied very openly, "No, I don't want to go with them; I don't like the way things are there either. The young fellow with the horn and the girl with the silk dress belong to each other that way, and they're said to have been very much in love. They say last week the girl was false to him for the first time, and he couldn't believe it; that is why he's so sad, and so cross with her and the others who laugh at him. She just pretends to be doing penance for it by dancing alone and talking to nobody, and she's making fun of him all the time. But you can tell by looking at the poor fellow that he'll make up with her before the day is over. I don't want to be where things like that go on; because I'd never want to be untrue to you, though I'd be willing to endure anything else to get you."

Meanwhile, however, poor Verena's love grew more and more feverish as she leaned on Sali's breast; for ever since noon, when the landlady had thought she was engaged and had introduced her as such without correction, the idea of being a bride had flamed in her blood, and the more hopeless she was, the wilder and the more uncontrollable it became. Sali's case was just as bad, since the fiddler's talk, however little he was inclined to heed it, had nevertheless turned his head, and he said in a halting, irresolute voice, "Come inside; at least we must have something more to eat and drink."

They entered the guest room, where there was nobody except the small company of the vagrants, who were already sitting around a table and having their meager meal.

"Here comes our bridal pair!" cried the fiddler. "Now be happy and cheerful, and get married!"

They were constrained to sit down at the table, in so doing they also took refuge from themselves; for they were happy merely to be among people for a moment. Sali ordered wine and more to eat, and great merriment set in. The sulker had become reconciled with his unfaithful companion, and they were caressing each other in amorous bliss. The other wild pair were also singing and drinking, and showing every sign of mutual affection; while the fiddler and the hunchback with the bass viol played away into the night.

Sali and Verena kept still, with their arms about each other. Suddenly the fiddler commanded silence and performed a jocose ceremony intended to represent a wedding. They were told to join hands, and the company rose and approached in procession to congratulate them and welcome them into the brotherhood. They submitted without saying a word, regarding it as a joke, though meanwhile hot and cold shivers ran through them.

The little gathering, inflamed by the stronger wine, was now growing more and more noisy and excited, when suddenly the fiddler insisted upon their breaking up.

"We have a long way to go," he cried, "and it's past midnight! Come on! We'll escort the bridal pair, and I'll march ahead and show you some real fiddling!"

As the confused and forsaken pair could think of nothing better to do, and were quite distracted anyway, they once more allowed things to take their course. They were stationed in front and the other two couples formed a procession behind them, the hunchback bringing up the rear with his bass viol over his shoulder. The black fiddler went ahead down the mountain, fiddling as if possessed, while the others laughed, sang, and leaped along behind.

Thus the wild nocturnal procession marched through the quiet fields, and through Sali's and Verena's home town, the inhabitants of which had long been asleep. When they entered the quiet streets and passed by their lost parental homes, a wild and painful feeling came over them, and they tried to outdo the others in dancing along behind the fiddler, kissing each other and laughing and crying. They also danced up the hill where the three fields were, as the fiddler led them there. On the crest of the hill the black fellow sawed his fiddle twice as wildly, and jumped and hopped about like a demon. His companions would not be outdone in boisterousness, so that the quiet hill was converted into a veritable witches' mountain. Even the hunchback sprang about with his burden, panting, and no one seemed to notice the other anymore.

Sali grasped Verena's arm more firmly and forced her to stand still; for he was the first to regain his senses. To silence her he kissed her vehemently on the mouth, for she had quite forgotten herself and was singing wildly. Finally she understood him, and they stood still and listened, while their wedding escorts rushed on madly along the field and passed out of sight up the stream, without missing them. The fiddle, the laughter of the girls, and the shouts of the men, however, continued to sound through the night for a long time, until finally it all died away and quiet reigned.

"We've escaped them," said Sali, "but how shall we escape ourselves? How shall we keep away from each other?"

Verena was unable to answer, and lay panting on his breast.

"Shouldn't I take you to town and wake up somebody and get you a place to stay? Then tomorrow you can be on your way, and you'll certainly be all right—you get along well everywhere!"

"Get along without you?"

"You must forget me!"

"I'll never do that! Could you?"

"That's not the question, my love," said Sali, caressing her hot cheeks as she tossed about passionately on his breast. "The only question now is you. You're still so young, and everything may still go well for you!"

"And not with you, you old man?"

"Come," said Sali, drawing her away; but they took only a few steps and stopped again, to hug and kiss each other, undisturbed. The stillness of the world sang and made music in their souls; they could hear nothing but the soft, pleasant gurgling of the river below, as it slowly flowed by.

"How beautiful it is all around us! Don't you seem to hear something like a beautiful song and a ringing of bells?"

"It's the swish of the water in the river. Everything else is still."

"No, there's something else—here, there, everywhere!"

"I believe we hear our own blood pounding in our ears."

For a while they listened to these sounds, imaginary or real, which proceeded from the intense stillness, or which they confused with the magic effects of the moonlight, playing near and far over the white, autumnal mist that lay deep on the lowlands.

Suddenly something occurred to Verena; she felt in her bodice, and said, "I bought you another keepsake that I meant to give you." She gave him the simple ring and put it on his finger herself.

Sali then produced his ring, and put it on her finger, saying, "So we had the same idea!"

Verena held out her hand in the pale, silvery light and contemplated the ring. "Oh, what a lovely ring!" she said laughing. "And so we're really and truly engaged now—you're my husband and I'm your wife. Let's think we are, just for a minute—only until that cloud over the moon has passed, or until we've counted twelve! Kiss me twelve times!"

Sali's love was certainly just as strong as Verena's, but for him marriage was not such a living, burning question—not so much a definite either-or, an immediate to-be-or-not-to-be—as it was for Verena, who was capable of feeling only the one thing, and saw in it with passionate decisiveness a simple issue of life or death. But now at last he saw the light, and what was womanly feeling in the young girl immediately became in him a wild and hot desire, and his senses were alight with a burning clarity. Vehemently as he had embraced and caressed Verena before, he now did it in a different and more tempestuous way, overwhelming her with kisses. In spite of her own intense feeling, Verena noticed this change at once, and a violent trembling thrilled her entire being; but before the streak of cloud had crossed the moon she too was convulsed by passion. With impetuous caresses and struggles their ring-adorned hands met and clasped each other tightly, as if celebrating a wedding on their own account, without the exercise of anyone's will.

Sali's heart now pounded like a hammer and the next moment stood still. He drew a deep breath and said softly, "There's only one thing for us to do, Verena—join in marriage this very hour, and then leave the world together. There's the deep water—there nobody can separate us again. We shall have been together— whether for a long time or a short time doesn't matter."

Verena at once replied, "Sali—I had the same idea long ago and I decided that we could die; then everything would be over. Swear you'll do it with me!"

"It's as good as done! Nothing but death shall ever take you from me now!" cried Sali, beside himself. But Verena drew a deep sigh of relief, and tears of joy streamed from her eyes. She jumped up and ran, light as a bird, across the field down toward the river.

Sali hurried after her, thinking that she was trying to run from him, while she thought he was trying to hold her back. And thus they raced along, Verena laughing like a child unwilling to be caught.

"Are you sorry already?" cried one to the other, as they reached the river and embraced.

"No, I'm happier and happier!" each replied.

Freed of all care, they walked downstream along the bank, outstripping the hurrying waters, so eager were they to find a resting place; for their passion now saw only the blissful intoxication of their union, and in this was concentrated the entire import and value of the rest of their lives. What was to come afterward, death and annihilation, was a mere breath, a nothing, and they thought less of it than a spendthrift thinks, squandering the last penny he has, how he is going to live the next day.

"My flowers shall go first!" cried Verena. "Look, they are all faded and withered!" She took them from her breast and threw them into the water, singing aloud: "But sweeter than the almond is my true love for thee!"

"Stop!" cried Sali. "Here is your bridal bed!"

They had come to a wagon road which led from the town to a river; here was a landing, where a large boat, loaded high with hay, lay moored. Impetuously, Sali began to untie the strong ropes. Verena laughed and caught his arm, crying, "What are you doing? Are we going to end up stealing the farmer's hay boat?"

"That's their wedding present—a floating bedstead, and a bed such as no bride ever had. Besides, they'll find their property down below, where it's headed anyway, and they'll never know what happened to it. Look!—it's already rocking and moving out!"

The boat lay in the deep water, a few steps from the bank. Sali lifted Verena high up in his arms and carried her through the water out toward it; but she caressed him with such boisterous vehemence, squirming like a fish, that he was unable to keep his footing in the current. Striving to get her face and hands into the water, she cried, "I want to try the cool water too! Do you remember how cold and wet our hands were when we shook hands for the first time? We were catching fish then—now we're going to be fish ourselves, two nice big ones!"

"Be quiet, you dear little devil!" said Sali; what with his lively sweetheart and the waves, he was having trouble to keep his balance, "or it'll carry me away!"

He lifted his burden into the boat and jumped in alongside; then he lifted her onto the high-piled, soft, sweet-smelling cargo, and swung himself up after her; as they sat there aloft the boat gradually drifted out into the middle of the river and then floated, slowly turning, downstream.

The river flowed through high, dark forests, which overshadowed it, through open fields, past quiet villages, past isolated huts. It widened out into a placid stretch, as calm as a quiet lake, where the boat almost stopped; it rushed around rocks and quickly left the sleeping shores behind. And as the glow of morning appeared, a city with its towers emerged from the silver-gray stream. The setting moon, as red as gold, made a shining path up the river, and crosswise on it the boat drifted slowly along. As it drew near the city, two pale forms, locked in close embrace, glided down in the frost of the autumn from the dark mass into the cold waters.

A short time afterward the boat floated unharmed against a bridge and stayed there. Later the bodies were found below the city, and when it was ascertained where they came from, the papers reported that two young people, the children of two poverty-stricken, ruined families that lived in irreconcilable enmity had sought death in the water, after dancing and celebrating together all day at a church fair. Probably—so the papers said—this occurrence had some connection with a hay boat from the same region, which had landed in the city without a crew; and the assumption was that the young people had stolen the boat to consummate their desperate and God-forsaken marriage—another sign of the increasing spread of moral and emotional degeneracy.

Translated by Paul Bernard Thomas and
adapted by Frank G. Ryder

Mirror, the Cat
A Fairy Story

W hen a citizen of Seldwyla has struck a bad bargain or been bamboozled, they say there: He bought the cat's fat! It's true that one also hears this proverbial expression elsewhere, but never as frequently as in Seldwyla and this may be due to the circumstance that in this town there is an old tale concerning its origin and meaning.

It is said that several hundred years ago an elderly woman dwelt alone in Seldwyla with a handsome black and grey cat that lived with her very contentedly and wisely, never harming anyone who did not harm it. Its only passion was hunting, but this passion the cat satisfied with reason and moderation, without attempting to glorify it or letting itself be carried to extremes of cruelty merely because hunting also served a useful purpose and was pleasing to its mistress. For this reason it caught and killed only the most importunate and insolent mice that ventured within a certain distance of the house. These it dispatched with unerring skill. Only occasionally would it pursue beyond its home territory an especially impudent mouse that had aroused its anger, and in such cases it always very politely asked permission of the neighbors to be allowed to mouse a bit in their houses. Such permission was gladly granted, for the cat left the milk jars alone and did not jump up on the sides of ham that might be hanging along the walls, but attended to its business quietly and efficiently and, when that was accomplished, decorously departed with the mouse in its mouth. Nor was the cat shy or ill-bred, but always friendly toward everyone and it did not run away from sensible people. On the contrary, from such persons it knew how to take a joke and would even let them pull its ears a bit without scratching. But from stupid persons of a certain stamp, whose stupidity, so it maintained, came from immaturity and a base heart, it would not put up with a thing and either avoided them or gave them a good whack across the hand if they molested it with some dumb trick.

Thus Mirror, for so the cat was called on account of his sleek, gleaming pelt, spent his days serenely, gracefully and contemplatively, in modest luxury and without arrogance. He did not sit too often on the shoulder of his friendly mistress, trying to snatch a morsel from her fork—only when he saw that she was not averse to such sport; only seldom did he lie and sleep the whole day long on his warm pillow behind the stove; rather, he kept himself alert and preferred to lie on a narrow railing or in the eaves-trough and devote himself to philosophical speculation and the observation of the world. Only once each spring and fall, when the violets were in bloom or the warmth of the Indian summer put one in mind of violet-time, was this peaceful life interrupted for the space of a week. Then Mirror would go his own ways, wandering in amorous intoxication over the rooftops and singing the loveliest songs. As a thorough Don Juan he then took hair-raising risks, and on the rare occasions when he showed up at home he had such a daring, devil-may-care, indeed, dissolute and disheveled appearance that his habitually mild-mannered mistress would be moved to cry out impatiently; "Why Mirror! Aren't you ashamed to be leading such a life!" But the one that was not ashamed was Mirror. As a man of principles, who well knew what he could permit himself in the way of a refreshing change, he would calmly busy himself with restoring the sleek luster of his pelt and the innocent cheerfulness of his looks, and without the least embarrassment would rub his damp paws over his nose as though nothing at all had happened.

But the even tenor of this life suddenly came to a sad end. Just when Mirror was in the prime of life his mistress unexpectedly died of old age, leaving her beautiful cat orphaned and ownerless. It was the first misfortune that had befallen him, and with those wailing notes that so keenly express anxious doubt concerning the true and just cause of a great sorrow he accompanied the corpse into the street and then wandered around all the rest of the day in and about the house, wholly at a loss. But his sound instinct, his reason and his philosophical nature soon bade him get hold of himself, bear the inevitable and show his grateful devotion to the house of his dead mistress by offering his services to her joyful heirs. He was prepared to stand by them with word and deed, continue to keep the mice in check and furthermore to impart much useful information, things these foolish people would not have disdained, had they not been what they were, namely fools. As it was, they did not even give Mirror a hearing, but threw the house slippers and footstool of his departed mistress at his head every time he showed his face, quarrelled among themselves for a week, finally brought a lawsuit and closed the house indefinitely, so that now no one lived in it at all.

Thus it was that Mirror was left sitting sad and abandoned on the stone step before the front door and had no one to let him in. At night, it is true, he found a way to get in underneath the roof, and in the beginning would stay hidden there a large part of the day, trying to sleep off his grief; but hunger soon drove him again into the light and forced him to appear in the warm sun and among people, in order to be on hand and on the watch for any chance mouthful of the slightest nourishment. The more infrequently such a mouthful came his way, the more watchful did Mirror become, and all his moral qualities were soon absorbed in such watchfulness, so that very soon he no longer resembled his old self. He undertook numerous excursions from his home base before the front door and stole shyly and furtively across the street, sometimes returning with a bite of unappetizing food that he would not have even glanced at before and sometimes with nothing at all. Day by day he grew thinner and more unkempt and at the same time greedy, servile and cowardly; his spirit, his graceful feline dignity, his reason and his philosophy, all were gone. When the boys came out of school, he crept into an obscure corner as soon as he heard them coming and only peeped out to see whether one of them might not toss away a crust of bread, carefully noting the spot where it fell. When the mangiest mongrel appeared in the distance, he quickly ran away, whereas formerly he had calmly looked danger in the eye and had often bravely given ill-tempered dogs deserved punishment. Only when a coarse and simple-minded member of the human race, such as he had once wisely avoided, came along, did he remain sitting, although the poor beast retained enough knowledge of human nature to recognize such oafs for what they were. But want forced poor Mirror to deceive himself and to hope that *this* evil person would prove an exception, that he would gently stroke him and offer him a bite to eat. And even if instead of such friendly treatment he received a slap or a pinch in the tail, he still did not scratch, but silently ducked aside and longingly gazed at the hand that had hit or pinched him and which smelled of sausage or herring.

When Mirror, so noble and sagacious, had declined to this degree he was sitting one day, downcast and emaciated, on the stone doorstep in front of his house, blinking in the sun. The city sorcerer Pineis happened to come along, saw the cat and stopped in front of it. Hoping for something good, even though this uncanny character was well known to him, Mirror humbly remained sitting on his stone and waited to see what Mr. Pineis would say or do. But when the latter finally cried out; "Well, cat, shall I buy your fat from you?" Mirror lost hope, for he thought the sorcerer was deriding him on account of his skinniness. Nonetheless, he answered with a meek smile, not wishing to get on the wrong side of anyone; "Oh, Mr. Pineis wants his little joke!" "By no means!" cried Pineis, "I'm quite in earnest! I have special need of cat fat for my wizardry, but it has to be ceded to me contractually and voluntarily by the worthy owners themselves, otherwise it is ineffective. It looks to me that if ever a brave little cat was in a position to conclude an advantageous bargain, it is you! Enter my service. I'll feed you splendidly, fatten you up and make you into a regular butterball with sausages and broiled quail. On the great high old roof of my house, which is, by the way, the most delightful roof in the world for a cat, full of interesting nooks and crannies, there grow superb shoots of grass, green as emerald, slenderly waving in the breeze, inviting you to bite them off and enjoy the tenderest tips when you've gotten a bit of indigestion from my delicacies. That way you'll keep in perfect health and one day furnish me with strong usable fat!"

Mirror had long since pricked up his ears and had been listening with his mouth watering, but the matter was not yet clear to his weakened understanding and he therefore replied; "That doesn't sound bad so far, Mr. Pineis! If I could only figure out how I then, since I have to give up my life to deliver you my fat, could collect the agreed-on price and enjoy it, when I'm no longer alive."

"Collect the price?" the sorcerer asked in puzzlement. "The price is precisely what you enjoy in the way of the plentiful and luxurious food with which I fatten you—that should be obvious. But I don't want to put pressure on you!" And he acted as though he were about to go on his way. Whereupon Mirror said hastily and anxiously; "You must at least grant me a modest period of grace beyond the time of my prime rotundity and obeseness, so that I don't have to leave this world so precipitately when that agreeable and oh so woeful point of time has been reached and determined!"

"It's a bargain!" said Mr. Pineis with apparent good humor. "You shall be permitted to rejoice in your agreeable condition until the next full moon, but no longer! The period of grace must not extend into the waning moon, because that would have a debilitating effect on my well-earned property."

The cat hastened to shake hands on this and signed a contract (the sorcerer was carrying one on his person) in his clear hand, his last possession and sign of better days.

"Now you can turn up at my house for the noon meal, tomcat!" said the wizard. "We eat at twelve o'clock sharp!" "I'll take the liberty, with your permission," said Mirror, and appeared promptly at noon at the house of Mr. Pineis. For several months there now began a most agreeable life for the cat; for it had nothing in the world to do but consume the good things that were set before it, watch the master at his wizardry, if it liked, and go for a stroll on the roof. The roof resembled a tremendous "fog-splitter" or stovepipe hat, like those of the Swabian peasants, and, just as such a hat shades a brain full of whims and sly tricks, so did this roof cover a great, dark house, full of angles and corners, together with a thousand things pertaining to wizard's work and uncanny business. Mr. Pineis was a jack-of-all-trades and filled a hundred and one petty offices: he doctored, exterminated lice, pulled teeth, and lent money at interest; he was guardian of the orphans and widows, cut quills in his leisure time at a dozen for a penny, and made fine black ink; he dealt in ginger and pepper, in axle grease and cordials, in notebooks and shoe nails; he kept the tower clock in repair and annually drew up a farmer's almanac with weather predictions, rules for planting and a small human figure showing where to let blood; by day he attended to a multitude of legal affairs for a modest wage and only by night to a number of illegal ones out of personal passion, though he might quickly add just the squiggle of an illegal tail, tiny as that on a young frog, to some piece of legal business before letting it out of his hands, purely for the fun of it, as it were. In addition to all this, he controlled the weather when times were bad, oversaw the training of witches and had them burned when they were ripe. He engaged in witchcraft himself only for the sake of scientific experiment and for his personal use; in an analogous fashion he secretly tried out and twisted the city laws—which it was his job to edit and make clear copies of—in order to test their durability. Since the inhabitants of Seldwyla always needed such a citizen, one who was willing to do all the unpleasant small jobs for them, he had been appointed city sorcerer and had already filled this post for many years with tireless devotion and skill, early and late. For this reason his house was crammed full from top to bottom with all things imaginable, and Mirror found much entertainment in examining and smelling everything.

But in the beginning he was interested in nothing but eating. He gulped down everything that Pineis offered him, and could hardly wait from one meal to the next. In so doing, he overloaded his stomach and actually did have to go out on the roof to bite off some of the green grass and cure himself of all sorts of indispositions. When the master noticed this ravenous hunger, he was highly pleased and thought that in this way the cat would soon get nice and fat and that the more he fed it now, the more he would save in the end. For this reason he built in his parlor a regular landscape for Mirror, setting out a little copse of fir trees, erecting small hills made of stones and moss and laying out a tiny lake. In the trees he placed savory broiled larks, finches, titmice and sparrows, according to season, so that Mirror always found something to take down and nibble on. In the little hills he hid in artificial mouseholes delicious mice, which he had carefully fattened with wheat flour, then cleaned, wrapped in tender bacon rind and broiled. Some of these mice Mirror could pull out with his paw; others, to heighten the pleasure, were hidden more deeply, but tied to string on which Mirror cautiously had to draw them out, if he wished to enjoy the sport of a mock hunt. The basin of the lake Pineis filled every day with fresh milk, so that Mirror could quench his thirst with this sweetish liquid, and in the milk he floated fried gudgeon, since he knew that cats sometimes like to fish. Now that Mirror led such a lordly life, could do or leave undone, eat and drink whatever he pleased and whenever he liked, he began, it is true, to prosper bodily quite visibly; his pelt again became sleek and shiny and his eyes alert; but at the same time, since his intellectual powers increased in like measure, he began to assume better manners; his wild greed was allayed, and because he had a sad experience behind him, he became wiser than before. He curbed his appetite and did not eat more than agreed with him, and he also again commenced to devote himself to reasoning and profound observation and to see through things again.

One day, for example, when he had fetched himself a fieldfare down from the branches and was pensively carving it up, he found its tiny craw stuffed to the brim with fresh, undigested food. Green herbs, cunningly rolled together, black and white seeds and a shiny red berry were stuffed in the craw as neatly and as closely as though a fond mother had packed her son's knapsack for a journey. As Mirror slowly devoured the fieldfare and hung the amusingly packed little craw on his claw and regarded it philosophically, he was touched by the fate of the poor bird, which had had to give up its life so soon after finishing its peaceable meal that it had not even had time to digest the things it had packed in. "What good did it do him, the poor chap," said Mirror, "to nourish himself so diligently and eagerly that this little sack looks like a day's work well done? This red berry is what tempted him out of his woodland freedom and into the fowler's noose. But he of course thought he could improve his lot by nourishing himself on such berries, and I, who have just eaten this unlucky bird, have thus only eaten myself a step nearer to death! Can one conclude a more miserable and cowardly contract than to lengthen one's life for a short span and then lose it for the sake of the price by which it was lengthened? Would not a swift, voluntary death have been preferable for a determined tomcat? But I did not think, and now that I'm thinking again, I see nothing before me but the fate of this fieldfare; when I am fat enough, I must bid life farewell, and for no other reason than that I am fat. A fine reason for a vital and thinking tomcat! Oh, if I could only get out of this noose!"

He brooded deeply on how this might be accomplished, but since the perilous moment had not yet arrived, he came to no conclusion and found no way out; but as a man of wisdom he in the meantime led a life of virtue and self-control, which is always the best propaedeutic and expenditure of one's time until something shall be decided. He scorned the soft pillows Pineis had laid down for him so that he would sleep long and soundly and grow fat and preferred to lie as formerly on a narrow ledge and in high dangerous spots, if he wanted to rest. He likewise scorned the broiled birds and bacon-seasoned mice and, employing his old ruses and skills, caught instead on the rooftops, since he now had a lawful hunting ground, a plain live sparrow or in the granaries an agile mouse, and such prey tasted more delicate to him than the cooked game in Pineis's artificial preserve and did not make him too fat. Also the exercise and daring and the renewed practice of virtue and philosophy prevented a too rapid increase in weight, so that Mirror, though he looked healthy and shiny, remained, to the surprise of Pineis, at a certain stage of portliness, a stage far from that at which the master was aiming with his tempting diet; for Pineis had in mind a spherical, sluggish beast that never left its restful cushion and consisted of pure fat.

But in this his wizardry had erred and for all his shrewdness he did not realize that if you feed a donkey, it remains a donkey, and if you feed a fox, it becomes nothing else than a fox; for every creature must grow according to its kind. When Mr. Pineis discovered that Mirror always stayed at the same stage of well-nourished, but supple and sturdy slenderness, and was not putting on enough fat, he suddenly took him to task one evening and said sternly; "What's the matter, Mirror? Why aren't you eating the good things I prepare for you with such culinary art? Why aren't you catching the broiled birds in the trees and hunting the tasty mice in the caves? Why don't you fish any more in your lake? Why aren't you taking care of yourself? Why don't you sleep on your pillow? Why do you wear yourself out and refuse to get fat?"

"Because, Mr. Pineis," Mirror replied, "I feel better this way.

Am I not to be permitted to pass my brief span in the manner most pleasing to myself?"

"What!" cried Pineis, "you're supposed to live in such a way that you get fat and round and not keep your weight down with hunting. I see what your scheme is! Do you think you can make a fool of me and make me let you run around forever in this in-between condition? Ah, no, my friend! It is your duty to eat and drink and take care of yourself, so that you put on weight and get nice and fat! Renounce this treacherous, breach-of-contract moderation immediately or I'll show you what's what!"

Mirror interrupted his self-satisfied purring, which he had begun in order to keep his composure, and said; "I think there is not a single word in our contract that says I am to renounce moderation and a healthful way of life. If you, Mr. City Sorcerer, were counting on me to be a lazy glutton, that's not my fault! You do a thousand lawful things every day, just add this to them and let us live nice and peaceably; for you know that my fat is useful to you only if it has been put on lawfully."

"Oh you gabbler!" Pineis cried out angrily, "are you telling me what to do? Let's just see how far along you really are, you idler! Maybe we can soon make use of you after all." He grabbed hold of the cat's belly, but Mirror, who felt himself disagreeably tickled, gave the sorcerer a sharp scratch on the hand. Pineis looked at him attentively, then he said; "Is that the way things stand, you beast? Very well, by virtue of our contract, I hereby solemnly declare that you are fat enough! I am satisfied with the result and shall take action accordingly. In five days there's a full moon; up to then you can enjoy life, as agreed in writing, but not a minute longer!" With that he turned his back on him and left him to his thoughts.

These were now very solemn and morose. Was it really true that the hour was near at hand when our good Mirror was to lose his hide? Was all his inventiveness of no more avail? With a sigh he climbed up on the high roof, whose ridges projected darkly into the autumn sky. The moon was just coming up and throwing its light on the town and the black mossy tiles of the old roof, when a sweet song resounded in Mirror's ears and a snow-white pussy-cat took her gleaming way along a neighboring roof-ridge. Mirror immediately forgot the prospect of his impending demise and replied to the praises of the promenading beauty with his loveliest tomcat song. He hastened toward her and was soon engaged in hot battle with three strange tomcats, whom he put to flight with wild courage. Then he paid court to the lady with ardor and devotion and spent day and night with her without giving Pineis a thought or showing himself at home. He sang like a nightingale all through the moonlit nights, pursuing his white beloved across the rooftops and more than once tumbling from a high roof in violent love-play or in a struggle with a rival and falling into the street. But then he would pull himself together again, shake his fur and begin anew the wild chase dictated by his passions. Periods of calm, moments of loud outcry, tender feelings and angry strife, intimate communings, witty conversations, the tricks and travails of love and jealousy, caresses and fisticuffs, exultant happiness and sorrowful misfortune kept lovesick Mirror from coming to his senses, and when the moon's disc had become full, he was in such a sad state from all this excitement and passion that he looked more miserable, more emaciated and disheveled than ever before. At this moment Pineis called to him from a little tower on the roof, "Mirror, my boy, Mirror, where are you? Come on home for a while!"

Whereupon Mirror took leave of his snow-white mistress, who went her way content and aloofly meowing, and proudly turned to his executioner. The latter descended to the kitchen, rustled the contract and said, "Come, Mirror, come!" Mirror followed him, seating himself defiantly in front of the master in the witch's kitchen in all his emaciation and disarray. When Pineis saw how he had been so ignominiously cheated of his reward, he jumped into the air as though possessed and cried out in rage, "What's this I see? You rascal, you shameless scoundrel! What have you done to me?" Beside himself with anger, he reached for a broom and was about to strike Mirror, but the tomcat hunched his dark back, made his hair stand on end and let a pale gleam crackle over it, meanwhile laying back his ears and glaring at the old man so fiercely that Pineis sprang back three steps in terror and dismay. He began to fear that he was in the presence of another wizard, who was making a fool of him and was more powerful than himself. In a timid and uncertain voice he said, "Is the honorable Mr. Mirror perhaps a member of our profession? Is it possible that a learned magician has taken a fancy to assume your honor's outward form, seeing that he can dispose of his physical appearance at will and become just as portly as he pleases, neither too fat nor too thin, or, before one realizes it, become as skinny as a skeleton, in order to escape death?"

Mirror resumed his calm and answered honestly, "No, I'm not a magician. It was the sweet power of love alone that brought me to this state and, I'm glad to say, robbed you of your fat. And if we want to start this business over again, I'll stick to it bravely and eat like a trooper! Just serve me a nice fat sausage, I'm starved and exhausted!" In a rage, Pineis seized Mirror by the scruff of the neck, and, locking him in a goose pen that always stood empty, shouted, "There now, let's see if the sweet power of love can get you out of this and whether it is stronger than the power of wizardry and my lawful contract! Now the motto is: Root, hog, and die!" He immediately broiled a long sausage, which smelled so appetizing that he could not refrain from nibbling off both ends himself before sticking it through the grating. Mirror ate it up from one end to the other, then smugly cleaning his whiskers and licking his pelt, he said to imself, " 'Pon my soul, I must say love's a fine thing! This time it got me out of the noose again. Now I'll rest up a bit and strive to return to reasonable thoughts through serenity and good nourishment. There is a time for everything! Today a bit of passion, tomorrow a bit of rest and reflection— everything is good in its way. My prison's not at all bad, surely I'll be able to think of something salutary in here." But Pineis now made every effort and each day prepared with all the skill at his command such delicacies and in such attractive sequence and of such digestibility that goose-penned Mirror could not resist them; for Pineis's supply of cat fat was decreasing daily and threatened to run out altogether, and without this chief ingredient the wizard was a beaten man. But the good sorcerer could not avoid nourishing Mirror's spirit along with his body; there was no way to get rid of this inconvenient additional factor, and thus did his wizardry prove itself less than perfect.

When Mirror in prison pent finally seemed fat enough to him, he hesitated no longer, but laid out his instruments before the eyes of the attentive tomcat and made a blazing fire in the fireplace to render the lard he had so long desired. Then he sharpened a great knife, opened the cage, pulled Mirror out, having first carefully closed the kitchen door, and said cheerfully, "Come here, wise guy! First we'll cut off your head and then we'll skin you. Your pelt will make me a warm cap, something I in my simplicity had not even thought of. Or shall I skin you first and then cut off your head?"

"No, if you don't mind," said Mirror humbly, "I'd rather you first cut off my head."

"Right you are, poor chap," said Mr. Pineis, "we don't want to torture you unnecessarily. Justice above all!"

"A truer word was never spoken!" said Mirror with a pitiable sigh and resignedly laid his head on one side. "Oh, if I had only always done what is just and had not so frivolously neglected such an important matter, then I could face death with a better conscience, for I'm glad to die; but an injustice makes my otherwise so welcome death hard to bear; for what has life to offer me? Nothing but fear, care and poverty and, as a change, a storm of consuming passion, which is even worse than silent quaking fear!"

"Aye now, what injustice, what important matter?" asked Pineis full of curiosity.

"Ah, what good to talk about it now," sighed Mirror, "done is done and it's too late for regrets."

"You see, wise guy, what a sinner you are?" said Pineis, "and how richly you deserve your fate? But what the deuce did you do, anyway? Did you perhaps steal something from me or turn someone against me or ruin something? Have you done me some outrageous injustice that I know nothing about, have no premonition or suspicion of, you Satan? That's a fine way to behave! A good thing I found out about it before it's too late! Confess to me at once or I'll skin you and render you alive! Are you going to talk or not?"

"Oh no," said Mirror, "I have nothing to reproach myself with on your account. It concerns ten thousand gold gulden that belonged to my deceased mistress—but why talk about that? To be sure—when I think about it and take a closer look at you, perhaps it isn't altogether too late—when I size you up, then I see that you are still quite a handsome and well-preserved man, in fact, in your prime. Tell me, Mr. Pineis, haven't you ever felt the desire to get

married, honorably and profitably? But what nonsense I'm talking! Why would such a clever and artful man ever have such idle
thoughts! Why should a usefully employed sorcerer think about
silly women! Of course it's true that even the worst of women has
something about her that may be of use to a man—you can't deny
that. And if she's worth anything at all, then a good housewife
has, let's say, a white body, a prudent disposition, a friendly manner, is faithful, a frugal housekeeper, but extravagant in the
care of her husband, amusing in her speech and pleasant in her
deeds, flattering in her actions! She kisses her husband with her
mouth and embraces him with her arms and scratches him behind
the ears, just the way he likes it; in short, she does a thousand
things one can't object to. She sticks close beside him or keeps a
modest distance, according to his mood, and when he is engaged
in his business, she doesn't disturb him, but sings his praise within
the house and without; for she allows no slight to rest upon him
and lauds everything about him. But the most charming part is the
marvelous constitution of her tender physical being, which nature
has made so different from ours for all the apparent human simi-
larity, so that it works a continual miracle in a happy marriage
and actually contains within itself the most uncanny witchcraft of
all. But why am I going on like a fool here at the threshold of
death! How can a wise man turn his attention to such vanities!
Forgive me, Mr. Pineis, and cut off my head."

But Pineis cried vociferously, "Won't you finally shut up, you
chatterbox! Tell me—where is such a woman to be found and
does she have ten thousand gold gulden?"

"Ten thousand gold gulden?" said Mirror.

"Well, yes," cried Pineis impatiently, "Weren't you just talking
about them?"

"No," replied Mirror, "that's a different story. They're buried
in a certain spot."

"And what are they doing there? Who do they belong to?"

"They don't belong to anyone. That's what's troubling my conscience, because I should have taken care of them. Actually, they
belong to the man who marries such a person as I've just described. But how is one to join these three things in this godless
town: ten thousand gold gulden, an excelling housewife white of

skin, and a wise and honest man? For that reason my sin is after all not so great, for to fulfill these conditions was beyond the powers of a poor cat!"

"If you don't stick to the subject and explain things in their proper order, I'll begin by first cutting off your tail and both ears! Now, let's hear it!"

"Since it is your command, I suppose I'll have to tell you the story," said Mirror and calmly sat down on his hind quarters, "although this delay only increases my sufferings." Pineis stuck the sharp knife in the floor between himself and Mirror and sat down on a cask to listen, full of curiosity. Mirror then went on, "You are aware, Mr. Pineis, that that excellent woman, my dear departed mistress, died unmarried, an elderly spinster who quietly did many good deeds and never harmed anyone. But she had not always led such a quiet and peaceful life, and although she was never bad-tempered, still she caused a lot of damage and suffering; for in her youth she was the most beautiful young woman far and wide, and every young gentleman or enterprising young journeyman who came her way fell in love with her and insisted on marrying her. Now there was no doubt that she was keen on getting married and taking a handsome, honest and prudent man for a husband, and she had a wide choice, for both the local lads and strangers were fighting for her and more than once put a sword through each other's bodies to gain an advantage. Gathered about and asking for her hand were bold and faint-hearted, wily and frank, rich and poor suitors, good, decent businessmen and cavaliers elegantly living on their private income; this one had these things, that one those in his favor, was eloquent or taciturn; one was jolly and amiable and another seemed to possess superior inner qualities, though he looked rather simpleminded; in short, the maiden had a choice as perfect as any marriageable young woman could wish for.

"However, in addition to her beauty, she possessed many thousand gold gulden and this was the reason she could not make up her mind and choose a husband, for she managed her estate with surpassing wisdom and prudence and valued it highly, and since it is human nature always to judge others by our personal inclinations, so it happened that, as soon as a respectable suitor who halfway won her approval showed up, she immediately imagined that he desired her only for the sake of her wealth. If the suitor was rich, she believed he wouldn't want her if she weren't rich also, and of those without means she assumed as a certainty that they had only her gulden in mind and intended to regale themselves at her expense, for the poor young woman, who herself placed such emphasis on worldly pelf, was not capable of distinguishing her suitors' love for money and possessions from their love for her person or, in case the former was really present, of making allowances and forgiving them for it.

"Several times she was as good as engaged and her heart finally began to beat faster, but then she would suddenly think she had discovered through some trait or other that she had been betrayed and that the man in question had his eye only on her wealth, and she would at once break off the relationship and retire from the scene full of sorrow but impervious to all pleading. All who did not displease her she tested in a hundred ways, so that great skill was necessary not to fall into a trap, until finally none could approach her with any hope of success who was not a thorough trickster and impostor. For this reason the choice at last became truly difficult, because such persons in the end arouse an uncanny sense of discomfort and leave a beauteous woman in the most painful uncertainty, the smoother and cleverer they are. Her chief means for winnowing out her admirers was to put their generosity to the test and make them lay out large sums every day for rich presents and philanthropic enterprises. But whatever they might do, they never did the right thing; for if they proved generous and self-sacrificing, if they gave splendid entertainments, offered her presents or entrusted her with considerable sums for the poor, then she would suddenly say they were doing all this just to catch the trout with a minnow or knock down the flitch of bacon with a sausage, as the saying goes. And she would then give both their presents and the money entrusted to her to some convent or benevolent society and use it to feed the poor, but her disappointed wooers she turned away without mercy. If the latter proved to be frugal or even stingy, sentence was passed on them at once, since she took that in much worse part and interpreted such an attitude as outright inconsideration and mean selfishness. Thus it came to pass that she, who sought a pure heart devoted to her alone, was finally surrounded by nothing but scheming, sly and selfish wooers, whom she could not fathom and who embittered her life.

"One day she was feeling so out of sorts and dispirited that she turned all her suitors out of the house, closed it up and departed for Milan, where a cousin of hers lived. As she rode across the St. Gotthard on a donkey, her mood was as black and forbidding as the wild rocks towering up from the abysses at her side, and she felt a violent temptation to cast herself from the Devil's Bridge into the raging waters of the Reuss. Only with the greatest effort did the two servant girls who were accompanying her (whom I later knew myself, but who are now long dead) and the guide manage to calm her and turn her mind from such a desperate undertaking. But she arrived pale and sad in the lovely land of Italy, and blue as the sky there was, her black thoughts would not leave her. But after she had spent a few days with her cousin, another melody was to resound unexpectedly and a burgeoning spring season, of which she had until then known but little, was to begin within her.

"For a young compatriot came to the cousin's house and she liked him so much at first sight that she now fell in love of her own accord for the first time. He was a handsome youth, well-bred and of noble bearing, neither rich nor poor at the time, for he possessed nothing but ten thousand gold gulden, which he had inherited from his deceased parents and with which, since he had studied commerce, he intended to establish a silk business in Milan; for he was ambitious, had a clear head and a lucky hand, as is often the case with persons of open and innocent disposition, and this the young man was: he seemed, well-educated though he was, as unsuspecting and innocent as a child. And although he was a merchant and of ingenuous mind—in itself a rare combination— yet he was firm and gentlemanly in his attitude and wore his sword at his side as boldly as any veteran. All this, as well as his fresh good looks and his youth, so conquered the maiden's heart that she could scarcely suppress her feelings and treated him with great friendliness. She grew cheerful again, and even if at times she was melancholy, this was only because of the alternation between fear of love and hope, and this was still a nobler and more agreeable feeling than that painful embarrassment she had formerly experienced in trying to decide among her many wooers. Now she knew only one care, namely, to try and please this handsome, kind-hearted young man, and the more beautiful she was, the humbler and more uncertain she now became, because for the first time she felt true affection. The young merchant had never seen such a beauty or at least had never been so close to one who treated him with such polite friendliness. And since, as I have said, she was not only beautiful, but also kind of heart and refined of manner, it is not surprising that the fresh, open youth, whose heart was still quite free and inexperienced, also fell in love with her with all the strength and lack of reserve that lay in his nature.

"But perhaps no one would have ever found out about this, if he, in his naiveté and encouraged by the young lady's confidential manner, had not ventured to interpret her posture, albeit with secret trembling and trepidation, as a reciprocation of his love, for he was himself a stranger to all dissembling. But he restrained himself for a few weeks and thought he was keeping the matter secret, though everyone could tell at a glance that he was head over heels in love, and if he chanced to come near the young woman or merely heard her name mentioned, then one immediately saw with whom he was in love. But he had not been in love long, indeed, he was just beginning truly to love with all the impetuosity of youth and to prize the object of his affections as the highest and best thing in the world, placing in her once and for all his salvation and personal worth. This pleased the young woman beyond measure; for in everything he said or did there was something different from anything she had known before, and this heartened her so much and touched her so deeply that she was likewise conquered by the strongest love and there was no longer any question of choosing.

"Everyone saw what was taking place and spoke and joked about it openly. The young woman enjoyed all this immensely and, though her heart was almost bursting with anxious expectation, she did her share to complicate the romance a bit and to spin it out, in order to drain its pleasures to the dregs. For in his confusion the young man did incredibly childlike things, such as she had never before experienced and these were for her more flattering and pleasing than all else. But he, with his direct and honest nature, could bear it no longer; and since everyone made references to their relationship and joked about it, it seemed to him to be on the point of becoming a comedy and for that he deemed his beloved much too good and too sacred; for what especially tickled her fancy made him worried, uncertain and embarrassed about her. He also thought that he was insulting and deceiving her by cherishing for so long such a strong passion for her and thinking of her constantly without giving her any inkling of it—this was not proper and he did not like it!

"So it was that one morning, when one could tell from afar that he had something on his mind, he confessed to her his love in a few words, resolved never to repeat his confession again, if she did not also declare her affection for him. For he could not imagine that such a beautiful and well-bred young woman might not tell him the truth at once and immediately give him an irrevocable Yes or No. Since he was just as tenderly disposed as he was violently in love, just as reserved as childlike and just as proud as open and natural, it was with him always a matter of life and death, yes or no, blow on blow.

"At the very moment, however, when the young lady was listening to his declaration of love, which she had so yearned to hear, her old mistrust came over her and she unfortunately recalled that her suitor was a merchant, who after all probably only wanted to get his hands on her money, in order to expand his enterprise. And even if he were a bit in love with her as a person, well, there was no special merit in that, seeing how beautiful she was, and only all the more disgraceful if he thought of her merely as an added attraction to her money. Instead, therefore, of making him welcome and confessing that she loved him in return, as she would have dearly liked to do, she conceived on the spot a new ruse to test his devotion, and assuming an earnest, almost melancholy, expression, she confided to him that she was already engaged to a young man at home whom she loved with all her heart. She had been wanting to tell him about this several times, she said, as he had probably noticed from her behavior, adding that she trusted him like a brother. But the graceless jokes that had become current in the community had made it hard for her to speak to him confidentially; however, now that he had himself surprised her with his forthright, noble heart and revealed his feelings to her, she knew no better way to thank him than to be as open with him as he was with her. She could only belong to the one she had chosen once and for all, she went on, and it would never be possible for her to give her heart to another man—this was written in her soul in golden letters of fire, and the man she loved did not himself know how dear he was to her, as well as he might know her!

"But their fortunes stood under an unlucky star, she said: her fiancé was a merchant, but poor as a churchmouse; for that reason they had decided that he should found a business with her funds; a beginning had already been made and everything was well under way, the wedding soon to be celebrated, when by a stroke of unexpected misfortune her wealth had suddenly been diminished and her right to it disputed—perhaps it was even lost forever. Meanwhile her poor fiancé had to make his first payments in a few days to the Milanese and Venetian merchants: on this depended his whole credit, his prosperity and his honor, not to speak of their happy union! She had journeyed in haste to Milan, she said, where she had well-to-do relations, to try to find financial support and some way out of their distress; but she had come at a bad time; nothing would work out, and meanwhile the day of payment was drawing nearer and nearer, and if she was unable to help her beloved, she would die of grief. For he was the dearest and best man one could imagine and would certainly become a great merchant, if one helped him, and she could conceive of no other happiness on earth than to then be his wife!

"Long before she had finished this tale, the poor, handsome youth had grown pale and was white as a sheet. But he uttered not a word of complaint and said not a thing more about himself and his love, but merely inquired sadly as to the amount of the sum pledged by her unfortunate betrothed. Ten thousand gold gulden! she replied much more sadly still. The unhappy young merchant rose, admonished the young woman to take heart, saying that certainly some way out would be found, and departed without daring to look at her, so taken aback and ashamed did he feel that he had cast his eye on a lady who loved another so passionately and faithfully. For the poor fellow believed every word of her story like the Gospel. Then he at once betook himself to his business friends and persuaded them by pleading and by the forfeiture of a certain sum to let him retract his orders and his purchases, which he was supposed to pay for just at that time with the ten thousand gold gulden on which he was basing his whole career, and before six hours had passed he appeared again before the young woman and begged her for God's sake to accept this aid from him.

"Her eyes gleamed with joyful surprise and her heart thudded like a sledgehammer; she asked him where he had gotten this capital, and he replied that he had borrowed it on his good name and would be able to repay it without inconvenience, since his affairs were taking a prosperous turn. She clearly saw that he was lying and that it was his sole fortune and only hope that he was sacrificing for her happiness, but she pretended to believe him. She gave her joyous feelings free rein, cruelly acting as though they concerned her happiness at now being able to rescue and marry the man she had chosen. She could not find words to express her gratitude.

"But suddenly she bethought herself and declared that she could accept this magnanimous gift only on *one* condition—nothing else could persuade her to do so. When he asked what the condition was, she demanded his sacred promise that on a certain day the young merchant would come to see her, in order to attend her wedding and to become the best friend and patron of her future husband as well as her own dearest friend, protector and advisor. Blushing, he begged to be excused from making this promise, but all the reasons he brought forward could not move her; in vain did she remind him that his affairs would not permit him to return to Switzerland at this time and that he would suffer considerable losses from such an out-of-the-way journey. She stubbornly insisted on her demand and even shoved his money back to him when he would not accede to it. Finally he made the promise; she made him give her his hand and swear to it by his honor and hope of eternal blessedness. She designated the exact day and hour when he was to appear, and to this he also had to swear by his faith as a Christian and his hope of salvation. Only then did she accept his sacrifice and contentedly had it carried to her sleeping quarters, where she herself locked it up in her trunk and stuck the key in her bosom.

"She now broke off her sojourn in Milan and journeyed back over the St. Gotthard, just as happy as she had been sad when she came the other way. On the Devil's Bridge, where she had wanted to cast herself into the abyss, she laughed like a person possessed and giving a ringing halloo with her melodious voice threw the blossoming pomegranate twig she was wearing on her bosom down into the Reuss. In short, her joy was not to be curbed and it was the merriest journey ever made. When she got home, she threw open the house and aired it from top to bottom and adorned it as though she were expecting a prince. At the head of her bed she placed the sack with the ten thousand gold gulden and at night laid her head on this hard lump and slept on it as blissfully as though it had been the softest down pillow. She could hardly await the appointed day, when she was sure he would come, since she knew that he would not break the simplest promise, much less his solemn oath, even if it were a matter of his life. But the day dawned and the beloved did not appear and many days and weeks went by and he sent no word. Then she began to tremble in every limb and grew full of fear and anxiety; she sent letter after letter to Milan, but no one could tell her where he was.

"Finally, however, it was discovered by accident that the young merchant had had a martial dress tailored for himself out of a piece of blood-red silk damask that he had lying in his house from the time he had begun his business and which he had already paid for and had gone to join the Swiss, who were just then fighting in the pay of Francis I of France in the Milanese War. After the Battle of Pavia, in which so many Swiss lost their lives, he was found lying on a heap of slain Spaniards, mortally wounded in many places and his red silk garment slashed from top to bottom. Before he gave up the ghost, he made a man from Seldwyla, who was lying beside him and who was less seriously wounded than he, memorize the following message, begging him to deliver it if he escaped with his life: 'Dearest Lady! Although I swore to you by my honor, my Christian faith and my hope of salvation to attend your wedding, it still has not been possible for me to see you again and to see another share the highest happiness there could ever be for me. I came to realize this only after your departure. I did not know before what a demanding, uncanny thing such a love is as that I bear for you; otherwise, I would no doubt have been more cautious. But since this is the way things are, I preferred to forfeit my worldly honor and my spiritual blessedness and resign myself to eternal damnation as a perjurer rather than appear again before

you with a fire in my heart that is stronger and more unquench-
able than the fires of hell and which will make me almost insensible
to them. Do not bother to pray for me, beauteous lady, for I cannot and shall not ever attain blessedness without you, either in
this world or the next. And so, dear lady, take my greetings and
live happily!' So it was that in this battle, after which King Francis
said: 'All is lost but honor!' the miserable lover lost everything:
hope, honor, life and eternal salvation, but not the love that was
consuming him.

"The man from Seldwyla was lucky enough to escape, and as
soon as he had recovered somewhat and saw himself out of danger, he faithfully wrote down the words of the slain man in his
notebook, in order not to forget them, journeyed home, announced himself to the unfortunate young woman and read out
the message to her as stiffly and as martially as he was in the habit
of doing when he called the roll of his platoon; for he was a second lieutenant. The lady tore her hair, ripped her clothes and began to scream and lament so loudly that one could hear her all up
and down the street and the people came running. Like a crazy
woman, she dragged forth the sack with the ten thousand gulden
and scattered them over the floor, threw herself down on them at
full length and kissed the gleaming gold pieces. Completely out of
her senses, she tried to gather the rolling treasure into a pile and
embrace it, as though her lost lover were present in it. She lay day
and night on the gold, refusing both food and drink, incessantly
caressing and kissing the unfeeling metal, until, in the middle of
one night, she suddenly got up and busily hastening to and fro
carried the treasure out into the garden and threw it, weeping bitterly, into a deep well and pronounced a curse on it, so that it
might never belong to another."

When Mirror had reached this point in his story, Pineis said,
"And is all that beautiful gold still lying in the well?"

"Yes, where else?" answered Mirror. "I'm the only one who
can get it out again and up to now I haven't!"

"Ah-hah, quite right!" said Pineis, "I'd completely forgotten
about that, listening to your story! You spin a good yarn, you
rascal! And I was beginning to fancy the idea of a little woman
who would be as prejudiced in my favor as that. But she'd have
to be very beautiful! Now tell me what the connection is."

"It was many a year," Mirror said, "before the lady recovered sufficiently from her bitter sorrow to be able to begin to become the resigned old spinster she was when I knew her. I can boast that I became her most intimate friend and the sole comfort of her lonely life up to her quiet demise. When she saw her end approaching, she recalled once more the distant days of her youth and beauty and again suffered, though more mildly and with resignation, first the sweet excitement and then the wild pangs of that time and quietly wept for seven days and seven nights over the love the young man had borne her, so that shortly before her death her old eyes grew blind. Then she rued the curse she had pronounced on the treasure, and said to me, giving me the following important commission: 'I've changed my mind, Mirror, and now give you full authority to carry out my decision. Look around until you find a beautiful but indigent woman who has no suitors because she has no means. And if then a sensible, honest and good-looking man should be found, a man with a good income, who wants to marry this virgin solely for her beauty and regardless of her poverty, then let him bind himself by the most solemn oaths to be as true, self-sacrificing and irrevocably devoted to her as my unfortunate lover was to me, and to accede to all her wishes his whole life long. Then give the bride the ten thousand gold gulden as a dowry, so that she can surprise her bridegroom with them on the morning of their wedding!' These were the words of my mistress, may she rest in peace! My untoward fate has prevented me from fulfilling her request and now I'm afraid the poor woman is resting uneasily in her grave, and that can have unpleasant consequences for me!"

Pineis looked at Mirror mistrustfully and said, "Would you be in a position, laddie, to give me proof of this treasure and let me have a glimpse of it?"

"Any time!" replied Mirror, "but you must remember, Mr. City Sorcerer, that you can't just go and fish it out! Your neck would be broken immediately, for the well is haunted; I know that from certain indications I can't specify more exactly."

"Who said anything about fishing it out?" said Pineis rather fearfully. "Just take me there and show me the treasure! Or rather, I'll take *you* there on a good strong cord, so you don't escape!"

"As you like!" said Mirror, "but take along another long cord and a lantern you can let down into the well, because it's very deep and dark!"

Pineis followed his advice and led the tomcat, who was now in a gay mood, to the garden of his deceased mistress. They climbed over the wall together and Mirror showed the sorcerer the way to the old well, which was concealed beneath neglected shrubbery. Pineis then lowered his lantern into the well, following it with greedy gaze and not letting go of Mirror's leash. And, sure enough, he saw the gold gleaming in the depths beneath the greenish water and cried out, "I see it, I see it, it's true! Mirror, you're one in a thousand!" Then he eagerly looked down again and said, "Do you think it's really ten thousand?"

"Well, I can't swear to that," said Mirror, "I haven't been down and counted it. It's possible the lady lost a few pieces when she was carrying it to the well; she was in a very disturbed state."

"Well, suppose it is a dozen or so less," said Mr. Pineis, "that makes no difference!" He seated himself on the coping of the well and Mirror also sat down and licked his paws.

"So that's the treasure," said Pineis, scratching himself behind the ear, "and here's the man for it; all that's lacking is the beauteous lady!"

"How's that?" said Mirror.

"I mean," answered Pineis, "all that's lacking is the woman who is to receive the ten thousand as a dowry, so that she can surprise me with it on our wedding morning, the woman that has all those attractive virtues you were talking about."

"Hm," said Mirror, "the matter's not exactly the way you say. The treasure is there, as you have seen; the beautiful woman I have, to be honest with you, already spied out; but so far as the man goes, who would want to marry her under these difficult circumstances? Aye, there's the rub; for these days beauty has to be gilded like nuts in a Christmas stocking, and the hollower the heads become, the more they strive to fill the empty space with their wives' fortunes, in order to pass the time better. They then examine a horse or buy a piece of velvet with a self-important air, order a good crossbow after much running back and forth, and the gunsmith never leaves their house; then they say: 'I've got to get my grapes harvested, my wine butts cleaned, my trees trimmed and my house roofed; I've got to send my wife to the spa, she's sickly and costing me a lot of money, and I've got to get my wood hauled and collect my debts; I bought a couple of greyhounds and traded in my setters, I acquired a fine extensible oak table and traded in my big walnut chest for it; I cut my bean poles, fired my gardener, sold my hay and sowed my lettuce'—nothing but my, my, my from morning to night. Some even say: 'I have my washing next week, I've got to air my beds, I must hire a maid and get another butcher, because I want to get rid of the old one; I bought myself the neatest little waffle iron, just by chance, and I sold my little silver cinnamon-box, I had no use for it anyway.' All those things are of course a woman's business, and that's the way such a fellow spends his time and wastes God's daylight, enumerating all these deeds and never doing a lick of work. At a pinch, if he has to give his wife some credit, such a fine monsieur may say: 'Our cows and our hogs,' but—"

Pineis gave Mirror's leash a jerk, making him yell "Meow!" and cried, "Enough, you chatterbox! Tell me now at once—where is this woman you know about?" For the recounting of all these splendors and dealings connected with a wife's dowry had only made the mouth of the dried-up wizard water all the more. Mirror asked in astonishment, "Do you really want to undertake this thing, Mr. Pineis?"

"Of course I do! Who else but me? So out with it: Where is the woman in question?"

"You want to go and woo her?"

"No doubt about it!"

"Just remember then that the matter goes only through my hands. You have to talk to me, if you want the money and the woman!" said Mirror coldly and indifferently and vigorously rubbed his paws over his ears, after he had licked them a bit. Pineis took serious thought, groaned a little and said, "I see you want to cancel our contract and save your neck!"

"Would that be so unfair and unnatural?"

"I'll bet you're a liar and a deceiver, you rascal!"

"That's also possible," said Mirror.

"I'll tell you this: don't deceive me!" cried Pineis in an authoritative tone.

"Good, then I won't deceive you," said Mirror.

"But if you do!"

"Then I will."

"Don't torment me, Mirror!" said Pineis, almost in tears, and Mirror replied seriously, "You're a strange man, Mr. Pineis. Here you have me on a leash, pulling on it so hard I can't get my breath. You've been dangling the sword of death over my head for more than two hours; two hours? no, for half a year! and now you say: don't torment me, Mirror! Allow me to tell you briefly: I would dearly love to fulfill my duty toward my dead mistress and find a suitable husband for the woman in question and I must admit you seem to me to fill the bill. Though it may seem so, it's no easy matter to find a good husband for a woman, and I'll say again: I'm glad you're prepared to take on the job! But you don't get something for nothing! Before I say another word or take another step, before I even open my mouth again, I want my freedom restored and my life assured! So take off this leash and lay the contract here on the well, on this stone, or cut off my head, one or the other!"

"Don't be so crazy and conceited, you hothead," said Pineis, "you can't expect me to accept such terms. We have to discuss the matter and in any event close a new contract!" Mirror made no reply, but sat there unmoving, one, two, three minutes. The wizard began to get anxious, he pulled out his wallet, extracted the contract with a sigh, read it through once more and hesitatingly laid it down in front of Mirror. Scarcely had he done so when Mirror snapped it up and swallowed it; and although it made him choke awfully, it still seemed to him the best and most healthful meal he had ever had the pleasure of eating, and he hoped it would agree with him for a long time and make him plump and prosperous. When he had finished this pleasant meal, he courteously took leave of the wizard, saying: "You will certainly hear from me. Mr. Pineis, and you shall have the woman and the money. But be prepared to fall head over heels in love, so that you can swear to and fulfill the conditions of steadfast devotion to the fond caresses of the woman who is already as good as yours! And now, for the time being, thank you for your hospitality and *au revoir!*"

So saying, Mirror went on his way, rejoicing at the stupidity of the sorcerer, who thought he could fool himself and everyone else by marrying the hoped-for bride not unselfishly, out of pure love for her beauty, but with full previous knowledge of the ten thousand gold gulden. Meanwhile, Mirror already had someone in mind whom he thought to palm off on the foolish wizard in return for the latter's broiled fieldfare, mice and sausages.

Opposite the house in which Mr. Pineis lived was another house whose front was neatly whitewashed and whose freshly cleaned windows always glistened brightly. The modest curtains were always white as snow and newly ironed, and just as white was the habit, headdress and kerchief of an old Beguine* who lived in this house, whose nun-like headgear, which covered her bosom, always looked like folded writing paper and made one want to jot something down on it right away, which would certainly have been easy to do on her chest, since it was hard and flat as a board. As sharp as the white corners and edges of her habit were also the long nose and chin of the Beguine, as well as her tongue and the wicked look of her eyes; but with her tongue she spoke but little and looked but little with her eyes, since she did not like extravagance and expended everything cautiously and only at the appropriate moment. She went to church three times a day, and when she crossed the street in her fresh, white, crinkly garments, following her white, pointed nose, the children scattered in fright and even the grown-ups disappeared into their houses, if there was still time. But because of her strict piety and retired way of life she had a great reputation and was especially respected by the clergy, though even they preferred to deal with her in writing, rather than orally, and when she went to confession the priest always shot out of the confessional afterwards dripping with sweat, as though he had just come out of an oven.

Thus the pious Beguine, who would stand for no jokes, lived in perfect peace, untroubled by anyone. She also troubled about no one and left people alone, provided they kept out of her way, except that she seemed to have conceived a special hatred for her neighbor Pineis; for as soon as he showed his face at a window, she gave him a wicked look and immediately closed her white curtains. Pineis feared her like the plague and ventured to make witticisms about her only when he was in the very back of his house and all the doors were locked.

As white and gleaming as the house of the Beguine looked from

* Member of a religious community dating from the thirteenth century, whose lay-women do not take vows, and retain property and independence.

the street side, just as black and dingy, strange and uncanny did it look from the back, where, however, it could only be seen by the birds in the sky and the cats on the rooftops, because it was built into a dark corner formed by high windowless fire walls, where no human face was ever seen. There under the eaves hung old tattered petticoats, baskets and sacks with herbs; on the roof grew regular little yew trees and thorn bushes, while a great sooty chimney rose weirdly into the air. And out of this chimney there not infrequently flew a witch on her broomstick up into the sky, young and beautiful and naked as the day she was born, the way God created woman and the way the Devil likes to see them. When she emerged from the chimney she would sniff about with her fine little nose and smiling cherry lips in the cool night air and then fly away in the white gleam of her body, her raven locks fluttering behind her like a nocturnal banner. In a chink in the chimney there sat an old female owl, and it was to her that Mirror now betook himself, a fat mouse he had caught on the way in his mouth.

"Good evening, dear Mrs. Owl! Busily on guard, are you?" he said, and the owl replied, "Have to be! Good evening to you too, Mr. Mirror! I haven't seen you for a long time."

"There were reasons for that, I'll tell you later. Here, I've brought you a little mouse, plain and simple, according to the season, if you will deign to accept it. Has your mistress ridden away?"

"Not yet, she doesn't intend to go out until towards morning for a little while. Thanks for the plump mouse! Alwas the polite Mr. Mirror! Here's an ordinary sparrow I laid aside—it flew too close to me today. If you like, have a taste! And how have things been with you?"

"Strange enough," answered Mirror, "they were after my neck. Let me tell you about it." And while they contentedly ate their supper, Mirror told the attentive owl everything that had happened to him and how he had freed himself from the hands of Mr. Pineis. "I heartily congratulate you, Mr. Mirror. Now you have it made and can go wherever you like, after all those experiences!"

"I'm not through yet," said Mirror, "the man still has to get his wife and his gold gulden."

"Are you out of your mind? You still want to do the scoundrel who was going to skin you a kindness?"

"Well, he could have skinned me legally and contractually, and since I can pay him back in the same coin, why shouldn't I? Who says I want to do him a kindness? That story I told was a pure fabrication; my dear departed mistress was a simple soul, who was never in love in her life and never surrounded by admirers, and the treasure is illegal property she once inherited and threw into the well, so that it would not bring her misfortune. 'Cursed be he that takes it out and uses it!' she said. That's the way it stands with doing a kindness!"

"That puts everything in a different light! But now where are you going to get a suitable woman?"

"Right here out of this chimney! That's the reason I came to discuss the matter with you. Wouldn't you like to be free again from the bonds of this witch? Think about how we can catch her and marry her to the old villain!"

"Mirror, your very presence is conducive to fertile ideas."

"I knew you were smart! I've done my part, now it's better that you put in your two cents' worth and employ fresh energies, then we're bound to succeed!"

"Since everything fits in so beautifully, I don't need to think long—my plan is already laid."

"How are we going to catch her?"

"With a snipe net made of good strong hempen twine. It has to be woven by a twenty-year-old huntsman's son who has never looked at a woman, and the dews of night must have fallen on it three times without a snipe having been caught in it, and the reason for this must each time have been a good deed. A net like that is strong enough to hold a witch."

"I'll be curious to see where you find such a net," said Mirror, "because I know you're not just talking through your hat!"

"It's already found, as though made for us. In a woods not far from here there lives a twenty-year-old huntsman's son who has never seen a woman because he was born blind. For that reason he can only be employed to weave nets, and a few days ago he just finished a new, very fine snipe snare. But when the old huntsman was about to set it for the first time, a woman came along who tried to tempt him to sin with her; but she was so ugly that he ran away in fright and left the snare lying on the ground. Thus dew fell on it without a snipe being caught, and a good deed was the reason for it. When he went out the next day to spread the net, a rider with a heavy portmanteau behind his saddle chanced along. In the portmanteau was a hole out of which a gold piece dropped from time to time. The huntsman again left his net lying on the ground and ran along behind the horseman collecting the gold pieces in his hat, until the rider saw him, wheeled about and angrily directed his lance at him. The hunter ducked in fright, held out the hat to him and said, 'Allow me, your grace, you have lost a lot of gold, which I have carefully picked up for you!' This was again a good deed, for to return what one has found is one of the hardest and best; but the hunter was so far from his net that he left it lying in the woods for another night and took a shortcut home. On the third day, finally, that is, yesterday, when he was again on the way to his net, he met a pretty female relation, who was in the habit of flattering the old man, who had given her many a nice hare. Talking to her, he completely forgot his snipes and said the next morning, 'I have given the poor snipes their life; one must also be merciful to the birds and beasts!' And because of these three good deeds he found that he was too good for this world and entered a monastery early this morning. So the net is still lying unused in the woods and I only need to fetch it."

"Fetch it at once!" said Mirror, "it will serve our purpose well!"

"I'll fetch it, you just stand guard for me meanwhile here in this chink, and if my mistress should call up through the chimney and ask if the coast is clear, you answer, imitating my voice, 'No, it doesn't stink yet in the fencing school!' " Mirror took up his post in the niche and the owl silently flew away over the town toward the woods. Soon she returned with the snipe net and asked, "Has she already called up the flue?" "Not yet," said Mirror.

They spread the net out across the chimney and sat down beside it quietly and demurely; the air was dark; there was a light morning breeze and a few constellations were twinkling. "You'll see," whispered the owl, "how skillfully she can shoot up through the chimney without getting her shining white shoulders sooty!" "I've never seen her this close," Mirror replied softly, "if only she doesn't get hold of us!"

At this moment the witch called from below, "Is the coast clear?" The owl replied, "All clear! It stinks gloriously in the fencing school!" and immediately the witch came shooting up and was caught in the net, which the cat and the owl swiftly closed and tied together. "Hold fast!" said Mirror and "Tie it well!" said the owl. The witch flopped about in silent rage, like a fish in a net; but it did her no good: the net proved secure. Only the handle of her broom projected out through the meshes. Mirror quietly tried to extract it, but received such a blow on the nose that he almost fainted and realized that one must not come too close to a netted lioness. Finally the witch ceased struggling and said, "What is it you want from me, you strange beasts?"

"You are to release me from your service and restore my freedom!" said the owl.

"So much ado about nothing!" said the witch, "you are free, open up this net!"

"Not yet," said Mirror, still rubbing his nose, "you have to promise to marry the city sorcerer Pineis in the way that I shall explain and never to leave him!"

At this, the witch began to struggle anew and to snort like a horse, and the owl said, "She doesn't like the idea!" But Mirror said, "If you aren't quiet and do what we want, we'll hang you up in this net from the waterspout on the street side of the house, so that people will see you in the morning and know you're a witch. So tell us, would you rather be roasted under the supervision of Mr. Pineis or roast him by marrying him?"

The witch then said with a sigh, "Tell me just what you mean." And Mirror carefully explained what they meant and what she had to do. "I guess I can submit to that, if there's no other way out," she said and swore by the strongest oaths that can bind a witch. Then the animals opened her prison and let her out. She at once mounted her broomstick, the owl perched behind her and Mirror behind the owl, holding fast to the bundle of twigs, and thus they rode to the well, into which the witch descended to bring up the treasure.

In the morning Mirror called on Mr. Pineis and announced to him that he could have a look at the person in question and woo her, but that she had already become so poor that she was sitting under a tree before the city gate, abandoned and outcast and weeping bitterly. Mr. Pineis immediately donned his threadbare yellow doublet, which he wore only on solemn occasions, put on his fur cap, buckled on his sword and took in his hand an old green glove, an empty balsam flask—which however still smelled a bit—and a paper carnation. Thus equipped, he went out with Mirror before the city gate to woo. There he found a woman of greater beauty than any he had ever seen sitting beneath a willow tree and weeping. Her garments were so scant and torn that however modestly she tried to conceal her nakedness, here and there her snowy body kept peeping through. Pineis' eyes almost popped out and he was scarcely able to make his proposal for pure delight. Then the beautiful creature dried her tears, gave him her hand with a sweet smile, thanked him in heavenly bell-like tones for his magnanimity and swore to be eternally faithful to him. At the same moment Pineis was overcome with such jealousy and envious rage in regard to his bride that he determined never to let her be seen by human eyes. He had the marriage ceremony performed by an ancient hermit and celebrated the wedding feast in his own house, with Mirror and the owl as sole guests, Mirror having requested permission to bring the owl along.

The ten thousand gold gulden were standing in a bowl on the table and Pineis put in his hand from time to time and let them run through his fingers; then he would again look at the beautiful bride, who was sitting there in a gown of marine blue velvet, her hair in a golden net wreathed with flowers, her white throat enclosed by a pearl necklace. He constantly wanted to kiss her, but she defended herself with modest shame and a seductive smile, swearing she would not do that in the presence of others and not before nightfall. This only made him all the more fond and blissful, and Mirror seasoned the meal with charming conversation, in which the beautiful lady gracefully joined in the most agreeable, witty and flattering fashion, so that the wizard was beside himself with satisfaction. When it had grown dark, the owl and the cat took their leave and modestly departed; Mr. Pineis showed them to the door with a candle and thanked Mirror again, calling him an excellent, polite gentleman, and when he came back into the room, there sat his neighbor, the old white-clad Beguine, at the table, giving him a wicked look. Horrified, Pineis dropped the candlestick and leaned trembling against the wall. His tongue was hanging out and his face had become as sallow and pointed as that of the Beguine herself. The latter now stood up, came toward him and drove him before her into the bridal chamber, where she tortured him with such infernal arts as no mortal ever experienced. Thus he was now insolubly wedded to the old woman, and when the news got about, people in the town said, "Still waters run deep. Who would have thought that the pious Beguine and the old city sorcerer would ever get married! Well, they're an honorable and respectable couple, even if they're not very amiable!"

From now on, Mr. Pineis led a pitiable life; his spouse at once fathomed all his secrets and ruled him completely. He was not allowed the slightest freedom or relaxation, but had to work at his wizardry from morning to night as hard as he could, and whenever Mirror came by and saw him, he would say in a friendly way, "Always busy, busy, Mr. Pineis?"

Since this time, people in Seldwyla say: He bought the cat's fat! especially when a man gets for his bargain a wicked, repulsive wife.

Translated by Robert M. Browning

Clothes Make the Man

On an unfriendly November day a poor tailor was strolling along the highway to Goldach, a small, wealthy town only a few hours distant from Seldwyla. The tailor carried in his pocket nothing but a thimble, which, for lack of a coin, he kept twirling between his fingers whenever he put his hands into his pockets because of the cold. His fingers were quite sore from this turning and rubbing. The bankruptcy of a master tailor in Seldwyla had compelled him to forfeit his wages and his job and to leave town. He had had nothing for breakfast except a few snowflakes which had flown into his mouth, and he saw even less ahead of him for lunch. Begging was something he found extremely difficult to do; in fact he felt it to be utterly impossible, because over his black Sunday suit, which was the only suit he had, he wore a full, dark-gray cape, faced with black velvet; and this gave him an aristocratic and romantic appearance, especially since his long black hair and small mustache were carefully groomed and he possessed pale but regular features.

This type of dress had become a necessity for him, without his intending anything evil or deceptive by it; on the contrary, he was satisfied to be left alone to do his job quietly. But he would sooner have starved than be parted from his cape and Polish fur cap, which he also wore with style.

He could therefore work only in larger towns, where such things did not attract too much attention; when he was on the road and carried no savings with him, he fell into the direst need. When he

152

approached a house, people looked at him in astonishment and curiosity and expected anything but that he would beg. And so, since he was not a glib talker either, the words died on his lips; so that he was the martyr of his cloak and suffered hunger as dark as its velvet facing.

As he was climbing a hill, worried and weakened, he came up beside a new and comfortable coach, which the coachman of a nobleman had fetched in Basel and was delivering to his master, a foreign count living somewhere in eastern Switzerland in an old manor house that he had rented or bought. The carriage was fitted with all sorts of devices for holding baggage and therefore seemed to be heavily packed, although it was completely empty. Because of the steep road, the coachman walked beside the horses; when he got to the top of the hill he mounted his box again and asked the tailor whether he did not want to get into the empty carriage. For it was just beginning to rain and he had seen with one glance that the pedestrian was making his weary and wretched way through the world.

The tailor gratefully and modestly accepted the offer, whereupon the carriage swiftly rolled away with him and, in little under an hour, rode stately and rumbling through the gateway of Goldach. The elegant vehicle pulled up suddenly in front of the first hotel, called the Scale, and at once the bellboy gave such a violent tug at the bell that the wire almost snapped in two. Thereupon the landlord and his help rushed out and pulled the carriage door open; children and neighbors were already surrounding the splendid vehicle, curious to see what sort of kernel would emerge from such an unheard-of shell. And when the astonished tailor finally came out, pale and handsome in his cloak, and looking mournfully at the ground, he seemed to them to be at least a mysterious prince or young count. The space between the carriage and the door of the hotel was narrow, and moreover, the way was virtually blocked by the spectators. Whether it was because he lacked presence of mind or courage to break through the crowd and simply go on his way, at any rate he did not do so, but passively allowed himself to be led into the house and up the stairs; and he did not really grasp his new, strange situation until he saw himself transplanted into a comfortable dining room and solicitously helped out of his dignified cloak.

"You wish to dine, sir?" he was asked. "Dinner will be served at once, we've just finished the cooking."

Without waiting for an answer, the landlord of the Scale rushed to the kitchen and cried: "The devil take it! Now we have nothing to serve except beef and leg of lamb. I daren't cut into the partridge pie, because it's reserved and promised to the gentlemen who are coming this evening. That's the way it goes. The only day we don't expect a guest and have nothing on hand, a gentleman like this one has to appear! And the coachman has a coat of arms on his buttons, and the carriage is like a duke's. And the young man can scarcely open his mouth from sheer nobility!"

But the calm cook said: "Well, sir, what is there to lament about? You can safely serve him the meat pie; he isn't going to eat it all! The gentlemen coming this evening will then get it in individual portions; we can certainly get six portions out of what's left."

"Six portions? You forget that the gentlemen are in the habit of eating till they're full," said the landlord. But the cook continued imperturbably: "And so they shall, too. We can send out quickly for half a dozen cutlets. We need these for the stranger anyhow, and what's left I'll cut into little pieces and mix with the meat pie. You just let me attend to it."

But the good landlord said earnestly: "Cook, I've already told you before this that we don't do such things in this town or in this house. We live solidly here and honorably, and we can afford to do so!"

"For Heaven's sake, yes, yes!" cried the cook in some excitement. "If we can't handle such a situation, we may as well give up. Here are two snipe which I just bought from the hunter; perhaps we can add these to the meat pie. The gourmets won't object to a partridge pie adulterated with snipe. Then there's the trout too. I threw the largest one into the boiling water when that remarkable carriage arrived, and the broth is already boiling in the pan; so we have a fish, the beef, the vegetables with the cutlets, the leg of lamb and the meat pie. Just give me the key so that we can get the preserves and dessert out. And, sir, you might with all honor and confidence let me have the key for good, so that I don't have to run after you everywhere and suffer the greatest embarrassment."

"Dear cook, don't be annoyed; I had to promise my late wife

on her deathbed that I would always keep the keys in my hands; so it's a matter of principle, not of mistrust. Here are the pickles and cherries, here, the pears and apricots; but the old pastry must not be served again. Let Lizzie run out quickly to the confectioner's and get some fresh pastry, three plates of it, and if he has a large cake he can send it along too."

"But, sir, you can't charge all that up to the one guest; you can't make money that way, not with the best will."

"No matter, it's for the honor of the thing! It won't ruin me; on the other hand, such a grand gentleman shall be able to say he nd a decent meal when he passed through ourcity, although he came quite unexpectedly, and in winter too. I don't want it to be said, as they say about the innkeepers of Seldwyla, that we gobble up all the good things ourselves and serve the bones to strangers. So step on it, get going, hurry up, everybody!"

During these elaborate preparations, while the table was being set with glistening silver, the tailor found himself in the most painful anxiety. And, however passionately the starving man had yearned a short while before for some nourishment, all he wanted now was to escape from the threatening meal. Finally he gathered courage, put his cloak about his shoulders and his cap on his head, and walked out of the dining room looking for an exit. But as, in his confusion, he did not find the stairway in the spacious house at once, the waiter, who was constantly driven by the devil, thought he was looking for a certain convenience and cried, "Your most gracious permission, sir, I'll show you the way!" and led him through a long passage, which ended nowhere else than before a beautifully lacquered door on which an artistic inscription was affixed.

So the owner of the coat went in without objecting, meek as a lamb, and modestly locked the door behind him. Inside he leaned against the wall, sighing bitterly, and wished once more to share in the golden freedom of the highway, which now appeared to him as the highest good fortune, bad though the weather was.

But instead, he now involved himself in his first deliberate lie, because he waited a while in the locked room and thereby set out on the precipitous road of evil.

Meanwhile the landlord, who had seen him walking around in his cloak, cried, "The gentleman is freezing! Put on a bigger fire in the room! Where's Lizzie, where's Annie? Quick, throw a basketful of wood into the stove and a few handfuls of chips, so that it'll burn properly! The devil! Are people in the Scale to sit at dinner in their overcoats?"

And when the tailor emerged again from the long passage, as melancholy as the ancestral ghost of a family castle, the landlord accompanied him into the cursed dining room, rubbing his hands and paying him a hundred compliments. He was invited to the table without further delay, his chair was moved into place behind him; and as the fragrance of the nourishing soup, the like of which he had not smelled for a long time, completely robbed him of his will power, he sat down resignedly and at once dipped the heavy spoon into the golden brown broth. In profound silence he refreshed his faint spirits and was served in respectful calm and quiet.

When he had emptied his plate and the landlord saw how much he had enjoyed the soup, he courteously encouraged him to take another spoonful, saying it was good in this raw weather. Then the trout was served, garnished with greens, and the landlord helped him to a handsome portion. The tailor, tormented by anxiety, did not dare, in his timidity, to use the gleaming knife but toyed shyly and fastidiously with the silver fork. The cook, who was peeping through the door to observe the grand gentleman, noticed this and said to those who stood about her, "Heaven be praised! he knows how to eat a delicate fish properly; he doesn't saw about in the tender creature with his knife as if he wished to slaughter a calf. This is a gentleman from a great family; I'd be willing to swear to it if it weren't a sin to swear. And how handsome and sad he is! I'm sure he's in love with a poor girl whom they won't let him marry. Yes, yes, the great have their sorrows too!"

Meanwhile the landlord saw that his guest was not drinking and said respectfully, "You don't like the table wine, sir? Would you like to order a glass of good Bordeaux, which I can recommend most highly?"

Thereupon the tailor committed his second deliberate sin, by obediently saying yes instead of no. At once the landlord of the Scale went down to the cellar personally to fetch a choice bottle; for it meant everything to him that people should be able to say there was something really good to be had in the place. When the guest, out of a bad conscience, again took very small sips from the wine that was poured out for him, the landlord joyfully ran into the kitchen, clicked his tongue and cried, "The devil take me, that man is a connoisseur! He sips my good wine on his tongue the way you put a ducat on the gold scale!"

"Heaven be thanked!" said the cook. "I told you: he knows."

So the meal took its course, but very slowly, because the poor tailor kept eating and drinking daintily and undecidedly; and the landlord let the dishes stand long enough to give him time. However, what the guest had consumed so far was not worth mentioning; only now did his hunger, which was being steadily and dangerously stirred, begin to overcome his terror. When the partridge pie appeared, the tailor's mood took a sudden turn and a firm resolve began to take shape in his mind. "Things are now as they are," he said to himself, warmed and stimulated by a new drop of wine. "I would be a fool if I were willing to bear the coming disgrace and persecution without having had a good meal for it. So make hay while the sun shines. That little tower they've set up before me may easily be the last food they'll serve me; I'll make the most of it, come what may. What I once have inside of me, not even a king can take from me."

No sooner said than done. With the courage of despair he plunged into the dainty meat pie without a thought of stopping, so that in less than five minutes it had half disappeared and things began to look very dubious for the evening guests. Meat, truffles, dumplings, bottom, crust, he swallowed everything indiscriminately, concerned solely with filling his belly before fate overtook him. He drank the wine, moreover, in vigorous draughts, and crammed large bits of bread into his mouth. In short, it was as hasty and lively a hauling-in as when, in a rising storm, the hay is rescued by being pitched on the fork from the meadow into the barn. Once more the landlord ran into the kitchen and cried: "Cook! He's eating up the meat pie, while he's scarcely touched the roast beef. And he's drinking the Bordeaux by the half-tumblerful!"

"May it agree with him," said the cook. "You just leave him alone; he knows what partridge is. If he were a common fellow, he would have kept to the roast."

"I think so too," said the landlord. "Of course, it doesn't look very elegant; but when I was traveling during my apprenticeship I saw only generals and canons eat like that."

Meanwhile the coachman had had the horses fed and had eaten a solid meal in the dining room reserved for common people; being in a hurry, he soon had the horses hitched up again. The staff of the Scale could no longer contain themselves and asked the nobleman's coachman straight out, before it was too late, who his master up there was and what his name was. The coachman, a sly, jocular fellow, replied, "Hasn't he told you himself?"

"No," they said, and he replied, "I can well believe it; that man doesn't say much in one day; well, he's Count Strapinski. But he's going to stay here today and perhaps a few more days; for he ordered me to ride ahead with the carriage."

He made this bad joke to get revenge on the tailor, who, as he thought, instead of repaying his favor with a word of thanks and a good-bye, had gone off into the house without turning around and was playing the lord. Carrying his prank to an extreme, he climbed up on his carriage without requesting the bill for himself or his horses, cracked his whip and drove out of the city, and everything was found to be in order and added to the tailor's account.

Now, it just so happened that the tailor, who was a native of Silesia, was really called Strapinski, Wenzel Strapinski. This may have been a coincidence; or perhaps the tailor had taken his guild book out in the carriage, forgotten it there, and the coachman had taken possession of it. In any case, when the landlord, beaming with joy and rubbing his hands, stepped up to the tailor and asked whether Count Strapinski would take champagne or a glass of seasoned Tokay with his dessert, and announced that his rooms were just being prepared for him, poor Strapinski turned pale, became confused again and made no reply.

"Most interesting!" the landlord grumbled to himself, hurrying to the cellar once more and taking, from a special locker, not only a small bottle of Tokay but also a little jug of Bocksbeutel and a bottle of champagne, which he put under his arm. Soon Strapinski saw a young forest of glasses before him, the champagne glass standing out like a poplar tree. These glasses glittered, rang and gave out a strange fragrance, and what was stranger still, the poor but elegant man reached into the little forest not unskillfully, and when he saw the landlord put a little red wine into his champagne, he put a few drops of Tokay into his. Meanwhile the town clerk and the notary had come to drink their coffee and play their daily game for it. Soon the older son of the House of Häberlin and Company, the younger son of the House of Pütschli-Nievergelt and the bookkeeper of a large spinnery, Herr Melcher Böhni also arrived. But instead of playing their usual game, all these gentlemen, their hands in their back coat pockets, walked around behind the Polish count in a wide arc, winking to each other and laughing up their sleeves. For although these members of prominent families stayed home all their lives, they had relatives and associates scattered all over the earth, and therefore believed they had adequate knowledge of the world.

So this was supposed to be a Polish count? Of course they had seen the carriage from their office chairs; besides, they didn't know whether the landlord was entertaining the count or the count the landlord; however, the landlord had done nothing stupid till now; on the contrary, he was well known as a fairly sharp fellow; and so the circles which the curious gentlemen drew about the stranger became smaller and smaller, until they finally sat down familiarly at his table and skillfully, but in an off-hand manner, invited themselves to the banquet simply by beginning to throw dice for a bottle.

However, they did not drink too much, as it was still early; the idea was to take a sip of excellent coffee and to wait on the "Polack," as they were already secretly calling the tailor, with good cigars, so that he might smell more and more where he really was.

"May I offer you a decent cigar, Count? I got it direct from my brother in Cuba," said one.

"You Polish gentlemen also like a good cigarette; here is some genuine tobacco from Smyrna, my business partner sent it to me," cried another, thrusting a little red silken pouch at him.

"This one from Damascus is finer, Count," said the third, "our agent there got it for me himself."

The fourth stretched out a big ungainly cigar, crying; "If you want something quite excellent, try this planter's cigar from Virginia, home-grown, homemade and absolutely not to be had for money."

Strapinski smiled a sickly smile, said nothing and was soon enveloped in fine fragrant clouds, which turned beautifully silver as the sun broke through them. In less than a quarter of an hour the sky cleared and the most beautiful autumn afternoon set in. The general opinion was that they should make the most of the favorable hour, as the year might perhaps not bring many more such days; so it was decided that they should drive out to visit the jovial district councillor on his estate and taste his new wine, the red must; for he had pressed grapes only a few days before. Pütschli-Nievergelt, Junior, sent for his dogcart and soon his young iron-gray horses were pounding the pavement in front of the Scale. The landlord himself also got a carriage ready, and they courteously invited the count to join them and get to know the region.

The wine had warmed his wits; he made a rapid calculation that this would give him the best opportunity for disappearing unnoticed and continuing his journey on foot; the expense would be borne by these foolish and insistent gentlemen. He therefore accepted the invitation with a few polite words and got into the dogcart with young Pütschli.

Now, it also happened that the tailor had occasionally worked for the lord of the manor in his native village as a young boy, had done his military service with the hussars, and therefore possessed an adequate knowledge of horsemanship. When, therefore, his companion asked him politely whether he would like to drive, he at once took hold of the whip and reins and drove through the gate and along the country road at a swift trot in a professional manner, so that the gentlemen looked at each other and whispered, "It is true, he certainly is a gentleman."

In half an hour they reached the councillor's estate; Strapinski drove up in a magnificent half-arc and let the fiery horses pull up short in the best style. The guests jumped from the carriages, the councillor came out and led the company into the house, and soon the table was loaded with half a dozen carafes full of carnelian-colored wine. The fiery, fermenting beverage was first tested, praised and then cheerfully attacked, while the master of the house spread the news that a distinguished count had come, a "Polack," and gave orders for a more elegant reception.

Meanwhile, to make up for the card game they had missed, the company divided into two parties. In this country men simply could not come together without gambling, probably from an innate urge for activity. Strapinski, who for various reasons had to decline to participate, was invited to look on; for even this seemed to them worthwhile, because they were accustomed to display much cleverness and presence of mind at cards. He had to sit down between the two games, and the participants now took pains to play cleverly and skillfully and to entertain the guest at the same time. And so he sat there like an ailing prince being entertained by his courtiers with a diverting spectacle depicting the course of the world. They explained to him the most significant changes, tricks and events, and when the one party had to turn its attention for a moment exclusively to the game, the other carried on a conversation with the tailor all the more solicitously. The best topic for this seemed to them to be horses, hunting and the like. Strapinski was perfectly at home in this area too; for he merely had to dig out the phrases he had once heard around officers and the landed gentry, and which had pleased him uncommonly even then. He produced these phrases only sparingly, with a certain modesty and always with a melancholy smile, and thereby achieved an effect that was only the greater. Whenever two or three of the gentlemen got up and stepped aside, they said; "He's a perfect squire!"

Only Melcher Böhni, the bookkeeper, the born doubter, rubbed his hands in glee and said to himself; "I see it coming, there will be another Goldach putsch; in fact, in a way it's here already. But it's time for one too; it's two years since the last one. That man has strangely pierced fingers; perhaps he's from Praga or Ostroleka. Well, I'll take good care not to disturb the course of events."

The two card parties had now come to an end, and the gentlemen's thirst for must had been satisfied. They preferred to cool off a little on the councillor's old wines, which were now served; but the cooling off was of a rather passionate nature, for, in order not to fall into base idleness, the guests proposed a general game of chance. The cards were dealt, everyone threw in a Brabantine taler, and when Strapinski's turn came, he could not very well put his thimble on the table. "I don't have such a coin," he said, turning red. But Melcher Böhni, who had been watching him, had already put in a stake for him without anyone's noticing; for they were all far too comfortably fixed to entertain the suspicion that anyone in the world could be without money. The next moment the whole pot was moved toward the tailor, who had won; in confusion he let the money lie and Böhni managed the second round for him, which another man won, as well as the third. But the fourth and the fifth were again won by the Polack, who gradually woke up and got into the spirit of the thing. By keeping quiet and calm, he played with changing fortune; once he came down to one taler, which he had to risk, won again, and finally, when they got tired of the game, he had a few louis d'or, more than he had ever owned in his whole life. When he saw that they were all pocketing their gains he took these, not without dreading that it was all a dream. Böhni, who was watching him carefully all the time, was now clear in his mind concerning him and thought: "The devil he rides in a coach-and-four!"

But because he observed, too, that the enigmatic stranger had shown no greed for the money and had in general conducted himself with modesty and sobriety, he was not ill-disposed toward him, and decided to let the matter take its own course.

But while they were taking a walk in the open air before dinner, Count Strapinski collected his thoughts and considered that the right moment had come to take a noiseless departure. He now had a tidy sum of money for traveling and planned to pay the landlord of the Scale from the nearest town for the dinner that had been forced on him. So he put on his cape, pressed the fur cap further down over his eyes and strode slowly up and down in the evening sun under a row of tall locust trees, contemplating the beautiful landscape, or rather, spying out which road he should take. He looked superb with his troubled brow, his attractive but melancholy moustache, his glistening black curls, his dark eyes and his pleated coat blowing in the wind. The evening light and the rustling of the trees above him heightened the impression, so that the company studied him from afar with attention and benevolence. Gradually he got farther and farther away from the house, and strode through a clump of bushes behind which a field path ran. When he saw that he was protected from the eyes of the company, he was on the point of moving into the field with firm step, when suddenly the councillor and his daughter Nettie came toward him from around a corner. Nettie was a pretty young lady, dressed most splendidly, perhaps overdressed, and decorated with much jewelry.

"We've been looking for you, Count," cried the councillor, "first of all, because I want to introduce you to my child here, and secondly to ask you if you'll do us the honor of taking a bite of supper with us. The other gentlemen are already in the house."

The wanderer quickly took his cap from his head and made reverent, indeed timid, bows, blushing deeply. For matters had taken a new turn; a young lady now occupied the theater of events. But his shyness and excessive reverence did not hurt him with the lady; on the contrary, the shyness, humility and reverence of such a distinguished and interesting young nobleman appeared to her to be truly touching, indeed enchanting. You see, the thought went through her mind, the more aristocratic they are, the more modest and unspoiled; mark this, you rude gentlemen of Goldach, who scarcely tip your hats to a young girl any more!

She therefore greeted the knight most graciously, blushing adorably too, and at once said many things to him hastily and rapidly, in the manner of smug, small-town women who want to show off to strangers. Strapinski, on the other hand, became transformed in a short time; while so far he had done nothing to enter into the role that was being thrust on him, he now involuntarily began to speak a little more affectedly and mixed all sorts of Polish scraps into his talk; in short, the tailor blood in him began to cut capers in the presence of the woman and to carry off its rider.

At dinner he received the place of honor near the daughter of the house; for her mother was dead. But he soon became melancholy again when he reflected that he would now have to return to town with the others or force himself to escape into the night, and when he further considered how transitory was the fortune that he now enjoyed. But he felt this fortune nevertheless, and told himself in advance, "Ah, once in your life, at least, you will have been somebody and sat beside such a higher being."

It was indeed no trifling matter to see a hand gleaming beside him on which three or four bracelets tinkled, and to perceive, at every fleeting side-glance that he took, a daring, charming coiffure, a lovely blush, a full glance. For no matter what he did or did not do, everything was interpreted by this young lady as unusual and aristocratic, and his very awkwardness was charmingly interpreted as remarkable ingenuousness—though usually she could chat for hours about social faux pas. As they were in good spirits, a few guests sang songs that were in fashion in the thirties. The count was asked to sing a Polish song. The wine finally overcame his shyness, although not his anxiety; he had once worked on Polish territory for a few weeks and knew a few Polish words; he even knew a Polish folk song by heart, without being aware of its meaning, like a parrot. So he sang in Polish with an elegant air, timidly rather than loudly, in a voice which quavered gently as though with a secret sorrow:

> "A hundred thousand pigs are quartered
> From the Desna to the Vistula,
> And Katinka, that filthy wench
> Walks in dirt up to her ankles.
>
> A hundred thousand oxen roar
> On Volynia's green pastures
> And Katinka, yes Katinka
> Thinks I am in love with her."

"Bravo! Bravo!" all the gentlemen cried, clapping their hands, and Nettie said with emotion, "Ah, national songs are always so beautiful!" Fortunately no one asked for the translation.

After this high point in the entertainment, the company broke up; the tailor was packed into the carriage again and carefully brought back to Goldach; but first he had to promise not to go away without taking leave. At the Scale they had another glass of punch; but Strapinski was exhausted and wanted to go to bed. The landlord himself took him to his rooms, whose splendor he scarcely noticed, although he was accustomed to sleep only in poor hostel rooms. He was standing, bereft of all personal belongings, in the middle of a beautiful carpet, when the landlord suddenly noticed the absence of all baggage and clapped his palm to his forehead. Then he ran out quickly, rang the bell, summoned waiters and bellboys, exchanged words with them, came back and said, "It's true, Count, they forgot to unload your luggage. Even the most essential things are lacking."

"Even the little package that was lying in the carriage?" asked Strapinski anxiously, because he was thinking of a little bundle the size of his hand, which he had left lying on the seat and which

contained a handkerchief, a hairbrush, a comb, a little box of po-
made, and a stick of wax for his mustache.

"That's missing too; there isn't a thing here," said the good
landlord in fright, because he suspected it was something very important. "We must send a special messenger after the coachman
at once," he cried eagerly. "I'll attend to it."

But the count grasped his arm in equal fright and said with
emotion, "Don't! You mustn't! All trace of me must be lost for
some time," he added, startled by this invention.

The astonished landlord went to the punch-drinking gentlemen
and told them about the incident and concluded with the assertion
that the count must undoubtedly be a victim of political or family
persecution; for just about that time many Poles and other refu-
gees had been expelled from their country for acts of violence;
others were watched and ensnared by foreign agents.

But Strapinski enjoyed a good sleep, and when he awoke late,
the first thing he saw was the landlord's splendid Sunday dressing
gown hanging over a chair, and farther on, a small table covered
with every imaginable toilet article. Then he saw a number of servants waiting to deliver, on behalf of his friends of yesterday, baskets and chests filled with fine linen, clothes, cigars, books, boots,
shoes, spurs, riding whips, furs, caps, hats, socks, stockings, pipes
and flutes and fiddles, and to make the solicitous request that he
be gracious enough to use these conveniences for the present. Since
his benefactors invariably spent their mornings at their places of
business, they announced their visits for the period after lunch.

These people were anything but ridiculous or simpleminded; they
were prudent businessmen, smart rather than dense. But since their
prosperous town was small and they sometimes felt bored in it,
they were always eager for a change, an event, a happening, which
they could embrace without restraint. The coach-and-four, the
alighting of the stranger, his luncheon, the statements of the
coachman were such simple and natural things that the people of
Goldach, who were not in the habit of harboring idle suspicions,
built an event on them as on a rock.

When Strapinski saw the assortment of merchandise spread out
before him, his first impulse was to put his hand in his pocket to
find out whether all this was a dream. If his thimble still dwelt
there in solitude, he was dreaming. But no, the thimble sat there

cozily among the coins he had won at gambling and was rubbing sociably against the talers; so its master bowed to circumstance once again and descended from his rooms to the street to inspect the town in which things were going so well for him. Behind the kitchen door stood the cook, who made a deep curtsy to him and looked at him with new pleasure; in the hall and at the front door stood other domestics, all with their caps in their hands, and Strapinski strode out with dignity and yet modesty, gathering his cloak chastely about him. Destiny was making him greater with every moment.

He studied the town with an entirely different mien than if he had gone out to look for work in it. It consisted mostly of fine, solidly built houses, all adorned with stone or painted symbols and supplied with names. In these names the customs of the centuries could be clearly discerned. The Middle Ages were mirrored in the oldest houses or in the new buildings that had taken their place but had retained the old names from the age of the warlike mayors and fairy tales. On them one could read: the Sword, the Iron Helmet, the Armor, the Crossbow, the Blue Shield, the Swiss Sword, the Knight, the Flint, the Turk, the Sea Monster, the Golden Dragon, the Linden Tree, the Pilgrim's Staff, the Nymph, the Bird of Paradise, the Pomegranate, the Camel, the Unicorn and so on. The Age of Enlightenment and Philanthropy was clearly to be read in the moral precepts which shone over the front doors in beautiful golden letters, such as: Harmony, Uprightness, Old Independence, New Independence, Civic Virtue A, Civic Virtue B, Trust, Love, Hope, Au Revoir 1 and 2, Joy, Inner Righteousness, Outer Righteousness, National Prosperity (a neat little house in which, behind a canary cage covered entirely with cress, a friendly old woman with a peaked bonnet sat spinning yarn), the Constitution (below lived a cooper who zealously and noisily bound little pails and kegs with hoops, hammering incessantly). One house bore the gruesome name Death; a faded skeleton stretched from bottom to top between the windows. Here lived the justice of the peace. In the house of Patience lived the clerk of debts, a starved picture of misery, since in this town no one owed anyone anything.

Finally, the newest houses announced the poetry of the industrialists, bankers and forwarding agents and their imitators in the euphonious names: Rosedale, Morningdale, Sunny Mount, Violet

Castle, etc. The valleys and castles attached to ladies' names always indicated to the initiated a handsome dowry.

At every street corner there stood an old tower with an elaborate clock, a colorful roof and a prettily gilded weather vane. These towers were carefully preserved, for the people of Goldach rejoiced in their past and in the present and were justified in doing so. All this splendor was encompassed by the old circular wall, which, although it no longer served any purpose, was nevertheless retained as decoration; it was completely overgrown with thick old ivy and surrounded the little town with a wreath of evergreen.

All this made a wonderful impression on Strapinski; he thought he was in another world. For when he read the inscriptions on the houses, the like of which he had never seen before, he assumed that they referred to the special secrets and habits of life in each house, and that behind every front door things really were what the sign indicated, and that he had fallen into a sort of moral utopia. Thus he was inclined to believe that the remarkable reception he had been given was related to this correspondence—for example, the symbol of the scale under which he lived meant that here uneven destiny was weighed and balanced and that occasionally a traveling tailor was transformed into a count.

On his stroll he came to the city gate, and as he looked over the open field, his conscience prompted him for the last time to continue on his way at once. The sun was shining, the highway looked fine and firm, not too dry and not too wet either, as if made for walking. He now had traveling money too, so that he could stop and get comfortable lodgings anywhere he wished to and no obstacle was discernible.

There he stood like the youth at the crossroads, and on a real crossroads; hospitable columns of smoke rose above the linden grove which surrounded the town; the golden knobs of the towers sparkled enticingly through the treetops; happiness, pleasure and guilt, a mysterious destiny beckoned from there. But from the direction of the fields there gleamed open space; work, deprivation, poverty, obscurity awaited him there, but also a good conscience and a serene way of life. Feeling this, he firmly resolved to turn into the field. But at the same moment a swift vehicle rolled by; it was the young lady of yesterday, who sat all alone in a trim light carriage; she was wearing a fluttering blue veil and driving a handsome horse toward the town. Strapinski immediately reached for his cap in surprise, and humbly held it before his chest; the girl bowed to him in an altogether friendly manner, her face reddened quickly, and she drove away in great emotion, whipping her horse to a gallop.

Strapinski, however, involuntarily made a complete turn and confidently went back to the city. On that very day he was galloping on the best horse in town, at the head of a large equestrian company, through an avenue that led around the green circular wall, and the falling leaves of the linden trees danced like golden rain about his transfigured head.

Now the devil took hold of him. With every day he became transformed, like a rainbow which becomes distinctly more colorful in the triumphant sun. He learned in hours, in moments, what others did not learn in years, since it had been latent in him, like the spectrum in the raindrop. He studied the manners of his hosts thoroughly and shaped them into something new and foreign, even as he studied them. He was especially anxious to learn what they really thought of him and what sort of image they had formed of him. This image he developed further to his own taste, to the contented entertainment of some, who wanted to see something new, and to the admiration of others, especially the ladies, who thirsted for edifying stimulation. So he swiftly became the hero of a pretty romance, at which he devotedly worked together with the town, but whose main ingredient was still mystery.

With all this, Strapinski spent one sleepless night after another, something he had never known previously in his obscurity, and it must be emphasized as a point of censure that what robbed him of his sleep was not merely his conscience, but his fear of being shamefully exposed as a poor tailor. His innate need to represent something elegant and extraordinary, if only in the choice of his clothes, had led him into this conflict and now produced that anxiety; and his conscience had only enough power over him to make him harbor the unwavering intention of finding some reason for leaving the place when a good opportunity arose. Then he planned to regain, through lotteries and the like, the means for repaying to the hospitable folk of Goldach, from a mysterious distance, the money he had cheated them of. In fact, he was already sending for tickets, at more or less modest stakes, from all the cities where there were lotteries or agents for them, and in the correspondence which ensued, the receiving of letters was again noted as a sign of important connections and relationships.

He had already won a few gulden several times and had promptly used these to purchase new tickets, when he received one day a substantial sum from a foreign lottery agent who called himself a banker; the sum was enough to permit him to carry out the plan of saving himself. He was no longer astonished at his luck, which seemed to be a matter of course; nevertheless he did feel relieved, and especially at ease concerning the good landlord of the Scale, whom he liked very much because of his good meals. But instead of putting a quick end to the matter, paying his debts outright and departing, he thought of using the pretext of a short business trip, and then announcing from some large city that inexorable fate forbade him ever to return again. At the same time he would meet his obligations, leave a good memory behind him and devote himself once more, and with more prudence and luck, to his trade as a tailor, or hunt out some other respectable vocation. Of course he would have liked best of all to remain in Goldach as a master tailor and would now have had the means for establishing a modest livelihood for himself there; but it was clear that he could live here only as a count.

Because the beautiful Nettie treated him on every occasion with obvious preference and pleasure, many comments were already circulating, and he had even noticed that the young lady was now and then called the countess. How could he now prepare such a sequence of events for this creature? How could he so criminally give the lie to the destiny which had forcibly elevated him to such heights, and disgrace himself into the bargain?

From the lottery man, called banker, he had received a draft which he cashed at a Goldach bank; this transaction strengthened even more the favorable impressions about his person and his affairs, since the solid businessmen did not have the slightest suspicion that it might be a lottery matter. On the same day Strapinski went to a grand ball to which he had been invited. Dressed in deep, simple black he appeared and promptly announced to those who welcomed him that he was obliged to take a trip.

In ten minutes the news was known to the whole assembly and

Nettie, whose eye Strapinski was seeking, seemed stunned and avoided his glance, turning first red, then pale. She danced several times in succession with young gentlemen, then sat down absently and breathed rapidly. When he finally did come up to her, she rejected the Pole's invitation with an abrupt bow, without looking at him.

He went away strangely worried and excited, draped himself in his famous cloak and walked up and down a garden path, his locks flowing in the wind. It now became clear to him that he had really stayed here so long only on account of this creature, that the vague hope of seeing her once more inspired him unconsciously, but that the whole affair was simply an impossibility of the most desperate kind.

As he was striding along he heard swift steps behind him, light but disturbedly agitated. Nettie went past him and, to judge by some words she called out, seemed to be seeking her carriage, although it was standing on the other side of the house, while here only heads of winter cabbage and wrapped-up rosebushes were dreaming away the sleep of the just. Then she came back again, and since he now blocked her way with pounding heart and imploringly stretched out his hands toward her, she threw her arms about his neck without further ceremony and began to weep pitifully. He covered her flushed cheeks with his delicately fragrant dark locks and his cloak encircled the slender, proud, snow-white figure of the girl as though with black eagles' pinions; it was a truly beautiful picture, which seemed to carry its justification wholly in itself.

But in this adventure Strapinski lost his reason and won fortune, which quite often smiles on the simpleminded. That very night on their way home Nettie revealed to her father that she would have no other man but the count; the latter appeared early next morning looking charmingly shy and melancholy as usual, to ask for her hand. The father made the following speech:

"And so destiny and the will of this foolish girl have been fulfilled. Even when she was a schoolgirl she constantly asserted that she would marry only an Italian or a Pole, a great pianist or a robber chieftain with beautiful locks; and now we're in for it. She has refused all serious local offers; only recently I had to send home that excellent Melcher Böhni, who will be a big businessman someday, and she even made terrible fun of him because he has reddish whiskers and takes snuff from a silver box. Well, Heaven be thanked, here is a Polish count from far away. Take the goose, Count, and send her back to me if she feels cold in your Polackland and if she ever becomes unhappy and howls. Ah, how happy her late mother would be if she had lived to see her spoiled child become a countess!"

Now there was great commotion; the engagement was to be celebrated in but a few days; for the councillor asserted that his future son-in-law must not allow himself to be held back in his business and planned journeys by matrimonial affairs, but must expedite the latter by advancing the former.

Strapinski brought to the engagement bridal gifts which cost him half his earthly wealth; the other half he spent on a banquet he wished to give for his fiancée. It was just carnival time and the late winter weather was wonderful beneath a bright sky. The country roads offered the most splendid sledding, the kind that occurs but rarely and never for any length of time; and so Herr von Strapinski arranged for a sleighing party and a ball in the stately hotel that was popular for such festivities; it was about two hours distant, situated exactly halfway between Goldach and Seldwyla on a high plateau that afforded the most beautiful view.

It so happened that about this time Herr Melcher Böhni had business to attend to in Seldwyla and therefore went there a few days before the winter banquet in a light sleigh, smoking his best cigar. And it happened further that the people of Seldwyla had arranged a sleighing party for the same day as the people of Goldach, and at the same place; it was to be a costume or masked sleigh ride.

The sleighing party from Goldach rode through the streets of the town at about noon amid the tinkling of bells, the sounding of postilions' horns and the cracking of whips, which made the signs of the old houses look down in astonishment, and left by the city gate. In the first sleigh sat Strapinski with his fiancée. He was wearing a Polish overcoat of green velvet, trimmed with cord and heavily edged and lined with fur. Nettie was completely enveloped in white furs; blue veils protected her face from the fresh air and the glare of the snow. A sudden development had prevented the councillor from going along; however, it was his team of horses and his sleigh in which they were riding, with its gilded image of a woman representing Fortune decorating the front; for the councillor's town house was named Fortune.

They were followed by fifteen or sixteen vehicles with a gay gentleman and lady in each, all dressed up, but none as handsome and stately as the betrothed couple. Just as ocean vessels have their figureheads, so each sleigh bore the insignia of the house to which it belonged, so that the people cried, "Look, here comes Bravery! How handsome Efficiency is! Perfectibility seems to be newly lacquered and Thrift is freshly gilded. Ah, Jacob's Well and the Pool of Bethesda!" In the Pool of Bethesda, which closed the procession as a modest one-horse vehicle, Melcher Böhni drove quietly and contentedly. The figurehead in front of his carriage was a picture of that little Jewish man who had waited for his salvation at the said pool for thirty years. So the squadron sailed along in the sunshine and, approaching their goal, soon appeared on the plateau, which gleamed from a great distance. At the same time gay music was heard coming from the opposite direction.

From a fragrant forest covered with hoarfrost there erupted a confusion of gay colors and forms which developed into a train of sleighs, delineating itself against the blue sky high up on the white edge of the fields. It, too, was gliding toward the center of the region, a grotesque sight. The procession seemed to consist mostly of large peasant freight-sleds, joined in twos to serve as the bases for extraordinary structures and displays. On the first vehicle a colossal figure towered, representing the goddess Fortune, who seemed to be flying out into the ether. She was a gigantic straw puppet full of shimmering gold tinsel, her gauze robes fluttering in the air. On the second vehicle, however, rode an equally gigantic billy goat, a black and gloomy contrast, pursuing Fortune with lowered horns. This was followed by a strange structure, which turned out to be a fifteen-foot pressing iron; then there was a mighty snapping pair of shears, which was opened and closed by means of a cord, and which seemed to regard the sky as a bolt of blue silken waistcoat material. Other such current allusions to the tailoring trade followed, and at the feet of all these structures, on the spacious sleighs, each drawn by four horses, sat the society of Seldwyla in the gayest clothes, indulging themselves in loud laughter and song.

When both processions drove up at the same moment on the square before the inn, there was a noisy scene and a great press of men and horses. The people of Goldach were surprised and astonished at this strange meeting; the Seldwylers, on the other hand, behaved good-naturedly and with friendly modesty. Their leading sleigh, the Fortune, bore the inscription "People Make Clothes," and so it was natural that the whole company represented nothing but tailors from all nations and all ages. It was, so to speak, a historical, ethnographic tailor festival, which closed with the converse and complementary inscription: "Clothes Make People." For in the last sleigh, with this sign, with the utmost gravity, there sat exalted emperors and kings, councilmen and staff officers, prelates and canonesses, as the products of the heathen and Christian knights of the needle who had preceded them.

This world of tailors was able to extricate itself skillfully from the confusion, and modestly allowed the ladies and gentlemen from Goldach to walk into the house, with the bridal couple at their head. The Seldwylers subsequently occupied the lower rooms of the inn, which had been reserved for them, while the Goldachers noisily trooped up the broad stairway to the large banquet hall. The count's company found this behavior proper; their surprise turned to merriment and approving smiles at the imperturbable good mood of the Seldwylers. The count alone experienced very obscure emotions which he did not at all like, although in his present state of mind he felt no definite suspicion and had not even noticed where the other people came from. In a loud voice, so that Strapinski could hear, Melcher Böhni, who had parked his Pool of Bethesda carefully at a side spot and found himself the tailor's attentive neighbor, named an entirely different place as the origin of the masked procession.

Soon the two companies were sitting at set tables, each on its own floor, and they gave themselves over to merry conversation and jokes in expectation of further joys.

These joys soon came for the Goldachers when they went in couples to the dance hall, where the musicians were already tuning their violins. But when they were all standing in a circle and were about to take their positions for the round dance, a delegation from the Seldwylers appeared, presenting the friendly and neighborly request that they be allowed to pay a visit to the ladies and

gentlemen of Goldach and to give a dance recital for their pleasure. This offer could not well be refused; moreover, they promised themselves some real fun from the merry Seldwylers, and so,
at the request of the delegation, they sat down in a large semicircle, in the midst of which Strapinski and Nettie glowed like princely
stars.

The aforesaid groups of tailors came in gradually, one after the
other. In an elegant pantomime, each one acted out the sentence
"People Make Clothes" and its converse, first by pretending to
make some stately articles of clothing: a prince's cloak, a priest's
gown and the like; and then by dressing some needy person in it,
who, suddenly transformed, stood up with the greatest dignity and
solemnly marched about in time to the music. Fable, too, was
staged in the same way: a tremendous crow appeared, decking
itself out in peacock's feathers and hopping about and quacking,
or a wolf who was tailoring a sheepskin, and finally a donkey that
wore a fearful lion's skin made of cotton waste, draping himself
in it heroically as if it were a Carbonari cape.

All who appeared in this way stepped back when they had finished their turn and thus transformed the semicircle of Goldachers
into a wide ring of spectators, whose center finally became empty.
Then the music went into a sad, serious tune and at the same time
a final pantomimist walked into the circle, the focus of all eyes.
He was a slender young man in a dark coat, with handsome dark
hair and a Polish cap; it was none other than Count Strapinski as
he had walked on the highway that November day and climbed
into the fateful carriage.

In silent suspense, the whole assembly looked at the performer
who, solemn and melancholy, took a few steps in time to the music, then strode to the center of the circle, spread out his cloak on
the floor, sat down on it tailor fashion and began unpacking a
bundle. He drew out a nearly finished count's coat exactly like the
one Strapinski was then wearing, sewed tassels and cords on it
with great speed and skill and ironed it professionally, testing the
seemingly hot iron with a moist finger. Then he slowly stood up,
took off his threadbare coat and put on the elegant garment, drew
out a little mirror, combed his hair and finished dressing, so that
he finally stood there the spit and image of the count. Unexpect-

edly the music changed into a swift, spirited air; the man wrapped up his belongings in his old coat and threw the bundle far over the heads of the assembled company into the depths of the hall, as though he wanted to separate himself from his past for good. After this he skirted the circle in stately dance steps as a proud man of the world, bowing graciously here and there to the company, until he came to the betrothed couple. Suddenly he fixed his eyes steadily on the Pole, who was immensely astonished, and stood before him immovable as a pillar, while simultaneously and as though by prearrangement, the music stopped and a fearful silence ensued like a mute flash of lightning.

"Oh! Oh! Oh! Oh!" he cried in a voice that was audible at a great distance, and stretched his arms toward the unhappy man. "Behold our brother Silesian, our water Polack, who ran away from his job because he believed, on the basis of a slight business fluctuation, that it was all up with me. Well, I'm happy that things are so merry for you and that you are celebrating such a happy carnival here. Do you have employment in Goldach?"

At the same time he held out his hand to the young count, who was sitting there pale and smiling; the latter took it unwillingly, like a glowing iron bar, while his double cried, "Come, friends, behold here our gentle journeyman tailor, who looks like Raphael and was so much admired by our maids, including our pastor's daughter, who is, to be sure, slightly mad."

Now all the people from Seldwyla came past and crowded around Strapinski and his former employer, shaking the tailor's hand innocently, so that he swayed and trembled on his chair. At the same time the music started up again with a lively march; the Seldwylers, as they passed the betrothed couple, lined up for departure and marched out of the hall singing a well-rehearsed diabolical laugh chorus, while the Goldachers, among whom Melcher Böhni had been able to spread the explanation of the miracle with lightning speed, ran about in confusion, crossing the ranks of the Seldwylers, so that a great tumult resulted.

When the commotion finally subsided, the hall was almost empty; a few people stood against the walls whispering to each other in embarrassment; a few young ladies stood at some distance from Nettie, uncertain whether to approach her or not.

The couple, however, sat motionless on their chairs like a stone Egyptian royal pair, silent and lonely; one could almost feel the endless, glowing desert sand.

Nettie, as white as a marble statue, slowly turned her face to her fiancé and gave him a strange sidelong glance.

Thereupon he got up slowly and, weeping great tears, went away with heavy steps, his eyes fixed on the ground.

He went through the ranks of the people from Goldach and Seldwyla, who lined the staircase, passing them like a dead man who steals away spectrally from an annual fair, and strangely enough, they allowed him to pass like such a ghost, avoiding him silently, without laughing or calling harsh words after him. He also walked past the sleighs and horses from Goldach, which were getting ready to depart, while the people of Seldwyla were having a really merry time of it in their quarters; and he walked down the same highway toward Seldwyla by which he had come a few months before, half unconscious, with the sole intention of never coming back to Goldach. Soon he disappeared in the darkness of the forest through which the road ran. He was bareheaded, for his Polish cap, together with his gloves, had been left on the window sill of the dance hall; and so he strode forward with bowed head, hiding his freezing hands under crossed arms, while his thoughts gradually collected themselves and attained some degree of reason. The first distinct feeling he became aware of was that of a monstrous sense of shame, as though he had been a real man of rank and prominence and had now become infamous through the irruption of some fateful misfortune. But then this feeling dissolved into a sort of consciousness of having suffered an injustice; until his glorious entrance into the cursed town he had never been guilty of a misdemeanor; as far back into childhood as his thoughts could reach, he could not remember ever having been punished or scolded because of a lie or deception; and now he had become a deceiver because the world's folly had overwhelmed him in an unguarded and, so to speak, defenseless moment and had made him its playmate. He saw himself as a child who has been persuaded by another wicked child to steal the chalice from an altar; he now hated and despised himself, but he also wept for himself and his unhappy aberration.

When a prince conquers a country and its people; when a priest professes the teaching of his church without conviction and proudly consumes the goods of his benefice; when a conceited teacher holds and enjoys the honors and advantages of a lofty profession without having the least conception of the dignity of his discipline or advancing it in the slightest; when an artist without virtue makes himself fashionable through superficial activity and empty jugglery and steals bread and fame from the true worker; or when a swindler, who has inherited or obtained by fraud the name of a great merchant, robs thousands of their savings or their emergency funds through his folly and unscrupulousness—all these do not weep at themselves but rejoice in their well-being, and they do not remain for one evening without cheering company and good friends.

Our tailor, however, wept bitterly over himself; that is to say, he suddenly began to do so when his thoughts unexpectedly returned to his abandoned fiancée by the heavy chain of associations from which they were suspended; and he writhed on the ground in shame before the invisible girl. Misfortune and humiliation showed him with one clear ray of light the happiness he had lost, and out of the confused, enamored, venial sinner they made a rejected lover. He stretched out his arms toward the coldly glittering stars and staggered rather than walked along the road; then he stood still and shook his head, when suddenly a red gleam lit the snow about him and at the same time the sound of sleigh bells and laughter resounded. It was the Seldwylers riding home by torchlight. The first horses were already approaching him; he pulled himself together, took a mighty leap over the ditch and ducked into the foremost trees of the forest. The mad procession rode by and finally died away in the dark distance without the fugitive's having been noticed; but he, after listening for a good while, motionless and overcome by the cold as well as by the fiery beverages he had enjoyed earlier and by his grievous stupidity, stretched out his limbs unthinkingly and fell asleep on the crackling snow, while an ice-cold breath of air began to blow in from the east.

Meanwhile Nettie, too, had stood up from her lonely seat. She had looked attentively after her departing lover, had sat motionless for more than an hour and now got up, shedding bitter tears, and walked helplessly to the door. Two friends joined her with dubious words of consolation; she asked them to fetch her coat, shawl, hat and such things, which she put on silently, drying her eyes vigorously with her veil. But, when you cry, you always have to blow your nose; so she found herself obliged to take out her handkerchief after all and to give her nose a vigorous blowing, after which she looked about proudly and angrily. Into her view came Melcher Böhni, who approached her kindly, humbly and smilingly and pointed out to her the necessity of having a guide and companion on her way back to her father's house. The Pool of Bethesda, he said, he would leave behind here at the inn while he guided Fortune securely back to Goldach, together with the venerated unhappy lady.

Without replying, she walked ahead with a firm step toward the courtyard, where the sleigh with its impatient, well-fed horses stood ready, one of the last vehicles still there. She swiftly took her place in it, seized the reins and whip, and while the unsuspecting Böhni, bustling about with happy officiousness, was getting a tip for the stable boy who had held the horses, she unexpectedly whipped up the animals, which dashed out on the highway with vigorous leaps that soon settled into a steady lively gallop. And to tell the truth she was not riding home but along the road to Seldwyla. Only when the light-winged vehicle had already vanished from his sight did Herr Böhni discover the fact, and he ran in the direction of Goldach with cries of "Whoa! Whoa!" and "Stop!" then rushed back, jumped into his sleigh and raced after the beauty who had fled, or, as he thought, had been carried off by the horses, until he reached the gate of the excited town, in which the vexatious event already had all tongues busy.

Why Nettie had taken that road, whether out of confusion or intentionally, cannot be reported with certainty. Two circumstances may cast a little light on the matter. For one thing, Strapinski's fur cap and gloves, which had been lying on the window sill behind the couple's seat, were now, strangely enough, in the sleigh Fortune beside Nettie. No one had noticed when and how she had taken these objects and she herself did not know; she had done it as though in a somnambulistic state. Even now she was not aware that the cap and gloves were lying beside her. More than once she said aloud to herself, "I must speak a few words with him, just a few words."

These two facts seem to prove that the fiery horses were not entirely guided by chance. It was also strange that when Fortune got into the road in the woods, where the full moon was now shining, Nettie pulled the reins tighter, so that the horses slowed up and almost pranced along at a walk, while the driver fixed her sad but sharp eyes on the road, and did not miss the slightest striking object to the left or right of her.

And yet it was as though she were in a deep, heavy, unhappy oblivion. What are fortune and life? What do they depend on? What are we ourselves, that we become happy or unhappy because of a ridiculous carnival lie? What guilt have we incurred, to harvest shame and despair because of a happy, credulous affection? Who sends us such silly, deceptive figures, which erupt destructively into our destiny, while they themselves dissolve in it like weak soap bubbles?

Such questions, dreamed rather than thought, were occupying Nettie's mind when her eyes were suddenly drawn to a longish dark object that stood out from the moonlit snow at the side of the highway. It was Wenzel stretched out full length; his dark hair mingled with the shadows of the trees, while his slender body lay clearly in the light.

Nettie involuntarily pulled up the horses, whereupon a deep silence came over the forest. She stared fixedly at the dark body, until it became almost unmistakably clear to her eye. She gently tied the reins fast, got out, stroked the horses for a moment to calm them and then approached the figure cautiously and noiselessly.

Yes, it was he. The dark green velvet of his coat looked beautiful and aristocratic even on the night snow; the slim body and the supple limbs, tautly laced and clothed; everything about him, even in his numbness, at the brink of ruin, in his helplessness, still cried out: Clothes make the man!

When the lonely beauty bent over him and recognized him beyond doubt, she immediately saw the danger that threatened his life and feared that he might already be frozen. And so she instinctively seized one of his hands, which appeared to be cold and without feeling. Forgetting everything else, she shook the poor man and shouted his Christian name in his ear, "Wenzel! Wenzel!" In vain: he did not move, but only breathed weakly and sadly. Thereupon she threw herself on him, moved her hand over his face and, in her anxiety, flicked her finger against the pale tip of his nose.

Then a bright idea struck her; she took handfuls of snow and vigorously rubbed his nose and face and fingers with all her strength until the lucky unhappy man recovered, awoke and slowly sat up.

He looked about him and saw his rescuer standing before him. She had thrown her veil back; Wenzel recognized every feature in her white face, which was looking at him with wide eyes.

He fell down before her, kissed the hem of her cloak and cried, "Forgive me! Forgive me!"

"Come, stranger!" she said, suppressing the trembling in her voice. "I'll talk to you and send you away!"

She motioned to him to get into the sleigh, which he did obediently; she gave him his cap and gloves just as instinctively as she had taken them with her, took the reins and whip and drove on.

Beyond the forest, not far from the road, was a farmhouse, in which there lived a farmer's wife whose husband had died not long before. Nettie was the godmother of one of her children, and the councillor, Nettie's father, was her landlord. Only recently the woman had visited them to wish the daughter luck and to get all sorts of advice; but she could not as yet know anything about the course which events had taken.

To this farm Nettie now drove, turning off the highway and halting in front of the house with a vigorous cracking of her whip. There was still light behind the little windows; the farmer's wife was awake and was still bustling about the house, although the children and servants had long been asleep. She opened a window and peered out in astonishment. "It's only me, it's us," cried Nettie. "We have lost our way because of the new upper road, which I have never traveled before. Make some coffee for us, mother, and let us come in for a moment before we go on."

Very pleased, the peasant woman hurried out, recognizing Nettie at once; she was apparently both delighted and overawed to see the "big shot," the foreign count, too. In her eyes the happiness and the splendor of this world had crossed her threshold in these two persons; vague hopes of winning a small part of this splendor, some modest gain for herself or her children, animated the good woman and gave her every agility in serving the young masters. She quickly woke a young servant to hold the horses, and soon she had also prepared some hot coffee, which she now brought in to Wenzel and Nettie, who sat facing each other in the half-dark room, a weakly flickering little lamp between them on the table.

Wenzel sat with his head in his hands, not daring to look up. Nettie leaned back in her chair and kept her eyes closed tight, and her bitter, beautiful mouth too, from which it could be seen that she was by no means asleep.

When the woman had set the coffee on the table, Nettie stood up quickly and whispered to her, "Now leave us alone for a little while; go and lie on your bed, dear woman; we've had a bit of a quarrel and have to talk matters over, and there's a good opportunity to do it here."

"I understand; you're doing the right thing," said the woman, and soon left the two of them alone.

"Drink this," said Nettie as she sat down again, "it will do you good." She herself touched nothing. Wenzel Strapinski, who was trembling slightly, straightened up, took a cup and drank it, more because she had told him to do so than to refresh himself. He looked at her now, and as their eyes met and Nettie's gazed searchingly into his, she shook her head and then said, "Who are you? What do you want with me?"

"I am not entirely what I appear to be," he replied sadly. "I am a poor fool; but I'll make everything good and give you satisfaction and not stay alive much longer." Such words he uttered with conviction and without any affectation, so that Nettie's eyes flashed imperceptibly. However, she repeated, "I wish to know who you really are and where you come from and where you're going."

"Everything has happened as I'm now going to tell you in accordance with the truth," he replied, and he told her who he was and how things had happened on his entrance to Goldach. He emphasized especially how he had wanted to escape several times but had finally been prevented from doing so by her appearance, as though in a bewitched dream.

Nettie was overcome by an impulse to laugh; however, the situation was too serious to permit such an outburst. Instead, she asked, "And where did you intend to go with me and what did you plan to do?" "I hardly know," he replied; "I looked forward to further remarkable or lucky events; also I sometimes thought of death in such a way that I would bring it on myself, after—"

Here Wenzel stopped and his pale face turned quite red.

"Well, continue!" said Nettie, also turning pale, while her heart beat strangely.

Then Wenzel's eyes flamed up big and sweet and he cried:

"Yes, now it is clear to me how it would have happened. I would have gone with you into the great world, and after living a few brief days in happiness with you, I would have confessed the deception to you and committed suicide. You would have returned to your father, where you would have been well cared for and would have forgotten me easily. No one need have known about it; I would have disappeared without leaving a trace—instead of pining away all my life, yearning for a dignified existence, for a kind heart, for love," he continued sadly. "I would have been great and happy for one moment and high above all those who are neither happy nor unhappy and yet never want to die. Oh, if only you had let me lie there in the cold snow, I would have fallen asleep so gladly!"

He had grown silent again and looked ahead of him gloomily.

After a while, when the beating of her heart, stirred by Wenzel's words, had somewhat subsided, Nettie, who had been studying his face silently, said, "Have you played the same or similar tricks before, and deceived strangers who have done you no harm?"

"I have asked myself this question this bitter night and can't remember that I've ever been a liar. I have never yet begun or experienced such an adventure. Yes, in those days when the impulse awoke in me to be or appear to be something decent, when I was still half a child, I controlled myself and renounced a happiness which seemed destined for me."

"Tell me about it," said Nettie.

"Before she married, my mother had been in service with a neighboring squire's wife and had accompanied her on journeys and to large cities. From this she had acquired a more refined manner than the other women in our village, and I suppose she was somewhat vain too; for she dressed herself and me, her only child, more attractively and more carefully than was the custom there. But my father, a poor schoolmaster, died early, and so, living in direst poverty, we had no prospect of enjoying the happy experiences my mother liked to dream about. Rather, she had to devote herself to hard work to keep us alive and make sacrifices so that the most precious thing she had might have better clothes and a somewhat better standard of living. Unexpectedly, when I was about sixteen years old, the squire's wife, who had recently become a widow, said that she was moving to the city permanently; she asked mother to send me along too; it would be a pity for me to become a day laborer or farmhand in the village; she would have me learn a refined trade that I fancied, and in the meantime I could live in her house and do various light chores. This seemed to be the most glorious thing that could happen to us. Accordingly, everything was discussed and ready, when mother became pensive and sad and suddenly begged me one day, with many tears, not to leave her but to remain poor with her; she would not live long, she said, and I would certainly still find something good after she was dead. The squire's wife, to whom I reported this gloomily, came over and protested to my mother. But mother now became quite excited and cried over and over that she would not allow herself to be robbed of her child; anyone who knew him—"

Here Wenzel Strapinski stopped again and did not know how to go on. Nettie asked, "What did your mother say—'anyone who knew him—?' Why don't you continue?"

Wenzel turned red and replied, "She said something strange, which I didn't really understand and which I have never heard since; she said that anyone who knew the child could never part from him again. I suppose she meant that I was a good-natured lad or something of the sort. In short, she was so excited that, in spite of all urging, I refused the lady's offer and stayed with mother, for which she loved me doubly, begging my pardon a thousand times for standing in the way of my happiness. But when I had to learn to earn my living, it turned out that there was not much else to do but become an apprentice to our village tailor. I didn't want to, but mother cried so much that I yielded. That is the story."

When Nettie asked why and when he had finally left his mother, Wenzel replied, "Military service called me away. I was put among the hussars and was quite a handsome red hussar, although perhaps the most stupid in the regiment, and certainly the quietest. After a year I was finally able to get a few weeks' furlough and hurried home to see my good mother; but she had just died. So when my time came, I went out alone into the world and finally met my misfortune here."

Nettie smiled and observed him attentively as he mournfully talked. Then the room was quiet for a while; suddenly a thought seemed to occur to her.

"Since you were always so esteemed and so charming," she said suddenly, yet in a hesitating, pointed manner, "you have no doubt had the usual love affairs or the like at various times, and probably have more than one woman on your conscience—to say nothing about me?"

"Oh Lord," Wenzel replied, turning very red, "before I came to you I never so much as touched the fingertips of a girl, except—"

"Well?" said Nettie.

"Well," he continued, "it was the same woman who wanted to take me with her and have me educated; she had a child, a girl of seven or eight, a strange, passionate child, and yet as sweet as sugar and fair as an angel. On many occasions I had to play servant and protector to her and she had become accustomed to me. I had to bring her regularly the long distance to and from the parsonage, where she was given instruction by the old clergyman. At other times, too, when no one else was available, I had to take care of her. When I was leading her home for the last time over the field in the evening sun, the child began to talk of her approaching departure, declared that I must really come with them and asked me whether I would. I told her it couldn't be. But the child continued to plead with deep emotion and persistence, clinging to my arm and hindering me in my walking, as children will do, so that I unthinkingly freed myself from her, probably somewhat harshly. At that the girl's head dropped, ashamed and sad, she tried to suppress the tears that now welled up in her eyes, and she could scarcely control her sobbing. In dismay I wanted to appease her, but she turned angrily from me and left in displeasure. Since then the beautiful child has always remained in my mind, and my heart has always clung to her, although I have never heard from her again."

Suddenly the speaker, who had fallen into gentle agitation, stopped as though frightened and, turning pale, stared at his companion.

"Well," said Nettie in a strange tone, also growing somewhat pale, "why do you look at me like that?"

But Wenzel stretched out his arm, pointed at her as though he were seeing a ghost and cried, "I've noticed this before. When that child was angry, her beautiful hair stood up slightly about her brow and temples, as yours does now, so that you could see it move. That's the way it was that last time in the field in the evening glow."

Indeed, those of Nettie's locks that were closest to her temples and over her forehead had stirred gently, as though a breath of air had blown into her face.

Mother Nature, always somewhat coquettish, had made use of one of her secrets here to bring the difficult affair to an end.

After a brief silence, during which her bosom began to heave, Nettie got up, walked around the table toward the man and threw her arms about his neck with the words, "I will not leave you! You are mine and I will go with you despite the whole world!"

So she celebrated her engagement only now, with a profoundly resolute mind, by keeping faith and taking a destiny upon herself in sweet passion.

However, she was by no means so dull that she did not want to guide this destiny a little herself; on the contrary, she made new resolutions swiftly and boldly. For she said to the good Wenzel, who was dreaming, lost in this new change of fortune, "Now we'll go straight to Seldwyla and show the people there, who planned to destroy us, that they have united us more than ever and have made us happy!"

The good Wenzel could not see it that way. He wished rather to move to unfamiliar distant parts and to live there in a mysterious romantic manner, in quiet bliss, as he said.

But Nettie cried, "No more romances! As you are, a poor wanderer, I will accept you and become your wife in my native city in defiance of all these proud and scoffing people. We'll move to Seldwyla and there, through our energy and intelligence, make the people who have mocked us dependent on us."

And they did as they had said they would. After the farmer's wife had been summoned and rewarded by Wenzel, who began to assume his new role, they continued on their way. Wenzel was now holding the reins. Nettie leaned against him contentedly as if he were a church pillar. For heaven is the fulfillment of our wishes and Nettie had come of age exactly three days before and could follow hers.

In Seldwyla they stopped before the Rainbow Inn, where a number of the sleigh riders were still sitting over their drinks. When the couple appeared in the drawing room, the word spread like fire: "Ha, ha, we have an abduction here; we have initiated a precious affair!"

Wenzel, however, walked through the room with his bride without looking about him, and after she had disappeared in her rooms, he went to the Wild Man, another good inn, and there walked proudly through the ranks of the Seldwylers, who were still carrying on, into a room which he ordered, leaving them to their astonished deliberations. They felt obliged to drink themselves into the most furious hangovers about this affair.

In the town of Goldach, too, the cry "Abduction!" was making the rounds.

Very early the next morning, the Pool of Bethesda was riding toward Seldwyla, with the excited Melcher Böhni and Nettie's perplexed father in it. In their haste they almost drove through Seldwyla without stopping; but just in time they saw the sleigh Fortune standing intact in front of the inn, and surmised to their consolation that the handsome horses would at least not be far away. And so, when their surmise had been confirmed and they had learned of Nettie's arrival and her presence there, they had their sleigh unhitched and went into the Rainbow.

But it took a little while before Nettie sent word to her father to come to her room for a private talk. It was said that she had already summoned the best lawyer in town, who would appear in the course of the morning. The councillor went up to his daughter somewhat heavy of heart, deliberating in what way he could best lead the desperate child back out of her confusion, and he was prepared for desperate behavior.

But Nettie came toward him with calm and gentle firmness. She thanked her father with emotion for all the love and kindness he had shown her, and then declared in determined sentences: first, after what had happened, she did not want to live in Goldach any longer, at least not in the next few years; second, she wished to take possession of her substantial maternal inheritance, which her father had long held in readiness in the event of her marriage; third, she wanted to marry Wenzel Strapinski, and on this she was absolutely inflexible; fourth, she intended to live with him in Seldwyla and help him establish a thriving business there; fifth and last, everything would turn out well, for she had become convinced that he was a good man and would make her happy.

The councillor began his task by reminding her that she knew, of course, how very much he wished to place her fortune in her own hands as the foundation of her true happiness, and the sooner the better. But then, with all the concern that had filled him since the first news of the catastrophe, he explained how impossible the relationship she wanted to perpetuate was. And finally, he showed how the serious conflict could be resolved with dignity. It was Herr Melcher Böhni who was prepared to put an end to the whole matter by stepping in promptly to fill the breach with his person and to protect and maintain her honor before the world with his irreproachable name.

The word honor finally succeeded in throwing his daughter into a state of greater excitement. It was honor, in fact, she cried, which commanded her not to marry Herr Böhni, because she couldn't stand him, and to remain faithful to the poor stranger to whom she had given her word and whom, moreover, she loved.

There now ensued some fruitless talking back and forth, which finally brought the steadfast beauty to tears.

Wenzel and Böhni burst into the room almost at the same time, having met on the staircase, and a great commotion threatened to ensue, when the lawyer, a man well known to the councillor, came in and urged peaceful cool-headedness for the present. When he heard in a few preliminary words what the issue was, he gave orders that Wenzel should withdraw to the Wild Man and remain there quietly; that Herr Böhni, too, should not interfere but go away; that Nettie, for her part, should observe the amenities of good tone until the matter was settled; and that the father should renounce any exercise of coercion, since his daughter's freedom was legally incontestable.

So there was an armistice and a general separation for some hours.

In town, where the attorney scattered a few words about the large fortune that might come to Seldwyla through this affair, there now arose a great commotion. The sentiment of the Seldwylers suddenly veered in favor of the tailor and his fiancée, and they decided to protect the lovers with all their power and to guarantee them the right and freedom of person in their town. And so, when the rumor spread that the beauty of Goldach was to be taken back by force, they banded together, placed armed protective and honor guards before the Rainbow and the Wild Man, and in general carried out another of their great adventures with tremendous merriment, a remarkable continuation of yesterday's event.

The frightened and irritated councillor sent his Böhni to Goldach for help. The latter rode off at a gallop, and the next day a number of men drove over from there along with a substantial police detachment to help the councillor, and it began to look as if Seldwyla was to become a new Troy. The parties faced each other threateningly; the town drummer was already tightening his tuning screw, practicing individual taps with his right drumstick. Then some higher officials appeared on the square, both ecclesiastical and worldly gentlemen, and negotiations were carried on on all sides. Since Nettie remained firm and Wenzel did not allow himself to be intimidated, encouraged as they were by the Seldwylers, it was decided that their marriage banns would be published formally after all the necessary documents had been collected, and that they would wait to see what legal objections might be raised during this procedure and with what success.

In view of the fact that Nettie was of age, such objections could be raised only in regard to the dubious character of the spurious Count Wenzel Strapinski.

But the attorney who was handling his and Nettie's case learned that, until now, not even the shadow of evil reputation had touched the strange young man, either in his native village or during his travels; from everywhere there came only good and well-wishing testimonials about him.

As far as the events in Goldach were concerned, the attorney proved that Wenzel had never really represented himself as a count, but that this rank had been forcibly bestowed on him by others; that he had signed all existing documents with his real name, Wenzel Strapinski, without any addition; accordingly there existed no other misdemeanor, except that he had enjoyed a foolish hospitality, which would not have been offered him if he had not arrived in that carriage and if the coachman had not played a bad joke.

And so the war ended with a wedding, at which the Seldwylers fired off their powerful so-called mortars to the annoyance of the Goldachers, who could hear the thunder of the cannon quite well, since a west wind was blowing. The councillor handed over Nettie's whole fortune to her and she said that Wenzel must now become a big *marchandtailleur* and cloth master in Seldwyla; for there the draper was still called a cloth master, the iron merchant an iron master, etc.

And this really happened, but quite differently from the way the Seldwylers had dreamed. He was modest, thrifty and diligent in his business, which he was able to build up substantially. He made their velvet vests for them, violet-colored or with white and blue checks, formal dress coats with gold buttons and cloaks faced with red; and they all owed him money, but never too long. For to get new, still more attractive clothes, which he imported or made for them, they had to pay their bills, so that they complained among themselves that he was squeezing the blood out of them.

With all this he became round and stately and almost stopped looking dreamy. He became more experienced and skilled in business from year to year and, in conjunction with his father-in-law, the councillor, who had soon become reconciled to him, he was able to invest his money so well that his fortune doubled, and after ten or twelve years, with as many children which Nettie had meanwhile borne him, he moved with her to Goldach and there became a prominent man.

But in Seldwyla he did not leave a penny, either from ingratitude or revenge.

Translated by Harry Steinhauer

The Lost Smile

Chapter 1

Give me three yards of good silk banner,
And fellow marchers, starry-eyed,
In Sunday best, these men of honor—
And then my heart is satisfied.

I'll rise when morning lights the mountains,
To end the brief rest summer brings,
And join the march toward those clear fountains
From which our joy of country springs.

And boats and wagons, decked with flowers,
Converge on by-ways everywhere,
Ahead our graceful town-hall towers,
No weight of stones, no weight of care.

And shining on the speaker's rostrum,
The silver cup, a lovely thing!
Free men, thank God, it's still our custom:
In ardent words let freedom ring!

From mouth to mouth, in songs and speeches,
From heart to heart the joyful sound
Through every festive hour reaches,
Until the golden dawn comes 'round.

And duty's every call is growing,
And every strong resolve is steeled,
And of the seed that we are sowing
No single fruit shall be concealed.

So choose your place where men of honor
In Sunday dress spend holidays,
Where fair and high the silken banner
In skies above them gently sways.

Where fun's a patriotic matter,
All joy is free of Satan's curse.
So, coming home, if I'm no better
At least I won't be any worse.

The color-bearer of the Seldwyla male choir sang this song as the men marched to a songfest one brilliant summer morning. They had started off the night before, making part of the trip by rail, but had decided to walk the rest of the way, in the cool of morning, since it was all through beautiful woodland.

The shining lake, with the flag-bedecked city along its shore, stretched out before them. They marched in scattered groups, sixty or seventy men, young and old, down through a splendid grove of beeches, rousing with shouts and verses of song the echos that dwell beyond the great tree trunks, or answering another troop of singers farther down the mountain.

First in line was their standard-bearer, the only one to sing his song through to the end. He was a tall, slim young man, with a face as handsome as a picture, his voice a joyous but tempered baritone. Resplendent in a large, richly embroidered scarf and an elegant feathered hat, he carried the silken banner, equally rich and heavy, half folded over his shoulder. The golden tip of it glistened now and again in the green shade, as the morning sun broke through the leafy canopy of the trees.

When he had finished his song he looked back smiling. No one could begrudge the happiness that shone on his handsome face, for he had a smile so pleasant it won people over the moment they saw it.

"Our Jocundi," said the men following after him, "is going to be the handsomest color-bearer at the festival." For he bore the cheerful sounding name Jocundus Meyenthal (that is, Mayvale) and was simply called, with general affection, Jocundi. And he confirmed their hopes; for when the Seldwylers arrived on the scene and joined the long lines of singers waiting to enter, his appearance aroused general delight wherever they went.

For those who had attended several festivals he was already well known, and favorably so, a model participant in such celebrations. Constantly cheerful and tireless, from the first moment to the last, Jocundi was calm and composure personified. He was to be seen everywhere, participating in the general merriment and in each particular activity as well, endlessly patient and helpful. He was never too loud, he never drank too much. He could tolerate the noisy prankster, or the ill-tempered guest who had over-extended himself, spoiling the pleasure of others. He also had the forbearance and friendliness it took to rescue such persons from all kinds of rough sailing, when the general patience wore thin, and to save them from the embarrassment of shipwreck. Adeptly and silently, ignoring abuse, he could even extract from the press of the crowd someone whose quick temper had got the best of his self-control. And what he gained was the gratitude and devotion of a sobered friend.

In this exercise he represented, incidentally, a very mirror of all Seldwylers when they were off celebrating. On such occasions they were as orderly, industrious, and well-mannered as they were, in the rest of their lives, idle and undisciplined. They made a dignified entrance and a dignified exit, an orderly, harmonious group, as long as the festivities lasted. All the while, of course, they were rejoicing at the thought of the less formal relaxation they might indulge in at length, once they were home and their serious exertions were over.

After their fashion they had carefully practiced the song with which they intended to compete for the prize on the day of the song-fest. Now, with great restraint, they were sparing their voices. They had chosen a composition with the title "Violets Awaken," based on some inconsequential little song, but so elaborate and difficult of execution that for months there had been much discussion here and there as to whether the Seldwylers hadn't taken on too much, thus exposing themselves to the risk of defeat.

But when the day of the competition came, with thousands of listeners sitting in the great wide hall before almost as many thousand singers, and when the little troop of Seldwylers, their hour at hand, came out alone with their banner, before this sea of people, they sustained their tender yet demanding song through all its difficult harmonies and complexities, without wavering, causing it to whisper forth so softly and with such purity that one could imagine hearing the blue buds of the violets gently burst open and the first touch of their fragrance waft through the hall.

After breathless quiet, the applause broke forth with a tumultuous roar. In full view, the august judges visibly nodded their heads and looked at one another, reaching for their golden snuffboxes, gifts of honor from far-flung princes and peoples and offering one another pinches of snuff. Among them were some of the great choir masters.

As for the Seldwylers, they withdrew with quiet dignity and managed to extract themselves inconspicuously from the order of battle, to take a modest champagne breakfast in a shady garden. No one desired to drink more than his usual three glasses; and when they showed up again in the hall no one knew they had been away or where they had gone.

They carried on in this dignified fashion for the entire duration of the festival, until the moment came for the awarding of prizes. The gold of the afternoon sun wove its light through the hall, which was filled to the last seat. Decorated with red cloth and greenery and hung with many flags, it seemed as if suspended in beauty. On a raised platform were the plates and cups designed as prizes or commemorative gifts, shining in gold and silver, and there too sat a number of young ladies, chosen to fix the wreaths on the choir flags of the winners.

To be more exact, they served as escorts for the loveliest and tallest among them, the beautiful Justine Glor of Schwanau, who had with some difficulty been persuaded to take over the fastening of the wreaths on the flags. She looked like one of the Muses: in the thick curls of her brown hair she wore a fresh garland of roses, on her white dress a red sash.

All eyes were upon her as she stood up and took the first wreath, which had just been awarded, with drums and fanfare, to the men of Seldwyla. But at the same time they also fell on Jocundus who suddenly stood before her with his flag, smiling in joy and happiness. And on the face of the girl with the wreath there shone, like a reflection, the same beautiful smile, the very image of his own. For it was evident that both of them were natives of the same part of the world, the home of those blessed with such a smile. Each of them was doubtless more or less aware of the trait; each was now seeing it in another. And since the people around them took startled note of the phenomenon, both of them blushed, but not without exchanging repeated glances, while the wreath was being affixed.

An hour later the last and noisiest procession got under way through the festival city, beneath countless pennants and wreaths, past the surging crowds, carrying on display the ceremonial gifts and the prize-winning banners. Now the two saw one another again, for Justine was watching the procession from the garden balcony of her hosts' house when Jocundus passed by, waving his flag. That evening, it being a busy day for Lady Luck, Jocundus happened to be seated during the closing banquet at the same table with the beautiful girl. By midnight they were happily comfortable in one another's company.

The next morning they met again, as good acquaintants, on one of the great flag-bedecked steamboats assigned to take the festival committee, along with a number of honored and distinguished guests and friends from afar, for a pleasure trip along the lake. A cloudless sky lay over water, land, and mountains, opening whatever last wellsprings of joy might still be untapped. The ship cut the deep-green crystal water, borne now on the strains of good music, echoing now with song. Words of greeting sounded and flags waved from the flowering towns right and left on the far-stretching shores. Guests were proudly shown the familiar countryside, the rich residences and hamlets. A lovely garland of ladies sat on a raised deck of the boat, among them Justine Glor in an attractive, simple but fashionable dress, her parasol in her hand. Jocundus, stepping up to her in his flag-bearer's costume, was surprised at her changed appearance, almost more elegant than before, and was nearly taken aback. They spoke together, but only a few words, as often happens when one knows there is a long summer's day ahead.

A bit later, when Jocundus came by again, she beckoned to him

and told him that her parents in Schwanau (which lay at the upper
end of the lake) had invited the entire company to their gardens
for the evening. The boat would lie at anchor there, and she hoped
he would stay and join them. This confidence, to which only a few
others were party, quickly gained him from bystanders a harvest
of hints and congratulations which he modestly rejected but gladly
heard.

It was soon announced that the boat would stop in Schwanau
toward evening and that all were invited to enjoy their final refreshments at the estate of the Glor family. The family had done
this in honor of their daughter, and to show that she had quite a
home of her own and really didn't need to sit at banquet tables
elsewhere but could give a good party herself. For the Glors, as
self-made people, were rather taken with their possessions.

To make sure that no part of such a promising evening would
be lost, the stops at other places along the shore where the boat
was expected were exactly timed and held to schedule. The boat,
with all its music and singing, crossed promptly over the sparkling
lake to Schwanau. Greeted by a salute of cannon, it docked at a
place where the tall trees of the Glor gardens were mirrored in the
water and where one could see their houses shining on the terraces
and hills beyond.

While the crowds of singers spread out beneath the trees Justine
disappeared into the house to greet members of her family, while
her father and brothers, on the other hand, devoted themselves to
the welcoming of their numerous guests. In arbors and verandas
there were places prepared for the ladies to sit, with appropriate
refreshments; in a freshly mowed meadow, under fruit trees, great
tables were set for the men. It was not long, however, before all
the women were out on the meadow, enticed by the carryings-on
of the crowd of young men, their jokes, pranks, and teasing, all
designed to attract attention. And there was enough to look and
laugh at, since the wit and skill of various individuals produced a
hundred pleasant inventions and fancies. The most naive of these
aroused the heartiest approval, for they were done in good form
and the prevailing mood was one of joy. Even a surprise somer-
sault found its patrons, and an unhappy virtuoso, who in all seriousness had tried—and failed—to blow a sentimental melody on
his hair-comb, rejoiced at the unalloyed merriment he occasioned

and never took off the wreath of straw that was placed on his head.

Only Jocundus felt somewhat isolated in this busy scene. For much too long a time he had had no glimpse of Justine and he felt he had something of a claim upon her, at least for this last day. But the matter was happily resolved, for there, suddenly, was the young lady, standing by his side, without his knowing where she had come from. She was introducing him to her father and her brothers, as the standard-bearer of the winning choir. The greeting he received from them was courteous and even friendly, but it was not without that cool, firm detachment which was incumbent on such wealthy businessmen in an encounter with a Seldwyler of little or no means—if, that is, he tried to pass for anything more than an attractive visitor to such festivities.

The affable young singer sensed this immediately and was somewhat embarrassed. So was Justine, who in compensation continued as his guide after the gentlemen left, and offered to show him the estate.

Two identically constructed villa-like houses of the most recent style, set in the shady park nearest to the lake, she identified as the residences of her two brothers, each of whom had already founded his own family, but without on that account separating from the larger clan. Then she climbed with him up paths and steps to the site, overlooking the lower treetops, of her parents' house, which was also where she lived. It was a building of somewhat older style but still a stately manor house, surrounded by farm structures and stalls. Farther on were long, tall commercial buildings, with innumerable windows, bordering on the dusty highway which led by the estate. On the other side of the road, however, on the rising slope of the hill, stretched fields, vineyards, and meadows with forests of fruit trees. High above, Justine pointed out the house of her grandparents, the ancestral seat of her family, shining out over the land in the light of the evening sun, a vast and impressive farmhouse of old traditional architecture with glistening rows of windows, white plaster walls, and bright-painted timber work on the roof and the barns, with stone entrance stairs and artistically fashioned iron balustrades. Here lived her grandfather and grandmother with their servants. Both were country folk in their eighties, working and guiding the work of others every day and hour, tough, vigorous, strict old people, living a life of utmost simplicity, always ready (as Justine described them to her companion) to pass judgment on younger persons. "Shall we just go on up and say hello? They wouldn't deign to come down from their heights and watch our amusements. And the view up there is splendid." This is what the girl said. But the old people made Jocundus feel apprehensive and he politely declined any further efforts by his guide, for in addition the whole vast establishment was more unsettling to him than pleasing.

So they went back again and joined their companions of the festival, who were getting progressively jollier. They stayed until the full moon rose in the east, facing the sunset, so that roses and silver were mingled in air and water, and the boat was readied for departure and soon boarded.

A crush ensued, since everyone wanted to shake hands with the hosts, who were standing on the shore, while the ship's crew urged people to hurry. So it came about that Jocundus Meyenthal was diverted from his plan to say good-bye to his beautiful Justine and compelled to follow the flow of the crowd, for she was not among those by the wayside. Father and brothers, to be sure, shook his hand, with a fleeting, "Pleased to have met you"; but one of them called him Mr. Thalmeyer, the second, Meienberg, and the third even called him Mr. Meierheim, and no one said, "We hope to see you again."

Nor did he catch sight of her as the boat moved out into the glow of evening, for she stood with the other women in the darkening shadows of the trees.

Jocundus lived at home with his mother, whose only son and Jocundi he was, and her one great hope. His father, having died early, had managed to use up only half of the outside resources represented by his wife's dowry, and she had been able to bring up her only son with the other half. There was still something left, even though he had made no decisive start at anything and had earned little. But he had also not squandered anything, because he was reasonably obedient to his mother, from whom he had his good looks and health, and accepted her guidance.

He had not yet fixed on any particular occupation. At first it had seemed that he showed an inclination to things technical, so he had for a time gone into an engineer's office. But then his mood shifted in favor of the merchant class, and he entered a business which, however, was soon dissolved as a result of bad luck, though he did not lose much himself. Now he was headed off in the direction of the military, training to be an instructional and staff officer. Since he had to spend the greater part of the year on the drill ground and also drew pay, he was in a position, for the time being, to afford a handsome existence, nor was he required to contribute any great amount from his own resources, given his modest style of life.

So now with the festival over he was mounted on his horse, in his handsome military uniform, his sabre at his side, and his mother gazed at him with pleasure, noticing as she did so that his smile had taken on a certain admixture of what was perhaps melancholy. He seemed to have the look of someone who has picked up a touch of homesickness or longing. She reflected on this and also made a few discreet inquiries, and when she heard of the adventure with the lady of the wreaths, and how the others had teased him about it, a light dawned, by the glow of which she immediately set to work fashioning a piece of good fortune, cut to measure, and well sewn.

Gathering more from his facial expressions than from the little Jocundi said that things were indeed as she imagined, but also that as a reticent person, aware of differing circumstances, he felt no great urge to take the initiative, she did not for the moment say anything. But as summer advanced she announced for the first time in her life that at her age she must start doing something for her health and that she felt the desire to visit a nice spa for a few weeks, provided that Jocundi was willing to join her, and economize afterward, to make up the cost. He quickly declared himself ready to do so; pleased at this, she set off on her trip, loaded down with all her finery.

She had given her son instructions about coming and bringing her home whenever she should inform him that it was time, but also told him to arrange it so that he might stay at the place for a few days.

Soon thereafter she appeared at a health resort of some reputation, splendidly located in a mountainous area. There she took her place, very well dressed but with a natural air, down at the end of the table at the head of which, presiding over everything, sat the wealthy and highly respected Mrs. Gertrud Glor of Schwanau, with her lovely daughter Justine. She was just as tall of build as Jocundi's mother but considerably stouter, with a wise and rather severe look, and she was more than happy to explain that not only in the circle of her family but also in the community, indeed in even wider reaches of the land, she was called a "Stauffacher," probably because her name was also Gertrud, like that of the housewifely pillar of sage advice and virtue in Schiller's famous play *William Tell*.

She did not mind having it pointed out to her that the meaning of the name was quite familiar, that it described the ideal Swiss woman, intelligent and strong, a star and jewel of the house and a solace to her country.

Mrs. Meyenthal heard all this in the first half a day she spent in the place, but she maintained her silence and reserve. Not until the end of the second day, when Gertrud could no longer bear the thought of a newcomer of the female sex whom she did not know, did Jocundi's mother let herself be intercepted and engaged in a polite but brief conversation. In the course of it, however, she found occasion to grasp the hand of the stout lady and tell her in heartfelt tones that she felt impelled to express her delight at having made the acquaintance of such a genuine Stauffacher type. One might expect at any moment, she said, to see her step out of a house of old Canton Schwyz, its walls painted with coats of arms and mottos, and place her consoling hand upon the shoulder of her worried husband.

While Mrs. Glor blushed in satisfaction, Mrs. Meyenthal, for her part, was startled. While she was speaking her eyes fell for a moment upon lovely Justine, the daughter, standing nearby; she saw her sweet smile, which was that of her own son, and mixed like his with the selfsame shadow of a gentle longing.

Mrs. Meyenthal was startled at this wondrous trick of Nature, this unmistakable expression of the will of Fate, indeed the whole obvious situation. Besides, when Justine saw Jocundi's mother and found her face pleasantly familiar, she did not doubt for a moment who stood before her and hearing her name and where she had come from she gazed for one brief, unguarded moment happily into her eyes with that very same smile.

When the sun set, it shone upon the figures of three tall women who, strangely moved by love for themselves or by love and concern for others, stood together on the hill top and then seemed to drift apart in apparent confusion.

Jocundi's mother, in any case, was the first to regain composure, writing that same evening to her son to say that he should visit her in about a week, so that they might return together after a few days' stay. With the ladies of Schwanau she acted henceforth as if she had no notion of the encounter on the singing trip. And Gertrud hardly remembered anything about it, having at the time not seen the handsome standard-bearer at all, since with her duties as hostess she had for the most part stayed inside one of the garden houses.

Only Justine felt oppressed and restless. She did not dare ask her new acquaintance about her son, yet she did not really care to think that he had had nothing to say at home about what happened at the festival and about her. Mrs. Meyenthal, however, wanted the next meeting of the young people to be quite unexpected and unanticipated and so held back, but without at the same time missing any opportunity to capture, by her wise demeanor, a piece or two in the game she was playing with the "Stauffacher." One could in fact call her the *"old* Stauffacher" inasmuch as the lovely, good Justine was in the fullest prime of her life and, for independent status as a "Stauffacher" on her own, lacked nothing but a husband concerned over the welfare of his country.

The fact that as yet no one of the sort had appeared was due to certain strange workings of fate, which so often cause precisely the finest young ladies to remain single even as they advance in years. This happens because of the seeming coldness for which their dignified calm is mistaken, because of the jealous protection their families bestow upon them, and above all because they defend the right they possess in greater measure than others, that of heeding only the voice of their hearts.

Over the mountains, at last, a lovely evening approached and with it arrived Jocundus. Since he came from one encampment and had to return to another, he was wearing his military uniform, with a bit of red and a bit of gold on his dark coat. After freshening up and after a long chat with his mother, he went walking with her, all unsuspecting, and she directed their steps to where she knew the two ladies of Schwanau would be, through the woods and onto a lonely point of projecting rock, with seats and railings, high over a deep valley shading now into blue.

The sudden happiness this unexpected reunion brought to the faces of the two young people, their identical expression and the special childlike smile which accompanied it—all so far exceeded what even mother Meyenthal had imagined and expected that any artifice, any playing of a part was quite out of the question. She was simply content to watch what developed, as quietly and discreetly as possible.

Gertrud, however, in her astonishment was unable to keep her eyes from the children; she cast her glance back and forth from one face to the other. The gentle waves of mutual and unforeseen agitation finally subsided, and there ensued a most pleasant chattering and babbling, in the course of which the moon rose, illuminating the brooks and ponds that had lain hidden in the depths of the valleys, so that they shone back up like golden stars.

Gertrud Glor felt a kind of blissful joy, as if she were reexperiencing some vanished youthful happiness of her own. She took Mama Meyenthal on her arm, as the children walked ahead side by side, on the path to the resort hotel, alternately silent or chatting. Mrs. Meyenthal, for her part, was touched and taken aback by the importance of the matter, equally in love with both children, and at the same time concerned as to how it would all end.

At evening table the happy mood was, if possible, heightened— as often happens when a fond hope, realized, animates everyone involved, whether as actor or confidant, inspiring them to let the secret bask safe and secure in the sunshine of shared happiness.

Gertrud Glor drank a bit of a nightcap with Jocundus, out of sheer pleasure in his fine, handsome bearing. When her daughter, on retiring, threw her arms around her neck and deposited a few weighty tears in the ruffles of the maternal collar, like interest payments in hard-won coin, Gertrud was not at all surprised, but stroked the girl's cheek in sympathetic understanding.

But barely had she slept off the nightcap, which took till only a bit after midnight, for it was a small one as befitting a "Stauffacher," when she awoke in concern and spent the rest of the night inspecting the damage. Nor did Justine sleep, for she was well aware that her mother was awake. However, she remained quiet as a mouse and was simply glad that, wasting no time with sleep, she could think about the whole business without interruption.

Her mother, on the other hand, saw ever more clearly in the growing light of dawn that there was no way a man from Seldwyla could be allowed to marry into the family—Seldwyla, where no one had ever yet amounted to anything, where no one had any property. She therefore remained awake, anxious but determined, waiting for morning so that she might nip in the bud this impending evil, an evil which seemed even greater to her when she considered the strict attitude of her menfolk on this point.

She was further confirmed in her resolve when at sunrise someone who was headed late for bed and obviously a bit drunk climbed up the stairs and was led past the doors of the various rooms by a servant of the hotel, not without stumbling over the shoes in front of the room belonging to the Glor ladies and knocking them aside with his feet. Mama's shoes flew down the entire length of the hall, one crosswise, the other heel-end first; her daughter's boots, on the other hand, took a scuffing blow from behind and traveled toward the stairs and down them, like two sailboats in a race.

"Aha," cried the wakeful lady within. "That's the Seldwyler for you!"

And her heart was lighter, thanks to this timely revelation.

Justine, however, was already sitting straight up in bed, listening in anxious suspense. Overhearing a couple of words from the passerby outside, however, she cried out in relief, indeed with wicked delight, "It isn't the captain! You can tell by the voice. It's our Rudolph."

The mother looked over in surprise at her daughter and said almost angrily, "Are you out of your mind? How could our Rudolph come here, and at this hour? And since when does he stumble around, drunk, in hotels? And isn't he away, on military duty, at this very moment?"

Nonetheless it was Gertrud's younger son, the apple of her eye, just going to bed, high up here on the mountain.

He had arrived in haste, late at night, accompanied by someone and apparently burdened by worry. He too was in uniform and had fled from his drill field, where he had been challenged by another officer, whom he had insulted. Since he was rather better informed on bookkeeping and brokerage lists than on duelling customs, and since he had a young wife and two little children, which made him feel very uneasy, he had arranged for a postponement and had hurried up here to ask his mother for advice on what to do.

In the dining room he had run into Jocundus who, feeling no desire for sleep, had stayed up for a while, alone, in pleasant reverie.

The common military career they were pursuing compelled the two gentlemen, as Lieutenant Glor sat down at the table for a second supper, to exchange greetings and start a conversation. Since he had recently heard of the respect Captain Meyenthal enjoyed in military circles, he was glad to renew his acquaintance and felt himself immediately and confidentially drawn to him. Carried away by the several glasses of wine he had quickly drunk in his agitation, he soon told Jocundus his troubles, and also told him how he had come here to seek the opinion of his mother, who was of course, and rightly, called a "real Stauffacher," being equipped to give advice on anything.

Jocundus, however, advised him not to do that if he didn't want to make the whole matter worse. He explained to him that, given the attitude which, like it or not, prevailed in such matters, he would risk making himself look impossible as an officer, if it should be noised about that in an affair involving a duel he had confided in his mother and was following her instructions.

Rudolph now sank into renewed anxiety, as (sensibly enough) he could see no reason at all that he should have to die and be taken from his wife and children, simply on account of such foolishness.

Jocundus now asked him about the precise nature of the quarrel and just what happened.

Rudolph had been playing a game of cards with three other soldiers. At the conclusion of a hand in which his partner had not played his cards as Rudolph wished, and while the new hand was being dealt, they took the occasion to review the course of play, conjugating after the fashion of the day, "So I play this, and you play that; now he's got to play this way and not that way, and I'll stick with him and play that, then you'll play that again. That's clear enough, if we want to win."

"No, that's not clear," Rudolph's partner had countered, "first I top his trump and then play that."

"If you did you'd be playing like a jackass," Rudolph had cried, whereupon the whole party had immediately disbanded, with the challenge following early the next day, in so ceremonious and so uncompromising a form as to leave the good young fellow with no opportunity to explain himself to anyone's satisfaction.

When Jocundus, already smiling over the story, also discovered the name of the challenger, he said, "Oh, him. Well, for heaven's sake, he has to fire off another challenge every year to keep his honor from getting moldy. But *yours,* Lieutenant, requires of course that you don't wager your life on this incident but do by the same token explain to your opponent that he would *not* have been playing like a jackass, but in whatever other capacity he might prefer. In any event you may draw from all this the conclusion that a person in uniform ought to use language rather precisely, even in moments of relaxation. However, it definitely mustn't seem as if your explanation were the result of a conversation with your mother, assuming, as I have already said, that you don't want to create even worse consequences. If it would be of service to you, I will volunteer as your adviser and assistant and will write the gentleman, right now, a couple of lines to say that you have spoken to me and have delivered to me, at my advice, a satisfactory explanation. Tomorrow morning the letter will go out and the matter will be resolved to everyone's satisfaction, that I can promise you!"

A great weight had now fallen from the heart of the young military man. In order to demonstrate his gratitude and at the same time to compensate himself for the anxieties he had endured, he had with some forcefulness ordered a lot to drink and detained his helpful friend until the break of dawn. The latter had been glad to sit with him and had willingly listened to the happy chatter of the young man, who was Justine's brother. The wine bubbled away harmlessly in the depths of his warm kindness, and he went off to his bed quietly, with his senses in order, while the other fellow was so noisily seeking his.

Consequently, while the "Stauffacher" had thought to triumph over this mischief with the rising of the sun, things had only got worse for her. For not only was it her own seed that had sprouted up here, slightly tipsy, but out of it had developed a good stalwart friendship and alliance with her enemy.

Through the half-open door Justine had managed to summon a maid and had learned from her that in fact her brother had arrived and had spent the whole night in good company, with the captain. She had then slipped back into bed and at last fell asleep, content.

Jocundus also slept rather late, and Rudolph was not to be roused until well into the forenoon, when his mother forced her way into his room and called him to account. Since he was in a position to regard his affair of honor as settled, he confided in his mother after all and told her how the good words and deeds of the captain from Seldwyla had solved the problem and, one might say, saved his life. For he could simply not picture himself being able to fire a real pistol shot at a healthy human being, yet he would have had to hold still for this other person. And in his excited and loquacious condition he extolled the wisdom and bravery of the Seldwyler so mightily that in a confusion of shock and vexation she hurried back to her room and for the time being locked herself in.

Furthermore, she was jealous of her fame as a "Stauffacher" and of her respect and rights as a mother, and also quite exasperated, from wondering how her advice could be worse for her son than that of a young Seldwyler. In no time she stormed back out of her hiding-place, planning to give the gratuitous counselor a dressing down and at the same time stir up some useful dissension with him, which would serve to disrupt the friendship. However, she found all three of them sitting together under an arbor, in joy and harmony, each one provided with a late breakfast of his own invention, and all engaged in trading food with one another. Scarcely had she caught sight of the young couple, side by side, lovely and happy once again, when all her resolve was forgotten and she joined in immediately with consultation and planning for a fine picnic that afternoon. She was after all a happy woman, like all "Stauffachers," as long as there didn't happen to be any storm clouds over their menfolk, for them to disperse.

Later during the day, to be sure, she demanded an accounting from Jocundus. As she listened to him explain in sensible, courteous words the affair of the duel, she could see that he was right and had done her son a great favor, which filled her with a sense of gratitude and trust.

She therefore went that very day to Jocundi's mother and put her as well to the test, pumping her with all manner of maxims and trying to nail her down on questions involving the two children.

Mrs. Meyenthal immediately caught the thread of her talk and ran it skillfully onto a little spool, which she handed back to her opponent in spades, saying she was quite familiar with the bad side of Seldwyla. But, she said, it all depended on circumstances. She too had married there from outside and was considered a good catch. And things had not gone badly, apart from the early demise of her husband, so that she felt her son, thank Heaven, had turned out well and was open to the promptings of a good and honorable life—with which Mrs. Glor agreed.

This concluded the decisive stage of secret negotiations, and what the voices of mighty Nature wished was under way. The difficulties still lodging in the minds of the rest of the Schwanau family were overcome, quietly and decorously, and in a few months the announcement was made of the engagement of Jocundus and Justine.

This was everywhere regarded as such a lovely and fitting occurrence that no dissenting voice was heard. The engaged couple did not receive a single anonymous note of abuse or warning, such as often seems to occur when great envy is aroused. The clearest morning sky smiled upon their engagement and the wedding itself became a festival of sunlight and sound, with flags and singing, all of which seemed to those present like an old sweet song.

Chapter 2

The young couple went to live in the family's home in Seldwyla. It was a fairly large house, with high-ceilinged rooms and halls, built during the last century by a resident of the city who had gone abroad and got rich, and had then decided to make a splendid addition to his property in his home town. But before it was furnished and readied for living the man had lost his entire fortune in the years of revolution and war which followed, so that instead of moving into his house he had gone away again to see whether he couldn't discover a new windfall where he had found the first one. The house, however, had since passed from hand to hand, following the same pattern: whichever Seldwyler felt the greatest desire and financial capability for a baronial existence took it over and occupied it for a time, without its ever being completely finished inside.

The Meyenthals had by now owned it longer than anyone else. In the course of time they had footed the bill for wallpaper here, a paint job there. Before the wedding Jocundus had had the outside of the house touched up and the garden put in good order, and now that Justine had moved in with her vast dowry of personal possessions, all beautifully distributed and set in place throughout the stately rooms, the fortunes of the house seemed finally to be more or less permanently established—or, in this case, sewed up. The initiator of it all, namely Mother Meyenthal, resided in her section of the house, proud and content, especially as she saw that the beautiful Justine had a clear, firm sense of property and its maintenance, and that Jocundus showed no signs, in reference now to his young wife, of abandoning his good-natured tractability.

Upon his marriage he had, by agreement, abandoned the military life as a career, because of the continual absences it entailed. To assure in its place an honorable source of income and a regular occupation he had set up a trading company based on the abundance of wood in the municipality and surrounding areas. The great forest commons created by the land apportionment of Alemannic times had later been augmented by the timberland of the castle and cloister along whose walls the town was built.

The town had always spared this source of its well-being, preserving it out of civic pride, just as it preserved in the cellars of its city hall a rich store of drinking vessels and old wine. However, through some opening or other, temptation and the thirst for gain had finally slipped in, and Death passed unseen through the wide corridors of the forest and crept along the edge of it, tapping with its bony fingers on the smooth tree trunks. So when Jocundus appeared at this very time to buy up and export lumber and firewood, his business immediately flourished, for the Seldwylers preferred the mediation of their honest, familiar fellow citizen to the aggressiveness of the outside dealers through whom the evil had first crept in.

Now the hundred-year-old stands of tall timber began to fall, in the process giving hailstorms an open line of access to vineyards and meadows. But the trees had once been young and low to the ground, perhaps several times, and they could mature and grow back up again. Soon, however, the ax came to the younger forests too, ever more attractive uses were found for the money flowing in, and the mountainside grew in proportion ever barer. Now Jocundus began to feel a chill deep inside him; since his youth he had been a friend and lover of the forest. Even as he was earning substantial profits from his business, he began to be more and more ashamed of it. He seemed in his own eyes an enemy and destroyer of all green beauty and pleasure. He became disillusioned and often sad. It almost seemed to his wife that his happy smile, which was like a twin of her own smile, had become increasingly rare, so in her concern she had asked him about it and he confided in her. It was her opinion, however, that things would take their course with or without her husband. Indeed they would probably just get worse, and her only aim was to see that he became prosperous and independent on his own, so that she might be proud of him in this regard as well as others. She did not, therefore, encourage her husband in his disillusionment but rather urged him to persist, and so he carried on.

At the time a piece of medium growth forest was being cut on a mountain slope which ran along at a steep, sharp angle and was called the Wolfhartsgeeren. From its midst there had always towered a massive leafy dome, an oak tree probably a thousand years old, called the Wolfhartsgeeren Oak. In older records it bore, in its capacity as a landmark and symbol, other names which pointed to the fact that its youthful crown had once been stirred by the early morning breezes of Germanic times. Now that the forest about it was felled—for they saved the mighty tree for special sale—the oak constituted a monument the like of which no earthly prince or people could have erected or even transplanted, with all their treasure. The lower trunk measured a good ten feet in diameter and its horizontally spreading limbs, which at a great distance seemed like delicate twigs sketched upon the sky, were at closer view themselves the equal of mighty trees. Miles away one could spot this beautiful, monumental tree, and many people came by to see it close at hand.

Now, as they all waited to find out which purchaser would offer the highest price for it, Jocundus took pity on the tree' and tried to save it. He advanced the argument that it would be appropriate for the community to preserve as national treasures such witnesses to the past, and to continue at public expense their right to air and dew and a plot of ground; and that the relatively limited proceeds from the sale could not be compared with the irreplaceable inner worth of such a jewel. But he gained no hearing. It was precisely the health of the old giant that was to cost it its life, because, so it was said, this was the right time to realize the highest return. Once the trunk became diseased, its value would fall significantly. Jocundus then appealed to the government, recommending as a general principle the preservation of individual trees of great beauty wherever they were to be found. The response was that the state had forest areas worth millions and could augment those as it saw fit, but it had no money and no authority whatever to buy a harvestable tree on town property and let it stand.

He could see that people were not generally receptive to his idea, that he was just showing himself up as a poor businessman and secretly becoming an object of amusement. So he bought the oak and the land it stood on, neatened up the grounds, and put a bench under the tree, where there was a lovely view into the distance. And people praised him for what he had done and took pleasure in the view. But from that moment people also tried to use him and to outwit him, as if he were a great lord who could be taken advantage of at will.

Distressed by the butchery of the forests, Jocundus changed businesses, gradually, but as quickly as possible, giving up the timber business and instead deciding to become a dealer in those treasures which come from the heart of the earth and take the place of wood. He built warehouses for hard and soft coal, imported clay and iron pipe to displace wooden waterways, also brick for lighter structures which were otherwise made with wood, and cement for all kinds of containers. He talked a rich farmer into having an enormous, solid, cool fermenting vat built for him out of concrete. When this turned out well he pictured in his mind the replacement of wooden barrels, in cellars everywhere, by such storage containers, resembling the great wine jars of antiquity that rested in the earth, and sparing the good oak lumber. He also bought quantities of worn-out railway track, iron rails which in hundreds of cases can take the place of wooden beams.

Of course the export of timber went on without him, indeed right past him, into the all-consuming cities. But he was now at peace with his conscience, that silent companion in whose absence he never felt happy as a businessman. Nor would his new undertakings in themselves have failed to show a profit, had not his change of occupation occasioned certain disruptions, and had not his business friends changed their attitude and showed their true faces, after he gave the oak tree board and room, like a pensioner.

Jocundus invariably told the truth and so believed everything others said to him. He always revealed from the start his entire opinion, what he could do, and what he could be counted on for. He implicitly accepted, as to the terms of purchase or sale and the condition of merchandise, whatever he was told by the other party, who for his part operated at first with the assumption that Jocundus would take pains to look more closely into the matter and then, when he didn't, with the immediate, barefaced intent to deceive. Repeated experience was of no help. Equally fruitless were all admonitions by his womenfolk not to be so gullible. The very next time he had a chance to believe something, he did, either because he couldn't help it or because he felt it repugnant and beneath contempt to spend a long time arguing and haggling. Besides, he was anything but a clever financier able to manipulate money and credit, and so it transpired that one day his resources were exhausted and the end had come. This happened suddenly, because he had never kited his debts, paying old ones by incurring new ones, nor engaged in any fictitious deals.

He wondered whether he should confide first in his mother or in his wife, or in both at the same time, to inform them that their prosperity was over and they must make a completely fresh start, of what sort and where he didn't know. He decided to tell his wife. Standing alone with her in his office, he began, sad at heart, to tell her about his situation, but when he did so she came up to him and stroked his anxious brow with her hand, interrupting him with the question: Had he kept his books accurately and fully? When he answered in the affirmative, she smiled at him so beautifully that it lifted his spirits. She told him that if that was the case she already knew how matters stood, for she had been curious and recently, in his absence, had studied his—or rather their joint—financial situation.

One quiet Sunday, when he was going away on a trip, he had left his keys on her work table as usual, and she had in fact taken them and locked herself in his accounting room, for she was aware that he was concealing some worry. There, being quite familiar with such things, she had investigated his books and papers. All was clear and transparent, every figure in place. She saw that things could not go on much longer, but that there was no danger of ending in disgrace, so long as a bottom line was drawn in time. Certain, given his candor, that his confession would not be long postponed, she had already acted and had taken her parents into her confidence. In the proud spirit of these wealthy people such an eventuality had been foreseen, even as they assented to the marriage, and it had been determined that if, as was likely, things did not work out in Seldwyla, the young people should come to Schwanau. So Justine had not been much surprised by her discovery, rather she felt a secret pleasure that she could bring her dear, sweet, good husband to her parental home and there wrap him solicitously in a cocoon of silk, like a fragile glass figurine.

So she told him of these plans and made it plain to him that all they had to do was to arrange a quiet and prompt liquidation of their business in Seldwyla and then move to Schwanau, where surely Jocundus could make himself useful. He paled and said, "That would be the end of my freedom and my self-respect. I'd rather chop wood."

"Well, then I can stay too," replied Justine. "And I can help you saw, and when we're standing there by the road and it's raining and the two of us are pulling the saw back and forth, we'll be quarreling with one another, and people will stop, just the way we saw it happen in the big city, on our wedding trip."

She sat down and continued, "Do you remember what a strange impression that made on us? It rained, it rained incessantly, the wood was wet, the saw was wet, and the man and his wife were soaked, and they pulled the saw back and forth endlessly and quarreled bitterly with harsh words. Do you know why? They were fighting about poverty, about misery, about worry, and they weren't the least bit ashamed that people were listening to them—"

"Be quiet," cried Jocundus, "how can you twist what I said and take unfair advantage of it, when you know how it's meant?"

"It could also mean what I said, too," answered Justine. "Come," she went on, putting her arm around his shoulder, "everyone loves you, everyone will help you. You'll be no less a man, once you've got your feet on solid, sensible ground. But we'll never prosper here."

Jocundus broke off the conversation, to collect himself. He was confused and disturbed, not having been so disconsolate, so discouraged in his view of things as his wife was, and he was hurt. He went to his mother, but she began to cry the moment she was informed of the situation. She felt that everything would be lost if her son did not stick by his wife and her people, and she implored him not to ruin his own and his family's happiness.

His good mother had been able to hold poverty at bay and now, she thought, to escape it forever, by arranging such a wise marriage for her son, and she feared poverty as she would fear a burnished sword.

Justine on the other hand hated and despised poverty as something in itself evil and despicable—except in the case of poor strangers, to whom one can conveniently do favors. Indeed she practiced an eager and well-ordered charity, went to the humble cottages of the poor and sought them out. But when poverty attempted to penetrate the closer circles of her blood relatives or her friends, she reacted with a sharp revulsion, as she would to the plague, and literally fled from it. So it was of no help that Jocundus went to her once again and suggested that she might still make some attempt to bear with him for a time the uncertainty of his fate, since she was after all secure in her parental refuge and her rich inheritance. Not for one moment was she willing to see him, or herself, exposed to need and humiliation. So when her father came and in a friendly way talked to him as he would talk of a course of action that was obvious, easily arranged, and in everyone's best interest, he had to yield.

Jocundi's workers were paid off and dismissed, and the property sold and all obligations were terminated, because his mother, though she was part owner, did not want to stay in Seldwyla alone. Now Jocundus had not a penny in hand for the immediate moment, which gave him a most curious feeling. Justine, however, was in good spirits and full of cheer as she managed the packing of their belongings and the arrangements for moving. At one time she was in Schwanau to set up their quarters, at another she was back in Seldwyla to see to things here. She was well provided with funds and in her joy and eagerness forgot even to think whether Jocundus might need money or have any in hand.

He began to feel like a person facing a journey, with no travel money, into some distant land, among total strangers, whose language he did not understand. He looked about anxiously to see where he might at least lay his hands on some pocket money, just in case. The great oak had been forgotten, the tree he had saved and preserved; with a melancholy smile he now sold the old giant after all, along with the ground on which it stood, and received a few thousand francs, which he carefully put aside.

The buyer of the tree immediately hired a dozen men who freed and undercut its roots, working at it for a good week. When things had progressed to the point where the tree could be dropped, all Seldwyla poured out to the hillside, to watch the fall, and thousands of people were camped round about, well provided with food and drink.

Strong ropes were fastened in its crown and handed over to long rows of men, who at command began to pull. The oak tottered, but only a little, and for hours the mighty roots had to be further loosened and sawed. All the while the people ate and drank and made a day of it, but not without tense expectation and feelings of excitement.

Finally the site was again cleared far and wide, the ropes again drawn taut, and after a mighty swaying which lasted minutes, in a veritable deathly silence the oak crashed down upon its face, its branches broken, the white wood staring out. After the first general outcry it was only an instant before people were swarming about the enormous trunk. Hundreds climbed up on it and into the green limbs of the crown, which lay in the dust. Others crawled about in the hole where the tree had stood and searched through the dirt. But all they found was a little piece of thick poured glass from Roman times, which because of its age shone like mother of pearl, and the rust-eaten tip of an arrow.

On a distant hill over which Jocundus and his people were slowly passing, farm workers suddenly cried out, pointing to the horizon, "Look how the old Wolfhartsgeeren Oak is swaying! Is there a storm over there?" Because of course they could not see the people who were pulling at it. Jocundus also looked over and saw that the tree was no longer there; in its place was only empty sky. Then a feeling pierced his heart as if he alone were at fault and must bear within himself the conscience of his land.

The Seldwylers spent the evening rather more in sadness than in joy, for the tree and Jocundi were no longer there.

At the beginning of his stay in Schwanau Jocundus spent most of his time on the mountain, with the same grandparents whose seemingly brusque, unfriendly manner and restless energy had once made him almost afraid of them. But in the course of time he found himself on a good footing with them and even became a favorite of the old people. It often happens that such country folk, in the security of their traditional lives, like to have about them an element of the leisurely, someone unlike them, to make them of good cheer. They saw in the young man something alien and impractical but also lovable, presumably ill-starred, and therefore deserving of sympathy and interest. This was the way it appeared to the "Ehgaumers," as people still called them, from the long forgotten office of marriage adjudicator (or "Ehegaumer"), which the grandfather had occupied half a century ago and which represented a sort of domestic court or office of public morality. The title was no older than the cut of the white cap and the large white shawl that adorned the "Ehegaumer's" wife. All of this stemmed from the time when Goethe, on a visit to the region, wrote of the place that it gave a charming, ideal picture of the finest and highest degree of cultivation: buildings set far apart, with vineyards, fields, gardens, orchards stretched out between them, etc. Further: What one hears agricultural economists wishing for, namely the highest level of cultivation together with a certain modest prosperity, this (he wrote) one could see here before one's very eyes.

That state of affairs had remained unchanged, here on this

mountain estate, right down to the house itself, the walnut furnishings in the good room, and the dishes in the cupboards. The modern age, with its altered countenance and its more elaborate lifestyle, had taken its stand down by the lakeshore. Jocundus enjoyed the clean air on the heights and helped with the work of the old people and their servants so devotedly that he was soon well informed about everything and became for these patriarchs a steward they had no wish to dismiss.

Justine rejoiced in the esteem her husband had gained from her grandparents and often climbed happily up the mountain to bring him down in the evening. Or she enjoyed staying and watching a storm at haying time, when its onset compelled the young people to stay up here for the night. Then she would take off her fashionable blouse, put on one of her grandmother's white shawls with the tips tied behind her and would cook the brown flour soup, bake the fragrant egg pancakes, or fry the savory cervelas sausage which she had taken it upon herself to steal from the larder for supper. When her lovely face glowed with such happiness, and especially when she took charge of the shining pewter mugs and the light clear wine, the old people swore that now at last she really looked like a true old countrywoman. And then there was the occasional game of masquerade, as the grandmother brought out her old-fashioned garnet jewelry and the Sunday caps and silk jackets she had worn in the flower of her youth, sixty years ago. She would dress her granddaughter in these things, to the delight of everyone there. But instead of looking in the mirror, Justine would then look, with her blissful smile, into the face of Jocundus, who gazed in surprise at this apparition that shone upon him as if from a faraway time.

On Sundays too, he generally went up on the mountain, since he felt more comfortable there than amid the sounds of loud but monotonous sociability produced by the talkative people and their gatherings down below.

Sundays and holidays on the mountain the Bible was always open on the table so that the "Ehgaumer's" wife could comfortably read in it from time to time, when it occurred to her, just as one keeps at hand a jug of wine, a dish with cherries or other tidbits as refreshment for such times of leisure.

When she placed her rosemary sprig and her glasses on the

book, tired of reading, Jocundus would often sit down behind the Bible and read in it. Otherwise the book was rarely at his disposal, as happens to people when there are newer and more necessary things one is always supposed to read, or when one assumes one has acquired quite enough of those old things during one's years of compulsory schooling. He contemplated the sultry, stormy atmosphere of the Old Testament and the passionate figures in it. He discovered the Hamlet-like scene in the Gospel of John, where Jesus reflectively writes something on the floor with his finger before he says, whoever is without sin should cast the first stone at the woman taken in adultery, where he writes again, and, looking up, finds that all the accusers have left and the woman is standing in solitude before him in the now silent temple.

The grandmother welcomed this sight, for she was of the old and orthodox faith, and convinced that Bible reading was automatically beneficial for anyone. Justine, in order to gloss over the unchurchly ways of Jocundus, pretended to the old people that he was a philosopher; for she herself was a devotee of the vague popular religion of the time, and her zeal was in direct proportion to the vagueness of her ideas.

Once, as he sat reading, the old woman affectionately took her seat beside him. The neatly folded lace wings of her cap grazed his cheek, and she stroked his hand, saying, "Well, philosopher, I still believe you have a bit of the fear of God in you."

Jocundus was surprised by the remark and thought it over. It seemed to him that he might well try to answer her. But should he confide in the old woman about something which, if he recollected rightly, his own wife had never inquired into? But for that matter, how could his wife inquire into something she knew nothing about? She did have a warm feeling for religion, but as far as the divine was concerned she was far too curious and indiscreet and she also had far too great a feeling of personal confidence to possess what, in the stricter sense, we mean by the fear of God. The idea that serious questions had been raised concerning the dear Lord himself was something she had already heard from the favorite pulpit orators of the day, whose lectures she travelled around to hear. Toward Christ, that fairest and most perfect of men (as these preachers called Him), she cherished feelings more on the order of sisterly regard or inspired friendship. She could have embroidered for Him the loveliest sofa pillow and the most splendid slippers for the sweet comfort of His head and His feet. Indeed, once on her travels she had been touched by profound emotion at the sight of that famous painting by Correggio which represents, with magic effect, the countenance of Christ on the kerchief of Veronica. Absorbed by the sight of this fixed and dreamlike expression of intense suffering, she had sighed aloud. Then, in search of shared compassion, she had smiled at her husband standing beside her, and to this day the moment was one of her dearest memories. However, all this was not the same as the fear of God.

When, however, the old woman insisted on an answer, Jocundus said, weighing his words: "I believe that as far as the concept itself is concerned I do have something like the fear of God, in that I am incapable of irreverence in speaking of fate or life. I don't believe I have any right to ask that things go well for me, everywhere and as a matter of course. Rather, I am afraid that here and there things may come out badly, and if they do I still hope that they may take a turn for the better. At the same time, in all I do and in all I think, unseen by others and unknown to them, I am conscious of the whole of the world. I have the feeling that, when all is said and done, everyone knows about everything, and that no man can lay claim to real secrecy of thought and action or to the privilege of silence for his follies and errors. That is born into some of us and not into others, quite apart from any teachings of religion. Yes, the greatest religious zealots and fanatics usually have no fear of God, otherwise they wouldn't live and act the way they do.

"How this business of everyone knowing about everything is possible, and how it is constituted, I don't know. I believe, however, that it has to do with a mighty republic of the universe, living according to one single, eternal law, where in the end everything is known in common. The brief insights we have today give us more than ever before an inkling of this possibility, because never have we had such tangible evidence of the inner truth of those words that are written in this book: 'In my Father's house are many mansions.' "

"Amen," said the old woman, who had been listening attentively. "What you're preaching there amounts to something after all; it's certainly better than nothing. Just keep reading in my Bible, and you'll find a president for your republic yet."

"It may be," Jocundus replied with a smile, "that occasionally someone like that is chosen by vote, and so the Lord God is a kind of elective monarch."

The old woman smiled at this thought, saying, "A regular, honorable World Governor, the way they have Land Governors over there!" As she spoke she pointed out through the open window toward the mountains, where in the old rural republics the highest officers of government were given that name.

She laughed more and more at the idea, for she loved, in her advanced years, to think constantly of God and eternity. Thus she welcomed an innocent play on God's name, as it served to keep Him close at hand.

While the two of them were laughing and enjoying their not quite orthodox conversation on religion, Justine looked in through the carnations in front of the window. Even with the carnations to compete with, her face glowed, because she had climbed all the way up the mountain to get her husband. But her face almost outdid the red of the carnations when her grandmother cried cheerily: "Come in quickly, child! I have news for you! Your husband here has more than a little fear of God in him; he just confessed to me!"

A strange jealousy seized her instantly, to think that her grandmother should know more about Jocundi's thoughts than she did, his wife. She said, "Probably that's why he doesn't ever do me the honor of going to church with me!"

"Be quiet," said Jocundus. "Don't argue! After all, we don't argue about the pure water we all drink, when and where we choose."

Justine picked up what he had said as she walked arm in arm with her husband along the twilit ridge, to descend by a more remote path.

"We won't argue about the water we drink. But we must see to it that we don't argue about the bread we eat, either between us or with others," she said, and she told him how she and her family wished that he would become involved in a substantial way, by accepting a position in the great industrial and commercial undertakings of the family. His rural preoccupation with the old people on the mountain was not in the long run fitting for him and would lead to nothing, while down there everyone was prepared to introduce him into the business and to share honorably with him in the labor and the profit.

Jocundus sensed clearly the plan behind all of this: No one was wanted in the family if he were not able and willing to get rich. Since basically he could ask for no better plan, he assented without further hesitation, though with secret mistrust of himself. He told Justine that he would begin the very next morning, since it was Monday, and try to earn a full week's pay.

Early the next day he was introduced to the offices and working areas of the firm, so that he might become acquainted with and master the various branches of the business. The House of Glor had for more than thirty years been engaged in silk manufacture, a business which had with the passing years grown to impressive scope. In a hundred rural dwellings on the sunny mountain slopes, behind bright windows, stood the looms of the girls and younger women of the local population, who with light and busy hands wove the shining pieces of material, and thus laid the foundation for widespread, if modest, prosperity. On every path, sturdy persons hurried along with loom-beams on their shoulders, delivering the finished material and getting the silk for a new piece. In great open rooms there were also machines set up, at which heavier, richer materials were produced and male workers employed.

The purchase of the raw silk, the preparation of it through its various stages, the supervision and evaluation of the work, the sale of accumulated stock, the assessment of the general market and the calculation of the right moment for every transaction, and finally the most advantageous use of incoming funds—all of this required unceasing, fast-moving activity and a whole series of interconnected skills.

Negotiations with a steady stream of jobbers offering silk thread from various parts of the world, or with the men who handled the export of finished fabric to other parts of the world and in so doing sought to make their own fortunes, also demanded constant adroitness and quick decision making. The daily growth of competition required meticulous calculation of available resources and at the same time extremely careful inspection, for quality and purity, of the goods being delivered. The same employees that did this work and had to be so strictly watched were eagerly sought after in other quarters and lured away when incentive and enterprise were running high. If, on the other hand, things were slowing down the same people had to be kept on, at some sacrifice, for better days ahead.

Again, changes in taste and demand in every region under the sun had to be followed attentively. Here, what was offered had to be attractive silk dresses of durable weave, for women of the middle class in established societies. There, it was a matter of cheap fancy dresses for the women of Californian or Australian adventurers, to adorn them for a few gala days, afterwards to be cast aside. Depending on the destination of their goods, they had to enlist the skills of the great dye works and battle with them to get the most beautiful, lasting colors for the expert eye of the real housewife, or the illusion of quality for the colorful beauties of the Farthest West.

Jocundus was now introduced into this whirlpool of activity, with the idea that he would learn to swim; and he did not pass the test well. In the beginning, with separate, less complicated aspects of management, things went well enough, because he worked attentively and carefully. But soon there were complaints about slowness, since his youthful flexibility and quickness of mind were things of the past, and the word was that he couldn't seem to get started. Now, in order forcibly to teach him to swim, he was pitched headlong into the maelstrom, where he swirled around with forced good cheer, or rather with a certain anxiety, until he lost his bearings. Workers cheated him on the silk he entrusted to them, by making the weave too light and loose and then lying to him about the cause. Others were able to talk him out of business secrets and then, on their own, engage in damaging competition. Against all his previous resolutions he again and again believed implicitly what jobbers and middlemen told him, and accepted their offers when other buyers were just halfway beginning to listen and talk. He actually seemed to work himself deeper into this pattern of clumsiness, beyond anything implicit in his personality. A kind of unnatural stupidity came over his spirit and clouded his thoughts the minute business matters were involved. Before half a year passed he had, like a marten in hiding, caused noticeable damage in the form of a deficit, which was soon tracked to its source.

When Justine noticed that strangers as well as employees no longer considered her husband a shining light and treated him with sympathetic smiles, she wept secretly, in distress and agitation. She fell into a state of oppressive anxiety, for fear that she too might begin to regard him as an unfortunate and limited person. What her father and her brothers said, whenever they discussed the matter in confidence, did nothing to lift her spirits or her self-esteem. She could not even be comforted by the consoling words of the "old Stauffacher," who allowed that a firm like theirs could afford to take along one non-paying passenger if he were otherwise well behaved.

If, however, she went to Jocundi's mother with her questions and complaints, the latter would weep with her and beg her to be patient, for Jocundus was certainly no dumbbell, he would sooner or later prove himself, and so forth.

Jocundus had no idea of all the talk that went on around him, yet he felt by no means comfortable about the situation. Everyone was convinced that it could not go on like this for long, that in any event the matter would soon be cleared up, so no one wanted to be the first to talk with him or the first to hurt him. All about him there settled a kind of light haze, which seemed to veil the eyes of people around him and muffle the sound of their voices.

One day, however, he again bought a supply of raw silk at a price which was the going one the day before but had since fallen. He was now told it would be better if he gave up this part of the business, and the suggestion was repeated a few days later in another context. At this he was taken aback and gave up completely. But no one asked him the reason for the time off he was taking, everyone went his way as if nothing had happened, and only then did Jocundus see the situation he was in and realize his complete isolation.

On the same day his realization was further confirmed.

Justine had been invited for the evening to the parsonage, where the pastor was going to deliver a disquisition on the contemporary revival and renewal of the church through the arts, a topic which greatly appealed to her and, on a small local scale, already occupied her attention. Jocundus himself was cool to the idea and preferred to spend as little time as possible within range of the pastor's voice. But since it was a dark fall day he had promised to come and pick up his wife.

The pastor stood in the very front line of those who fought for the church as it was to be reformed for the religious community of the future. Throughout his early years his preaching had been both excellent and generally liberal, so that the flocks he tended were much edified, even if not completely clear as to precisely what ground they stood on. Under the protection of the temporal powers and following the example of established leaders, the younger generation had struggled for and won a freer view of the world as seen from the pulpit, as well as greater freedom of movement in life. Strictly orthodox forces had been pushed imperceptibly over to a position where they were simply defending their existence, although all of this did not have much noticeable effect on the outward form of worship. The old songs, the old forms of prayer, the old Bible texts still prevailed, and only on certain occasions was the super-human treated as human. For the rest, Christ remained the Lord and Savior, and there was no tampering with the unity and personal quality of universal order or with the immortality of the soul. Theology still passed for a closed science, even where those who were its pillars had long since begun to hold quietly with all manner of skeptical views, letting the dear Lord fare for himself, and even contemplating with secret sighs the possible finiteness of their own personal identities.

At the same time the early Enlighteners and Rationalists were looked down upon with condescension, although with their dry courage they had paved the way for the present day. And those Philistines who sought explanations or understanding in miracles were the object of smug amusement, although these same new believers always made an exception for this or that miracle, allowing it to happen half naturally, half supernaturally.

But this happy time, when things went so comfortably and famously for anyone who was skillful of speech and not lacking in boldness, began to change like everything else in the world.

The very force and growing spread of the liberal way of thinking nourished a desire for firmer community and stricter forms, and generated a wish for power, all of which brought with it a clearer statement of what people professed and meant.

This, however, was precisely the time when physicists were making a series of remarkable observations and discoveries, and people were giving in to the tendency to confuse seeing with comprehending, and to draw natural conclusions from the partial phenomenon to the whole—more often than not, however, failing to do so where it was most necessary.

New philosophies, which hung their slogans like old hats from one peg to another, filled the air with bold and wicked phrases, and there arose a great compulsion for repeating the opinions and sayings of others.

Those among the priesthood who were calmer and more restrained saw no need to get upset over a modestly greater or lesser degree of clarity. They wisely took their peaceful stand on ground already gained, militant only against the old enemies and oppressors. Others, however, were determined at any cost to avoid the appearance of being left behind on any issue, of not knowing everything, or of not being at the forefront of things. So it was that they armed themselves with heavy weapons and got out on the farthest limbs of the tree, from which they would, in due time, fall down with a great clatter.

The pastor of Schwanau had joined this flock because it was impossible for him to lead a life contrary to the spirit and culture of the times as he understood them.

So he taught the necessity of conceding to science that a personal ruler of the universe did not exist, and that there could no longer be a theology about such things. But where science left off, faith began, he said, and so did the sense of the inexplicable, the indefinable, which alone could fill out the spirit. This very filling out was religion, which now as before required administering, and the administration of this area was what we now call theology, clergy, and church. The divine word was accordingly immortal and sacred and the administering of it sacred and solemn. Now as before the tabernacle was lifted up for all those to gather around who would not perish from desperate emptiness of heart. Yes, the mysterious insides of the tabernacle needed more than ever the consecrating, incense-burning priest, as ruler and guide of the helpless herd. No one could approach the tabernacle from behind, rather one must turn in trust to the custodian thereof. In return, those of the priesthood must not hold themselves aloof from any aspect of human nature, which they were still in the best position to understand. They were always available to help and assist people, and to see that the first cut was made at the right end of the sausage. All they asked in exchange was strict respect for the tabernacle of the Unknown and general attentiveness to the proclaiming and description thereof.

In saying this the pastor also expressed in moving terms his distress at lack of candor in the pulpit, not calling things by their right name, not daring to serve pure wine to the people, as if they couldn't tolerate it. He described this lack of candor, and the art of obscuring the issue, so aptly that his parish audience cried out in renewed transport: "How beautifully, how truly and profoundly he's said it again!"

At other times, however, he would challenge the gathering to cast out all dross and purify themselves for the thought of immortality through the sanctification of every action. Science must of course be granted the possibility that the continued existence of the soul was a dream of the past. But if anyone still felt he wanted to or had to keep this hope, it should not be taken from him; for that matter immortality was now and at all times present. It consisted in the unceasing chain of consequences which ran from one breath to the next and in which lay the guarantee of eternal continuity. From what he described, the aged spinster could conclude that we continue to live on in our children and grandchildren. The poor in spirit consoled themselves with the immortal efficacy of their words and deeds. A person frequently tormented by thoughts of economizing or frugality would rejoice that not an atom of his physical being would be truly wasted but rather be forever honorably employed in the domestic economy of Nature, in ever changing form, and would contribute lavishly to the production of a thousand new buds and shoots. Finally, the weary and overburdened could hope for decisive relief from all their troubles.

In conclusion he would decorate the structure of his sermon with a thousand little verses and images from poets of àll times and nations, so beautifully that no one had ever seen the like. It resembled the inside of a toll-collector's booth, the poverty of its four walls pasted over with picture cutouts, bits and pieces, letterheads and logos on checks and drafts from every corner of the globe, and in the window a toy monk with a cowl that keeps taking its cap off and putting it on again.

But adorning the temple of the spoken word was not the only thing; the temple with real walls must be restored in keeping with modern times. The church in Schwanau had been built a couple of centuries before the Reformation and still retained the unadorned state it had been left in by the Iconoclasts and by the strict clerical tradition. For centuries the outside of the ancient grey structure had been twined about with ivy and wild grape, while the inside was brightly whitewashed. Through the clear windows, which had always been kept plain, the light of the heavens flooded freely in upon the congregation. No statuary was to be seen, except perhaps the walled gravestones of earlier generations. The word of the preacher alone held sway, without any further help from the senses, in the bright, simple, yet venerable space. The congregation had for three centuries felt itself strong enough to scorn all external sensuous adornment, in order to worship with increased devotion the inward spiritual image of the story of salvation. Now that this latter had also fallen to the ravages of time, external ornamentation had to be called upon to help beautify the tabernacle of the Indefinable.

All this had a special appeal to Justine, who, to compensate as much as possible for the lukewarm attitude of her husband, redoubled her dedication to this strange labor of reformation. She became vigorously involved, indeed she led the way with gifts of her own, and with the zealous solicitation of contributions from others.

The sunny white walls, framed by summer green and by flowers that peeked in at the windows, had first to yield to a varicolored paint job of Gothic ornamentation, the work of unqualified hands. The vaulted spaces of the ceiling were painted in several colors and strewn with golden stars. Then they took up a collection for stained-glass windows, and soon the bright window arches were filled with anemic figures of evangelists and apostles which could at best produce, with their dimly colored modern surfaces, not a deep glow but a pallid haze.

Then they had to get themselves a covered altar and an altar painting. Thus the imperceptible cycle of icon worship could begin again by way of "esthetic stimuli," though it was unfailingly destined to evolve at some time into miracle-working, blood- or tear-sweating statuary, in fact into idolatry, so that future reforms would not be left without a target.

Finally, the chalices of white maple wood, the neat white trays for the host, and the pewter wine pitchers were banished, and at every great family celebration in the houses of the rich, gifts were made to the church in the form of silver chalices, platters, and ewers, all this at the initiative of Justine, whose wealth-proud spirit took pleasure in such splendor. She had no feeling for the fact that she was helping the new church lay the groundwork for a good old-fashioned treasury, which could be augmented every day, quietly but persistently, and could be used to entice further contributions from field and vineyard and a tithe of the product of every pair of hands, for an empty tabernacle has more room in it than a full one.

By now there was an example, even to sculpture with figures in painted plaster, of every possible art form, the sole exception being music, which was therefore dragged in without delay. In the absence of sufficient funds for an organ, one person contributed a squeak-box with a trumpet register, a mixed choir did some hurried practicing of old Catholic pieces for the mass, which were sung in Latin for the sake of heightened solemnity and also because no one could understand the words. This choir was split into various segments. Children's groups were brought in and trained; just as an experiment, in the name of a liturgy designed to reinvigorate divine worship, they staged a brave little skit, out of which there could again develop, in time, the pomp and ceremony of a universal mystery play.

Everything they had created would have been an unsalted sacrifice without the practice of a little wholesome discipline. To fill his renovated temple the pastor would tolerate no one who did not desire to enter. He turned his pike-staff above all against those who stayed on the outside and presumed already to know on their own what he was proclaiming inside.

"It is not the Jesuits or the superstitious," he cried with a loud voice from the pulpit, "who are now the most dangerous enemies of the church, but those cold and indifferent persons who, in their vain arrogance, in their sad superficiality, believe they can dispense with our church and our religious community and scorn our teachings, while in their base worldliness they chase after the things of the world and their material interests and pleasures. Why is it that we never see this or that person among us, when, united in our temple, we strive to lift ourselves above the temporal and find the divine, the everlasting? Because now that we have freed the church, after a century of struggle, from the armor of dogma, he believes that there is nothing for him to believe, to fear, to hope, nothing, that is, which he could not say better than any priest. Because he does not know that all past and present faith and the cognizance of divine things form nothing less than a great, coherent, profound body of knowledge, which lives on and must be governed through the work of those who have studied it and now understand it. Because, finally, he does not know that in the bitter hour of his death he will long for our support and stand in need of the mysterious consolation of the tabernacle.

"But now he is caught up in selfishness and vanity. Being through *our* good efforts free and unencumbered, he refuses ungratefully and scornfully to take part in our resistance to the forces of darkness and lies, refuses to fight together with us the battle for life, to make our joy his own and, calling himself a Christian, join us in adorning the altar. So he simply goes his way, our 'this or that person', our Mr. Aloof, our indifferentist, our pillar of pride. To be sure, he has no idea how impoverished, how sad he seems to us in his sense of security, which of course we neither can nor would take from him, although it comes to him only through us! To be sure, he does not know how barren the path is along which he wanders, by which no Sunday bells will ring, beside which no Easter will ever bloom, no resurrection. And I do not mean the resurrection of the flesh but the resurrection of the spirit, the eternal Easter of the heart! He will fare accordingly. No blessing will accompany him, his spirit will grow bitter and he will bear malice toward us, as we rejoice in the rewards of our struggle and the work of our Lord Jesus Christ and enjoy the lamb of Easter now and every day. And when streams and brooks are freed of ice and, 'laden almost to sinking, our last vessel leaves,' then he will stand sadly upon the shore and as we depart, look on defiantly, self-exiled and self-condemned! But *we* condemn no one, we pass sentence on no one. No, we grant every man his freedom, mindful of the words, awful to be sure in their double meaning:

> Before the slave whose fetters break,
> Before the free man do not quake!

"But do not Thou permit him to escape the adamantine chains of Thine eternal moral law, which Thou hast established, oh all-loving Creator and Lord, origin of the fundaments of the land and the girdling flood of the sea, oh Thou erector of the eternal tent of heaven! Lead him back into Thy protecting sanctuary, which we have built according to Thy commandment, proclaimed unto us through the mouth of Moses:

> And every wise hearted among you shall come, and make all that the Lord hath commanded;
> The tabernacle, his tent, and his covering, his taches, and his boards, his bars, his pillars, and his sockets,
> The ark, and the staves thereof, with the mercy seat, and the vail of the covering,
> The table, and his staves, and all his vessels, and the shew-bread,
> The candlestick also for the light, and his furniture, and his lamps, with the oil for the light,
> And the incense altar, and his staves, and the anointing oil, and the sweet incense, and the hanging for the door at the entering in of the tabernacle,
> The laver and his foot.
> The cloths of service, to do service in the holy place, the holy garments for Aaron the priest, and the garments of his sons, to minister in the priest's office.

"Bring him into Thy tabernacle, that he may pray with us:

> Thou loving spirit, universal soul, paternal ear,
> No flock that lifts its voice to praise Thee
>   wilt Thou fail to hear.
> One strand of prayerful gratitude, one thread
>   of hymnal praise
> Extends from scented morning to the evening
>   bright and clear.

One strand of hymned praise, one thread of
    prayerful gratitude
Extends from scented evening to the morning
    bright and clear.
So grant, oh Lord, that as we fan the fires
    of prayer their flames
May make in this poor soul Thy light of inner
    life appear.

"Grant that he may seek the land of immortality with the longing
of Goethe's virgin priestess, who said:

And so I stand for days beside the sea,
Seeking with my soul the lands of Greece!

so that he may sometime sing, with the dying flower of the poet:

Ever-burning heart of world,
Let me fade away with thee!
Heaven's blue tent shall be unfurled;
Mine, once green, will cease to be.
Springtime, may thy light be blest;
Breezes, blest, in morning skies!
Without care I go to rest
Without hope to rise.

and he shall be answered:

Undesigning soul, pay heed!
Be consoled, the grand design
Gives to all that blooms its seed,
Storms of death blow as they must!
Let thy dust of life be strewed,
You will rise up from the dust,
Hundredfold, renewed. Amen."

At the conclusion of such eloquence, which frequently left him
moist about the eyes and in a state of excitement over his own
gibberish, his parishioners would often run up to him on the church

path and press his hand in gratitude. At well-set dinner tables he would be lauded by fair lips hungry for emotion, and praised by men of wisdom. Now, they said, one could at last be churchly and Christian again, without exposing oneself to the suspicion of being narrow-minded and behind the times.

Among those chastised for their indifference and lack of concern was Jocundus. He was not hostile to the new church, nor did he try to place obstacles in its way, knowing full well that everything in the world must run its own course. Yet with his naive devotion to the truth he found it impossible to join in maintaining the appearance of a churchliness which, at least for men accustomed to thinking for themselves, was false. So he made silent and unostentatious use of his personal freedom; and he was the more stubborn in this as it represented virtually the sole domain where he still preserved full independence from anxiety—and from love.

But the pastor counted Justine among his main pillars of support, since with her respected position she could almost be considered a church elder, and he did not like the fact that her husband seemed, by staying away, to express disapproval and a determination to be above it all. He took all such staying away as an unspoken personal reproach and as silent criticism of his activities. Hence he had taken offense at Jocundus and preached against him. This flaw of character was another thing some of the new preachers had taken over from the old, namely their habit of standing in the pulpit, where they alone had the word and no one could contradict them, and speaking out on anything that bothered them personally, accusing and denouncing at will. Jocundus, however, knew nothing of this, for he paid little attention to people's talk and did not inquire into the meaning of vague innuendos.

When he came to the parish house late that evening to pick up his wife, as they had agreed, the minister had just finished his lecture to a few friends, on the mutual rejuvenation of the church and the fine arts, and Jocundus had to sit down and wait for a while.

"If you had done me the honor of being among the audience for my little paper," said the pastor, "perhaps you would have found a point of compromise in my thought that this is the time for art to give thanks to religion for its existence and so to pay back its dear, once rich mother, who is now so poor. You might even find some personal satisfaction in the prospect of being able to sing your heart out in a significant piece of music, perhaps in company with us. You could be thinking whatever you please, leaving us the right to do the same."

As he spoke, Justine looked hopefully at her husband. Her happiest memory was of working with him in the first year of their marriage on a music festival in one of the larger cities. During the presentation of a mighty Biblical oratorio they had stood so close to one another, each in his own section, that they could hold hands during the pauses. That evening Jocundus had taken his wife tenderly in his arms and confessed to her that even with all they had experienced together he had never been so happy as he had been today, singing as part of this beautiful flood tide of music and song, and all the while hearing beside him her lovely voice.

But now in a sombre mood and hardly cheered by the clergyman's aggressiveness, he answered rather drily, "I do not share your view that religion is the source of art. Rather I believe that art is there on its own and always has been, and it is art that has taken religion along the way with it and brought it quite a distance."

The pastor turned red. In the close circles of his congregation he did not easily tolerate such contradiction. He said, "Well, we shall not pursue the matter further. You are certainly a layman in more ways than one, otherwise you would be aware that we theologians nowadays have incorporated into our theological science many areas of knowledge which were formerly not under our surveillance and on which you, given your position in life, have no perspective."

Jocundus replied rather brusquely, "You theologians may feel a need for this sort of thing, but I do not believe it will help your theology regain the status of a living science, any more than old cabbalistic doctrines or alchemy or astrology deserve that name."

This struck and offended the clergyman in his inmost being, and he said, "Your hatred of us makes you blind, and foolish! But enough of that; we stand above you and your life, and you in your blind conceit will simply crack your skull against our solid walls."

"You're already going to extremes," said Jocundus, who had in the meantime calmed down completely. "We don't run our heads into walls. And it's not a question of hate or anger. The question is simply whether we can continue to create teaching positions in matters where no one person, if he's going to be honest and truthful about it, can teach another, and then handing such a position over to anyone who reaches his hands out for it. This at the moment is my individual opinion, but I wish you well anyway. I ask only that you leave me completely in peace; I'm deadly serious about this."

He said these last words as his wife took his arm, ready to leave. His voice was firm, and it broke her heart. In the new culture of the church, which seemed to her so open-minded, so cultivated, so right, she had found virtually her only defense against the secret worries that oppressed her. Now her husband had broken out against it in open rebellion. She considered him, in comparison with the minister, uninformed, inadequate, a poor unfortunate! And here, in the midst of this enlightened and well-spoken world of the church, the double crisis of conflicting religious beliefs and incipient domestic strife was suddenly at hand.

Hardly had they reached the street when Justine let go of her husband's arm and walked or almost stumbled along, softly weeping. Jocundus thought she had found it easier to walk alone because of the autumn storm and rain, and he paid no attention to her state. By the time they reached home she had gained outward control; inside, however, she trembled with emotion and indignation.

Jocundus, quickly forgetting the incident and filled with other worries, wanted to talk over with her the situation in which they found themselves and explain to her how he felt: that his right place was not in this house, that he must try to stand on his own two feet, and this would come in good time; that she should follow him to the city, where he had excellent connections and friends. If, to help them in starting out, she could take along some of her family funds, perhaps no more than what she had already expended for the cultural activities of the church and for her other favorite pursuits, he would have no worries for the future.

He touched on this latter point with some embarrassment, because he did not feel he needed anything for himself but was only considering Justine's fear of being without money.

No sooner had he mentioned the matter, however, than she broke her silence. The latent lower-class coarseness of the nouveau riche, which the men of the family sometimes revealed, now broke out in her, unexpectedly and in its full caustic power. Passionately and ruthlessly, without reflection, she cried that he could go wherever he wished. Why should she follow him if he could not prosper in her house, where he had lacked for nothing, had encountered only kindness, had everything, every consideration? It would never occur to her or to her family to risk making the slightest sacrifice for such a lost life, or to throw good money after such a . . .

Here she used an expression which had scarcely ever passed her lips and which, though it was not an outright term of abuse, was one that no real man could tolerate from his wife.

Hardly had the word escaped her when Justine blanched. She looked with wide eyes at her husband, who had already turned pale and was now leaving in silence.

Justine hurried out to look for her mother but she was at the house of one of the brothers; so Justine went there to seek advice and refuge.

Jocundus waked his own mother, who had already gone to bed, tired. He told her to get dressed, packed up a few necessities, and in the middle of the night got a rented carriage and drove off unnoticed, in the storm and rain, with his mother, taking with him what little money he had saved and put away from the sale of the old oak tree.

From this moment on, that graceful and happy smile was gone from the face of both husband and wife; it vanished as completely as if it had never been there.

In the dark carriage, sitting beside his aging mother, who in resignation and heavy with slumber had fallen back to sleep, Jocundus saw before his eyes the beautiful face of Justine as she had first smiled at him. This smile, he said bitterly to himself, is the trick of a muscle formed just so and no other way; cut through it with the merest little cut and everything is gone forever!

In the early light of dawn, Justine, who had not gone to bed, stood before a mirror and saw her stiff, pale lips. She tried painfully to smile at the fair, cruel dream of vanished happiness. But her mouth and both her cheeks were stiff and motionless as marble, and her mouth remained from then on closed, from morning to evening and from one day to the next.

Chapter 3

Jocundus had gone to the capital of the province, where his first responsibility was to care for his mother and to bury her; for she had fallen sick from shock and worry and never recovered, having no further hope for her son's prosperity or the wearing qualities of what she had once spun and woven for him.

On the way back from her grave he met an army officer, once his superior, who knew him well but had not seen him for a long time. The officer inquired into his present circumstances and, being informed of them (insofar as they could be revealed), he told Jocundus that he was precisely the man he was looking for to fill a vacant spot in his extensive business and capital ventures. What he sought was a calm and dependable person, someone on whom he could count to fulfill his obligations with dispatch and on time, looking neither to the right nor to the left but never off guard and, most important, engaging in no speculations of his own.

Jocundus signed up with this man and immediately took over the position arranged for him. From the very first things went well. The work assigned him was of such nature that he had neither to deceive or lie nor to believe the lies of others. He had no need to ask too much or offer too little, to haggle, to outwit or resist being outwitted. Whatever else was required in the way of knowledge of human nature, or in the application of that knowledge, came as smoothly as ever to him, now that with the loss of his naiveté the scales had fallen from his eyes.

His days flowed quietly and seriously; no joy lit his face. He had lost all touch with Justine; in vain he waited for some sign from her that she regretted the wrong she had done him and wished to take him back. She, meanwhile, was kept from doing so by her family, who felt it better not to stir things up, preferring to wait and see what further luck Jocundus might have and whether it would last. Nor were they really wrong to call it luck; in times of trouble, finding oneself is generally more a matter of luck than people are inclined to admit. In this case it had perhaps depended entirely on a chance encounter with an experienced and perceptive stranger.

Jocundi's time of cold and bitter calm, however, was brief. Everyday, to be sure, he proved himself more useful in his job and virtually without help or favor was soon promoted beyond the level first assigned him, so that the greater gain that had once seemed so elusive, and the solid prospect of material possessions seemed to materialize of their own accord. At the same time, however, there arose in society at large a movement into which he was passionately drawn, as a function more of his embittered spirit than of his real inclination.

Forty years had passed in the life of the Republic since the last of those political reforms through which the people had reasserted their lost rights or had enhanced existing ones. There had developed in the younger generation a will for change, but without any awareness or acceptance of that will on the part of the ruling representatives of the earlier order. For them, the world and the state as at present constituted were in good order. They refused with a firm "No" to cooperate in substantial changes of any kind. Rather, they confined themselves to continuing efforts aimed at gradual extension of what already existed and had once been so highly praised. By their opposition, however, they gained the appearance of stand-patters, indeed enemies of progress, and aroused against themselves an ever more violent mood of irritability. But they managed affairs in a straightforward and honest way and expended great effort on all manner of things which in themselves seemed by no means regressive, so it was hard to find an opening for large-scale political action. In such a situation people may lack the impetus to violent action, through which their desires will automatically be realized in a single day. But to reach the same goal on the path of law and order, by setting aside a self-made constitution and self-elected representatives in favor of the new, requires that massive moral energies be aroused.

In times of violent change, a few drops of steaming blood will generate this level of excitement. A people bent on decisive action can attain it in a different way, but only by committing the first wrong, levying false charges, and then, true to the principle that the offender persecutes the injured party with ever-increasing hatred, not resting until the stumbling block is out of the way and the desired change in the constitutional setup has been effected.

But there was no real handle available for stirring up a great wholesale indictment, adequate to the creation of such a general and all-consuming flood of emotion. The various individual points of dissatisfaction involved no questions of dishonesty or breach of public trust, but rather questions of disagreement as to reasonable and proper means to an end.

However, a populace or a republic determined to quarrel with its leaders and its officials is never long at a loss for ways of starting things and will invent ever new means for doing so. So what finally happened was that people simply stood up to those involved and said, "We just don't like your looks."

This came about by way of a strange, demonic movement, one which contained within itself more terror and persecution than many a bloody revolution, although not a hair of anyone's head was harmed, nor a blow struck.

First came the ridiculing of certain unimportant persons, for whatever reason. Then came jabs at certain others, of greater importance, for characteristics that were in a way foolish, in a way unseemly—but were in either case distorted. A mocking and sadistic attitude became more and more widespread, giving rise to a breed of instigators and virtuosi of derision and distortion. Soon what was once amusing mockery turned into grim calumny, raging about, marking the houses of its victims, and dragging private lives out into the streets.

These victims were kneaded into a doughy mass of absurdities, consisting of imagined physical infirmities and bad habits invented for the purpose, but mostly of nothing more than inept behavior; after these had been well mixed, they were suddenly accused of mysterious crimes committed long ago, of a repugnant way of life, and of depravity in thought and action. This was made to contrast all the more sharply and intolerably with the respect they had previously enjoyed. Of course any charges of specific wrongdoing, which would obviously call for extensive criminal investigation, were dropped with a smile at the first outcry from those affected. But the feeling of revulsion was there and the person was stuck with it; and all the rest of this amorphous mischief was kept alive by the very confusion of its victims. Widespread fear and repugnance produced a veritable immunity from punishment, particularly since all law suits began to turn into holidays for the attackers and were greeted with counter-threats of a most serious nature.

The parties to this general parliament of slander hurried forth out of every crack and hiding place. Persons whose own physiognomies, life-style, and conduct were well suited to make them the butt of caricature, ill will, and mockery took up positions in the very front rank. Like regular captains of calumny and defamation, they raised their voices on high, and the louder the angry racket, the quieter and more timid were the victims of this abuse. Regarding them, idle and unthinking onlookers used a frightening cliché in reference to those involved: If only a hundredth part of the charges were true, they said, that would be more than enough. They did not pause to think that by any fair measure each one of them bore such a hundredth part on his own shoulders.

Besides those who were respected and well known in the land, some poor unknown would occasionally be destroyed in one corner or another; the sound of it was like the scream of a chicken being throttled alone at night by a marten. Or a couple of the leaders among the ravening beasts would attack one another on their particular hunting ground. Yet when they returned to the general congress, with their jaws torn and bloody, they seemed to have suffered no loss of reputation. They licked their battered hides and arrogantly took the floor again.

The entire phenomenon was so new and unusual that no student of history could find anything in the past to compare it with, even though there was more than one case where constitutional change or the extension of liberty had proceeded from unjust causes or false pretexts.

These troubles and persecutions occurred without bloodletting, without harm to life and limb, but men whose reputations were disfigured in the process found themselves deserted by old friends, who heard their protestations of innocence but could not act—which did *them* no good either.

Others, who might have spoken out decisively and courageously, kept silent to avoid being made the victims of base slander in the presence of wives or fiancées. Others remained silent out of concern for the peace and innocence of children still growing up. More than one man, realizing he had perhaps shown a touch of some human weakness sufficient to provide the trouble-makers with a point of attack, simply thanked God he had been spared thus far and kept as quiet as a mouse. Right beside him there stood a blatant villain, just as quiet, but so notorious he could not join the prosecution, waiting with his eyes peeled to see what would happen to him. And he was spared too, not only because as a dangerous villain he was feared by the slanderers, but also because this remarkable movement, for all its excesses, maintained a certain law of economy of effort and demanded no sacrificial victims who weren't directly in its way.

Further, there was an unmistakable awareness that all this was in fact a great big, rather crude joke. The masses of people were in no way reluctant to represent their country to the world as a land undermined, packed-full, and dominated by evil. But there is a true subterranean layer of depravity which no country lacks; this they left unmolested, and so it lay there quietly—except when it came up on its own initiative into the light of day, to join the general movement and assist in the despoiling of that integrity it found hateful. The active pack of liars resembled the popular village gossip who as part of her humor takes it for granted that everyone will decide what to believe, and that those with blackened reputations won't take the joke too seriously.

Jocundus was not of this humor. In his present state he was doubly inclined to believe anything and everything, even if he hadn't been predisposed to do so by his simple nature. Although he had become more cautious in business matters, his reaction to this movement was one of childish surprise. He accepted as gospel truth every scandal that was served up, puzzled beyond measure how such a thing could happen or was possible in a republic.

His particular fellow citizens, the Seldwylers, had from the beginning welcomed these events as a new golden age. Nothing could provide them greater happiness than mocking and dragging down such gloomy, long-faced individuals who had so long claimed to be better than other people. They were not exactly leaders in the invention of horrors but they were all the more active in the marshalling of absurdities. Separately or in large groups, they kept coming to the capital to see what was new and to play their part in the rising tide of the movement. Because Jocundus was the most

respectable person among them they made him their chieftain, and
he marched in complete earnestness at the head of the laughing
and ever carousing guild of Seldwylers, sad and worried, but also
incensed and punitive.

For he had never seen the world in this light. He felt as if
springtime had fled from it, leaving behind a gray, hot, hopeless
desert, at the far, veiled rim of which the lonely shadow of his
wife slowly receded. In clubs and gatherings he saw, along with
tough and well-known agitators, all manner of characters who had
crawled out of dark holes, intent on using their dirty hands to
drown their own long-standing misfortunes in the general deluge,
or taking fiery tongs, as it were, to drag the upper classes down
to their own level. He could see that those who held out a hand
to him were no church wardens. What he really felt, however, was
a kind of deep sympathy for such saintly fellows, whom he regarded as victims of the world, a world about which he had his
own sad song to sing—or so he thought. Just as Saint Elizabeth
showed a preference for the unclean, the sick, the wretched, and
even lay down in a leper's bed, so Jocundus felt a real tenderness
for his mangy companions and associated every day with people
he ordinarily wouldn't have touched with a ten-foot pole, as they
say.

He did this at the very time when the popular movement had
already passed through its initial swirls and eddies and people were
on course toward their goal. They were beginning to leave the
shadowy types behind and to affirm their new rights, the way lovely
colors and fragrances are produced from dark and filthy sub-
stances, and the latter thrown out. Jocundus hardly noticed that
he was already standing off to the side of the main road, with the
losers. When he did begin to realize it, he was overcome by renewed pity for the poor prophets who were to be betrayed once
more. It was of no use that a few of the smarter Seldwylers whispered to him that these slanderers and foes of decency had already
gone out of fashion, that people were sticking to straight politics
and matters of state, so he shouldn't make a fool of himself. What
was needed now, they said, was a state with real institutions and
something to respect once more, where you didn't have to take up
with lousy no-goods. Jocundus believed the poor and outcast, not
those who warned him.

To prove his courage in public and to show that he was their protector, he invited a fine assortment of his friends to dinner one day in an inn and treated them so lavishly that they were soon in the best possible mood.

Shyster lawyers down on their luck, dishonest and convicted petty bureaucrats, fraudulent salesmen, idle merchants and bankrupts, unacknowledged wits, and humbuggers of various sorts were all gathered around him, singing and celebrating as if the Holy Roman Empire had been restored. But the jollier they got the more serious Jocundus looked, and not a trace of a smile crossed his sad face. He thought of the days when he too had been happy, with the innocent pleasures of life, and now it was all gone! As the wine increasingly loosened their tongues and deadened their minds, the jolly comrades began to talk about their deeds and their fate, and to tell of the injustice they had suffered. However, now and then one of them would contradict another, then a third refused to go along, a fourth raised objections, a fifth offered detailed explanations. This gave rise to a confusing jumble of mutual recriminations and reproaches. The resulting impression, for an impartial observer, was that of a rather large, snarled fabric of petty, unedifying activities, for which they were all calling one another the most refined of crooks. It was such an elaborate crisscross and crossover that if you could have made a visible depiction of it, for example like Chladni's sound diagrams, it would have looked like the finest Brussels lace or the most ornate Genoa silver filigree, so wonderful and manifold are the works of God.

Jocundus tried, at first out of love, then in amazement, to understand and untangle the fabric. His face grew more and more earnest as his renewed gullibility became increasingly apparent to him. The dubious welter of conversations grew louder and more threatening and at various times turned violent, so that several pairs of men had one another by the throat or were pulling each other's beards, though they were still separated by the table. Their experienced host, however, intervened with a sure method of averting the threat of stormy weather. He quickly had the table set with a second meal he had held in readiness; it consisted of a cold platter, not fancy but generous in quantity, made up of ox feet, beans, potatoes, onions, herring and cheese. No sooner had the disputants caught sight of these refreshments than they calmed down and indulged themselves in complete silence until everything was eaten up.

There followed a solemn and general reconciliation, as after a spiritual love feast, and they all deplored the folly of having assaulted one another as they did, when harmony was so much needed.

It would be far better, they said, and more to the purpose if they could hold one of their trials, convict some oppressor and enemy of the people, and launch a merry chase after him. Plenty of them were still running around with head unbowed and defiant, or keeping themselves out of sight, with the idea that the storm would pass them by. Well, it was time to drag them out, time to revive the Terror.

They decided in principle to take action and moved directly to the designation of the individual victims who were to be deprived of fortune and honor. Soon they had selected the names of two or three such persons, each of whom had at one time or another got in the way of some member of the company and was therefore hated by him. When it came to determining the manner of the attack and the person's weakness or crime to be attacked, the gathering found itself at a loss, either because their imaginations were no longer lively enough or because the natural wit of the deliberating parties had been adversely affected by the late night hour. After several futile and pointless suggestions had been offered and rejected, someone finally shouted: "The Oil Wife will have to help. There is no other way."

Jocundus, paying closer attention now, asked who or what the Oil Wife was. This was an old woman, they explained, whose name came from the Biblical widow with the inexhaustible oil cruse, because she never ran out of good ideas and bad gossip, any more than the widow did of oil. Whenever it seemed there was no more information to be gotten or rumors to be spread about someone, this woman, who lived in a remote hut, could always squeeze out another drop of thick oil to befoul him with. In a few days she could fill the whole country with rumor.

Jocundus volunteered to undertake the mission and go to the Oil Wife; it was granted him gladly. He had them repeat clearly the names of the prospective victims. As far as he was aware, these were law-abiding people, who had not caused much talk; he wrote them down carefully in his notebook.

Thereupon he ordered a new round of good wine to inspire the gathering to further loquacity and leaned back with a sigh, to listen. But the gentlemen were now weary of serious work and more inclined to singing. So they sang with loud voices, the first verse of every song they knew.

The room in which they were gathered was large but low-ceilinged, more on the dark side than bright, and strangely decorated, for the innkeeper had bought the discarded wallpaper from a rather large house and adorned his public room with it.

It was a panoramic representation of the grandeur of a Swiss landscape, running around all four walls, and depicting a world of mountains with snowy peaks, alpine meadows, waterfalls, and lakes. However, the hall for which this splendid wallpaper was originally designed was half again as high as the room into which it was now transplanted, so they had enough to cover the ceiling with it too. Consequently the mighty giants among the mountains, namely the Jungfrau, the Mönch, the Eiger, and the Wetterhorn, the Schreck- and the Finsteraarhorn, were bent over half way up and bumped their snow-covered heads together in the middle of the low ceiling, where they were, however, somewhat darkened by lamp soot and smoke. Enthroned on the walls were green alpine meadows, strewn with red and white cows; farther down glistened the blue lakes, and ships with colorful pennants sailed on them. On the terraces of inns one could see ladies and gentlemen walking in yellow skirts and blue frock coats, and wearing old-fashioned tall hats. Soldiers stood in rank and file, wearing white trousers and beautiful shakos. In one whole row, straight as a ruler, all the left cheeks (which were colored red) were offset a bit from their proper place or printed that way by the wallpaper printer, and the commanding colonel with his great cocked hat and outstretched arm seemed to be expressing his disapproval; for the little red arcs located halfway off the empty cheeks gave the appearance of the earth's shadow as it moves away from the disc of the moon during an eclipse.

Along the entire painted countryside, however, at the height of a sitting man, there ran a dark dirty streak from the greasy heads of all the steady patrons who had rubbed against it in the course of time.

Suddenly a pale-faced fellow who liked to be called "The Idealist" discovered this painted nighttime wallpaper fatherland and used it as an occasion for a fiery toast to the glorious, beloved, beautiful Fatherland, which here surrounded this society of sturdy Swiss patriots like a sort of closer, more familiar homeland. And since these poor in spirit and fortune also loved their country, he roused a loud echo of approval and they tuned up with all the patriotic songs they knew. A few of their comrades, who were unimpressed, viewed the whole thing lightly and, since they were at the time eating herring, threw the backbones skillfully up at the eternal glacial snows above their heads, where they landed and stuck.

The others grumbled in protest; the idealistic toastmaster reproached the evildoers for their vulgar attitude and cried out that they were casting herringbones in the face of their country and fouling the pure alpine glaciers. But they only laughed and shouted, "Herringbone yourself," so that once again there was discord and racket.

Jocundus leaned his arms on the table, rested his head on them and sighed deeply.

Now in the midst of the tumult rose the thin falsetto of a former town treasurer who was vainly trying to sing the song Jocundus had sung on the way through the woods to the song-fest. At last the singer remembered the final verses and screeched in a shrill voice:

> "Where fun's a patriotic matter,
> All joy is free of Satan's curse.
> And coming home, if I'm no better
> At least I won't be any worse."

Then Jocundus remembered the fair and happy day when he had seen Justine for the first time, and he hid his face even deeper, trying hard to hold back the bitter tears.

Justine, meanwhile, also thought back longingly to the days when she had first met Jocundus; she would gladly have sought him out and made up for the wrong she had done him, had circumstances not always interfered. The primary obstacle now was his participation in the people's movement and in particular his association with the little troop of lost souls. All her family and friends stood on the opposite side, where the view taken of the whole matter was somber indeed.

In order to occupy her thoughts and gain peace of mind she had devoted herself with renewed zeal to the pastor and to efforts on behalf of the church and had also extended her activities into worldly things. She went everywhere and became chairman of everything; she had to have many pairs of good shoes, more sturdily built than before, because she was always to be seen on the street, going from school to school, house to house, meeting to meeting. She sat in the front row of seats at all ceremonies and business sessions, at all public lectures and festivities, but she found no peace, nor did the slightest smile return to her pale face. Her restlessness even drove her back into a music society she had long ago left, and she sang with a serious face and pleasant voice but without attaining any happiness at all. Her doctor even became concerned and announced that the melodic, vibrant sound of her voice suggested the onset of a chest disorder, and it was important to see that she spared herself.

Everyone sensed what her trouble was but no one was able to help her, and soon the others were in need of help themselves. For one of those grim crises from overseas broke upon the whole business world and in the process shook the House of Glor to its apparently solid foundations, with such sudden fury that it was nearly destroyed and survived only with great difficulty. In the space of a few weeks, the reports of disaster struck these proud people, blow after blow, making their nights sleepless, their mornings terrible, and the long days a time of endless trial. Their stock in trade lay in great piles, across the oceans, valueless. Money owed them was as good as lost, and their accumulated fortunes dropped from hour to hour, along with the high-yielding paper it was invested in. Finally all that was left was the main estate and some modest family holdings in the form of old titles to land. And this too was to be sold, sacrificed to meet those of their own obligations which, with so large a business, were still outstanding at the time the storm hit.

The men figured and consulted together, pale and still, for days and nights. Household affairs seemed to have come to a standstill. The servants worked without instructions and served meals, but no one ate or knew what he was eating. The clocks ran down and were wound back up again, sadly, after they had stood still for days. Time had to be husbanded, the way candles are lit, one from the other, to see in the darkness. Some kittens who had, up to the day of misfortune, been the playthings and the amusement of young and old, were suddenly not noticed any more and drew back shyly, with their little leaps, into a corner. When after a considerable time some degree of peace of mind returned to the house, everyone was amazed to see that the cats had suddenly grown up while they weren't looking.

It was clear that, if the honor of the house was to be saved and all debts paid, not a penny would be left in the family's possession and they would have to make a new start, from nothing. Gertrud, the "Stauffacher," was standing there when the word came; she trembled in every limb and had to sit down.

But Justine, with the terror and fear of poverty in her heart, turned directly to thoughts of self-help. She said she would immediately go out into the world and, with the knowledge and skill she had, support not only herself but also her father and mother. And she devised visionary schemes in feverish haste.

Now, however, her mother spoke up again, declaring that she would claim dower rights to a good part of the family fortune, which would allow her to save the firm and make possible its continued existence. Let the men make some agreement with the creditors; that was being done almost everywhere nowadays.

The men shook their heads darkly and said they could not and would not do that. They would rather be poor and emigrate, and work day and night in some foreign country, in order to get ahead again.

But the "Stauffacher" had regained her strength and her eloquence. She insisted that she was right and cited many examples to show how such a well-considered course of action had seen people through the storm, secured the future, and later permitted the release or honoring of every legitimate obligation.

The whole matter was to some extent still the family's secret. Their many workers continued to come as usual with their fabrics and their weaving, and received their pay and new work to do, for all decisions were anxiously postponed. With every passing day of delay, the men wavered in their resolve to follow the strict line of duty, although this would have allowed them to look everyone in the eye, as truly free men. The "Stauffacher" was at the point of winning out, and she was firmly convinced that she had every right to act as she did, for after all she had her dower rights. Then the old people came down from the mountain, the "Ehgaumer" and his wife, to protest these financial maneuvers and put a stop to them. The old man could not speak because, attached to possessions himself, he was appalled by the disaster that had struck his children. He sat down in a chair, coughing, and asked his wife to speak.

She placed on the table a bundle of yellowed certificates and said, here was what they, the old folks, had saved; they were bringing it to help preserve their good name. But what was owed had to be paid, and there must be no financial maneuvers involving the dowry. She spoke in such eloquent and powerful terms that it was she, in her white peaked cap, who seemed to be the true "Stauffacher." The other one stood by the window in tears.

For this lack of bravery she was reproached by the old woman, who at the same time remarked that there was dust all over the piano and the mirror tables in the beautifully furnished room where the family had gathered. She took her handkerchief and began forthwith to wipe them off.

The family decided upon the course of action that was strict and hard on them; but they retained their peace of mind and respect. The freehold estate was mortgaged; the business went on without interruption, but for the time being all members of the household were poor as church mice and none of them had a franc to spend for their favorite pursuits or for anything other than necessities.

Justine's positon of leadership in church and society was also gone, and she remained in seclusion, quiet and ashamed. But she could not bear this total lack of resources, so after the fashion of impoverished upper-class women she took in the various kinds of handiwork that women do, to earn a little pocket money. She did not realize that, in order to satisfy her desire for possessions, she was taking bread from the mouths of completely helpless widows and abandoned orphans who supported themselves precariously by the same means. As the modest sums of money she earned began to accumulate perceptibly, she redoubled the zeal and industry with which she did this work; and with her energy and skill she was able to attract and handle a substantial amount of it. The people who ordered and sold her things could hardly give her enough in the way of consignments and had to take some work away from others.

Being constantly occupied was all the more precious to her as she was able during work to be alone with her weighty thoughts, either concentrating on them or brushing them aside, to assess in her mind her slender hopes for a return of happiness. Her mother was in on the secret. In her pride she had started to fight against it; but she found in Justine's earnings the means of affording many minor expenditures of her own, for which she no longer dared make any demands on the cash accounts of her menfolk, who were working so anxiously and tirelessly. So she adapted herself without difficulty to her daughter's way of thinking.

Justine's father and brothers finally took notice; they had begun to wonder what was becoming of the many pieces of embroidery and needlework constantly being produced, and at last they discovered the secret. Even though they had saddled themselves with every kind of deprivation and had sold their carriages, their elegant horses, and the like, they did not want to be thought the kind of people who couldn't support a couple of women. They found it unseemly for the two to go out in search of manual labor, while poor working girls were looking for and finding the same thing in their firm.

So the whole business was resolutely suppressed and Justine was instructed to ask for whatever was required to meet her needs, as before, and not force herself to do anything; she must know that she was not for sale at such a price anyway. Justine's pattern of thinking, however, was so set that she could not escape it. There is an almost pathological urge for independence which runs like a fever through the women of this time, in consequence of the relative uncertainty that men leave the world in; increasingly Justine fell victim to it. She brooded and racked her brains, and finally devised the plan of seeking a job elsewhere, to support herself as a teacher. These thoughts of hers were directed to the capital, with its many schools. But part of the reason was the quiet hope that she was more likely to meet her husband there than she would be in her family home, where he was judged more harshly now than before, even though they knew he was doing well.

No sooner was this decision made than she moved without hesitation to carry it out, going first to the pastor to ask for his advice and his intercession. Only when she was part way to the parsonage did it occur to her, with some surprise, that this man of the cloth, always in the past a friend of the family, had not put in an appearance since the disaster struck, and that no one had missed him or thought of communicating with him or seeking his solace.

A shivering sensation went through her as she suddenly realized further that she had for months not even been in the church she had helped decorate. She stopped and tried to get this curious situation straightened out, but she could not manage it in such a hurry. She hastened ahead all the faster, as if seeking light.

In the garden of the parsonage she met the clergyman's wife, an inconspicuous woman, who was quietly picking parsley. She was informed that the pastor had just returned from the bedside of a dying person and that he seemed not to feel well. But Justine should go in anyway; he would be happy to have her visit. She hurried directly to his study and, as was her habit, knocked vigorously and went right in.

The pastor sat pale and exhausted in his armchair, leaning his head on his hand. When he turned and rose he seemed to her really thin and ailing. "You can tell," said the pastor after greeting Justine, "that I am not in very good shape, and that may explain why you haven't seen me for so long. In fact I am a patient in the same hospital as you and your family—and more so than you imagine."

On Justine's puzzled request for clarification, he continued, "I wanted to be rich and so in the course of my association with you and your family, in your house, I listened and made note of how your capital was put to use. I wrote down the stocks and bonds that you expected the largest profit from, and I secretly copied the investment operation I saw going on, using my wife's modest fortune. When I suspected the fact that the House of Glor was badly shaken I knew at the same time that I had lost everything and had squandered and gambled away my wife's inheritance and that of her children. She does not know yet and I can't tell anyone, lest I dishonor my calling. But with you, as you come to me so unexpectedly, I feel the need to be frank."

Justine was shocked. This new loss caused her real vexation and annoyance; so she said, rather angrily: "But what in the world compelled you to take risks in business matters when you have a pastorate and an income?"

"I told you," the pastor replied sadly, "that I could not disgrace my vocation by the admission of my sinful folly. Inwardly I no longer even belong to this vocation. I have left it, and so I wanted to become rich in order to live independently. Since that unhappy evening when I argued with your husband here, there has been a thorn lodged in my heart, though I have tried to talk it out, or brazen it out—in vain. I saw that Jocundus, however ill at ease or ill-fated he may have been, in a religious sense led a confident and irreproachable life. So I was forced to rethink and reexamine everything, something which, on the moral side of the question, as it concerns my own heart, I had unfortunately not done for years. I found that I was no longer leading a religious or Christian life; I was no longer a priest!

"I had to confess to myself that year in, year out, I felt not the slightest impulse to remember the man on the cross, whose name is the name of my life's vocation, and who sustained me. I had to confess that my heart and all my faculties were centered on the world and its pleasures and comforts, oh yes, if you wish, on its troubles and duties, but without feeling, whether by day or by night, the slightest tremor of individual, personal reverence, the slightest awe of Him whom we routinely preach as our Lord and Redeemer.

"Indeed when I did occasionally think in solitude of the person of Christ, whom I proclaim as sanctified, and did so as other than a function of my profession, it was more in the haughty spirit of a protector or patron, who for example takes on responsibility for some poor devil and tells him confidentially: 'My dear fellow, you cause me a lot of trouble!'

"Finally I sensed that without being aware of it I had become a platform artist, thirsting for applause, a windbag; that without having in my possession the golden key of the truly eternal word of God I could understand no more of the secret being of my fellow man, could have no more power over his spirit than a child would, indeed that the half-truth and ambiguity of my words left me, compared to a child, in a very bad way.

"I began to feel ashamed at the mindless applause that came my way. In addition, my occupation made it impossible for me to put my thoughts in order for the good of my still, inner being, for my own peace. Because there was no way to harmonize that with the loud urgency of my profession and its demands; and so I wanted to leave it and hang up my threadbare Reformer's coat for good.

"But that has become impossible, at least for now, because in trying to escape by the path of wealth I have actually robbed myself of the means of establishing any sort of secure existence."

Justine sat there petrified. She had come to get advice and help and witnessed instead the collapse of one more thing that had given support and meaning to her life. For she saw, as if in a flash of lightning, how things really stood and why, even in her misfortune, she had not sought out her colorful church. Her breast rose and fell, and bitter torment welled up in it. But she could not give in, because now she needed even greater compassion, as the clergyman broke into tears, saying, "Today the worst thing of all happened to me; I was turned away from the bedside of a dying person! A tough old woman has been struggling with death for hours. She stubbornly hopes to see all her children again, particularly her oldest son, who died in poverty. I arrive, full of worries and distracted, and get ready to offer my prayers for the dying, which I have composed myself and which are, as you know, rather pantheistic-sounding. She asks me questions about the certainty of eternal life and I answer her with vague, irresolute words; so the dying woman turns her back on me. And the people around her, with the doctor's support, take me aside and quietly beg me to cease my pastoral mission."

The pastor told this story in broken words and at the end covered his face with his handkerchief. He was deeply shaken, because no one likes to have it said, even of the kind of profession he does not love, that he is unable to practice it according to the rules of the game.

The impression this scene made on the horrified Justine was like witnessing the collapse of a mountain. What she thought was as solid as a rock, she now saw waver and die, as the self-confidence of this priest collapsed and she beheld him fleeing his temple. She sensed, no doubt, the oppressive force that lay, still hidden, in this far from momentous occurrence, one perhaps destined soon to be repeated, here, there, in a hundred places. She did not, however, understand its broader significance but felt only its painful pressure.

Confused, perplexed, she left without mentioning the request that brought her here, without trying or wanting to console the pastor with gentle words. Only when she reached the street and gave more thought to what the clergyman had said, comparing it with earlier, isolated statements and events, did she feel truly chilled. She realized first of all that she had no church; in her feminine mind, and given the force of habit, she felt like a lost bee, hovering over endless ocean waves in a cold autumn night. Abandoned by her husband, her property lost, and now without the community of the church—taken all together it seemed the equivalent of being banished and virtually stripped of honor.

The absence of a church, however external her churchliness may have been, seemed to wrap up and seal all the rest of her misfortune. Remarkably enough, she believed the pastor implicitly at the first word he uttered about his tabernacle being empty, while on the other hand she had never been willing to accept her husband's views, precisely because for her he possessed no spiritual authority.

She walked home without uttering a sound; there, to spend the next hour and fill it with something, she took out her knitting and sat down by the garden gate near the road, as if to show that she was still around and had no need to be embarrassed. But she spoke to no one and looked wanly at her work, while her lips mechanically counted the stitches.

The evening drew on; ships moved homeward on the quietly shining lake, and on the road workingmen passed by. But Justine never looked up until a little old lady, ancient as the hills and laboring along as if on a pilgrimage, stopped in front of her to rest and catch her breath. This person had a tall yellow straw hat on her head, a short red skirt, and stockings to match, a little white bag on her bent-over back, and in her hand a walking stick. It was apparent that she was in fact a pilgrim from some remote region, journeying to the famous shrine located in the mountains, a few hours ahead.

When Justine saw that she could hardly stand, she asked the little old woman to join her on the bench. "I'd be glad to, with your permission, lovely lady," said the pilgrim and promptly settled down beside her. She rummaged in her travelling bag and pulled out a piece of bread, looking about her for a well that might provide her with a drink of water to go with it. But Justine went to the house and got a glass of good wine to give her; she accepted it happily and took comfort in it.

"Why are you walking alone like this on a hot, hard road, at your age, when all the other pilgrims go by train or by steamship and sit together in a group?" Justine asked.

"Oh, that would be no credit, no proper sacrifice for a poor sinner like me," replied the pilgrim. "The others nowadays, they travel for the pleasure and curiosity of it, and the most they do is say a decent prayer at the shrine. But I walk to the blessed Mary, Mother of God, on my two old feet. I'm not just with her at the holy altar—she goes with me on the path, every step of the way and holds me up when I'm about to fall, the way a good daughter holds her weak old mother. Just now she gave me this refreshing drink, by your white hand. If only you knew how sweet and kind she is, how beautiful, how bright! And what power she has, what wisdom! She always knows what to do, she can do everything!"

During this hymn of praise the old woman did not drop her rosary for a moment. Justine watched her curiously as she played incessantly with the beads; she asked how they were used and how they were wrapped around one's hand. Promptly the old lady showed her, winding the poor little string of beads around Justine's hands. She held her hands folded for a few moments, pensively, and stared ahead as if lost in thought. But then she shook her head slowly and returned the rosary to the pilgrim woman without saying a word.

Now the little old pilgrim had had enough of resting and wanted to walk on for a good hour or so before she sought lodging. She gave thanks, promised to say a prayer for the dear kind lady, whether she wanted it or not, and wandered out into the dusk on her feeble legs, as cheerful and assured as if she had been at home, walking around in her own room.

Justine leaned back and watched the tottering red-clad figure until it disappeared in the blue shadows of evening.

"Catholic," she cried, forgetting herself, and fell back into deep, searching thought. She shook her head again.

But her homeless feminine heart kept searching and searching. She went to bed without eating and spent a sleepless night. No longer could she even say she was as poor as a churchmouse; for she was nothing but a plain fieldmouse. In her distress she thought of a poor little working family, a widow and her daughter, who had the reputation of quite special piety and despite the most impoverished living conditions enjoyed complete contentment and peace of mind. Even the pastor, although they belonged to what he called a foolish and ignorant sect, had expressed the opinion that they gave one a quite reasonable idea of the primitive Christians of earliest times. These two persons had previously lived in Schwanau and the daughter had worked in the factory rooms of the House of Glor. Justine felt a certain attraction to these poor folk and had at various times thought of converting them and winning them over to her nice, well-appointed, intelligent church. But she had always abandoned this resolve, though not intentionally, just as she was on the point of carrying it out. Then both mother and daughter left the area and moved near the capital; and now sleepless Justine decided to seek them out and explore the secret of their peace and their faith and, if possible, to share in their happiness. She also decided to put this plan in operation the very next day.

Chapter 4

The morning promised a beautiful day, and Justine got up early to prepare for a long hike. For though she would have to walk for almost three hours she meant to do her pilgrim's journey on foot, in all humility, inspired no doubt by the little old woman and her pilgrimage, and also because in this way she was most likely to be left alone with her thoughts. She put on a pair of her heavy old "committee chairman" shoes, which really came into their own now. She also added to her burden a basket holding gifts for her dear "early Christians": a bottle of good pure cream, a fresh loaf of wheat bread, a little bag of snuff for the mother (who was known to like a pinch when she could get it, for all her renunciation of the world), and for the daughter a pair of nice new stockings. So she tucked up her dress and set out, no pilgrim's staff in her hand to be sure, but a parasol, which together with her broad-brimmed straw hat gave her plenty of shade.

As she walked she thought over everything she knew about the two women and was more and more taken with the decision she had made.

Ursula, the mother, had come to the area as a poor housemaid and had devoted herself to a quiet, respectable life of duty. But at that time she had loved the world, as she put it, and had lent a willing ear to the son of well-to-do farm people, because she was touched by his kindness and simplicity of heart. So they got together, poor as little creatures of the field, and became a couple. The man was promptly cast out and disowned by his family, who did not even give him an empty wood basket to take with him. The two now led a bare existence as day laborers in a remote, miserable hut, and were more deserted than all the Robinson Crusoes on all their islands. They were simple and long-suffering, so in this rich and gentle Christian countryside they drew upon themselves, as a magnet draws iron, all the hardheartedness of which men are capable. Every bit of arrogant misunderstanding that existed round about seemed to be gathered together and directed against these poor folk, so that if some people thought of helping, others kept them from doing so; on top of it all they laughed, and no one knew why, which is the way it sometimes is in the world.

Still the little woman was filled with her love of worldly pleasures. She enticed a fat barn cat from the field near the hut where it was slinking around, skinned its fur coat off and boiled the cat in water, to still her bleak hunger. She also carefully separated off the fat to cook up some soup stock in case a little flour or bread should show up in the house. However, this act of violence did not escape discovery, and the fine imposed on the woman for committing it took away all the pay her husband had earned for a whole month's work on a road-building job he had finally found after a long search. So he, in his good-hearted simplicity, and on the advice of others, used his next pay to get drunk before they could take the money away from him. In the process he was struck by a mass of undermined earth, and killed, since he did not run from the landslide in time. This was also the end of Ursula's days of sinfulness and worldly pleasure.

Around this time there appeared a number of poor, nameless preachers who went among the lesser folk in search of adherents for some sect or other and would baptize those they converted. They taught the pure original Christianity; in their opinion this could be found in the Bible, without benefit of learning, if only each word were interpreted literally, in the German translation of course, which was what they had available to them. The main thing was to live a new and sanctified life, in deed and in truth, every hour of the day and in every place, and also to form among the faithful a firm bond of love and mutual attachment, so as to be strengthened and readied for the great hour of promised Judgment soon to come.

These preachers had soon gathered about them a congregation comprising dark and dismal souls in need of help, natural head-hangers, the prideful weak who even in their low station sought a vantage point from which they could be better than their neighbor, also kind hearts driven by their love, and the unfortunate, who hoped to find here a solace denied them everywhere else. Some of them, had they been Catholics, would simply have gone into a cloister. Others, if their circumstances had been such as to permit it, would have become Freemasons. Still others, if they had had means and an education, would have joined some charitable or service organization or a scholarly or musical society in order to lift themselves up out of the dust of ordinary life. Their substitute for all those things was this quiet, pious fellowship, where they found not only sanctity and eternal life, but also plenty of pastime and entertainment in the form of constant talking, teaching, debating, praying, and singing.

By no means, however, were they esteemed and beloved, rather they were persecuted and mocked from all sides by the church, by the liberals, by the orthodox, by the pious upper class, by the common people, and by the authorities. Particularly in rural areas their meetings were disturbed and disrupted, and the intolerance toward others which had taken early root among *them* was now returned in full measure.

In the town where the poor widow lived, the sectarians had been persecuted with particular severity and were not permitted to gather in areas under municipal administration; so they held their services in a remote wilderness area, in the ruined walls of an old fortified castle known as the Devil's Kitchen. This was the occasion for renewed mockery but they paid no attention to it, and went on preaching and singing reverently among the weeds and bushes.

In her tumbledown cottage one Sunday evening Ursula heard their pious songs, carried on the silent air, coming from where the golden clouds lay over the forest. She felt a comforting urge to follow the light and the sound. So she took her two-year-old daughter, little Agatha, in her arms and walked until she found the hidden congregation. Then she sat down, unassuming, on a bit of ruined wall in the back of the Devil's Kitchen, holding the child in her lap, and listened attentively to every word that was spoken. Various preachers rose to talk; besides tending to the offices of salvation each one had a simple trade he worked at and an equally simple way of dealing with the Word. For they were not even aware yet of the theological distinction between Peter and Paul, nor did anyone among them really know exactly who the Romans were, whose soldiers crucified the Savior.

At first the poor widow was covered by the shadow of a hazel bush, but as the sun sunk deeper in the sky it scattered its dancing light over the widow and the child, who now shone like a golden picture against the fiery green. This caught the eye of the man who was then preaching. He interrupted himself when he saw the silent, attentive woman and instructed her to approach and take a seat within the circle of the faithful, and he did so in a loud voice, so that the whole congregation turned their heads and took notice of the stranger.

As for her, she did not move but sat there shyly. At last someone rose from a row of five or six elderly washerwomen sitting ceremoniously in a prominent spot on a downed tree trunk, like so many bishops; and this person came to fetch the lost sheep and its young and lead them back by the hand.

Thus she was taken into the congregation and grew to be a respected member of it, special and different from all of the others, just as the same earth grows the most varied plants, each according to its nature.

The washerwomen were the first to include her in their company. They got her plenty of work to do, so that she became a washerwoman in the Lord, working in people's houses for forty years without cease, laboring day and night until her strength was more than exhausted. During this period the congregation had long since achieved recognition and tolerance and had also developed a degree of dignity. The members, sustained by their mutual aid and their orderly life, were all in comfortable circumstances. Their preachers now appeared more in the guise of clergymen with some claim to learning and wore better robes. Their gatherings took place in a bright, friendly prayer hall. They even engaged in a bit of church politics vis-à-vis the official church and other expanding sects as well.

Ursula and her little daughter Agatha, however, were untouched by change, sticking to the simplicity of their earliest days and becoming, without their knowledge, models of human piety. The daughter had a weak constitution and was sickly. She was employed at the silk reels in the workrooms of the House of Glor and lived with her mother, who took in laundry. As long as they could continue working this way, they earned enough to afford what they needed and could even give aid and financial help, where necessary and without being asked, to their fellow believers. What is more, they still had the means to show their friendliness and gratitude toward the world for any little service, any friendly treatment accorded them. Without consciously intending it, they had mastered the art of being rich in their poverty, simply through unceasing work and their own self-sufficiency and contentment. The only battle they waged between them consisted in vying with one another over the same kind of friendly favors and good deeds as they did for strangers. Because as soon as either one of them was on the receiving end she resisted, claiming that it was unnecessary and too generous.

In every other way, they lived in profound peace with the whole world. They forgave every injury at the point of its commission and never returned a harsh word in the same tone, for they drew from their piety the kind of self-control otherwise gained only through birth and education. In the same sense they suppressed without effort any immodest curiosity or faultfinding, or whatever the rest of those little social vices are called. Toward unbelievers and children of the world they were benevolent and tolerant in proportion to their certain conviction that such people were deeply unhappy or even lost.

Wrongs that were done them they accepted, not exactly with

pleasure but still without resistance. Brothers of the deceased husband and father had pulled themselves up in the world to the point where they lived in apparent prosperity and respect, but they had never paid out the little inheritance to which the child and her mother were entitled, nor had they even given them a share of what came in as interest. These men had high-flying ambitions and were always under financial pressure. They perhaps wished, without admitting it, to avoid depriving themselves of even the most modest sums, and therefore acted as if they did not acknowledge the debt, as clear as it was. It would have cost the women only a single word to force them into compliance and to strip them of public respect. But they were not to be persuaded even by their fellow believers; they remained all their lives the poor, patient debtors of their imperious and unjust relatives, so that it might truthfully be said that they were the rich ones, while the latter were the poor.

Time left them older, then simply old. Their work began to be a burden to them, a daily trial, but they did not want to give it up. The sickly daughter redoubled and trebled her exertions, so that she might at least secure for her mother the relief she most urgently needed. With all this they remained cheerful and composed and were far more likely to render solace and small favors to others than to demand such for themselves.

This was the time when the House of Glor was struck by its great misfortune and when numerous workers were kept on, despite the lack of demand for them and of resources to pay them. While many such workers who had houses and land and were quietly aware of the situation continued to draw their pay, and while the poorer ones expected their earnings to continue just as if they had a right to them, poor weak Agatha alone made it a matter of conscience.

She and her mother told each other that their stricken employers were making an involuntary sacrifice with every day's pay they disbursed, a sacrifice they had no right or desire to accept. They decided, quite without presumption, out of the pure goodness of their hearts, to shun this sacrifice, and went so far as to leave the area and move elsewhere. Actually, in doing this, Agatha, the aging spinster, planned secretly to spirit her mother away from her clientele, for in serving them she was beginning to show signs of collapse, as the great attacks on the laundry would be launched at three in the morning and would go on for three days. She had the idea of getting a reel or a winder into the house so that she could tend her mother all day, giving her a chance to rest, and at the same time work to support the two of them.

Near the capital city she found the situation she was looking for and a little house, which the head of the silk works gave her to live in. This tiny building was located in a remote orchard and contained two little rooms so arranged that one opened onto the orchard and could be reached only through the other, which was by the roadside. The former was a sunny, cheerful spot amid the greenery, for the field with the orchard began near the window. The other, however, was a dark, cheerless room, the entrance of which was at the same time the front door, opening onto the dusty highway. Beside the door there was a little hole in the wall with an iron grating—a sort of window.

In this gloomy shelter lived an ugly, discontented old woman who should have cleared out but was left there because the pious women requested it. They lived in the more cheerful room. In fact they had once exchanged it for the dark hole because the wicked old person complained and bickered about it and they had let her occupy the bright little room. But she hadn't wanted to stay there either because then she couldn't keep watch on the entrance and see what was going on along the road. So the two long-suffering ladies had to move into the rear of the house again, and the old woman was back in the hole once more, where she never stopped scolding and threatening. She would lie in wait for anyone who entered or left, pumping them for information, and trying to turn them against the good little ladies, for the two of them had all sorts of visits from friends and from people who were in need of a gentle word. Whatever small tokens of friendship they received (and accepted with sincere thanks) they also shared immediately with the old monster, who in her ill-humor checked the division of the spoils, and rudely rejected her share if it wasn't quickly and punctually forthcoming.

For their part, they had no fear of the old nuisance and lived in immediate proximity to her, as pious hermits might to a wild beast or a terrible demon.

Now this woman was the Sibyl of Slander called the Oil Wife, the person Jocundus Meyenthal was looking for as he tried to get to the bottom of the evil he had uncovered that happy night.

When Justine, having found out where the little house was, came walking up, the Oil Wife was sitting at the side of the road in front of her door, grumbling as she scoured a pan.

According to legend, at the time when Attila appeared with his Huns there lived near Augsburg a witch who was so repellently ugly she had been banished. As the vast army was about to ford the River Lech, this woman, it is said, rode out to meet them, alone and naked, on a scrawny, dirty horse, and screamed, "Get out of here, Attila!" Whereupon Attila and his whole army, filled with terror, turned straight about and took off in another direction. So the old witch they banished had saved the city—which rewarded her with a nice new shift. But this witch scarcely deserved a new shift from *her* country.

Justine too nearly turned around and fled when she saw the Oil Wife sitting in front of the door, with her great yellowish rectangle of a face, on which envy, vengefulness, and malice lay framed around broken vanity like gypsies around a burned-out fire on the heath.

The old dragon hissed at beautiful, stately Justine and, straightening up, asked her what business she had with these people. Justine took courage and pressed on past her through the darkness; suddenly there she was with the gentle ladies in the sunshine, the fresh green before her eyes.

"Oh, how beautiful it is here," she exclaimed, as she set down her basket and other things, put away her hat, and drew up a chair. Ursula and Agatha, for their part, were in a state of purest joy, so amazed were they at such a surprise visit. Ursula sat in her armchair, paralyzed by her arthritis, unable to rise. Agatha stopped her half-dozen spools, which had been turning in the sun with the shiny red silk wound on them. An expression of cordiality, composed and almost aristocratic, shone in the pale face of the daughter, who had certainly enjoyed no aristocratic upbringing. Justine noticed that she also was none too steady on her feet. They had in fact begun to hurt her and were occasionally a bit swollen, Agatha explained with a smile. But she did not utter a single word of complaint, any more than her mother did. Rather they described with innocent merriment the queer old witch at the door,

Justine having asked about the mysterious apparition. They said that one must be patient with the poor creature, who was inhabited by evil spirits and was certainly suffering enough already.

But they were really amazed when Justine got out her simple gifts. Nothing could have pleased Agatha more than the stockings, for she confessed she could hardly find any time for knitting, particularly since her eyes could no longer really see well at night in the light of their little lamp. Meanwhile her mother had already opened the package of fresh snuff and, with almost too eager a show of delight, filled her horn snuffbox from it. This was the one point where the child had a measure of control over the mother, for she would not allow her quite as much of this black worldly pleasure as she might have been capable of using, were she free to relapse into the sins of her youth. But now even Agatha smiled at Justine as her mother, with such obvious joy, took a fresh pinch.

Agatha promptly filled a saucer with the cream and cut a piece of the fresh-smelling white bread, to take it to the poor woman outside. "Not too fast," said the mother softly, "so she won't be knocked over if she is listening at the door again. Make a bit of noise with your feet."

"Oh, they'll hurt too much if I stamp," replied her daughter, and she laughed at the harmless trick she was supposed to play. But she did cough a bit before she opened the door, and, sure enough, out there in the dusk of the little front room the shapeless figure of the old woman was visible, scuttling along more nimbly than one might have expected of her.

When things had quieted down again, mother and daughter wanted to know how the young gentlewoman had got here and where she was headed, for they could not imagine that she had meant to come so far just to see them.

The light of the sun, alternating with the shadows of the swaying tree limbs, played over the floor and walls of the little room. Before the open window bees hummed, and a little green lizard that had climbed up from the grass was looking curiously into the room; a second one joined him, both of them, it seemed, in expectation of things to come. Justine saw all of this, and the feeling of peace did not escape her. She could not, however, find the courage to break the silence, until finally she began to cry and now in her affliction and distress confided in the two women, telling them that she had lost her religion and was seeking their advice and instruction as to the nature of their happiness and the source of their peace of mind. She hoped to experience something new and overpowering, something she had never before encountered, and to which she could surrender without having to mull it over. Ursula immediately set her snuffbox aside and Agatha put down what she had in her hand. The two looked at each other, shocked; they folded their hands involuntarily. Justine saw how each was praying softly to herself, her lips moving, Agatha with tears flowing, her mother with the greater composure of age. Neither had the confidence to say a word; they were quite shaken by the demand placed upon them, that they should win salvation for a person of such learning and brilliance, but there was no mistaking or doubting the design of Providence.

Ursula was the first to begin speaking, slowly, and only a few words, while Agatha pushed a footstool over toward Justine, sat down at her feet, took her hands, and patted them. Justine had always been her secret love and the very aristocratic object of all her goodwill and admiration.

Things were soon on the right track, tongues were loosened, and the two older women now vied in explaining to the worldly young one this matter of great moment, taking up one another's words and adding to them, like two children telling to a third some fairy tale they just heard from their grandmother. What they brought forth, however, was nothing new or unheard of, only the harsh and barren old story of Original Sin, of the Atonement, the reconciliation of God through the blood of his Son, who would soon come to judge the quick and the dead, of the resurrection of the flesh and the bones, of Hell and eternal damnation, and of the necessity of absolute belief in all these things. They said this as if it were something no one understood as well or as truly as they and their congregation did. Nor did it issue forth from them with the gentle human grace that marked them in everything else they did and said, but rather with dry haste, colorless and monotonous, like something memorized. At no point did their words become softer or more kindly, nowhere were their faces warmer or more animated. Even the suffering and death of Christ they treated as if it were a school lesson, not a matter of feeling or of the spirit. It was a lifeless world they spoke of, off by itself; and what they were in the other aspect of their own being was another world again.

Besides, in simpleminded imitation of their preachers, they spoke awkwardly and without grace; indeed they were imperious in their insistence, at every second word, upon belief.

Justine now realized that the good ladies drew their peace of mind from some other source than the doctrines of their church and were in no position to bestow it upon others by dint of those doctrines. Or rather Justine saw that only they, with their particular natures, could have flourished on this barren soil, because they drew their nourishment from the free winds of the heavens. She had come here in vain. Her heart tightened within her until it threatened almost to stop; she leaned back on her wooden chair to recover, while the preacher-women kept on talking. And she did gradually recover, but she was still as pale as the whitewashed walls that surrounded her. She tried to imagine how, without hurting the women, she might bring it all to an end and make her escape.

Suddenly there came an ugly scream from the doorway, as if someone had stepped on a cat's tail. In fright, Agatha ran out and opened the door, so that light flooded into the dark front room, and they saw a tall slim man holding the Oil Wife fast by the throat and practically forcing her against the wall. Just as the light fell on this scene, he let the old witch go, out of chagrin and embarrassment, but also out of disgust, because in her fear and rage she was slobbering on his hand, and he was now wiping it off. The next sound, by contrast, was a joyful exclamation from Justine, who recognized the man as Mr. Jocundus Meyenthal. He turned toward her; instantly the two of them embraced and for a long time held one another tight. Then attentively and anxiously, they contemplated their sad, serious faces and finally went for the moment into the women's little parlor, into the sunlight.

While Justine was taking her religion lesson, Jocundus had come just in time to the witch's cavern. At first she had smiled a delighted and spiteful smile, for she thought that this handsome man and the beautiful woman were using the pious women's house for a forbidden rendezvous, and that these ladies were thus at last exposing their weak spot. The adventure ought to provide her with oil of roses by the pitcher-full.

Jocundus pulled out his list of good folk to be libeled and told her what the job was, and in whose name and behalf he had come; he asked her, at first rather dryly and briefly, what she knew about each one, what could be done to label him a villain, get some well-deserved rumor started about him, and bring him to punishment. She said sullenly, "I don't know him. They never did anything to me."

This creature at least has the instinct to bite only those who have touched it or kicked it, thought Jocundus; so he inquired about certain of the previous victims of these attacks and asked what they had done to her.

She laughed hoarsely the moment she heard their names, recalling the important role she had been allowed to play in the merry chase. But she gave no answer to the question: rather she began, with heavy-handed eloquence, to describe how she had gone about initiating and spreading evil rumors and false charges. All that was needed to start with, she said, was some particular quality, innocent in itself, some habit or characteristic of the person in question, an incident, the conjunction of two circumstances or chance occurrences, anything that was in itself true and unquestionable and thus capable of providing the nucleus of reality for the fabrication at hand. Also, she said, pure invention was not the only way to go; one could profitably transfer to a given person the crimes and atrocities committed by someone else, thanks to those fortuitous combinations that exist in real life anyway. Or one could hang on another person the sort of thing one always felt like doing oneself, or perhaps had even done a bit of. To compensate in this fashion for an often unjust fate, and to improve on it, offered one a kind of god-like satisfaction. For example, say there were two people, one of whom you liked fairly well while you hated the other, but the first was a poor, mean failure, a ne'er-do-well, while the latter was an insufferable do-gooder who never left himself open to gossip. Well, you felt a bit like Providence itself if you could relieve your good friend and fellow sufferer of his uncouth traits and shortcomings and dump them on the insufferable stuffed-shirt. Yes, there was something great about using a carefully planted word or two to pull a proud family down into shame and disgrace, greater than it would be if a magician could cause a storm and send ships to the bottom of the sea.

Her words revealed far more knowledge of the world and people than the woman's misshapen figure and impoverished appearance might lead one to expect. But all this knowledge was dry and withered and crippled and only grew rankly on the surface of things like a matted network of moss. She herself, despite her devious cunning, was often like a child who in its ignorance plays with fire and starts a city burning.

With some difficulty one could gather from her often confused words and hints that she was accusing her own parents or grandparents of having frittered away a heritage of some distinction, leaving her exposed to misery and darkness, that she had once been married to a shoemaker who had fought with her for a long time but finally bested her and chased her away, that she now supported herself as a peddlar. Every now and then she would locate merchandise of various kinds, with which she could rove about the byways, when she felt like it, creeping from house to house and tending to her sinister trade.

Suddenly the witch interrupted her own flow of words and asked to see again the names of those who were to be the new objects of slander, for while she was talking she had unexpectedly felt the desire to get busy again and play Providence.

For good measure, Jocundus put the list in her hands just to see how she would go to work in specific terms, for he had already determined for himself the general basis on which this large-scale public harassment was built.

At the very first name, which was that of an honest burgher, she cried, "Wait, I *do* know him! How could I overlook him? That is the dear gentleman who showed me the door when I was in his kitchen, talking with the servants. He received one inheritance after another in quick order, and got rich while poor relatives of his were starving. He'll turn out to be a nice case of fortune-hunting, if we investigate the matter a bit and get it into the proper perspective. A couple of old cousins of his, whose money he inherited, died unexpectedly—but what am I saying? His own father died a few years ago, and he wasn't even very old or sick. Most unusual!"

Now Jocundus was frightened at the consequences of his own actions, and he snatched the list from the old woman, crying, "Quiet, you disgusting Oil Witch. Don't you dare repeat a single word of those lies you're telling, or you'll have me to answer to."

"You?" replied the old monster, glaring at him with her eyes suddenly wide open. Then she hissed, "What's wrong with you? What do you want from me, you dog? You cursed spy! Are you trying to bribe me? Are you trying to take advantage of me and get me to do something bad? You wait, we'll get you in hand. We know you! We know you, you rotten evil man!"

Angered by the woman's ugly rage and the hideous face she made, Jocundus, who had already turned to go, forgot himself for a moment and seized her by the neck, wringing from her that very scream which brought about his reunion with Justine—with the result that he did not regret his violation of the Oriental commandment (which came to his mind in retrospect), forbidding us to strike a woman even with a flower.

Ursula and her daughter were touched and pleased that the separated couple were rejoined in their house. They regarded it as further evidence of God's will, but they were in some doubt whether the religious instruction they had begun was destined to continue, for they did not entirely trust Mr. Meyenthal. They therefore referred the matter to a higher power and modestly said nothing more about it. Ursula immediately picked up her snuffbox again.

Jocundus and Justine meanwhile did not say much either; they were eager to leave the house and get outside. With only the most necessary words of explanation to account for their having met here, they took their leave of the good Christian ladies (whom Jocundus remembered well) and promised them further news and their continued sympathy. When they went through the Oil Wife's room she was not to be seen and must have hidden. But hardly had they reached the street when her face appeared beneath the iron grating of the little window, where she shouted horrible curses and threats at them. However, they heard none of it because they were sufficiently occupied with one another, walking side by side, with a new and different feeling of happiness, but still in deep seriousness.

Jocundus had a horse waiting at an inn; he had ridden the rather long distance up here. Justine had arranged to meet her brother on one of the steamboats from the city, when it reached the landing, and make the return trip with him. The two of them therefore agreed to meet the next morning and to do so at the home of the grandparents on the mountain by Schwanau, where Jocundus would head, starting at daybreak. They intended to spend the whole day there and talk things out. So they parted for today, looking into one another's eyes with candor and affection but still with the deepest seriousness.

The next day was a Sunday and it began with a beautiful June morning. Justine rose with the sun. She got herself outfitted and dressed up as if there were a festival in the offing. Contrary to her recent custom, she arranged her hair in thick curls and put on a sheer summer dress of bright colors, not forgetting some attractive jewelry for her neck. So with her family still asleep she set out, unnoticed, on the way to the heights, her stride vigorous, her face lightly flushed. Her grandmother was startled by her lovely, youthful appearance and also pleased with the apparent turn fate had taken. Since she was at breakfast she made her granddaughter drink a cup of coffee, for she had had nothing that morning. Yet Justine did not pause for long, but started off again to walk along the mountain path Jocundus would have to take, in order to meet him part way. And so she walked in anxious, happy expectation, into the silence of the Sunday morning. The ground wherever she looked was covered with flowers, the blossoms were floating down from the budding trees with every breeze that blew. Now the church bells everywhere began to ring, all along the distant shores of the great lake, in the gleaming white towns. The deep full notes of the mighty bells blended together and filled the air far and wide like an endless sea of sound, swelling up to touch Justine's heart and threatening to draw it down into their depths. However, she did not turn back but hurried on, borne by the waves of sound, toward her husband, who was now approaching with rapid steps in the light of the morning sun. As soon as they saw one another the long lost smiles returned to their faces and they embraced and kissed lovingly.

Without watching where they were going they came upon a forest path and climbed arm in arm to the topmost height of the mountain, chatting away together, telling one another everything that had happened to them, what they had lived through and thought about during the time of their separation. The sound of the bells, meanwhile, was gradually lost in the intervening forest, or perhaps they were finally through ringing. When the last tone, with its single reverberating note, died away, they were aware of the deep silence that took over. They found themselves at the edge of a vast forest clearing which enclosed a well-tended planting of young trees. In orderly rows stood thousands and more thousands of tiny white fir, red spruce, pine, and little larches, barely three or four inches tall, lifting high their bright green tips, looking like a festive convention of nursery schools. Next came the gathered files of knee-high, then chest-high young trees, like sturdy grammar schools, followed by a host of man-high saplings of beech, oak, and maple, until beyond them a guardian community of tall old forest trees rounded off the assembly. The whole plantation was tended as carefully and neatly as the garden of some great noble, though it belonged to a cooperative society of simple farmers. The solemn stillness heightened the impression produced by this vision of loving care, care directed to the welfare not of their own lives but of a coming century, for grandchildren and great-grandchildren.

In the translucent shade of the young maples, foresters had set a bench as a resting spot; here Jocundus and Justine sat down to enjoy this comforting sight in silence and peace.

"You see," said Jocundus at last, as he took Justine's hands, "no sooner do we find each other again than we see that the world is not as bad as it likes to pretend. All these hasty, cold, selfish people actually work as hard as they do just for their children and they even assume the duty of providing for future generations they do not know."

"Do you still love me a little bit?" Justine replied, for at this moment she felt more like providing just for herself. Jocundus looked off into the distance and saw, through the tops of a couple of fir trees a stretch of blue horizon with the shining reflection of a long white building, its presence more to be surmised than recognized.

"Can you see that white shiny thing?" he asked. "It was once a cloister, founded seven hundred years ago by a knight in memory of his wife when she died. He entered it himself and never left it again all his life. I love you as much as he loved his wife, although I would not enter a cloister if I lost you. The whole gleaming, silent edifice of the world would be the temple of your memory, your shrine. But let us settle the little affair of honor that still stands between us. As penance and atonement, my rude little sweetheart, you shall call me that coarse name again, the word that drove us apart, but with a smile on your lips, so that it loses its bad meaning. Quick! What was it?"

As he said this he put one arm around her shoulder and with the other held her chin tight. But she shook her head and closed her mouth as hard as she could. Then he tapped gently on her cheek, tried to open her mouth and kept saying, "Quick, out with it, loosen your tongue!" until she spoke the word quickly, full of tenderness and humor, but almost inaudibly: "Fool!" Whereupon Jocundus kissed her.

Now, as they held each other close and were silent for a while, Justine said, suddenly and unexpectedly, "Jocundus, what shall we do about religion or about the church?"

"Nothing," he answered. After some reflection he continued, "If the Eternal and Infinite keeps its silence and hides itself, why shouldn't we be able to keep happily and peacefully still for a while too? I'm tired of all the importunities and banalities of these people who come without our calling for them and who have themselves no calling, who don't know anything, yet always want to shepherd me around. If you remove the individual persons from a religion, its temples fall and the rest is silence. But the silence and peace we gain is not death but life, blossoming and glowing, like this Sunday morning. And we make our way through it in good conscience, awaiting those things that will come or not come. In good conscience and undivided we will walk on ahead, we will not let head and heart or knowledge and spirit be torn in two by the familiar miserable commonplace. We must go whole and indivisible to that judgment that awaits all men."

Justine looked straight at her husband, unblinking, her face flushed, because she sensed that she might long ago have heard him talk to her as openly as this if she had entrusted herself to him rather than to a churchman.

Whether Jocundus's words were wise or foolish, they seemed to her inordinately pleasing—proof that she now belonged wholly to him.

"Amen!" said Jocundus. "I almost believe I'm beginning to preach."

"Not amen!" cried Justine, "Go on and talk more! Imagine that this nursery is your congregation and preach to it as that saint did to the rocks or the other one to the fish."

"No, church is over! Did you hear the sign?" Jocundus answered with a smile, as here and there in the distance the bells actually did proclaim the end of worship.

They got up and walked slowly to the house of their grandparents; it was noon before they got there. The old people, however, had summoned the whole family up from Schwanau so that they might have a real feast of reunion and reconciliation there, and they had prepared a simple, hearty meal in country fashion. Everyone was already gathered together when the handsome, reunited couple arrived. A degree of tension and awkwardness prevailed at first, but when they saw that the lost smiles had returned, the sunshine of former happiness spread through the whole house. The "Stauffacher" shone like a star and seized the helm firmly, to steer the refurbished ship of fortune.

Justine moved to join her husband in the city where he now prospered without a break, shedding his gullibility in matters of business and commerce but without therefore becoming false and deceitful.

They had a son and a daughter, whom they called Justus and Jocunda, and who are sure to pass on the heritage of fresh and smiling beauty.

Frequently, when they went for a walk, they would visit those pious women, Ursula and Agatha, and see to it that they lacked for nothing. The Oil Wife had moved away, for she could not stand perfect innocence and kindness.

The pastor, whose hour of weakness Justine had witnessed, came by occasionally to visit the couple again and enjoyed confiding in them. He continued for a time, with a heavy heart, his dubious dance on the swaying tightrope and then was glad to be able, through Jocundi's intercession, to enter a worldly business in which he proved himself a good deal sharper and more useful than Jocundus had been in Seldwyla and Schwanau. For he, the pastor, did not easily fall for what people tried to make him believe.

Translated by Frank G. Ryder

From
STORIES
OF
ZURICH

The Banner of
the Upright Seven

Kaspar Hediger, master tailor in Zurich, was at an age when the industrious artisan begins to allow himself an hour or so of rest after meals. And so he was sitting one fine March day not in his bodily but in his intellectual workshop, a tiny den which he had allotted to himself these many years. He was glad he could occupy it again without a fire; for neither his old habits as tradesman nor his income permitted him to have an extra room heated during the winter, merely for reading. And this at a time when there were tailors who could afford to hunt and to go riding daily; so closely dovetailed are the shades of culture.

Master Hediger, however, cut no mean figure in his orderly back room. He looked almost more like an American squatter than a tailor: a powerful and intelligent face with heavy side-whiskers, surmounted by an imposing bald dome, was bowed over *The Swiss Republican,* reading the leading article with a critical expression. At least twenty-five neatly bound folio volumes of this *Republican* stood in a small walnut cabinet, and they contained almost nothing which Hediger had not experienced or fought through in the last twenty-five years. Besides these the cabinet contained Rotteck's *Universal History,* a Swiss history by Johannes Müller, and a handful of political tracts and the like; an atlas and a small portfolio of caricatures and pamphlets, mementos of bitterly passionate days, lay on the bottom shelf.

The walls of the little room were adorned with portraits of Columbus, Zwingli, Hutten, Washington, and Robespierre; for he was a bitter partisan and sanctioned the Terror after the event. Besides these international heroes, some Swiss Progressives also adorned the walls, with highly edifying and prolix memorials appended in their own handwriting, regular little essays. Against the bookcase leaned a well-kept, shining musket, on which hung a short side arm and a cartridge box that always contained thirty ball-cartridges. This was *his* hunting-piece, with which he went gunning not for hare and partridge, but for aristocrats and Jesuits, for constitution-breakers and betrayers of the people. Until now his good angel had preserved him from bloodshed, through lack of opportunity; yet more than once he had seized his gun and hurried to the square in the days of the riots, and the weapon had to remain permanently stationed between bed and cabinet; "For," he was wont to say, "no government and no battalions can protect freedom and justice unless each citizen is prepared to step outside his door and see what is going on."

Just as the doughty tailor was deeply buried in his article, now nodding approval and now shaking his head, in came his youngest son, Karl, a budding official in one of the government offices.

"What is it?" asked Hediger gruffly, for he did not like to be disturbed in his den.

Karl asked, somewhat uncertain of the success of his request, whether he might have his father's gun and cartridge box for the afternoon, to drill with.

"No, you can't; not a chance!" said Hediger curtly.

"Oh, why not? I won't hurt it," continued the son, intimidated but persistent, for he absolutely had to have a gun or he would be put under arrest. But the old man only replied the louder, "Not a chance! I only wonder at the persistence of these gentlemen, my sons, who are so unpersistent in other things that no one of them stuck to the calling of his own choice. You know that each of your three older brothers wanted this gun as soon as they had to begin to drill, and that not one of them got it. And yet here you come slinking along after it. You've got your own fine wages, and nobody to provide for—buy your own weapons like any other man of honor. This gun won't leave the spot, except when I use it myself!"

"But it's only for a few times. You surely don't expect me to buy an infantry rifle, seeing I'm going to join the sharpshooters later on and buy a carbine for that."

"Sharpshooters! That's good too. Just how do you explain the necessity of joining the sharpshooters, when you've never fired a bullet in your life? In my day a man must have burned up a lot of powder before he could apply for membership; now lads turn marksmen, hit or miss, and there are fellows wearing the green coat that couldn't knock a cat off a roof, though to be sure they smoke cigars and play the gentleman instead! That's not my affair."

"Oh, let me have it just this once," said the boy, almost whimpering, "tomorrow I'll see about getting another; I can't any more today."

"I give my gun to nobody," responded his father, "who doesn't know how to handle it; if you can take off the lock of this gun and take it apart properly, then you can have it, otherwise it stays here."

And he hunted in a drawer for a screwdriver, gave it to his son, and handed him the musket. Desperate as he was, Karl tried his luck and began to loosen the screws of the lock. His father looked on derisively; but it was not long before he cried, "Now don't let the screwdriver slip so, you'll ruin the whole thing. Loosen all the screws first, then take them out, that's easier. There, at last!"

Now Karl held the lock in his hand, but did not know what else to do with it and laid it down with a sigh, already seeing himself in imagination in the guardhouse. But old Hediger was now warmed up and he picked up the lock to give his son a lesson on it by explaining it as he took it apart.

"You see," he said, "first you take away the trigger-spring by means of this spring-hook—this way; then comes the screw of the sear-spring, which you unscrew only halfway, and then tap on the sear-spring this way, so that the pin comes out of the hole; now you take out the screw. Now the sear-spring, the sear-screw, and the sear; then the bridle-screw and the bridle-hammer; then the tumbler-pin, the trigger, and finally the tumbler; this is the tumbler. Hand me the neat's-foot oil from that little cabinet there, I'll just oil up the screws a bit right now."

He had laid all these parts on the newspaper, and Karl looked on eagerly and handed him the bottle, saying that the weather had changed for the better. But when his father had wiped off the parts of the lock and freshly moistened them with the oil, he did not put them together again, but threw them helter-skelter into the cover of a small box, saying, "Well, this evening we'll put the thing together again; now I want to finish reading the paper."

Disappointed and savage, Karl went out to tell his woes to his mother; he felt a mighty fear of that public power to which he was now going to school as recruit. Since he had outgrown school, he had not been punished, nor in fact during the last years of school, and now it was to begin again on a higher plane, simply because he had relied on his father's gun.

His mother said, "Your father is really quite right. All you four boys get more than he does, and that by reason of the education he has given you; but not only do you spend the last farthing on yourselves, but you're forever coming to plague him with borrowing every sort of thing: black swallowtail, field glass, drawing instruments, razor, hat, rifle, sabre; everything that he keeps in good order you carry off, only to bring it back ruined. It's just as if you were studying the year round what else could be borrowed of him; but for his part he never asks anything of you, although you owe him your life and everything else. But I'll help you this once more."

Hereupon she went in to Master Hediger and said, "Dear husband, I forgot to tell you that Frymann the carpenter sent word that the Seven would meet today to transact some business, I think something political."

"Is that so?" said he, at once agreeably stirred, and he got up and walked back and forth. "I wonder that Frymann didn't come himself to speak with me first about it, to consult me."

After a few minutes he dressed hastily, put on his hat, and left with the words, "Wife, I'm going out right now, I must know what is up. Besides, I haven't once put my foot outside the door this spring, and it's so lovely today. So goodbye."

"There, now he won't come back before ten o'clock tonight," said his wife laughing, and she bade Karl take the gun and be careful of it, and be sure to bring it back in season.

"Take it!" lamented her son, "why, he's taken the lock apart, and I can't fix it."

"Then I can," cried his mother, and she went into the den with him. She tipped over the boxful of parts, picked out the springs and screws, and began to put them together very skillfully.

"Where the dickens did you learn that, mother?" cried Karl quite dumfounded.

"I learned it in my father's house," she said. "He and my seven brothers had trained me to clean all their guns and rifles for them after they had been shooting. I often cried over it, but in the end I could handle the stuff like a gunsmith. In the village they simply called me the Gun Girl, and almost always my hands and the tip of my nose were black. My brothers shot away and drank away house and home, so that poor me, I was glad to have your father the tailor marry me."

During this narrative her dexterous fingers had actually assembled the lock and fastened it to the stock. Karl hung the shiny cartridge box about him, took the gun, and hurried at top speed to the drill ground, where he just barely escaped being late. After six o'clock he brought the things back, and attempting now to take the lock apart himself, put the parts back into the box cover, shaking them into disorder.

When he finished his supper it was dark. He went to the lake front, hired a boat, and rowed along the shore until he came opposite some yards used partly by carpenters, partly by stonecutters. It was a perfectly glorious evening; a mild south wind lifted tiny ripples on the water, the full moon lit up its distant surface and sparkled brightly on the little waves close by, and in the sky the stars stood out in clear, brilliant shapes; the snowy mountains looked down into the lake like pale spectres, divined rather than seen; and on the other hand, the folderol of commerce, the petty and restless lines of the buildings vanished in the darkness and were united under the influence of the moonlight into large, quiet masses—in short, the landscape setting was worthily prepared for the coming scene.

Karl Hediger rowed rapidly until he neared a large lumberyard; there he sang a couple of times in a quiet voice the first verse of a short song, then rowed slowly and quietly out into the lake. From the piles of lumber a slender girl who had been sitting there arose, untied a skiff, stepped into it, and rowed gradually, with several turns, after the boatman of the gentle voice. When she had reached his side, the young people spoke to each other by name and then rowed without further delay side by side out into the flowing silver, far out upon the lake. Glorying in youthful power, they described a mighty curve with several spirals, the girl leading and the youth following with easy pulls of his oars, without leaving her side, and one could see that the couple was not unpractised in rowing together. When they had got to complete stillness and solitude, the young girl drew in her oars and stopped. That is, she laid only one oar down, the other she held over the gunwale as if playing with it, but not without a purpose; for as Karl also stopped rowing, but tried to approach her and even to grapple her skiff, she very skillfully managed to keep off his boat with her oar, by giving it a single push from time to time. This practice also seemed not to be new, since the young fellow soon resigned himself and sat still in his little craft.

Now they began to chat, and Karl said, "I must say, Hermine, I can turn the proverb around and declare that what I enjoyed to the full in youth I vainly wish for in old age. When I was ten years old and you were seven, how often we used to kiss; and now that I am twenty, I don't even get your fingertips to kiss."

"Once and for all, I refuse to listen to another word of these impudent lies," answered the girl, half angry, half laughing, "it's all made up and false, I absolutely don't remember any such familiarities."

"Unfortunately," cried Karl, "but I remember them all the better. And more than that, you were the leader and the temptress."

"Karl, how horrid," Hermine interrupted him, but he continued pitilessly, "Just remember how often, when we had got tired of helping poor children to fill their baskets with shavings—and how it always vexed the foremen—how often I'd have to build out of small sticks and boards in among the big piles of lumber, and all in secret, a tiny little hut with a roof and a door and a little bench inside. And then when we'd sit on the bench with the door shut, and I'd finally lay my hands in my lap, who would throw her arms around me and kiss me more times than you could count?"

At these words he came near falling into the water; for as he had sought to approach imperceptibly during this talk, she suddenly gave his skiff such a violent shove that it almost overturned. She burst into a ringing laugh as his left arm plunged into the water to the elbow, drawing a curse from him.

"You wait," he said, "some day I'll certainly get even with you for this."

"Lots of time for that," she replied, "don't be in too much of a hurry, please, my fine gentleman!" Then she continued somewhat more seriously, "Father has learned our story; I didn't deny it, at least in essentials; but he won't hear of it, and forbids us any further thought of it; so that's how we stand."

"And do you intend to yield to your father's command as dutifully and as irrevocably as you make out?"

"At least I shall never do the exact opposite of his wish, and still less shall I risk a hostile relationship with him; for you know that he bears a grudge a long time and is capable of a hatred that eats into his very soul. You also know that he has been a widower these five years past, and has stayed so for my sake; I think a daughter might well consider that. And now that we're talking about it, I must also tell you that under these circumstances I regard it as improper for us to see each other so often; it's bad enough when a child can't obey its father in spirit; but to do every day what would hurt your parents if they knew it has something hateful about it, and so I wish we wouldn't meet alone oftener than once a month, instead of every day as we've been doing, and for the rest, let time take its course."

"Take its course! And can you and will you really let things go that way?"

"Why not? Are they so important? Perhaps we can still have each other and perhaps not. The world will go on just the same, and perhaps we'll easily forget each other, for we're young still; but in any case it doesn't seem to me that there's any great cause for making a fuss."

This speech the seventeen-year-old beauty delivered in a matter-of-fact tone and with apparent coldness, as she seized her oars again and steered for the land. Karl rowed along beside her, full of anxiety and alarm, and not less full of anger at Hermine's words. She was half glad to know that her young scamp was anxious, but on the other hand she too was pondering upon the substance of their conversation, and especially the four weeks of separation she had imposed on herself.

Thus he finally succeeded in surprising her and forcing his boat up to hers with one stroke. Instantly he clasped her slender body in his arms, drawing her half toward him, so that they both leaned partly over the deep water, while the boats were tipped quite decidedly, so that any movement might overturn them completely. The girl consequently felt herself defenseless and had to allow Karl to imprint seven or eight passionate kisses on her lips. Then he gently and carefully righted her and her skiff; she swept the loose hair from her face, seized her oars, drew a deep breath, and with tears in her eyes cried angrily and threateningly, "Just wait, you rascal, until I have you under my thumb. As true as God is in heaven, you shall know that you've got a wife!"

Hereupon she rowed with rapid strokes back to her father's land and dwelling, without looking around at him again.

Karl however, filled with bliss and triumph, called after her, "Good night, Miss Hermine Frymann! That tasted good!"

Mrs. Hediger had, however, not made a false report to her husband when she caused him to go out. The news which she communicated to him had only been saved up for suitable use and then utilized at the right moment. As a matter of fact a meeting did take place, a meeting of the Society of Seven, or of the Strong, or of the Upright, or of the Freedom-loving, as they variously called themselves. This was simply a circle of seven old and tried friends, all master artisans, patriots, arch-politicians, and stern domestic tyrants after the pattern of Master Hediger. Born in the previous century, every man of them, they had as children witnessed the downfall of the old régime and had then experienced through many years the storms and birth pangs of the new period, until the latter cleared up in the late forties and once more brought Switzerland to power and unity. Some of them came from the common domains, the former subject-land of the Swiss Allies, and they could remember how as peasant children they had had to kneel down by the roadside when a coach came driving by with barons and the court usher in it; others were more or less distantly related to imprisoned or executed revolutionaries. In short, all were filled with an inextinguishable hatred toward all aristocracy, which since the downfall of the latter had simply been transformed into a bitter scorn. But when it once more appeared in democratic garb, and, allied with those old-time purveyors of power, the priests, stirred up a struggle lasting several years, then to their hatred of the aristocrats was added that of the clerics; indeed, their martial sentiment now had to turn not only against lords and priests, but against their own brothers, against entire masses of the agitated people—causing them in their old days an unexpected expenditure of compound energy, which however they made valiantly.

These seven men were anything but insignificant; in all popular assemblages, union meetings, and the like, they helped to form a solid center, stuck unweariedly to their posts, and were ready by day or night to do for their party commissions and transactions which could not be intrusted to hirelings, but only to perfectly reliable persons. Often they were consulted by the party leaders and taken into their confidence, and if a sacrifice was necessary, then the seven men were the first with their mites. For all this they desired no other reward than the victory of their cause and their good conscience; never did one of them thrust himself forward or seek an advantage or a position, and for them the greatest honor was a fleeting handshake from this or that "famous Confederate"; but he must be a genuine one, and "clean to his kidneys," as they put it.

These valiant men had been learning each other's ways for decades; they all used each other's Christian names, and came in the end to form a close corporation, but without any other statutes than those they bore in their hearts. Twice a week they met, and since two of even this small company were innkeepers, these alternated in having the meetings. Very entertaining and sociable they were; quiet and serious as the men showed themselves in large gatherings, they were both noisy and gay when by themselves; none of them put on airs, and none minced matters; at times they all spoke at once, then again they would listen attentively to a single speaker, according to their state of mind and their fancy. Not only politics was the topic of conversation, but also their home life. If one of them was in sorrow and anxiety, he would lay before the society what distressed him; the affair would be discussed, and its remedy became common cause. If one of them felt himself injured by another, he would make his complaint to the Seven, who would sit in judgment, and the offender would be admonished of his wrongdoing.

In all this they were alternately very passionate or very calm and dignified, or perhaps ironical. On two occasions traitors, unclean fellows, had sneaked in among them, been recognized, and in solemn assembly condemned and cast out, that is sadly thrashed by the fists of the valorous graybeards. If a great misfortune came upon the party to which they belonged, that transcended all domestic unhappiness, and they would hide singly in the darkness and shed bitter tears.

The most eloquent and prosperous of them was Frymann the carpenter, a veritable Croesus with a very fine establishment. The most impecunious was Hediger the tailor, but in oratory second only to Frymann. His political ardor had long since lost him his best customers, yet he had nonetheless given his sons a good education, and so he had no means left. The other five were well-established people, who did more listening than talking in the society when important business was on, but made up for it by speaking all the more weightily in their houses and among their neighbors.

Today there actually were important transactions on hand, which Frymann and Hediger had previously discussed. The time of unrest, of conflict, and of political trouble was past for these brave fellows, and the conditions which had been secured seemed to conclude for good and all their long political activities. All's well that ends well! they were able to say, and they felt successful and contented. And so on this evening of their political life they wished to indulge in a grand final festivity, and attend in a body, as the Seven, the Swiss national shooting match which was to be held the next summer at Aarau, the first one to follow the adoption of the new constitution of 1848. Now most of them had long since been members of the Swiss Marksmen's Association, and all but Hediger, who contented himself with his musket, had good rifles with which they had in previous years gone shooting on Sundays. They had also already attended other festivals, though not together, so that the matter did not seem exactly strange. But a spirit of outward pomp had come over some of them, and it was a question of no less a matter than appearing in Aarau with their own banner and presenting a handsome memorial trophy.

When the small company had drunk several glasses of wine, and good humor held full sway, Frymann and Hediger came out with their proposal, which nevertheless startled the modest gentlemen somewhat, so that for some minutes they wavered irresolutely. For they did not quite see the propriety of attracting such attention and marching out with a banner. But as they had long since forgotten how to vote against any bold flight or daring undertaking, they did not hold out longer than it took the speakers to paint to them in glowing colors how the flag would be a symbol and their procession a triumph of tried and true friendship, and how the appearance of seven such old war horses as they with a banner of friendship would surely make good sport. Only a small banner of green silk was to be made, bearing the Swiss coat of arms and a good legend.

After the banner question had been settled, the memorial gift was taken up; the value of it was fixed fairly easily: about two hundred francs, old style. But the choice of the object caused a lengthy and almost vexatious debate. Frymann began the general inquiry and invited Kuser the silversmith, as a man of good taste, to express his opinion. Kuser solemnly drank a deep draught, coughed, bethought himself, and then said that as luck would have it, he just happened to have a handsome silver cup in his shop, which he could heartily recommend, if that was satisfactory to them, and which he could give them at a very great discount. Hereupon there followed a general silence, interrupted only by brief utterances such as "That sounds good," or "Why, yes." Then Hediger asked if there was any further proposal to be made. Whereupon Syfrig, the skillful smith, took a swallow, plucked up courage, and said, "If it is agreeable to the gentlemen, I will express an idea, too. I have forged a very ingenious plow of solid iron, which as you know was praised at the agricultural exhibit. I am willing to deliver this fine piece of work for the two hundred francs, although that would not pay for the labor on it; but I am of the opinion that this implement and symbol of agriculture would be a memorial gift that would genuinely represent the common people. Not that I wish to cast reflections on any other proposal."

During this speech, Burgi the crafty cabinetmaker had also been thinking about the matter, and when a short silence again prevailed and the silversmith was beginning to make a long face, the cabinetmaker delivered himself thus: "An idea has come to me too, good friends, which might perhaps make great sport. Years and years ago I had to make for an out-of-town bridal couple a double four-poster bed of the finest walnut, inlaid with bird's-eye veneering; day after day the young couple hung around my work-shop, measuring the length and breadth of the thing, and billing and cooing before journeymen and apprentices without minding their jokes and broad hints. But when the wedding was to come off, suddenly they began to fight like cats and dogs, though not a soul knew why; one went off this way, the other that, and my bedstead stood there like a rock. At the very lowest valuation, it's worth a hundred and eighty francs; but I'll be glad to lose eighty and give it for a hundred. Then we'll have a featherbed made for it and set it up in the trophy room, all fitted up, with the inscription: For the encouragement of some unmarried Confederate. How's that?"

A merry peal of laughter rewarded this idea; only the silver-smith and the blacksmith smiled coolly and acidly; but Pfister the innkeeper at once raised his strong voice and said with his wonted frankness, "Well, gentlemen, if the point is to have every man bring his own corn to market, then I know something better than anything proposed yet. In my cellar lies a fine solid cask of 1834 claret, so-called Swiss Blood, which I bought myself in Basle more than twelve years ago. In view of your moderation and modest ways, I never ventured to tap the cask, and yet two hundred francs are tied up in it, for there are exactly a hundred quarts. I'll give you the wine at cost price, and reckon the cask as cheaply as pos-sible, for I'll be only too glad to get room for better-selling goods, and may I never leave this spot if that trophy doesn't do us honor."

This speech, during which the three foregoing movers had al-ready begun to murmur, was scarcely ended when Erismann, the other innkeeper, took the floor and said, "If this is the way it's going, then I won't stay in the background, but will say that I think I have the best thing for our purpose, namely, my young milch cow of pure highland breed, that I'm ready to sell if I get a good purchaser. Tie a bell around the neck of this splendid ani-mal, hang a milkpail between her horns, deck her out with flow-ers—"

"And put her under a glass globe in the trophy room" the pro-voked Pfister interrupted, and with that there burst one of those storms which occasionally made the sessions of the Strong Seven somewhat tempestuous, but only to result in all the brighter sun-shine. All spoke at once, defended their own proposals, attacked those of the others, and accused each other of self-seeking. For they always told each other plainly what they thought, and disposed of their affairs by means of frank truth and not disingenuous hushing up, as men of a certain kind of false culture are wont to do.

Now when a perfectly fiendish din had arisen, Hediger clinked his glass noisily and raised his voice to speak. "Ye warriors, do not become heated, but let us make quietly for our goal! The objects proposed are then a cup, a plow, a complete four-poster, a cask of wine, and a cow. Permit me to consider your proposals a little more closely. That cup of yours, my dear Rudi, is a fixture in your place and I know it well; it's been standing for years and years behind your show window, and I actually believe you got your master's title with it. But its shape is antiquated and will not permit us to choose it and pretend it is new. Your plow, Connie Syfrig, doesn't seem to have suited its purpose very well, after all, or you'd certainly have sold it three years ago. But we must plan to have the winner of our trophy take unfeigned pleasure in it. Your four-poster, however, is a new idea, Henry, and certainly a delicious one, and would surely give occasion for the most proverbial turns of speech. But to carry it out properly would require handsome and sufficient bedding, and the excess over the sum we have fixed would be too much for only seven people. Your "Swiss Blood," Lienert Pfister, is fine and will be still better if you put a more reasonable price on it and end by tapping it for us, so that we can drink it on our memorial days. Against your cow, Felix Erismann, there is nothing to be said except that she regularly upsets the milkpail. That's why you want to sell her; for that vice is certainly not agreeable. But how about it? Would it be right now if some honest farmer won the animal, led her joyfully home to his wife, and she joyfully sat down to milk her and then saw the sweet foaming milk poured out on the ground? Just imagine the vexation, the anger, and the disappointment of the good woman, and the embarrassment of the good marksman, after this scene had been repeated two or three times.

"Yes, dear friends, do not take it ill of me, but I must say it: all our proposals have the common fault of hastily and thoughtlessly trying to make the honor of our country a source of calculation and of profit. What if this be done a thousand times over by big and little—we in our circle have never yet done it, and let us not begin now. So let each man bear equally, without thought of gain, the costs of the trophy, so that it can really be a trophy of honor."

The five gain-seekers, who had let their heads hang in shame, now cried with one voice, "Well said! Kaspar has spoken well," and they said it was his turn to make a suggestion.

But Frymann took the floor and said, "It seems to me still that a silver cup is most fitting for an honor trophy. It always keeps its value, cannot be worn out, and remains as a handsome memento of happy days and of the valiant men of the house. A house in which such a cup is preserved can never wholly decay, and who can say whether many other things are not preserved simply on account of such a memorial? And is not the opportunity given to art to mold many of these vessels into ever new and beautiful forms, and so to exercise its inventiveness and to send a ray of beauty into the most distant vales, so that little by little a mighty store of noble prize cups is treasured up in the fatherland, noble in form and in substance? And how appropriate that such treasures, scattered through the whole country, cannot be utilized for the common uses of everyday life, but in their pure brilliance, in their refined forms, continually keep the higher things before our eyes, and seem to hold fast the idea of the common good and the sunlight of days of ideal beauty! Away then with the rubbish of the annual fair that is beginning to pile up in our trophy chambers, the prey of moths and of the most ordinary uses, and let us abide by the time-honored venerable drinking cup! Truly, if I lived in a day when Swiss liberties were nearing their end, I could not imagine any more exalted crowning festivity than to gather together the thousands and thousands of cups belonging to all the corporations, clubs, and private citizens, cups of every kind and shape, in all the splendor of days departed, with all their recollections, and to drink a last toast to the declining fatherland—"

"Silence, rude guest! What unworthy thoughts are these?" cried the Upright and Strong, and fairly shivered. But Frymann went on, "As it is fitting for a man at times to think of death in the midst of his prime, so too in an hour of reflection let him fix his eye upon the certain end of his fatherland, that he may love it all the more fervently in the present day; for all things upon this earth are transitory and subject to change. Or have not much greater nations than we perished? Or would you one day care to drag out an existence like that of the Wandering Jew who cannot die, serving all the new upstart nations, he that buried the Egyptians, the Greeks, and the Romans? No, a nation that knows that one day it will live no more, uses its days all the more actively, lives so much the longer, and bequeaths a glorious memory; for it will grant itself no rest until it has brought to light and to fruition the capabilities that lie dormant in it, like an indefatigable man who puts his house in order before he departs this life. This is in my opinion the main consideration. When a nation has performed its task, then a few years more or less of existence do not matter; new manifestations will already be waiting at the portals of time.

"And so I must confess that once a year I fall a prey to such thoughts during a sleepless night or on quiet paths, and try to imagine what type of nation will one day hold sway in these mountains, after we are gone. And each time I go at my work with so much greater haste, as if I could in that way accelerate the labor of my nation, so that that future commonwealth may walk with respect over our graves.

"But away with these thoughts, and let us return to our joyful project. What I think is that we ought to order a new cup of our silversmith, on which he promises to take no profit, but which he will make as valuable as possible. And for this purpose let us have an artist execute a good design, which shall avoid all humdrum emptiness; but in view of our limited means let him pay more heed to the proportions of it, to a beautiful outline and rhythm of the whole piece, than to profuse ornamentation. According to this design Master Kuser will furnish a neat and substantial piece of work."

This proposal was accepted and the transactions ended. But Frymann immediately took the floor again and began, "Now that we have dispatched the general business, worthy friends, permit me to bring up a special matter and to lay a complaint before you, the friendly adjustment of which we will undertake in common after our time-honored custom. You know that our good friend Kaspar Hediger is the progenitor of four specimens of handsome jolly boys, who endanger the whole region with their premature bent for marriage. And sure enough, three of them already have wife and child, although the oldest is not yet twenty-seven. Now there is still the youngest, just twenty, and what does he do? He makes up to my only daughter and turns her head! Thus these frantic marriage-devils have now forced their way into the circle of intimate friendship, and threaten to break it up. Apart from the excessive youth of the children, I frankly confess that such a marriage goes contrary to my desires and intentions. I have a large business and a considerable fortune; therefore when the time comes I shall seek out a son-in-law who is a man of business, and who can furnish a corresponding capital and carry on the large building operations which I have in mind; for you know that I have bought up extensive building lots and am convinced that Zurich is going to expand very considerably.

"But your son, my good Kaspar, is a government clerk and has nothing but his meagre income, and even if he rises it won't become much larger, and so once and for all his account is settled. Let him stick to it, he's provided for if he's economical; but he doesn't need a rich wife, for a rich official is absurd, taking the bread out of other people's mouths; and on the other hand I'm still less inclined to give my money for the loafing or the experimenting of inexperience. Besides all this, it goes against my grain to turn my old and tried relation to my friend Kaspar into kinship. What, are we to load up with family vexations and mutual dependence? No, my friends, let us remain till death intimately linked, but independent of each other, free and answerable to none for our actions; down with kinsman and cousin and all such titles! And so I call upon you, Kaspar, to declare in the bosom of friendship that you will support me in my purposes and oppose those of your son. And no offense, we all know each other."

"We know each other, well said," said Hediger solemnly, after he had dwelt long over a pinch of snuff. "You all know what bad luck I have had with my sons, although they are active and lively lads. I had them taught everything that I wish I had learned myself. All of them knew some language, could write a good essay, figured splendidly, and had enough grounding in other branches of learning to keep, with a little effort, from sinking into complete ignorance. Thank God, I thought, we can at last educate our boys to be citizens that can't have the wool pulled over their eyes any more. And thereupon I let each of them learn whatever trade he chose. But what happened? Scarcely did they have their indentures in their pockets and look about them a little, when the hammer got too heavy for them, and they thought they were too clever for the trades and began to run after clerking positions. The devil knows how they managed it, but the young scoundrels went like fresh rolls! Well, evidently they can be used. One's in the post office, two are with the railroad, and the fourth perches in a government office and claims he's an administrative official. Not that I really care. He who doesn't want to be master must stay a journeyman and have superiors all his life. But since money passes through their hands, all of these young clerking gentlemen had to furnish security; I have no property myself, and so all of you have given my boys security in turn, amounting altogether to forty thousand francs—the old tradesmen, friends of their father, were good enough for that! And now how do you think I feel? How can I look you in the face if only one of all the four makes a single false step, or does something careless or incautious?"

"Fiddle-de-dee," cried the old men, "drive all those notions out of your head. If they hadn't been good boys, we shouldn't have given security, rest easy about that."

"I know all that," answered Hediger, "but a year is a long time, and when it's over another begins. I can assure you that I am terrified every time one of them comes into the house with a fine cigar. Won't he succumb to luxury and self-indulgence? I think. If I see one of the young wives coming along with a new dress, I am afraid she is getting her husband into bad ways and into debt; if one of them talks to a bad debtor on the street, a voice cries out in me: won't that man mislead him into some indiscretion? In short, you see that I feel myself humble and dependent enough, and am far from wanting to become indebted to a rich kinsman to boot, and to make of a friend a master and patron. And why should I wish my young swell-headed son to feel rich and provided for and to run about before my nose with the corresponding arrogance, when he's never been through anything yet? Shall I help to close the school of life for him, so that even in his youth he shall become a hard-hearted boor and lubber, who doesn't know what it means to earn one's bread, and who thinks he's a man of marvelous merit? No, my friend, rest easy; here's my hand on it. Let's have no talk of kinship, down with your in-laws!"

The two old men shook hands, but the others laughed, and Burgi said, "Now who would believe that you two, who have just spoken so wisely in the cause of the fatherland and given us a good dressing down, would do such foolishness the very next minute! God be praised, then I still have some prospect of finding a taker for my double bedstead, and I propose that we give it to the young couple as a wedding present."

"Voted!" cried the other four, and Pfister the innkeeper added, "And I demand that my cask of Swiss Blood be drunk at the wedding, which we shall all attend."

"And I shall pay for it, if it comes off," shouted Frymann angrily, "but if nothing comes of it, as I know nothing will, then you'll pay for the cask, and we'll drink it at our meetings until it's gone."

"We take the wager," they said; but Frymann and Hediger pounded on the table with their fists and kept crying, "Down with kinship! We don't want to be kinsmen, but independent good friends."

With this declaration the weighty session was finally terminated, and the Lovers of Freedom were strong and upright as they wandered homeward.

The next day at dinner, after the journeymen had left the table, Hediger announced to his son and his wife the solemn decision of the day before, namely that for the future no contact between Karl and the carpenter's daughter would be tolerated. Mrs. Hediger was so amused by this authoritative pronouncement that the small remnant of wine which she was just going to drink ran into her windpipe and caused her a terrific coughing spell.

"What is there to laugh at?" said Hediger angrily.

His wife answered, "Oh, I can't help laughing to think that the proverb 'Cobbler, stick to your last' might be applied to your club. Why don't you stick to politics, instead of meddling with love affairs?"

"You laugh like a woman and you talk like one," replied Hediger with great seriousness. "The family is just where true politics begin; of course we are political friends; but in order to stay so we must be careful not to turn the families upside down and play communism with another's wealth. I'm poor and Frymann is rich and that's the way it's to be; we get all the more pleasure out of our spiritual equality. Now shall I stick my nose into his house and his affairs by marriage, and arouse jealousy and embarrassment? Far be it from me!"

"Well, well, well, these are queer principles," answered Mrs. Hediger, "a fine friendship, if one friend doesn't want to give his daughter to the son of the other! And since when is it called communism when prosperity comes into a family through marriage? Is it a blameworthy piece of policy, when a fortunate son is able to win a beautiful and rich girl, because that enables him to attain property and influence, to walk beside his aged parents and his brothers and lend them a helping hand, so that they too can get into clover? For when once good fortune has entered a house, it easily widens its scope, and without damaging the one, the others can throw out their hooks in his shade to advantage. Not that I am looking for a fool's paradise. But there are lots of cases where a man who has got rich can with decency and justice be taken into counsel by his poor relatives. We old folks shall need nothing more; but the time might come when one or the other of Karl's brothers could venture on a good undertaking, a fortunate change of life, if some one lent him the capital. And perhaps one of them will have a talented son who could rise high if there were means enough to send him to college. One would perhaps become a favorite physician, another an influential lawyer or even a judge, another an engineer or an artist, and for all of these, once they had got that far, it would be easy to make good matches and so finally form a respected, numerous, and happy family.

"Now what would be more natural than to have a prosperous uncle, who could open up the world to his industrious but poor relatives, without harming himself? For how often it happens that through one fortunate person all the rest of the people in that house get something of the world and become wise and shrewd. And will you plug up all this opportunity and choke the well-spring of fortune?"

Hediger emitted a vexed laugh and cried, "Castles in the air! You talk like the girl with her milk pail. I see another picture of the man grown rich among poor relations. He to be sure denies himself nothing and always has a thousand notions and desires which cause him all sorts of expenditures and which he satisfies. But whenever his parents and his brothers come to him, as quick as a wink he sits down in importance and ill humor at his rent-book, sticks his pen askew into his mouth, sighs, and says: 'Thank God that you don't have the annoyance and the burden of administering such a fortune! I'd rather herd a flock of goats than watch a pack of malicious and dilatory debtors. No money comes in anywhere, they keep trying to break through and slip out everywhere, and day and night you are in fear of being grossly cheated. And if you get a rascal by the collar, he sets up such a howl that you have to let him go again the next minute, unless you want to be decried as an inhuman usurer. Every official paper, every legal summons, every abstract, every advertisement you have to read over and over, so as not to miss one petition or overlook one term. And never is there any money on hand. If somebody repays a loan, then he puts his money bag on the table in a dozen taverns and brags of his payment; and before he's out of your house there will be three men after that money, one of them without even any security. And then the demands made on you by the community, the philanthropic institutions, the public undertakings, subscription lists of every sort—you can't dodge them, your position demands it; but I tell you, often you don't know where your head is.

" 'This year I'm especially hard pressed, for I have had my garden trimmed and beautified and had a balcony built; my wife has wanted it for a long time, and now the bills are here. I can't even think of keeping a saddle horse, as my physician has advised me to do a hundred times, for new expenses keep coming along. Look there, I had a little winepress of the latest type built for me, to press out the Muscatel that I grow on trellises—devil take me if I can pay for it this year. Well, my credit is still good, thank heaven.'

"This is the way he talks, with cruel ostentation, and so intimidates his poor brothers and his old father that they say nothing about their request and simply take themselves off again, after they have admired his garden and his balcony and his ingenious winepress. And they go to strangers and pay higher interest, simply to escape hearing so much gabble. His children are expensively and elegantly dressed, and walk with a springy step along the street; they bring little gifts to their poor cousins and come twice a year to take them to dinner, and this is a great lark for the rich children; but when the guests lose their shyness and begin to make a noise too, their pockets are filled with apples and they are sent home. There they tell all that they have seen and what they had to eat, and everything is criticized; for ill-will and envy fill the hearts of the poor kinswomen, who none the less flatter the prosperous one and praise her finery with eloquent tongue.

"Finally some misfortune strikes the father or the brothers, and the rich man must enter the breach willy-nilly, to avoid gossip. And he does it, without needing much persuasion; but now the bond of brotherly equality and love is completely rent asunder. The brothers and their children are now the slaves and slave-children of their master; year in, year out they are hectored and badgered, they have to dress in coarse cloth and eat black bread, in order to make good a small part of the damage, and the children are sent to orphan asylums and pauper schools, and if they are strong enough they have to work in the master's house and sit at the lower end of his table without the privilege of speech."

"Whew," cried the wife, "what a terrible tale! And will you really take your own son here for such a scoundrel? And is it written in the Book that it has to be just his brothers who are to meet with such a misfortune that will make them his slaves? They who have always got along by themselves till now? No, for the honor of our own blood I must believe that a rich marriage wouldn't turn us topsy-turvy to that extent, but that on the contrary my more hopeful view would prevail."

"I don't mean to say," replied Hediger, "that it would go just that way with us; but we too should find an outward and finally also an inward inequality entering in; he who seeks after wealth, tries to rise above his equals—"

"Stuff and nonsense" interrupted his wife, as she took up the tablecloth and shook it out of the window. "Has Frymann, who owns the property we are quarreling about, risen above the rest of you? Are you not one heart and one soul and forever putting your heads together?"

"That's different," cried her husband, "entirely different. He didn't get his property underhandedly, nor win it in the lottery, but he earned it dollar by dollar through the toil of forty years. And besides, we're not brothers, he and I, and we have nothing to do with each other, and don't want to, that's the point. And finally, he's not like other people, he's still one of the strong and upright. But don't let's keep considering nothing but these petty private concerns. Fortunately there are no monstrously rich people among us, prosperity is fairly well distributed; but just let fellows with many millions spring up, who have political ambition, and you'll see what mischief they will do. There's that well-known spinner-king, he really has got many millions and they accuse him of being a bad citizen and a skinflint, because he is said not to care anything for the common weal. But on the contrary, he's a good citizen, who lets other folks do as they please just as he always did, and who governs himself and lives like anybody else.

"But let this gold-bug be an ambitious political genius, give him some amiability, pleasure in spending money, and an understanding of all sorts of theatrical display, let him build palaces and houses of public utility, and then see what damage he will cause in the commonwealth and how he will ruin the character of the nation. A time will come when in our country, as elsewhere, great masses of money will accumulate without having been sturdily worked for and saved up; then the time will come to show the devil our teeth; then it will be seen whether the thread and the color of our banner cloth are sound. The long and the short of it is that I don't see why a son of mine should put out his hands for another man's goods without having lifted a finger to earn it. That's as much of a fraud as anything."

"It's a fraud that has been going on as long as the world has," said his wife laughing, "namely that two people who love each other marry. And with all your big, stilted words, you'll never change that a particle. Anyway, you alone are the one to be made a fool of; for Master Frymann is wisely trying to prevent your children from becoming equal to his. But the children will have their own policy, too, and will carry it out if there's anything in the affair—as to that I don't know."

"Let them," said the master tailor, "that's their affair; but mine is not to favor it, and in any case to refuse my consent as long as Karl is a minor."

With this diplomatic declaration and the latest number of the *Republican* he withdrew into his study. Mrs. Hediger on her part was curious now and wanted to get after her son and call him to account; but only now did she perceive that he had cleared out, as the entire negotiation seemed to him wholly superfluous and irrelevant, and he besides felt disinclined to reveal his love affairs to his parents.

All the earlier did he enter his skiff that evening and row out to where he had been on many previous evenings. But he sang his little song once and twice and even down to the last verse without any one appearing, and after he had vainly cruised about for more than an hour in front of the lumberyard, he rowed back perplexed and depressed, and thought his affair was indeed in a bad way. The next four or five evenings he had a similar experience, and now he gave up lying in wait for the faithless girl that he took her to be; for although he recalled her resolve not to see him more than once a month, he merely regarded this as preparing him for a complete dismissal, and fell into an angry gloom. So he found it very opportune that the drill season for the sharpshooter recruits was just beginning, and on several afternoons beforehand he went out to a shooting range with a sharpshooter he knew, to get at least a little practice and to be able to show the number of hits necessary for his application. His father looked on at this rather derisively, and unexpectedly came out there himself, in order to dissuade his son from his foolish audacity before it was too late if, as he suspected, Karl had no ability.

But he happened to come just after Karl had had his half dozen misses and so made a number of fairly good shots.

"You needn't try to make me believe," said Hediger, astonished, "that you have never done any shooting; you've secretly spent many a franc at it, that's certain."

"Well, I have done some secret shooting, but it hasn't cost anything. Do you know where, father?"

"I thought so."

"Even as a boy I used to watch the men shoot, and listened to what they said about it, and for years I've had such a desire for it that I used to dream about it, and while lying in bed I would think for hours of handling a gun, and I've aimed hundreds of good shots at the target."

"That's capital. In the future they'll order whole companies of marksmen into bed and order them to execute such mental exercises; that will save powder and shoes!"

"It is not so ridiculous as it seems," said the experienced sharpshooter who was instructing Karl. "It is certain that of two marksmen who are equally gifted as to eye and hand, the one who is used to reflection will be the master. You need to have an inborn knack at pulling the trigger, and there are lots of queer things about it, as in all exercises."

The oftener and the better Karl shot, the more did old Hediger shake his head; the world seemed to him to be turned upside down, for he himself had only attained to what he was and what he could do by industry and strenuous practice; even his principles, which most people manage to cram in as easily and as numerously as sardines, he had acquired only by dint of persevering study in his back chamber. But now he no longer ventured to raise opposition, and left, not without an inward satisfaction at numbering one of his sons among his country's sharpshooters; and by the time he reached his dwelling he was determined to make Karl a fine-fitting uniform of good cloth. "He'll have to pay for it, of course," he said to himself; but he knew well enough that he never demanded any return from his sons and that they never offered to repay him anything. That is wholesome for parents and allows them to reach a green old age, so that they may live to see their children gaily fleeced by their grandchildren, and so it passes on from father to son, and all survive and enjoy good appetites.

Now Karl was put into barracks for several weeks and developed into a handsome and skilled soldier who, although he was in love and neither saw nor heard anything further of his sweetheart, nevertheless applied himself attentively and cheerfully to his service as long as the daylight lasted; and by night the conversations of his roommates and the pranks they played allowed him no chance to pursue his thoughts in solitude. There were a score of lads from different districts, who exchanged and made capital of their native tricks and jokes long after the lights had been put out and until midnight came on.

Besides Karl, only one of them was from the city, and him he knew by hearsay. He was some years older than Karl and had already served in the light infantry. By trade a bookbinder, he had for some time not done a stroke of work, but lived on the exorbitant rent of old houses, which he skillfully managed to buy without capital. Sometimes he would resell one to some simpleton at an outrageous price, and then when the buyer could not hold out, he would put the forfeit and the paid installments in his pocket and take the house back again, once more raising the rents in the process. He also had a neat trick of adding a small chamber or bedroom to an apartment by simple alterations and then demanding a further considerable increase in rent. These alterations were by no means well advised or suitable, but quite arbitrary and stupid; and he likewise knew all the bungling artisans who did the cheapest and poorest work, and with whom he could do what he pleased. When he got to the end of his ideas, he would have one of his old buildings whitewashed outside and raise the rent again.

In this manner he enjoyed a neat annual income without doing an hour's actual work. His commissions and agreements did not take long, and he would stand in front of other people's buildings as long as he did before his own bungled affairs, play the expert, stick his nose into everything, and was in general the stupidest fellow in the world. Consequently he passed for a shrewd and prosperous young man, who would be a rich man before long, and he denied himself nothing. Now he considered himself too good for an infantry private and had wanted to become an officer. But as he was too lazy and too ignorant for that, they had not been able to use him, and by dint of obstinate insistence he had now got among the sharpshooters.

Here he sought to force his mates to respect him, but without exerting himself, simply by using his money. He was forever treating the subalterns and his comrades to drinks, and by clumsy liberality he thought he could procure himself indulgence and freedom. But he got nowhere except to make a butt of himself, though to be sure he did enjoy indulgence of a sort, in that they soon gave up trying to make anything of him, and let him alone as long as he did not disturb the rest. A single recruit attached himself to him, and he acted as Ruckstuhl's servant, cleaned his weapons and accoutrements, and took up the cudgels in his defense; this was a wealthy farmer's son, a young miser who always had a fearful appetite for food and drink when he could satisfy it at another's expense. This lad thought himself in clover to be able to carry back home all his shining crowns and nevertheless boast that he had had a merry life during his time of service and had caroused like a true sharpshooter; at the same time he was jolly and of good cheer, and entertained his patron, who had far less than he, with his thin treble voice, delivering all sorts of popular rustic songs oddly indeed from behind his bottle; for he was a merry niggard. So Ruckstuhl, the young robber, and Spurri, the young country miser, lived on in the most glorious friendship. The former always had meat and wine before him, and did as he pleased, and the latter left him as little as possible, sang, and cleaned his boots, and did not even scorn the small tips which the other bestowed.

Meanwhile the other soldiers had their sport with them, agreeing among themselves not to let Ruckstuhl stay in any company. But this did not apply to his famulus, for he was a fine shot, strangely enough, and in the army every man who knows his business is welcome, whether he be a Philistine or a scapegrace.

Karl was the ringleader in all joking about the two; but one night he lost his taste for jokes when the wine-bibber Ruckstuhl boasted to his follower, after the room was all quiet, what a fine gentleman he was and how he was soon planning to marry a rich wife to boot, the daughter of the carpenter Frymann, who could not escape him, or he missed his guess.

Now Karl's peace of mind was at an end, and the next day, as soon as he had a free hour, he went to his parents, to find out what was going on. But as he himself did not want to be the first to mention the matter, he heard nothing about Hermine until, just as he was leaving again, his mother told him she had sent him her regards.

"Why, where did you see her?" he asked as coolly as possible.

"Oh, she comes to market every day with the maid now, and learns how to buy. When we meet, she asks me to give her advice, and then we walk around the whole market and have lots of things to laugh at, for she's always jolly."

"Oh, ho," said Hediger, "so that's why you sometimes stay away so long? And what sort of matchmaking are you doing, hey? Is it becoming for a mother to act that way and to go around with persons who are forbidden to her son, and to take messages from them?"

"Forbidden, nonsense! Haven't I known the dear child since she was a baby, haven't I carried her in my arms, and now I'm not to go around with her! And isn't she to be allowed to send her regards to the people in our house? And can't a mother take such a message? And shouldn't a mother be allowed to marry off her children? It strikes me that she's just the proper authority to do it. But about such things we never talk, we womenfolk are not half so keen on you ill-bred men, and if Hermine takes my advice, she won't marry anybody."

Karl did not hear the conversation out, but went his way; for he had got his message and there had been no talk of any suspicious development. But he did put his finger to his nose and ask himself why Hermine had been so jolly, for she didn't usually laugh so much. He finally decided the question in his own favor and assumed that she had simply been jolly because she met his mother. So he resolved to keep quiet and give the girl credit for good will, and let things take their course.

Some days later Hermine came with her knitting to visit Mrs. Hediger, and a great friendliness prevailed, with much talk and laughter, so that Hediger, who was just cutting out an elegant holiday coat, was almost disturbed in his workshop, and wondered what gossip it was that had come. But he did not pay much attention to it until he heard his wife go to a cupboard and rattle the blue coffee cups. For she was making as fine a pot of coffee as she ever brewed; also she took a good handful of sage leaves, dipped them in an egg batter, and fried them in butter to make so-called mice, since the stems of the leaves looked like mouse tails. They rose splendidly, so that it made a heaping dish full, whose odor rose to the master's nostrils with that of the strong coffee. But then when he heard her pounding up sugar lumps, he became most impatient until he was called in to drink with them; but he would not have gone a moment earlier, for he was of the Strong and Upright.

As he now entered the room, he saw his wife and the dainty "forbidden" girl sitting in the closest friendship behind the coffee-pot, and he saw that it was the blue-flowered one, and that besides the "mice" there was butter there, and that the blue-flowered pitcher was full of honey; to be sure it was not real honey, but cherry conserve, about the color of Hermine's eyes; and it was Saturday, too, a day when all respectable city wives clean and scour, sweep and polish, and do not cook a bite that is fit to eat.

Hediger looked very critically at all these preparations and said good-day somewhat sternly; but Hermine was so gracious and yet resolute that he sat there dumfounded and ended by going in person to fetch up a "glass of wine" from the cellar, which he actually took from the little cask. Hermine repaid this mark of favor by asserting that a plateful of the mice must be kept for Karl, as he did not have much that was good in the barracks. She took her plate and kept pulling out the finest mice by the tail with her own dainty fingers until the mother herself finally cried that it was enough. Now the girl put the plate beside her, regarded it with satisfaction from time to time, and would now and then take a piece from it and eat it, saying that she was now Karl's guest; whereupon she would faithfully make good the theft from the dish.

Finally this got too much for worthy Mr. Hediger; he scratched his head, and urgent as his work was, he nevertheless quickly pulled on his coat and ran out to look up the father of the young sinner.

"We must be on our guard," he said to him. "Your daughter is sitting with my old woman, as thick as thieves, and the whole goings-on look mighty suspicious to me: you know the very devil's in the women."

"Why don't you chase the little minx away?" said Frymann angrily.

"I chase her away? You won't catch me trying it: why, you never saw such a witch! You come yourself and try it."

"All right, I'll come right along with you, and give the girl a proper notion of what she's supposed to do."

But when they arrived, they found instead of the young girl the sharpshooter, who had unbuttoned his green coat, and was enjoying the cookies saved for him and the remains of the wine with all the greater relish for the fact that his mother had incidentally told him that Hermine would go rowing on the lake again that evening, since the moon was so fine and since she had not been out for four weeks.

Karl rowed out on the lake earlier than usual, for at the sound of taps, which the buglers of Zurich were wont to send forth in heavenly harmonies on fine spring and summer evenings, he must be in his quarters again. It was not yet wholly dark when he arrived at the lumberyard; but alas, Master Frymann's skiff was not floating on the water as usual, but lay upside down on two horses, a good ten paces from the shore.

Was that a hoax of hers, or one of the old man's tricks? he thought, and was just going to row back, saddened and indignant, when the great golden moon rose out of the forests on Mt. Zurich, and at the same moment Hermine stepped out from behind a blossoming willow loaded with yellow cattails.

"I didn't know our boat was being freshly painted," she whispered, "so I'll have to get into yours, row away fast." And she lightly sprang in, and sat down on the other end of his skiff, which was scarcely seven feet long. They rowed out until they were out of sight of any spying glance, and Karl lost no time in questioning Hermine about Ruckstuhl, telling about his words and deeds the while.

"I know that this 'gentleman' wants to marry me," she answered, "and that my father is actually not indisposed to agree to it; he has talked about it."

"Is he possessed of the devil, to give you to such a vagabond and idler? What about his weighty principles?"

Hermine shrugged her shoulders and answered, "Father has simply got the notion of building a number of big houses and speculating with them; and that's why he wants a son-in-law who will help him in this, especially in regard to the speculation, and who will know that he is working for his own advantage if he takes pains with the whole enterprise. He is dreaming of an agreeable partnership in work and scheming, such as he would have liked to share with his own son, and now this man seems to him to have just the right talent for it. All he needs, he says, is a thorough business life and he'll be a regular expert. Father doesn't know anything about his silly way of living, because he doesn't watch people's doings and never goes out with anybody except his old friends.

"In short, Ruckstuhl has been invited to dinner tomorrow, as it's Sunday, in order to establish our acquaintance, and I'm afraid he's going to come right out with his proposal. Besides, I hear he's a shameless flatterer and an impudent fellow, when he wants to snap up something he's after."

"Oh well," said Karl, "you'll trump his ace for him."

"I shall indeed, but it would be better if he didn't come at all and left my father in the lurch."

"It would be better, surely, but that's a pious wish, for he'll take good care not to stay away."

"I've thought of a plan, though it's rather peculiar. Couldn't you get him into some piece of folly today or tomorrow morning, so that you'd both get arrested for a day or two?"

"How kind you are to put me into the clink for a couple of days, to save you a No. Can't you do it cheaper?"

"It's necessary for you to suffer with him, so that our consciences won't hurt us too much. As for my No, I don't want to be forced into saying aye, yes, or no to that fellow; it is bad enough that he talks about me in the barracks. He shan't get any further than that."

"Right you are, my sweetheart. Nevertheless, I think I can manage to have the rogue trot into jail alone; a scheme dawns on me. But no more of this, it's a pity to waste our precious time and the golden moonlight. Aren't you thinking anything?"

"What should I be thinking?"

"That we haven't seen each other for four weeks, and that you doubtless won't step ashore tonight unkissed."

"Are you going to kiss me, I wonder?"

"I myself; but I'm in no hurry, I've got you too securely. I want to look forward to it for a few minutes, perhaps five, six at the most."

"Oh, ho! Is this your gratitude for my confidence in you, and do you really mean it? Will you not let me bargain with you?"

"Under no circumstances, though you speak with the tongues of angels. Here's a bad situation for you, my young lady."

"Then I too will make a statement, good sir. If you touch me this evening with so much as a fingertip against my will, then it's all over between us and I will never see you again; I swear it by God and by my honor. For I mean it."

Her eyes sparkled as she said it. "That will take care of itself," answered Karl, "just keep still, I'll be coming over soon."

"Do as you like," said Hermine curtly and was silent.

But whether he really thought her capable of keeping her word, or whether he himself did not want her to break her oath, he stayed obediently where he was and looked over at her with sparkling eyes, peering through the moonlight to see if the corners of her mouth were not twitching and she making fun of him.

"Then I must seek consolation in the past again, and find compensation in my recollections," he began after a short silence. "Who would believe that this stern and tightly shut little mouth knew how to give such sweet kisses so many years ago?"

"Will you begin your shameless inventions again? But let me tell you that I won't listen to that annoying stuff any longer."

"Quiet, be quiet. Just this once let us direct our meditations backward into that golden time, and let us speak of the last kiss you ever gave me; I recall the circumstances as clearly and distinctly as if it were yesterday, and I am convinced that you do too. I was thirteen years old at that time, and you about ten, and some years had passed without kissing, for we now thought ourselves big folks. But there was to be an agreeable epilogue after all; or was it the early lark proclaiming the new morning? It was a fine Monday, the day after Pentecost—"

"No, Ascension—" interrupted Hermine, but broke off in the middle of the word.

"You are right, it was a glorious Ascension Day in the month of May, and we were on an excursion with a company of young people, we being the only children among them; you stuck to the big girls and I to the young men, and we didn't deign to play or even to speak with each other. After we had already walked a good way, we sat down in a tall, bright grove, and began to play forfeits; for evening was not far away, and the crowd didn't want to go home without some kissing. Two people were sentenced to kiss each other with flowers in their mouths, without dropping them. When this couple failed to perform the feat, and the next couple also, you suddenly came running up to me quite unaffectedly with a lily-of-the-valley in your mouth, stuck another between my lips and said, 'Try it.' Sure enough both the flowers fell on the ground to join their sisters, but in your eagerness you deposited your tiny kiss just the same. It was like having a light-winged, pretty butterfly rest there, and I involuntarily put up two fingertips to catch it. But they thought I wanted to wipe my mouth and laughed at me."

"Here we are at the shore," said Hermine and jumped out. Then she turned around amiably and faced Karl again.

"Since you have kept so quiet and have given my word the honor due it," she said, "I will row out with you again, if necessary, before the four weeks are up, and will make the appointment in a little note. It will be the first writing I have ever confided to you."

With that she hurried to the house. Karl on his part rowed hastily to the landing, so as not to miss the taps of the worthy buglers, which cut the mild air like a jagged razor.

On the way he encountered Ruckstuhl and Spurri, who were slightly tipsy; saluting them amicably and heartily, he grasped the former by the arm and began to praise and laud him: "What the deuce have you been doing again? What sly dodges have you been thinking up, you bad customer? If you aren't the grandest sharpshooter in the whole canton—what am I talking about, in all Switzerland."

"Thunderation!" cried Ruckstuhl, highly gratified to have some one beside Spurri make up to him and praise him, "thunderation, but it's too bad we have to turn in so soon. Haven't we got time to drain a bottle of some good wine?"

"Ssh, we can do that in our room. It's the custom among the sharpshooters anyhow to trick the officers at least once during their enlistment and carouse all night long in their room. And as recruits we'll show them that we're worthy to be full members."

"That would be a capital joke. I'll pay for the wine, as sure as my name is Ruckstuhl. But we must be sly about it, as crafty as serpents, or we're done for."

"Never fear, we're the right ones for that. Just let's march in very quietly and sanctimoniously and make no fuss."

When they got to the barracks, their roommates were all in the canteen getting their nightcaps. Karl took some of them into his confidence, these passed it on, and so each provided himself with a few bottles, which they took out unnoticed, one after the other, and hid under the beds. When it struck ten, they quietly lay down on their beds, until the inspection of the lights had been made. Then all got up again, hung coats over the windows, lighted the lights, got out the wine, and began to carouse like mad; and Ruckstuhl felt as if he were in paradise, because they all drank to him and made him out a great man. For his ardent desire to have the soldiers as well as others think him somebody, without his doing anything to deserve it, made him stupider than he was.

When he and his satellite seemed to have been completely drunk under the table, various drinking feats were carried out. One of the men had to stand on his head and drink up a casting-ladle full of wine held to his mouth; another was to sit on a chair, with a lead ball suspended from the ceiling, circling about him, and drink three glasses before the ball touched his head; a third had some similar test, and every one who failed got some droll penalty. All this was done in perfect stillness; whoever made a noise was penalized also, and all were in their nightshirts, so that they could quickly crawl into bed in case of surprise.

Now as the time for the sentries to go the rounds drew near, the two friends were also assigned a drinking feat. Each was to hold a full glass to the other's mouth on his sword blade, and these must be emptied without spilling a drop. Boastingly they drew their short swords and crossed the blades with the glasses on them; but they trembled so that the glasses fell off and they did not catch a drop. They were therefore directed to stand guard before the door in undress for a quarter of an hour, and this undertaking was lauded as the boldest that had been carried out in those barracks in the memory of man. Haversack and short sword were hung crosswise over their shirts, and in addition they had to put on their shakoes and pull on their blue leggings, but without shoes, and thus, with rifles in their hands, they were led outside the door and posted at either side. Hardly were they there when the door was bolted, all traces of the carousal removed, the windows cleared, the lights extinguished, and every man slipped into his bed and lay as if he had been sleeping there for hours.

Meanwhile the two sentries walked up and down in the gleam of the corridor lamp, rifle on shoulder, and looked about them with bold glances. Spurri, whom the free carousal had put ito the most blissful humor, became quite merry and suddenly burst into song, and this hastened the steps of the officer on duty, who was already on the way. As he approached, they tried to slip hastily into the room; but the door did not open at once, and before they knew what to do, the foe was there. Now everything fairly danced in their heads. In their confusion each placed himself at his post, presented arms, and cried, "Who goes there?"

"What does this mean, in the devil's name? What are you doing there?" cried the patrol, but without getting a sufficient answer, as neither of the two loons could get out a sensible word. The officer quickly opened the door and looked into the room; for Karl, who had been listening sharply, had hastily jumped out of bed, shot back the bolt, and as hastily crept back under the covers. When the officer saw that everything was dark and still, and heard nothing but puffing and snoring, he cried, "Hallo, men!"

"Go to the devil," cried Karl, "and go to sleep, you drunkards!"

The others also acted as if they had been wakened, and cried, "Aren't those beasts in bed yet? Throw them out, call the guard."

"The guard is here, it is I," said the officer, "one of you light a light, quick!"

It was done, and when the light was thrown on the two lunatics, loud laughter came from under every counterpane, as if the entire company had been surprised to the utmost. Ruckstuhl and Spurri joined in like fools, marching around and holding their sides; for their spirits had again wandered off in a different direction. Ruckstuhl snapped his fingers in the officer's face time after time, and Spurri stuck out his tongue at him.

When the derided guard saw that nothing could be done with the "happy" couple, he took out his tablet and wrote down their names. Now as misfortune would have it, he was just then living in one of Ruckstuhl's houses and had not yet paid the rent—for it was just after Easter—whether because he had not been in funds or because he had neglected it while on military duty. At all events, Ruckstuhl's evil genius hit upon this topic, and reeling toward the officer he laughed and stuttered:

"Pa-pay your de-debts fir-first, Lieutenant, before you wr-write other fo-folks' names down. You know?"

And Spurri laughed still louder, tottered and stepped crabwise backward, wagging his head and piping, "Pa-pay your de-de-de-debts, Mr. Officer, tha-that is we-well said, well said."

"Let four men get up," said he calmly, "lead these men under arrest to the guardhouse, and have them locked up tight; in three days we'll have a look at them and see if they have slept this off. Throw their cloaks over them and hang their trousers on their arms. March!"

"The tr-tr-tr-tr—the tr-trousers," shouted Ruckstuhl, "we must have; there-there's some-something in them that fa-fa-falls out when you shake them."

"Fa-falls out when you sh-shake them, Mr. Officer," repeated Spurri, and both swung their trousers around till the coins rattled. So they marched laughing and shouting with their escort through the corridors and down the stairs, and soon vanished in a cellar-like chamber on the ground floor, whereupon it became quiet.

Master Frymann's table was unusually richly set the following noon. Hermine filled the cut-glass decanters with wine of '46, put the gleaming glasses beside the plates, laid handsome napkins on the latter, and cut a loaf of bread fresh from the bakery at the Sign of the Hen, where it was baked after an old traditional recipe, and was the delight of all the children and gossips of Zurich. She also sent an apprentice, all in his Sunday best, to the pastry cook to fetch the macaroon tart and the coffee cake, and finally she arranged the dessert on a small side table: crisp cookies, both flat and curled, pound cake, fruit tarts, and conical raisin bread.

Frymann, whom the fine Sunday air had put in a cheerful mood, gathered from this zeal that his daughter would oppose no serious resistance to his plans, and he said to himself with amusement: That's like all women. As soon as an acceptable and definite opportunity comes to them, they make short work of it and catch it by the forelock!

According to ancient custom, Mr. Ruckstuhl was invited for twelve o'clock sharp. When he had not arrived at a quarter past twelve, Frymann said, "Let's eat; we must accustom this gentleman to punctuality from the start."

And when the soup was eaten and he still had not come, the master called in the apprentices and the maidservant, who were to eat alone that day and were already half through, and said, "Come and eat with us, we don't want to sit here and look at the stuff. Dig in and enjoy yourselves:

> Whoever late for meal-time comes
> Can take what's left or suck his thumbs!

This invitation did not need to be repeated, and they were all jolly and of good cheer, and Hermine was the sprightliest of all, and found her appetite getting better, the more vexed and put out her father was.

"That seems to be a boor of a fellow," he growled to himself.

But she heard it and said, "No doubt he couldn't get leave, we mustn't condemn him right away."

"Leave indeed! Are you sticking up for him already? Why shouldn't he get his leave, if he wants to?"

In the utmost dudgeon he ended his meal and immediately went to a coffeehouse, contrary to his habit, simply to avoid meeting the neglectful suitor, if he should finally come. Toward four o'clock he returned again, instead of seeking out his usual Sunday companions, the redoubtable Seven, curious to know whether Ruckstuhl had not put in an appearance. As he came through the garden, there sat Mrs. Hediger with Hermine in the summerhouse, as it was a warm spring day, and they were drinking the coffee and eating the raisin bread and the fruit tarts, and seemed in the highest of spirits. He bade the woman good day, and although the sight of her annoyed him, he immediately asked her whether she had any news of the barracks, and whether the sharpshooters were perhaps gone on an excursion together.

"I think not," said Mrs. Hediger. "This morning they went to church and afterward Karl came home to dinner; we had roast mutton, and he never leaves that in the lurch."

"Didn't he say anything as to what's become of Mr. Ruckstuhl?"

"Mr. Ruckstuhl? Yes, he's under strict arrest with another recruit, for getting terribly intoxicated and offending his superiors; they say it was a regular comedy."

"Devil take him!" said Frymann and went off like a shot. Half an hour later he was saying to Hediger, "Now your wife is squatting in the garden with my daughter, and they're both tickled because a plan for her marriage is ruined."

"Why don't you chase her away? Why didn't you growl at her?"

"How can I, when we're old friends? You see, that's the way these accursed affairs are already mixing up our relations. And so hold fast: down with kinship!"

"Down with in-laws!" affirmed Hediger, and shook his friend's hand.

July and the shooting match of the year 1849 were at hand; there were scarcely two weeks left. The Seven were again in session, and cup and banner were finished and both were displayed and approved. The banner was set up and towered aloft in the room, and in its shadow was held the most difficult deliberation that the Upright had ever had. For suddenly the evident fact had come to light that there could not be a banner without a speaker, and it was the choice of this speaker that almost stranded the little ship of the septuple crew. Thrice did the choice fall upon each member of the crew, and thrice did each most decisively decline.

All were indignant that none would take it upon himself, and each was angry that he was just the one on whom they wanted to put the burden and of whom they expected this unheard-of thing. As eagerly as other men crowd forward when some one must open his head and let himself be heard, just so timidly did these men shun the opportunity for a public address, and each alleged his incompetence, declaring that he had never done such a thing in his life, nor ever would. For they still venerated speechmaking as an art which required talent as well as study, and they still cherished an unbounded and honest esteem for good speakers who could stir their souls, and everything such a man said they held as indisputable and sacred. These speakers they sharply distinguished from themselves, and ascribed to themselves the merit of attentive listening, of conscientious deliberation, and of agreement or rejection, which seemed to them a sufficiently glorious task.

So when they found that no speaker could be obtained by vote, a tumult and general uproar arose in which each sought to convince his neighbor that he ought to sacrifice himself. Hediger and Frymann in particular were the ones on whom they had designs, and these they bombarded furiously. They, however, defended themselves mightily and each put it off on the other, until Frymann called for silence and said, "Fellow warriors, we have committed a thoughtless act, and we cannot but see that we had better leave our banner at home after all, and so let us quickly make up our minds to that and attend the festival without ostentation."

A great gloom settled on them after these words.

"He is right," said Kuser the silversmith.

"There is nothing left for us to do." Thus Syfrig the plowmaker.

But Burgi cried, "It's impossible: our project is known, and the fact that the banner is made. If we give it up, we'll get into the almanac."

"And that's true," remarked Erismann the innkeeper, "and our old opponents the reactionaries will work the joke for all it's worth."

A sudden terror thrilled their old bones at this idea, and the company renewed the attack on its two most talented members; but they again protested and finally threatened to withdraw.

"I am a simple carpenter and will never expose myself to ridicule," cried Frymann, whereupon Hediger interposed, "Well, and how should a poor tailor like me risk it? I should make you all a laughingstock, and harm myself to no purpose whatever. I propose that one of the innkeepers be called upon—they have the largest experience with crowds."

But these protested most vehemently, and Pfister nominated the cabinetmaker, as being a great joker.

"Joker nothing," cried Burgi, "do you think it's a joke to address a Swiss festival chairman in presence of four thousand people?"

A universal sigh answered this utterance, which again brought to their minds the difficulties of the task.

Little by little they now took to running in and out, and to whispering together in corners. Frymann and Hediger were left alone at the table and looked gloomy enough, for they saw that they would once more have to battle for their lives. Finally, when all had reassembled, Burgi stepped forth in front of them and said, "Fellow soldiers Kaspar and Daniel! You have both of you spoken so often to our satisfaction when we were together that either of you, if he only will, can very well deliver a short public address. It is the vote of the society that you two draw lots, and that's the end of it! You will yield to a majority vote of five to two!"

A fresh tumult confirmed these words; the victims looked at each other and finally succumbed dejectedly, but each not without hoping that the bitter lot would fall to the other. It fell to Frymann, who for the first time left a meeting of the Freedom-lovers with a heavy heart, whereas Hediger rubbed his hands in delight—so inconsiderate does selfishness make the oldest friends.

Frymann's pleasure in anticipating the festival was now destroyed, and his days grew dark and cheerless. Every moment he thought of his speech, without getting the barest shadow of an idea, because he kept seeking it afar off, instead of seizing on the obvious and acting as if he were simply among his friends. The words he was wont to speak to them seemed trivial to him, and he fumbled about for something special and high-sounding, for a political manifesto, and this not from vanity, but from a dogged sense of duty. Finally he began to scribble up a piece of paper, not without many interruptions, sighs, and curses. With infinite labor he filled up two sheets, although he had only intended to compose a few lines; for he could not see how to end it, and the complicated phrases clung to each other like sticky burrs and would not release the writer from their tenacious claws.

With the folded paper in his vest pocket he went despondently about his business, and would occasionally read it over behind a shed and shake his head over it. At last he confided in his daughter and declaimed to her this rough draft, to observe the effect. The speech was an accumulation of thunderous words against Jesuits and aristocrats, profusely interspersed with Freedom, Human Rights, Servitude, Oppression, and the like; in short it was a bitter and unnatural declaration of war, without a word in it about the Seven and their banner, and moreover confusedly and awkwardly put together, whereas otherwise he could deliver an extemporaneous address ably and correctly.

Hermine said it was a very strong speech, only it seemed to her somewhat out of date, as the Jesuits and aristocrats had been beaten for the present, and she thought a cheerful and pleasant announcement would be more suitable, since everyone was contented and happy.

Frymann was somewhat taken aback, and although the ardor of battle was strong enough in his old bones, still he pulled at his nose and said, "Perhaps you are right, but you don't quite understand it. When you speak publicly, you have to make a bold showing and put it on thick, something like a scene painter, whose work looks like an ugly daub close by. Still perhaps it can be softened down here and there."

"That would be good," continued Hermine, "for it has so many 'therefores' in it. Let me see it. Look, almost every other line has a 'therefore' in it."

"That's just the mischief of it," he cried, and took the paper from her and tore it into a thousand pieces. "That ends it: I can't do it and I'm not going to make a fool of myself."

But Hermine now advised him not to write anything at all, but to let it go and about an hour before the celebration to get hold of an idea and make a brisk extempore speech on that, just as if he were at home.

"That's the best thing to do," he answered, "and then if it goes badly, at least I haven't made any false pretenses."

Nevertheless he could not refrain from continually prodding and stirring up the aforesaid idea, without causing it to develop, however; he went about distracted and anxious, and Hermine observed him with great satisfaction.

All at once the week of the festival had begun, and in the middle of it the Seven drove off to Aarau before daybreak in a special four-horse omnibus. The new banner fluttered gloriously from the box; on the green silk gleamed the words: "FRIENDSHIP IN FREEDOM!" and all the old men were merry and gay, jocose or serious together, and only Frymann exhibited a depressed and dubious appearance.

Hermine was already at the house of a friend in Aarau, as her father was wont to reward her for her model housekeeping by having her share all his trips; and more than once she had graced the merry circle of the old men like a rosy hyacinth. Karl was also present; although his time and money were sufficiently taxed by his military schooling, still at Hermine's suggestion he had gone there on foot, and had strangely enough found quarters quite near hers; for they had to attend to their affair, and no one could say whether this festival could not be used to advantage. Incidentally he also wanted to shoot, and carried with him twenty-five cartridges, all he could afford; these he intended to use, but no more and no less.

He had soon scented the arrival of the Upright Seven, and followed them at a distance, as they marched with tightly furled banner to the festival grounds. It was the day of largest attendance, and the streets were covered with promenading throngs in gala dress; large and small shooting clubs marched along, some with bands, some without; but none so small as that of the Seven.

They had to wind their way through the press, but none the less they marched in step with short paces, and held their arms rigid with clenched fists. Frymann walked ahead with the banner, and his face looked as if he were being led to execution. Occasionally he looked about him on all sides, to see if there were no escape; but his companions, glad that they were not in his shoes, encouraged him and called out to him vigorous and pithy words. They were already approaching the festival ground; the crackling rifle fire already sounded close at hand, and high in the air floated the Swiss marksmen's flag in sunny solitude, and its silk now stretched out quivering to all four corners, now flipped with graceful little snaps over the people's heads, now hung down sanctimoniously along the pole for an instant; in short, amused itself with all the tricks that a flag can think of in a week; but the sight of it stabbed the bearer of the little green banner to the heart.

As Karl saw the gay flag waving, he had paused a moment to watch it, and so had suddenly lost the little group from sight; when he looked around for it he could no longer discover it anywhere: it was as if the earth had swallowed it. Rapidly he forced his way to the spot and then back to the entrance of the grounds and swept them with his eyes; no green banner peeped out of he throng. Back he went, and for greater speed took a side street parallel to the main road. There stood a tiny tavern whose proprietor had planted a few lean pines before the door, set up a few tables and benches, and stretched a piece of canvas over the whole, like a spider that stretches her web close beside a great pot of honey, to catch an occasional fly that goes to it. In this little house Karl accidentally saw the gilt tip of a flagpole shining behind the dirty window; he went in at once, and lo! there sat his dear old men in the low-ceiled room as if driven there by a thundercloud, lying limply athwart chairs and benches, and hanging their heads, and in their midst stood Frymann with the banner, saying, "I won't do it and that ends it! I'm an old man and I won't bear the stigma of folly and be pestered with a nickname for the rest of my days!"

And with that he planted the banner in a corner with a vigorous thud. No answer ensued, until the pleased innkeeper came and placed a vast wine bottle before the unexpected guests, although they had all been too startled to order it. Hediger filled a glass, stepped up to Frymann and said, "Old friend, brother soldier, here, drink a swallow of wine and pull yourself together."

But Frymann shook his head and would not say another word. They sat in great distress, such as they had never known; all the riots, counterrevolutions, and reactionary movements they had ever experienced were child's play compared with this defeat before the gates of paradise.

"Then in God's name let us turn around and drive home again!" said Hediger, who feared that fate might turn against him after all. But Karl, who had hitherto stood in the doorway, now stepped forward and said gayly, "Give me the banner, gentlemen! I will carry it and speak for you, I don't mind doing it at all."

All looked up in astonishment, and a ray of relief and joy quivered on all their faces; only old Hediger said sternly, "You? How did you get here? And how can an inexperienced greenhorn like you speak for us old men?"

But from all sides came the cry: "Well done! Forward, undaunted! Forward with the youngster!" And Frymann himself handed him the banner; for it took a weight off his heart and he was glad to see his old friends snatched out of the distress into which he had led them. And forward they went with renewed pleasure; Karl bore the banner majestically aloft, and at their rear the innkeeper looked dejectedly after the disappearing mirage which had for a moment deluded him.

Hediger alone was now gloomy and discouraged, as he did not doubt that his son would get them into a worse fix. But they had already entered the grounds; the men of Graubünden were just marching off, a long brown train, and past them marched the Seven through the people, and the time they kept to the Graubünden band was as true as it had ever been. Once more they had to mark time—the technical expression for going through the motions of marching in one spot—as three fortunate marksmen, who had won cups, crossed their path with buglers and followers; but all this, together with the noisy shooting, merely heightened their solemn intoxication, and finally they bared their heads at sight of the trophy temple, which was ablaze with trophies and on whose ramparts a close array of flags was fluttering, in the colors of the cantons, cities, counties, and parishes. In their shade stood some gentlemen in black, and one of them held the silver goblet of wine in his hand, to welcome the new arrivals.

The seven old heads floated like a sunlit ice cake in the dark sea of people, their scanty white hair shook in the pleasant east wind, and was blown in the same direction as the red and white flag high above them. On account of their small numbers and their advanced age they attracted universal attention, the smiles they caused were not disrespectful, and all were attentive as the young standard bearer stepped forward and delivered briskly and audibly the following address:

"Beloved Swiss! We have come here with our banner, eight of us in all, seven graybeards and a young ensign. As you see, each has his rifle, without our claiming to be remarkable marksmen; to be sure none of us would miss the target, and occasionally one of us might hit the black; but if any of us should hit the bull's eye, you can swear that he didn't mean to. So for all the silver we shall carry away from your trophy room, we might just as well have stayed at home!

"And still, even though we aren't extraordinary shots, we couldn't bear to huddle at home in the chimney corner; and we have come not to take away, but to bring trophies: a modest little cup, an almost immodestly cheerful spirit, and a new banner that trembles in my hand with the desire to float on your flag tower. But the banner we shall take away with us again, for it is simply to be consecrated here. See what is written on it in golden letters: FRIENDSHIP IN FREEDOM! Indeed it is friendship personified, so to say, that we are bringing to the festival, friendship through patriotism, friendship through love of freedom. That is what brought together these seven bald heads that are shining here in the sun, thirty, no forty years ago, and kept them together through every storm, through good and evil times. It is a society which has no name, no president, and no statutes; and its members have neither titles nor offices; it is unmarked timber from the primeval forests of the nation which now for a moment is coming out of the woods into the sunlight of its national holiday, only to step back into them again and to rustle and roar with the thousand other treetops in the cosy forest twilight of the people, where but few know or can name each other, and still all are familiar and acquainted.

"Look at them, these old sinners! Not one of them is in the odor of particular sanctity. Rarely is one of them seen in church. About things clerical they haven't much good to say. But I can confide to you, fellow countrymen, here under this blue sky a strange truth: as often as their country is in danger, they begin quite gently to believe in God; first each one quietly and by himself, then louder and louder, until one confesses to the other and they finally practice together a remarkable theological system, whose first and only dogma is this: Help yourself, then God will help you! On days of joy like this, when crowds of people are met together and a real blue sky smiles on them, they revert to these theological ideas and imagine that the dear God has hung the Swiss standard high in the heavens and has made the fine weather simply for us. In both cases, in the hour of danger and in the hour of joy, they suddenly become content with the initial words of our constitution: In the name of God the Almighty! And then they are inspired by such a gentle tolerance that, however refractory they may be at other times, they do not even ask whether it is the god of the Roman Catholic or of the Reformed hosts that is meant!

"In short, a child who has been given a little Noah's ark filled with bright-colored animals, male and female, cannot be more pleased with it than they are with the dear little fatherland, and the thousand good things in it, from the moss-covered old pike at the bottom of its lakes up to the wild bird that flutters about its ice-capped peaks. Oh, what different sorts of people swarm here in this little space, manifold in their occupations, in manners and customs, in costume and language! What sly dogs and what mooncalves don't we see running around, what noble growth and what weeds bloom here merrily side by side—and all of it is good and splendid and dear to our hearts, for it is our fatherland.

"So they become philosophers, considering and weighing the value of earthly things; but they cannot get over the wonderful fact of the fatherland. To be sure they have traveled in their youth and seen many lands of men, not with arrogance, but honoring every country in which they found the right sort of people; but their favorite expression is, now and always: respect every man's native land, but love your own.

"And how graceful and rich it is! The closer one examines it, the finer seems its warp and woof, beautiful and durable, God's wonderful handiwork!

"How agreeable it is that we have not simply one monotonous Swiss type, but that there are men of Zurich and Berne, Unterwalden and Neuchâtel, Graubünden and Basle, and even two kinds of Baselers; and that there is one history for Appenzell, and another for Geneva. This variety within our unity, which may God preserve to us, is the genuine school of friendship and only when political homogeneity becomes the personal friendship of a whole country has the highest goal been reached; for what citizenship should fail to accomplish, friendship can perform, and both will be united to form a single virtue.

"These old men here have spent their days in toil and labor; they are beginning to feel the weakness of the flesh, and one is pinched in one place, another in another. But when the summer comes, they do not visit the baths, but the national festival. The wine of the Swiss festival is the fountain of health that refreshes their hearts; the summer life of the Confederation is the breath that strengthens their old nerves; the wave-beat of a happy nation is the ocean bath that makes their stiff bones active again. You will soon see their white heads become immersed in that bath. So give us the draught of honor! Long live friendship in our fatherland. Long live friendship in freedom!"

"Long life to it! Bravo!" was the cry all around, and the welcoming speaker replied to the address and hailed the peculiar and striking appearance of the old men.

"Yes," he wound up, "may our festivals never become less than a school of manners for our youth, and for the old a reward for a pure public conscience and consistent civic loyalty, and a bath of rejuvenation. May there remain one festival of inviolable and active friendship in our land from canton to canton and from man to man. Worthy men, long live your nameless and statuteless society!"

Once more the cry was repeated round about, and amid general applause the little banner was set up on the ramparts with the others. Hereupon the little troop of the Seven wheeled about and marched straight to the great festival hall, to refresh themselves with a good luncheon, and scarcely had they arrived when they all shook their speaker's hand and cried, "It was as if our very hearts were talking. Hediger, friend Jakob, there's good stuff in that boy of yours, he'll turn out well, just give him a chance. Just like us, only with more ability, for we're old fools; but be steadfast and undaunted, Karl," and so on.

Frymann was quite dumfounded; the boy had said exactly what he ought to have thought of, instead of taking on the Jesuits. He too shook hands with Karl quite amicably, and thanked him for helping him out. Last of all, old Hediger stepped up to his son, took his hand likewise, fastened his eyes keenly and firmly on him, and said, "My son, you have revealed a fine but dangerous gift. Nurse it, cultivate it, with loyalty, with a sense of duty, with modesty. Never lend it to the spurious and the unjust, the vain and the trivial; for it can become a sword in your hand which will turn against you or against the good as well as the evil. It can also become a fool's bauble. Therefore look before you, modestly, eager to learn, but firm and undaunted. As you have done honor to us today, think always of doing honor to your fellow citizens and your country, of giving them joy; think of this, and it will be the surest way to preserve you from false ambition. Undaunted! Do not think you must speak on every occasion; let some of them go by, and never speak for your own sake, but always in some elevating cause. Study men, not to outwit and plunder them, but to awaken the good in them and set it in motion, and believe me, many that listen to you will often be better and wiser than you who are speaking. Never use sophisms and petty hairsplitting, with which one can stir only the chaff; the real heart of the people you can touch only with the full impetus of truth. Therefore do not solicit the applause of the noisy and restless, but look upon the calm and the strong, undaunted.

Hardly had he finished this speech and released Karl's hand, when Frymann quickly grasped it and said, "Seek to become a man of all round knowledge and enrich its foundations, that you may not lapse into empty words. After this first beginning let a good space of time pass without thinking of such things again. If you have a good idea, do not speak merely to make use of it, but put it away; there will always be opportunities when you can employ it more maturely and to better advantage. If some one gets ahead of you with this idea, be glad of it instead of being vexed, for it is a proof that you have felt and thought a universal truth. Train your mind and watch over your disposition, and study in other speakers the difference between a mere braggart and a man of truthfulness and spirit. Do not travel about the country and do not run about all the streets, but accustom yourself to understand the course of the world from within the stronghold of your house and among tried friends; then you can appear when it is time for action with more wisdom than agitators and vagabonds.

"When you do speak, don't speak either like a witty janitor nor like a tragic actor, but keep your own natural character pure and then always speak in that character. Don't be affected, don't strike attitudes, don't look around you like a field marshal before you begin, or as if you were watching the audience. Don't say you aren't prepared when you are; for people will know your style and will detect it at once. And when you have spoken, don't go around gathering applause, or beam with self-satisfaction, but sit down quietly in your place and listen attentively to the following speaker.

Save up your strong words as if they were gold, so that if you do some time get righteously indignant and use them, it will be an event and strike your opponent like an unforeseen thunderbolt. But if you think you may ever become reconciled to an opponent and work with him, then be careful not to let your anger carry you to extremes, so that people will not say: Cads will fight but for a night!"

Thus spake Frymann, and poor Karl sat astonished and thunderstruck with all these speeches, and did not know whether to laugh or be puffed up. But Syfrig the smith cried, "Now just look at those two, who wouldn't speak for us, and here they are talking like books."

"Right you are," said Burgi, "but we have gained new growth by it, and have sent out a vigorous young shoot. I move that the lad be admitted to the circle of us old men and henceforth attend our meetings."

"Voted!" they all cried, and they clinked glasses with Karl; somewhat heedlessly, he drained the entire glass, which however the old men let pass without murmuring, in view of the excitement of the moment.

After the company had sufficiently recovered from the adventure by means of a good lunch, it dispersed. Some went to try a few shots, others to see the trophy room and the other sights, and Frymann went to fetch his daughter and the ladies whose guest she was; for at noon they planned to meet again at a table which was nearly in the centre of the hall, and in the neighborhood of the speakers' tribune. They all noted the number of the table, and separated in high spirits and free of all care.

Exactly at twelve o'clock the company of several thousand, which changed every day, sat down to dinner. Country and city folk, men and women, old and young, learned and unlearned, all sat gaily side by side and waited for the soup, opening bottles and cutting bread the while. Nowhere appeared a malicious face, nowhere was to be heard an outcry or noisy laughter, but only the hum of a happy wedding feast, magnified a hundred times and evenly distributed through the hall—the quiet wave-beat of a self-satisfied ocean.

Here was a long tableful of marksmen, there a double row of blooming country girls, at a third table a gathering of so-called "old boys" from all parts of the country, who had finally passed their examinations, and at the fourth a whole emigrated town, men and women together. But these sitting companies formed only half of the assemblage; an unbroken stream of spectators, as numerous as the diners, flowed through the aisles and passages and circled about them in a perpetual movement. These were, God be praised and thanked, the cautious and economical ones, who had figured the thing up and had satisfied their hunger elsewhere for still less money, that half of the nation which manages everything more cheaply and frugally, whereas the other half kicks so terribly over the traces; there were also the excessively exclusive ones, who were afraid of the cooking and didn't like the forks; and finally there were the poor and the children, who did not look on by choice.

But the former made no invidious remarks, and the latter displayed neither torn clothes nor ugly looks; the prudent found pleasure in the imprudent, and the aristocrat who found the dishes of peas in July too ridiculous walked along as charitably as the pauper to whose nose they brought a tempting odor. Here and there to be sure a piece of culpable selfishness could be seen, when for instance some niggardly farmer succeeded in occupying on a sudden a vacated seat, and eating on with the best of them, without having paid; and, what was even worse for order-loving eyes, there was not even an altercation or a forcible ejection as a result.

The chief festival steward stood before the broad kitchen door, and blew on a hunting horn the signal for the serving of a course, whereupon a company of waiters burst forth and dispersed to the right and left and straight ahead with carefully practised evolutions. One of them found his way to the table at which the Strong and Upright were sitting, together with Karl, Hermine, and her friends, cousins or whatever they were. The old men were just listening eagerly to one of the principal speakers who mounted the tribune after the drummer had beaten a loud roll. Sober and serious they sat, with forks laid aside, stiffly upright, all seven heads turned toward the tribune.

But they blushed like young girls and looked at each other as the speaker began with a phrase from Karl's speech, narrated the appearance of the seven graybeards, and then took this as a beginning and text for his own address. Only Karl heard nothing, for he was softly jesting with the ladies, until his father nudged him to show his disapproval. When the speaker had finished amid great applause, the old men looked at each other again; they had attended many gatherings, but this was the first time that they themselves had ever been the topic of a speech, and they did not venture to look around, so embarrassed were they, though at the same time in the seventh heaven of happiness. But as things often go in this world, their neighbors round about did not know them, nor dream what prophets were in their midst, and so their modesty was not offended. With all the greater contentment did they press each other's hands after each had gently rubbed his own, and their eyes said: Undaunted! That is the sweet reward of virtue and enduring excellence.

Whereupon Kuser cried, "Well, this we owe to master Karl. I think we really shall have to promise him Burgi's four-poster, and put a certain doll into it for him. What do you think, Daniel Frymann?"

"I'm afraid so too," said Pfister, "and that he'll have to buy my Swiss Blood and lose his wager."

But Frymann suddenly wrinkled his brow and said, "A good tongue doesn't get rewarded with a wife so quickly. In my house at least there has to be a good hand to go with it. Let us not extend this jest, my friends, to unseemly things."

Karl and Hermine had grown red and looked out over the crowd with embarrassment. Just then boomed the cannon shot which announced the resumption of the shooting, and for which a long line of marksmen, gun in hand, had been waiting. Immediately their fire crackled along the whole line; Karl rose from the table, saying that he was now going to try his luck, too, and betook himself to the shooting range.

"And I'm at least going to watch him, even if I can't have him," cried Hermine jestingly, and followed him accompanied by her friends.

But it happened that the ladies lost sight of each other in the crowd, and at last Hermine was left alone with Karl and marched faithfully along with him from target to target. He began at the farthest end, where there was no crowd, and without much thought he hit the target two or three times running. Turning around to Hermine, who stood behind him, he said laughing, "Well, that's doing pretty well."

She laughed too, but only with her eyes, while her mouth said seriously, "You must win a cup."

"Impossible," answered Karl, "I'd have to shoot at least fifty shots to win twenty-five numbers, and I only have twenty-five cartridges with me."

"Oh well," she said, "there's plenty of powder and ball to be bought here."

"I don't want to do that, though, it would be a pretty expensive cup with all that shooting. To be sure, lots of them burn up more powder than the prize is worth, but I'm not such a fool."

"My, how nice and high-principled you are, and how economical," she said almost tenderly. "I like that. But it's better still when you do with a little as much as others manage with their tremendous preparations and their terrible exertions. So pull yourself together and do it with your twenty-five shots. If I were a marksman, I'd manage it!"

"Never, it simply never happens, little simpleton."

"That's just why you men are only holiday marksmen! But do at least begin again and try it."

He shot again and got a number, and then a second. Again he looked at Hermine, and her eyes laughed still more, as she said still more earnestly, "See? You're doing well, keep right on now."

Steadfastly he gazed at her and could scarcely turn his eyes away, for he had never seen such a look in her eyes; something stern and tyrannical gleamed amid the laughing sweetness of her glance, and two spirits spoke eloquently in the gleam: one was the commanding will, but with it was fused the promise of a reward, and out of that fusion arose something new and mysterious. "Do my will. I have more to give than you dream," said those eyes, and Karl looked into them, questioning, curious—until these two came to an understanding in the midst of the noise and tumult of the festival.

When he had satiated his eyes with this gleam, he turned again, aimed quietly, and once more struck the target. Now he himself began to think it possible; but because people began to gather about him, he went away and sought a quieter and more solitary range, and Hermine followed him. There he again hit the target several times, without missing once; and so he began to handle the cartridges as deliberately as gold pieces, and each one Hermine accompanied with greedy shining eyes as it vanished into the gun barrel; but before Karl aimed, which he did without haste or nervousness, he always looked into the face of the beautiful creature. As often as his success became noticeable and people gathered around him, he would go on to another range; and the tickets he got he did not put into his hat, but gave them to his companion to keep; she held the entire bundle, and never did a marksman have a prettier ticket-holder. Thus he actually fulfilled her desire, and made such fortunate use of his twenty-five shots that not one of them struck outside the prescribed circle.

They counted over the tickets and found this rare good fortune confirmed.

"I could do that once, but I shall never be able to do it again in all my life," said Karl. "Moreover, that is what your eyes did. The only thing I am wondering is how much else you intend to accomplish with them."

"You'll have to wait and see," she answered, and now her mouth laughed too.

"Go and find the old men now," he said, "and ask them to come to the trophy room for me, so that I can be escorted from it, since there is no one else with me—or will you walk with me?"

"I'd almost like to," said she, but still she went rapidly away.

The Seven were sitting deep in cheerful conversation; nearly all the places in the hall had been taken by other people, but they clung firmly to their table and let the general life surge about them. Hermine stepped up to them and cried mirthfully, "Karl wants you to escort him—he has won a cup."

"What, what?" they cried, bursting into a shout, "is that the way he's going on?"

"Yes," said an acquaintance who had just come up, "and what is more, he won the cup with twenty-five shots, which doesn't happen every day. I watched the young couple while they did it."

Master Frymann looked at his daughter in astonishment.

"Did you shoot too, I want to know? I certainly hope not; for women sharpshooters are all right in general, but not in particular."

"Don't be alarmed," said Hermine, "I didn't shoot, I simply ordered him to shoot straight."

Hediger however grew pale with wonder and satisfaction, to think that he should have a son both oratorically endowed and famous in the use of arms, to go forth with actions and deeds from his obscure tailor shop. He held his peace and thought to himself that he would no longer play the guardian in that quarter. But now they all set out for the trophy temple, where they actually found the young hero, sure enough, standing beside the buglers with the shining cup in his hand, waiting for them. And so to the air of a lively march they tramped away with him and into the dining hall, to wet the cup, as they say; and again they took short, firm steps and clenched their fists, looking triumphantly about them. Once more arrived at their headquarters, Karl filled the cup, set it in the middle of the table, and said, "Hereby I dedicate this cup to the society, that it may always remain with the banner."

"Accepted," they said; the cup began to circle, and new merriment rejuvenated the old men, who had been in high spirits since daybreak. The evening sunlight floated in under the countless roof beams of the hall and gilded thousands of faces already transfigured with pleasure, while the resounding strains of an orchestra filled the room. Hermine sat in the shadow of her father's shoulders, as modest and quiet as if butter would not melt in her mouth. But from the sun, which caressed the cup before her so that both its golden lining and the wine sparkled, golden lights played over her rosy, glowing face, lights that moved with the wine when the old men pounded on the table in the fire of their speech, and then one could not tell whether she herself had smiled or only the playing lights. She was now so beautiful that she was soon discovered by the roving glances of the young men.

Merry troops of them sat down near by in order to keep their eyes on her, and the question passed around: "Where is she from? Who is the old man, does nobody know him?" She's from St. Gall, from Thurgau, was the answer here; no, they are all from Zurich at that table, was the word over there. Wherever she looked, the merry youths took off their hats, to show the proper esteem of her charm, and she smiled modestly, but without affectation. But when a long train of youths passed the table and all bowed, she had to cast down her eyes after all, and still more so when suddenly a handsome young student from Berne came up, cap in hand, and said with polite frankness that he had been sent by thirty friends, who were sitting at the fourth table from her, to declare to her, with her father's permission, that she was the most charming girl in the hall. In short, every one fairly paid court to her, and the sails of the old men were swelled with new triumph, so that Karl's glory was almost dimmed by Hermine's. But he was to rise to the top again.

For there arose a murmur and a crowding in the central aisle, caused by two herdsmen from Entlibuch, who were pushing through the throng. They were veritable grizzly bears, with short pipes in their mouths, their Sunday coats under their big arms, small straw hats on their great heads, and silver hearts fastening their shirt bosoms. The one in advance was a clodhopper of fifty, and pretty tipsy and unmannerly; for he was eager to try feats of strength with all the men and kept trying to hook his clumsy finger into everything, while his little eyes blinked amiably or at times challengingly. So there arose offense and confusion wherever he went.

Close behind him walked the other, a still more powerful fellow of eighty, with his head covered with short, tight yellow curls, and this was the father of the fifty-year-old. He guided his gay son with iron hand, never letting his own pipe go out, and saying from time to time, "Laddie, keep the peace. Laddie, don't be disorderly," and at the same time giving him the corresponding shoves and guidance. So he steered him with skilled hand through the turbulent sea until just at the table of the Seven there was a dangerous blockade, as a crowd of farmers happened along who wanted to take the quarrelsome fellow into their midst and make him talk. Fearing that his laddie would attempt some monstrous deviltry, the father looked about him for some refuge and noticed the old men.

"Among these old shiny heads he'll be quiet," he grumbled to himself, and with one fist he grasped his son in the small of the back and steered him in through the benches, while he used the other behind him gently to fan off the angry pursuers; for short as the time was, more than one had already been considerably irritated.

"With your permission, gentlemen," said the ancient one to the

326 · Gottfried Keller

old men, "let me sit down here a minute, so I can give my laddie another glass of wine. Then he'll get sleepy and be as quiet as a lamb."

So he wedged himself into the company with his young scapegrace, and his son did indeed look about him meekly and respectfully. But he said at once, "I'd like to drink out of that little silver cup there."

"Will you be quiet, or I'll drive you into the ground without sharpening you!" said the father; but when Hediger shoved the filled cup toward him he said, "Well, all right then. If the gentlemen will allow it, drink away, but don't swill it all."

"That's a gay lad you have, good man," said Frymann. "How old is he?"

"Oh," said the father, "at New Year's he'll be something like fifty-two; at least he was yelling in my cradle in 1798 when the French came and drove away my cow and burned my house. But because I cracked a couple of their heads together, I had to run away, and my wife died of misery in the meantime. That's why I have to bring up the boy myself."

"Didn't you give him a wife, who could help you?"

"No, so far he's been too clumsy and wild; it won't do, he beats everybody to jelly."

Meanwhile the youthful ne'er-do-well had drained the fragrant cup, without leaving a drop in it. He stuffed his pipe bowl and smiled about the circle most cheerfully and peacefully. Thus he discovered Hermine, and the radiance of womanly beauty that issued from her suddenly rekindled in his heart the old ambition and his propensity for feats of strength. As his eye fell simultaneously on Karl, who was sitting opposite him, he invitingly stretched his crooked middle finger across the table toward him.

"Stop there, lad; has the devil got you again?" cried the old herdsman in anger, and was about to take him by the collar; but Karl bade him let his son be, and hooked his middlefinger in that of the young bear, and now each sought to pull the other over to him.

"If you hurt the gentleman or sprain his finger," said the old man, "I'll take you by the ears so that you'll feel it for a month."

The two hands hovered for some time over the middle of the table; Karl soon stopped laughing and grew fiery red in the face;

but in the end he gradually drew the arm and the body of his opponent perceptibly toward his side, and that decided the victory.

The man from Entlibuch looked at him quite disconcerted and discomfited, but did not have much time for it; for his aged father, nonetheless infuriated at his defeat, boxed his ears, and the son looked at Hermine in utter shame; then he suddenly began to weep and cried, sobbing, "And now I want a wife!"

"Come, come," said his parent, "you're ready for bed now." He grasped him by the arm and made off with him.

After the retreat of this queer couple, a silence fell upon the old men, and all wondered anew at Karl's deeds and achievements.

"That comes simply from gymnastics," he said modestly, "it gives you training, strength, and skill for such things, and almost any one can learn it if he hasn't been neglected by nature."

"So it is," said Hediger senior, after some reflection, and continued with animation, "Therefore let us praise for ever and ever the new time which is again beginning to train men to be men, and which commands not only the squire and the herdsman, but the tailor's son as well, to train his limbs and ennoble his body so that it can bestir itself."

"So it is," said Frymann, who had also aroused himself from reflection, "and we too have all helped in the struggle to bring in this new time. And today we are celebrating with our little troop, as far as we old fellows are concerned, the end, 'cease fire'; and the rest we leave to the young ones. But men have never been able to say of us that we have obstinately clung to error and misunderstanding. On the contrary our efforts have been to the end of always remaining open to the reasonable, the true, and the fair; and therefore I withdraw freely and frankly my declaration with regard to our children, and I invite you, Friend Kaspar, to do the like. For what better establishment, plantation, and foundation can we choose in memory of this day than that of a living shoot sprung straight from the bosom of our friendship, and a house whose children will preserve and transmit the undaunted faith and the principles of the Upright Seven? Well, then, let Burgi hand over his four-poster for us to fit up. I will put into it charm and womanly purity; and you, power, resoluteness and skill. And now forward with the unfurled green banner while they are young! That banner shall be theirs for all time, and they shall preserve it after we are dissolved. So make no further opposition, old Hediger, and give me your hand as kinsman."

"Accepted," said Hediger solemnly, "but on condition that you give the lad no funds for foolishness or boasting. For the devil goeth about and seeketh whom he may devour."

"Accepted," cried Frymann, and Hediger said, "Then I salute you now as kinsman, and let the Swiss Blood be tapped for the wedding."

All seven now arose, and amid great shouts Karl's and Hermine's hands were put together.

"Good luck; here's a betrothal, that's right," cried some of the nearest diners, and at once a throng of people came up to clink glasses with the young couple. Now the orchestra started up, as if ordered; but Hermine extricated herself from the press, without, however, dropping Karl's hand, and he led her out of the hall upon the festival ground, which already lay in nocturnal stillness.

They walked around the flag citadel, and as no one was near they stood still. The flags were waving talkatively and animatedly together, but the banner of friendship they could not discover, as it had disappeared in the folds of some large neighbor and was well taken care of. But high up among the stars flapped the Swiss banner, always lonely, and the rustle of its cloth was now distinctly audible. Hermine put her arms around the neck of her betrothed, kissed him unbidden, and said tenderly and with emotion, "But now our life must be good and right. May we live as long as we are good and capable, and not a day longer!"

"Then I hope to live a long time, for I imagine such a good life with you," said Karl and kissed her in return. "But how about government: are you really going to get me under your thumb?"

"As much as I can! However, law and constitution will surely develop between us, and they will be good in any case."

"And I shall guarantee the constitution, and claim the first position as godfather," suddenly rang out a powerful bass voice.

Hermine stretched her little neck and seized Karl's hand; but he stepped closer and saw one of the sentries of the sharpshooters of Aargau, standing in the shade of a pillar. The metal of his equipment gleamed through the darkness. Now the young men recognized each other: they had been recruits together, and the sentry was a handsome farmer's son. The betrothed couple sat down on the steps at his feet and chatted with him for a full half hour before they returned to the company.

Translated by B. Q. Morgan

From
SEVEN
LEGENDS

Eugenia

The woman shall not wear that which pertaineth unto a man,
neither shall a man put on a woman's garment: for all that do so
are abomination unto the Lord thy God.

Deuteronomy 22:5

When women renounce their ambition of beauty, grace, and womanly charm in order to distinguish themselves in other directions, it sometimes ends in their disguising themselves in men's clothes and disappearing from the scene.

The desire to ape the man often emerges even in the pious legendary world of early Christianity, and more than one female saint of those days was impelled by the desire to free herself from the common round of home and society.

The patrician Roman maiden Eugenia offers an example of this kind, with, it must be owned, the not unusual result that, reduced to the greatest extremity by her masculine predilections, she was forced after all to summon up the resources of her own sex in order to save herself.

She was the daughter of a Roman gentleman who resided with his family at Alexandria, a city which swarmed with philosophers and learned men of every description. Accordingly, Eugenia was very carefully educated and instructed, and this was so much to her taste that, as soon as she began to grow up, she frequented all schools of philosophers, grammarians, and rhetoricians as a student. In those visits she was always attended by a bodyguard of two good-looking lads of her own age. They were the sons of two of her father's freedmen, who had been brought up in her company and made to share in all her studies.

Meanwhile she became the fairest maiden that could be found, and her youthful companions, who, strangely enough, were both named Hyacinth, grew likewise to two graceful flowers of youth. Wherever the lovely rose Eugenia appeared, the two Hyacinths were always to be seen rustling along on her right hand and her left, or following gracefully in her train while their mistress maintained a discussion with them as they followed.

Never were there two better-bred companions for a bluestocking; for they were never of a different opinion from Eugenia, and they always kept a shade behind her in learning, so that she was in the right in every instance, and was never uneasy lest she should say something less clever than her companions.

All the bookworms of Alexandria composed elegies and epigrams on this apparition of the Muses, and the good Hyacinths had to inscribe these verses carefully in golden tablets and carry them after her.

Every season she became more beautiful and more accomplished, and she had even begun to stray in the mysterious labyrinths of Neoplatonic doctrines, when the young proconsul Aquilinus fell in love with Eugenia and demanded her of her father to wife. But the latter entertained such a respect for his daughter that, despite his authority as a Roman father, he did not venture to make the slightest suggestion to her, but referred the suitor to her own decision, although no son-in-law could have been more welcome to him than Aquilinus.

But Eugenia herself had had her eye upon him secretly for many a long day; for he was the most stately, most illustrious, and most gallant man in Alexandria, and, what was more, had the reputation of a man of intelligence and heart.

Yet she received the enamored consul in complete calm and dignity, with her parchment rolls about her and her Hyacinths behind her chair. The one wore an azure-blue, the other a rose-red robe, and she herself one of dazzling white. A stranger would have been uncertain whether he saw three fair, tender boys, or three fresh, blooming maidens before him.

Before this tribunal the manly Aquilinus now came in the simple toga of his rank. He would much rather have uttered his passion in more intimate and tender fashion; but when he saw that Eugenia did not dismiss the young men, he took his seat on a chair facing her and made his request for her hand in words which it cost him an effort to make few and simple, for he kept his eyes fixed immovably upon her and beheld her great beauty.

Eugenia smiled imperceptibly, and never even blushed, so tightly had learning and culture fettered all the finer impulses of ordinary life in her. Instead, she assumed a serious, profound expression, and made answer to him, "Your wish, O Aquilinus, to have me for your wife, honors me in a high degree, but is powerless to induce me to an act of unwisdom; and such it would justly be termed, if we were to follow the first crude impulse without examining ourselves. The first condition which I have to demand from a husband, whoever he be, is that he understand and honor and participate in my intellectual life and aims. So you will be welcome to me if you choose to be often in my society, and to exercise yourself in emulation with these my young companions in the investigation of the highest things along with me. By this means we shall not fail to ascertain whether we are suited for each other or not, and, after a period of intellectual activity in common, we shall know each other as beseems god-created beings who are meant to walk not in the darkness, but in the light."

To this high-flown demand Aquilinus answered, not without secret indignation, but still with proud tranquillity, "If I did not know you, Eugenia, I would not desire you for my wife; and, as to myself, great Rome knows me, as well as this province. If your learning does not suffice to recognize what I am by this time, I fear it will never suffice. Besides, I did not come here to go to school again, but to find a helpmeet; and, as for these two children, my first request, if you gave me your hand, would be that you would let them go and restore them to their parents, that they might help them and be of use to them. Now I entreat you, give me your decision, not as a person of learning, but as a woman of flesh and blood!"

This time the fair philosopher had indeed turned red, red as a carnation, and said with fast-beating heart, "My answer is soon given, for I gather from your words that you do not love me, Aquilinus. That might be a matter of indifference to me, were it not an outrage for the daughter of a noble Roman to be lied to!"

"I never lie!" said Aquilinus coldly. "Farewell!"

Eugenia turned her back without returning his farewell, and Aquilinus walked slowly out of the house to his own abode. She tried to take up her books as if nothing had happened; but the letters grew blurred before her eyes, and the two Hyacinths had to read to her while she, full of hot indignation, wandered with her thoughts elsewhere.

For, although up to that day she had regarded the consul as the only one among all her suitors whom she might have taken for a husband, supposing she had been so inclined, he had now become a stumbling block which she could not get over.

Aquilinus for his part attended calmly to his affairs of state, and sighed in secret over his strange folly, which would not suffer him to forget the pedantic beauty.

Almost two years passed, during which Eugenia became, if possible, more and more notable and a positively brilliant personage, while the two Hyacinths were now two sturdy rustic figures with growing beards. Although people everywhere began to take notice of this strange attachment, and, instead of the admiring epigrams, others in a more satiric vein began to appear, still she could not bring herself to part with her bodyguard; for Aquilinus, who had presumed to order her to do so, was still there. He went quietly on his own way, and appeared to concern himself no more about her; but he looked at no other woman, and no other wooing was heard of, so that he also came in for censure because, being so high an official, he remained unmarried.

Eugenia refrained all the more obstinately from offering any outward sign of reconciliation by dismissing her obnoxious companions. Besides, it pleased her to set ordinary custom and public opinion at defiance and be responsible to herself alone, and to preserve the consciousness of a pure life in circumstances which would have been perilous and impossible for any other woman.

Such eccentricities were in the air around that time.

Eugenia, meanwhile, felt anything but well and happy. Her well-trained servitors had to philosophize through heaven and earth and hell, only to be suddenly interrupted and forced to wander about in the country with her for hours together without being favored with a single word. One day she was seized with the desire to make an excursion to a country seat. She herself drove the carriage, and was in an amiable mood, for it was a bright spring day, and the air was full of balmy fragrance. The Hyacinths were delighted at her good humor. So they made their way through a country suburb where the Christians were permitted to hold their worship. They were in the act of celebrating Sunday; from the chapel of a monastery came the tones of a devout hymn. Eugenia checked her horses to listen, and caught the words of the psalm, "As the hart panteth after the water brooks, so panteth my soul after thee, O God. My soul thirsteth for the living God."

At the sound of these words, sung by humble, pious lips, her artificial life was made simple at last; her heart was touched, and seemed to realize what it desired; and slowly, without a word, she went on her way to the country house. There she secretly put on men's clothes, signed to the two Hyacinths to come with her, and left the house unobserved by the menials. She went back to the convent, knocked at the door, and presented herself and her companions to the abbot as three young men who desired to be received into the convent that they might bid farewell to the world and live for eternity. Thanks to her good training, she was able to answer the abbot's searching questions so cleverly that he received all three, whom he could not help taking for refined and distinguished persons, into the convent, and permitted them to assume the monastic habit.

Eugenia made a beautiful, almost angelic monk, and was called Brother Eugenius, while the two Hyacinths also found themselves transformed into monks for better or worse, for they were never even consulted, and they had long been accustomed only to live according to the will of their female paragon. Still, they did not find the monkish life amiss; they enjoyed incomparably more peaceful days, did not require to study any more, and found no difficulty in surrendering themselves entirely to a passive obedience.

Brother Eugenius, on the other hand, did not remain idle, but became a notable monk, his visage white as marble, but with glowing eyes and the presence of an archangel. He converted many heathen, tended the sick and destitute, became profound in the

Scriptures, preached in a golden bell-like voice, and on the abbot's death was actually chosen to be his successor. So now the tender Eugenia became abbot over seventy good monks, great and small.

During the time that she and her companions were thus mysteriously vanished and were nowhere to be found, her father had made enquiries of an oracle as to what had become of his daughter, and it answered that Eugenia had been taken away by the gods and placed among the stars. The priests utilized the event to contrive a miracle as a counterblast to the Christians, who all the time had the bird safely caged. They went so far as to point out a star in the firmament with two smaller stars adjacent as the new constellation, and the Alexandrians stood in the streets and on their house tops to gaze at it, while many, who had formerly seen her going in and out, recalled her beauty, became enamored of her memory, and looked up with moist eyes to the star, which swam placidly in the purple sky.

Aquilinus too looked up; but he shook his head and was not altogether satisfied about the business. The father of the vanished maiden was all the more obstinate in his credence, felt himself not a little exalted, and contrived, with the support of the priests, to have a statue erected and divine honors decreed to Eugenia. Aquilinus, from whom official sanction had to be obtained, granted it subject to the condition that the image should be made an exact likeness of the lost one. That was easily accomplished, as there was quite a collection of busts and portraits of her in existence, and so her statue in marble was set up in the forecourt of the temple of Minerva, and challenged the inspection of gods and mortals, for, in spite of being a speaking likeness, it was an ideal work in features, pose, and drapery.

When this news was discussed among the seventy monks of the convent, they were bitterly chagrined at the trump card played by the heathen, as well as at the erection of a new idol and the shameless worship of a mortal woman. Their most violent rebukes were showered upon the woman herself as a renegade and juggling impostor, and they made a most unaccustomed noise during their midday meal. The Hyacinths, who had become two good little priestlings and had their abbot's secret concealed in their hearts, glanced significantly towards him, but he signed to them to keep silent, and suffered the outcry and abuse to pass as a penance for his former heathenish sinful mind.

But when that night was half run, Eugenia rose from her couch, took a heavy hammer, and went softly out of the convent to find the statue and break it in pieces. She easily found her way to the quarter of the city, all glistening with marble, where the temples and public buildings were situated, and where she had passed her youth. Not a soul stirred in the silent world of marble. Just as the female monk ascended the steps to the temple, the moon rose above the shadows of the city, and cast its beams as bright as day among the pillars of the forecourt. There Eugenia saw her statue, white as new-fallen snow, standing in wonderful grace and beauty, the finely folded draperies chastely drawn over the shoulders, and looking straight forward with rapt eye and gently smiling mouth.

Full of curiosity the Christian advanced towards it, the hammer uplifted in her hand; but a sweet shudder went through her heart when she obtained a clear view of the statue. She let the hammer sink, and breathlessly fed her gaze on the vision of her own former existence. A bitter regret took possession of her, a feeling as if she had been thrust out of a fairer world and was now wandering, an unhappy shade, in the wilderness. For although the image was elevated to the ideal, still the very ideal represented Eugenia's genuine inner nature, which had only been obscured by her pedantry, and it was a nobler emotion than vanity which now led her to recognize her better self by the magical moonlight. She suddenly felt as if she had played the wrong card—to use a modern expression, for of course there were no cards in those days.

Suddenly the quick step of a man was heard. Eugenia hid herself involuntarily in the shadow of a pillar, and saw the tall form of Aquilinus approaching. She saw how he stationed himself before the statue, gazed long upon it, and finally flung his arm about its neck to imprint a light kiss upon the marble lips. Then he wrapped himself in his mantle and slowly departed, more than once turning round to gaze at the gleaming image.

Eugenia trembled so violently that she could feel her agitation. Full of wrath and violence, she gathered herself together and once again advanced toward the statue with uplifted hammer to make an end of the sinful idol; but, instead of shattering the beauteous head, she burst into tears as she too imprinted a kiss upon its lips, then hastened away, for she could hear the steps of the night watch. With heaving bosom, she slipped into her cell, and slept none that night until the sun arose, when, absenting herself from early prayers, she dreamt in rapid succession of things which had nothing in common with her devotions.

The monks respected their abbot's sleep as the result of spiritual vigils. But at last they were obliged to interrupt Eugenia's slumbers, as there was important business for her to attend to. A widow of rank, who professed to be lying sick and in need of Christian aid, had sent requesting the spiritual comfort and counsel of abbot Eugenius, whose deeds and person she had long revered. The monks did not wish to give up this conquest, which would help the fame of their church, and they wakened Eugenia. Half dazed, with handsomely reddened cheeks, such as she had not been seen with for many a day, she set out, her thoughts on her morning dreams and the pillars of the midnight temple rather than on the business before her.

She entered the heathen lady's house, and was conducted to her room and left alone with her. A beautiful woman, not yet thirty years old, was lying stretched upon a couch; but, so far from being sick and contrite, she was full of assurance and vitality. She could scarcely behave herself with bare quietness and modesty until the supposed monk, at her direction, had taken his seat close beside her; then she caught both his white hands, pressed her brow upon them, and covered them with kisses. Eugenia, who, absorbed in far other thoughts, had not observed the woman's unsaintly appearance, and had taken her behavior for humility and pious devotion, let her have her way; and the heathen, thus encouraged, flung her arms about Eugenia's neck, imagining that she was embracing the handsomest of young monks. In short, before he was aware, he found himself clasped tight by the amorous creature, and felt his mouth the target for a storm of passionate kisses. Completely dumbfounded, Eugenia awoke at last from her reverie; and even then it was some minutes before she could disengage herself from the wild embrace and rise to her feet.

But at the same instant the heathen Satan's tongue began to wag. In a storm of words the she-devil declared her love and desire to the indignant abbot, and sought by all manner of means to impress upon him that it was the duty of his youth and loveliness to assuage her desires, and that he was there for no other purpose. She did not fail to accompany her words with fresh assaults and tender allurements, so that Eugenia was scarcely able to defend herself. At last she rallied herself in indignation, and with flaming eyes read the shameless woman such a lesson and so answered her with such vigorous denunciations as only a monk has at command, that the latter recognized that her wicked intentions had failed, changed her tone in a twinkling, and took the way of escape which was once taken by Potiphar's wife, and has been taken a hundred and a thousand times since. She sprang like a tigress on Eugenia, clasped her again with arms like steel, pulled her down to her upon the couch, and at the same time set up such an outcry that her maids came running into the room from all quarters.

"Help! Help!" she screamed. "This man will force me!" And at the same time she released Eugenia, who got to her feet breathless, confused, horrified.

The women who had rushed to the rescue straightway screamed more desperately than their mistress, hastened hither and thither, and called for male assistance. Eugenia could not utter a word for horror; but made her escape from the house full of shame and disgust, followed by the outcries and curses of the infuriated rabble.

The fiendish widow lost no time in proceeding at once with a goodly following to the consul Aquilinus, and accusing the monk of the most disgraceful crime, to wit that he had come hypocritically to her house, first of all to molest her with efforts for her conversion, and, when these failed, to rob her of her honor by violence. Since all her following testified to the truth of her assertion, the indignant Aquilinus immediately caused the convent to be surrounded by troops, and the abbot along with his monks to be brought before him for trial.

"Is this what you do, you low hypocrites?" he said in severe tones. "Are you so high and mighty, you who are barely tolerated, that you have to assault our womenfolk, and prowl about like ravening wolves? Did your Master, whom I honor more than I do you liars, teach or command you such things? Not at all! You are a gang, a horde of wretches, who assume a name in public that you may abandon yourselves to corruption in secret. Defend yourselves against the charge, if you can!"

The infamous widow then repeated her lying tale, interrupted by hypocritical sighs and tears. When she had finished and had wrapped herself again demurely in her veil, the monks glanced fearfully at one another and at their abbot, of whose virtue they had no doubt, and they raised their voices with one accord to repel the false accusation. But not only the numerous menials of the lying woman, but also several neighbors and passersby, who had seen the abbot leaving the house full of shame and confusion and who had thereupon taken him for guilty, now came forward and testified one after the other with loud voices to the fact of the crime, so that the poor monks were shouted down ten times over.

Now they glanced once more, this time full of doubt, at their abbot, and his very youth suddenly appeared suspicious to the greybeards among them. They exclaimed that, if he were guilty, God's judgment would not be backward, no more than they were backward in abandoning him there and then to the secular arm!

The eyes of all were now directed upon Eugenia, who stood forsaken amid the throng. She had been lying weeping in her cell when she was arrested with the monks, and had stood all that time, her eyes downcast and her cowl drawn deep down over her head, and felt herself in a most awkward predicament. For, if she preserved the secret of her family and sex, she would succumb to this false testimony, while if she revealed it, the storm would break out against the convent more furiously than ever, and she would consign it to destruction, since a convent which had a beautiful young woman for abbot was bound to become the butt of the most unholy suspicion and mockery on the part of the malicious heathen world. She would not have experienced this timidity and indecision had she still had a pure heart, according to monkish notions; but the events of the previous night had already made a division in her mind, and her unfortunate encounter with the wicked woman had only increased her wavering, so that she no longer possessed the courage to step forward with determination and bring about a miracle.

Yet, when Aquilinus called upon her to speak, she remembered his former tenderness for her, and, as she had confidence in him, she hit upon a way of escape. In gentle and modest tones she said that she was not guilty and would prove it to the consul, if she might speak with him alone. The sound of her voice moved Aquilinus, though he knew not why, and he acceded to her request to speak with him in private. He accordingly had her conducted into his house, and repaired alone with her into a room. Then Eugenia fixed her eyes upon him, threw back her cowl, and said, "I am Eugenia, whom you once desired for your wife."

He recognized her at once, and was convinced that it was she; but at the same time a great anger and a burning jealousy rose up within his breast to think that the lost one so suddenly recovered should make her appearance as a woman who had been living all that time in secrecy with seventy monks. He therefore restrained himself with a violent effort and scrutinized her narrowly, while he made as if he did not believe her assertion in the slightest, and said, "You certainly do seem rather like that foolish young woman. But that does not concern me; I am much more anxious to know what you did to the widow!"

Eugenia shyly and anxiously told all that had passed, and from the whole tone of her story Aquilinus perceived the falsehood and malice of the accusation, yet he answered with apparent indifference, "But if you are Eugenia, then how did you contrive to become a monk? What was your intention, and how was it possible?"

At these words, Eugenia blushed and looked on the ground in embarrassment. Still, it seemed to her not so unpleasant after all to be there, and to be talking once again with a good old acquaintance about herself and her adventures. So she lost no time, but told in unstudied words all that had happened to her since her disappearance, except, strangely enough, that she never uttered a syllable about the two Hyacinths. He found the story not unsatisfactory, only every minute made it harder for him to conceal his joy in finding his beloved again. But nevertheless he controlled himself, and determined to see the matter out to the end and to ascertain from her subsequent behavior whether he had the old Eugenia before him, with her chaste and pure manners.

So he said, "All that is a well-told story: still, in spite of her eccentricities, I do not consider that the maiden you pretend to be was capable of such very astonishing adventures. At least, the real

Eugenia would certainly have preferred to become a nun. For how in the world can a monk's cowl and living among seventy monks be a merit and salvation for any woman, even the most learned and pious? No, I still hold to my opinion that you are a smooth-faced beardless fellow of an impostor, whom I don't trust in the slightest! Besides, Eugenia has been proclaimed as deified and dwelling among the stars; her image stands where it was dedicated in the temple, and things will go badly for you if you persist in your slanderous assertion."

"A certain man kissed that image last night," retorted Eugenia in a low voice, casting a curious look at the disconcerted Aquilinus, who gazed upon her as upon one inspired with superhuman wisdom. "How can the same man torture the original?"

He fought back his confusion, appeared not to hear her words, and continued, coldly and severely, "In one word, for the honor of the poor Christian monks, who appear to me to be innocent, I cannot and will not believe that you are a woman. Prepare yourself for judgment, for your statements have not satisfied me."

At that Eugenia exclaimed, "Then God help me!" and, ripping her monk's robe in two, pale as a white rose, she collapsed in shame and despair. But Aquilinus caught her in his arms, pressed her to his heart, and wrapped her in his mantle, while his tears fell upon her lovely head; for he was convinced that she was an honorable woman. He carried her into the next room, where there was a richly furnished guest bed, laid her gently down in it and covered her to the chin with purple coverlets. Then he kissed her on the lips, perhaps three or four times, went out, and locked the door securely. Next he picked up the monk's robe, which lay still warm on the floor, and betook himself again to the waiting throng outside, and addressed them thus, "These are strange happenings! You monks are innocent and may go to your convent. Your abbot was a demon who would have ruined you or seduced you. Here! Take his robe with you and hang it somewhere for a memorial; for, after he had changed his form in the oddest fashion before my eyes, he dissolved into nothing before these same eyes, and vanished without a trace. As for this woman of whom the demon made use in order to ruin you, she is under suspicion of witchcraft and must be put in prison. Now begone all of you to your homes, and behave yourselves!"

All were astounded at this speech, and gazed fearfully at the demon's garment. The widow turned pale and veiled her face, and by so doing made ample betrayal of her bad conscience. The good monks rejoiced over their victory and retired most thankfully with the empty husk, little suspecting what a sweet kernel had been hidden within it. The widow was cast into prison, and Aquilinus summoned his most faithful servant and went through the city, sought out merchants, and purchased a perfect load of the most expensive female attire, which the slave had to convey to the house as secretly and quickly as possible.

Softly the consul slipped into the chamber where Eugenia lay, seated himself on the edge of her bed, and saw that she was sleeping quite contentedly, like one recovering from difficulties undergone. He could not help laughing at the black pile of her shorn monk's head, and passed a gentle hand over the thick, short hair. Thereupon she awoke and opened her eyes.

"Will you be my wife now, at last?" he inquired gently; whereupon she said neither Yes nor No, but shivered a little beneath the purple coverlets in which she lay wrapped.

Then Aquilinus brought in all the clothes and ornaments that a fine lady required in those days to array herself from head to foot, and left her.

After sundown that same day, he took her with him, attended only by his faithful servant, to one of his country houses, which lay in a secluded and charming situation amid the shade of thick trees.

In the country house, the pair now celebrated their nuptials with the utmost privacy; and, for as long as it had been until they found each other again, still no time seemed to have been lost, rather they felt the most hearty thankfulness for the good fortune which had preserved them for each other. Aquilinus devoted the days to his official business, and at night drove as fast as horses could take him home to his wife. Only now and again on unkindly, stormy, wet days, he loved to hasten back earlier than he was expected to the country house to cheer Eugenia.

Without making many words about it, she now devoted herself to the study of connubial love and fidelity, with the same thoroughness and perseverance which she had formerly spent upon philosophy and Christian discipline. But when her hair had grown again to its proper length, Aquilinus, having devised a cunning fable, took his spouse at last back to Alexandria, brought her to her astonished parents, and celebrated a brilliant wedding.

Her father was certainly surprised to find his daughter again, not as an immortal goddess and a heavenly constellation, but as a beloved, earthly, wedded wife, and it was with regret that he saw the consecrated statue removed from the temple; but, to his praise, his disappointment was overcome by his fondness for his living daughter, who now proved fairer and more lovable than ever. The marble statue Aquilinus set in the finest room in his house; but he refrained from kissing it again, now that he had the warm, living original close at hand.

After Eugenia had investigated the nature of marriage to her satisfaction, she applied her experience to converting her spouse to Christianity, which she still continued to profess; and she did not rest until Aquilinus had made public acknowledgment of his adhesion to her faith. The legend goes on to relate how the whole family returned to Rome about the time when that enemy of the Christians, Valerian, came to the throne; and how, during the persecutions which then broke out, Eugenia added to her fame that of a famous heroine of the faith and martyr, and only then made full manifestation of her great strength of soul.

Her influence over Aquilinus had become so great that she was able to bring the two clerics, the Hyacinths, with her from Alexandria to Rome, where they also won the martyr's crown at the same time as she. Her intercession is said to be specially efficacious for dull schoolgirls who are backward in their studies.

Translated by Martin Wyness

The Virgin and the Devil

Friend! be alert, look out, the Devil's all around;
If he gets hold of you, he'll surely pull you down.

Angelus Silesius,
The Cherubinic Wanderer,

Book VI, 206

There was a certain Count Gebizo who possessed a won-
drously beautiful wife, a magnificent castle and town, and so
many valuable possessions that he was esteemed one of the richest
and most fortunate nobles in the country. He seemed to be aware
of and thankful for his reputation, for he not only kept a splendid
and hospitable board, at which his fair and virtuous wife warmed
the hearts of his guests like a sun, but he also practiced Christian
beneficence in the most comprehensive fashion.

He founded and endowed convents and hospitals, beautified
churches and chapels, and on every high day gave clothing, meat,
and drink to a great number, often hundreds, of poor; and several
dozen had to be present every day, almost every hour, about his
courtyard, regaling themselves and praising him, otherwise his
dwelling, fair as it was, would have seemed to him deserted.

But by such unbounded liberality even the greatest wealth is
exhausted, and so it came to pass that the count was obliged to
mortgage all his properties one after the other in order to indulge
his passion for grandiose beneficence and the more he got into
debt the more eagerly he redoubled his almsgiving and feasts to

the poor, hoping thereby, as he imagined, to turn the blessing of Heaven once more in his favor. In the end he impoverished himself entirely; his castle became deserted and fell into ruin; ineffective and foolish foundations and deeds of gift, which from force of habit he could not desist from writing, brought him nothing but ridicule; and any tattered beggar whom he might now and again lure to his castle would throw the meager pittance at his benefactor's feet and take off with scornful words of abuse.

One thing only was left to him unimpaired, the beauty of his wife Bertrade; indeed, the barer things looked in his house, the more brilliant did her beauty seem to grow. She increased too in grace, love, and goodness the poorer Gebizo became, so that all the blessings of Heaven seemed to be comprehended in his wife, and thousands of men envied the count this one treasure which still remained to him. He alone was blind to all this, and the more the fair Bertrade exerted herself to cheer him and sweeten his poverty the less he prized that jewel, and he fell into a bitter and obstinate dejection and hid himself from the world.

One day, when a glorious Easter morning dawned, a day on which he had once been accustomed to see joyous throngs making pilgrimage to his castle, he felt so ashamed of his downfall that he had not even heart to go to church, and was perplexed how to pass the bright sunny feast days. In vain his wife, with pearly tears and smiling lips, begged him not to grieve or be discouraged but come with her to church; he tore himself away crossly, and took himself off to hide in the woods until Easter was over.

Up hill and down dale he wandered, until he came to a primeval wilderness, where monstrous bearded firs surrounded a lake whose depths reflected the gloomy trees in all their length so that everything looked dismal and black. The ground about the lake was thickly carpeted with strange long-fringed moss in which no footfall could be heard.

Here Gebizo sat himself down and complained to God of his wretched ill fortune, which no longer enabled him to still his own hunger sufficiently, after he had gladly satisfied thousands and, worst of all, which recompensed his efforts with the scorn and ingratitude of the world.

Suddenly he observed in the middle of the lake a skiff, and in it a man of lofty stature. As the lake was small and one could easily see across it, Gebizo could not comprehend where the boatman could have come from so suddenly, for he had not observed him anywhere before. Enough, he was now there, gave one stroke of his oar, and immediately was on the shore beside the knight, and, before the latter could gather his wits, had enquired of him why he turned such a rueful face to the world. In spite of his extremely handsome exterior, the stranger had an expression of deep-seated discontent about his mouth and eyes; yet this was the very thing which gained Gebizo's confidence, and without any reserve he poured out the tale of his misfortunes and grievances.

"You are a fool," the other responded, "for you possess a treasure greater than all that you have lost. If I had your wife, I should never give a thought to all the riches and churches and convents, nor to all the beggar folk in the world."

"Give me back those things, and you are welcome to my wife in exchange!" retorted Gebizo with a bitter laugh, and the other exclaimed quick as lightning, "A bargain! Look under your wife's pillow; there you will find what will suffice for all your lifetime to build a convent every day, and feed a thousand people, though you should live to a hundred. In exchange, bring me your wife here to this spot without fail the evening before Walpurgis!"

With these words, such a fire spurted from his dark eyes that two reddish beams glanced over the count's sleeve, and thence over moss and fir trees. Then Gebizo saw whom he had before him, and accepted the man's offer. The latter plied his oar, and sailed back to the middle of the lake, where he and his boat sank into the water with a din which resembled the laughter of many brazen bells.

Gebizo, all gooseflesh, hastened back by the shortest path to his castle, searched Bertrade's bed at once, and found under her pillow an old, shabby book which he could not decipher. But, as he turned over the leaves, one gold piece after another fell out. As soon as he observed this, he went with the book to the deepest vault of a tower, and there, in the utmost secrecy, set to work and spent all the rest of Easter in turning out an ample heap of gold from the pages of this most interesting work.

Then he appeared in the world once again, redeemed all his possessions, summoned workmen who restored his castle more magnificently than ever, and dispensed benefactions on every hand like a prince who had been newly crowned. The principal of his works, however, was the foundation of a great abbey for five hundred capitulars of the utmost piety and distinction, a regular town of saints and scholars, in the center of which his burial place was one day to be. He considered this provision requisite for his eternal salvation. But, as his wife was otherwise provided for, no burial place was prepared for her.

The midday before Walpurgis he gave the order to saddle, and bade his fair wife mount her white hunter, as she had a long journey to ride in his company. At the same time he forbade a single squire or servant to attend them. A great dread seized the poor woman; she trembled in every limb, and for the first time in her life she lied to her husband, pretending that she was unwell, and begging him to leave her at home. As she had been singing to herself only a little time before, Gebizo was incensed at the falsehood, and considered that he had now acquired a double right over her. She was forced therefore to mount her horse, dressed in her best finery, and she rode away sadly with her husband, not knowing where she was going.

When they had accomplished about half their journey, they came to a little church which Bertrade had happened to build in former days and had dedicated to the Mother of God. She had done it for the sake of a poor mastermason whom no one would employ, because he was so surly and disagreeable, that even Gebizo, whom others could not help approaching in a pleasant and respectful fashion, could not tolerate him, and sent him away empty-handed despite all the work which he had to give out. She had caused the little church to be built secretly, and in his gratitude the despised mastermason had with his own hands wrought a remarkably beautiful image of Mary in his spare time, and set it over the altar.

Bertrade now craved to enter this church for a moment and say her prayers, and Gebizo allowed her, for he thought she might have much need of them. So she dismounted from her horse and, while her husband waited outside, went in, knelt before the altar, and commended herself to the protection of the Virgin Mary. Thereupon she fell into a deep sleep; the Virgin sprang down from the altar, assumed the form and garments of the sleeper, went gaily out by the door, and mounted the horse, on which she continued the journey at Gebizo's side and in Bertrade's stead.

The wretch thought to continue to deceive his wife and, the nearer they came to the journey's end, to lull her and hoodwink her by an increase of friendliness. Accordingly he talked with her of this and that, and the Virgin chatted pleasantly and gave him confiding answers, and behaved as if she had lost all her timidity. So they reached the gloomy wilderness about the lake, over which dun evening clouds hung; the ancient firs bloomed purple with buds, as only happens in the most luxuriant springtides; in the thicket a ghostly nightingale sang as loud as organpipes and cymbals; and out from among the fir trees rode a familiar gentleman, mounted on a black stallion, in rich knightly array, with a long sword at his side.

He approached very courteously, although he suddenly shot such a ferocious look at Gebizo that his flesh crept; still, the horses did not appear to scent anything dangerous, for they stood quiet. Trembling, Gebizo flung his wife's reins to the stranger and galloped off alone without so much as a glance back to her. The stranger grabbed the reins and away they went like a whirlwind through the firs, so that the fair rider's veil and garments fluttered and waved, away over mountain and valley, and over the flowing waters so that the horses' hoofs scarcely touched the foam of their waves. Hurried along by the boisterous storm, a rosy, fragrant cloud, which shone in the twilight, was wafted in front of the steeds; and the nightingale flew invisible before the pair, settling here and there upon a tree and singing until the air rang again.

At last all hills and all trees came to an end, and the two rode into an endless heath, in the midst of which, as if from afar, the nightingale throbbed, although there was no sign of bush or bough on which it could have perched.

Suddenly the rider halted, sprang from his horse, and helped the lady out of the saddle with the manner of a perfect cavalier. Scarcely had her foot touched the heath, when round about the pair there sprang up a garden of rose bushes as tall as a man, with a splendid fountain and seat, above which a starry firmament shone so brilliantly that one could have seen to read by its light. But the fountain consisted of a great round basin in which, like modern *tableaux vivants,* a number of devils formed, or represented, a seductive group of nymphs in white marble. They poured shimmering water from their hollowed hands—where they got it from, their lord and master only knew. The water made the most lovely harmony; for every jet gave out a different note, and the whole seemed in concert like string music. It was, so to say, a water-harmonica, whose chords were thrilled through and through with all the deliciousness of that first night of May, and melted into unison with the charming forms of the group of nymphs; for the living picture did not stand still, but changed and turned imperceptibly.

Not without tender emotion, the stranger cavalier conducted the lady to the seat and invited her to be seated; but then he gripped her hand with a violent tenderness, and said in a voice that pierced to the marrow, "I am the Eternally Forlorn who fell from Heaven! Nothing but the love of a good mortal woman on May-night can make me forget Paradise and give me strength to endure my eternal discomfiture. Be my helpmeet, and I will make thee eternal, and grant thee the power of doing good and preventing evil to thy heart's content!"

He flung himself passionately on the bosom of the beauteous woman, who smilingly opened her arms. But at the same instant the Blessed Virgin assumed her Heavenly form, and enclosed the entrapped Deceiver in her radiant arms with all her might. In a twinkling, the garden had vanished with its fountain and nightingale; the cunning demons, who had formed the tableau, took flight in the form of evil spirits, uttering cries of anguish, and left their lord in the lurch; while he, never uttering a sound, wrestled with titanic strength to free himself from the torturing embrace.

But the Virgin held on bravely and did not let him go, though indeed she had to summon all her strength. She intended nothing less than to bring the outmaneuvered Devil before Heaven, and there expose him, bound to a gatepost in all his wretchedness, to the laughter of the blessed.

But the Evil One changed his tactics, kept still for a brief space, and assumed the beauty which he had once possessed as the fairest among the angels, so that he almost rivalled the celestial beauty of Mary. She exalted herself as much as possible; yet, if she was radiant as Venus the fair Evening Star, he shone like Lucifer the Son of the Morning, so that it began to be as bright on that dusky heath as if the heavens themselves had descended upon it.

When the Virgin perceived that she had undertaken too much, and that her strength was failing, she contented herself with releasing the Fiend on condition that he renounce the count's wife, and the celestial and infernal beauties forthwith separated with great violence. The Virgin, somewhat wearied, went back to her little church; the Evil One, incapable of any further disguise and mauled in every limb, crawled away over the sand in horrid, degraded form, the very embodiment of long-tailed sorrow. So badly had his intended hour of dalliance turned out for him.

Meantime Gebizo, after abandoning his lovely wife, had gone astray in the darkening night, and horse and rider had fallen into a chasm, where his head was dashed against a stone so that he promptly departed this life.

As for Bertrade, she remained in her sleep until the sun rose on the first of May; then she awoke, and was surprised to see how the time had flown. Still, she quickly said her Ave Maria, and, when she came out of the church hale and hearty, her horse was standing before the door as she had left it. She did not wait long for her husband, but rode home blithely and quickly, for she guessed that she had escaped from some great peril.

Soon the count's body was found and brought home. Bertrade had it entombed with all honor, and founded innumerable masses for him. But all love for him was in some inexplicable way eradicated from her heart, although it remained as kind and tender as ever. Accordingly, her exalted patroness in Heaven looked about for another husband for her, who should be more worthy of such gracious love than the deceased Gebizo had been. How this business came about is written in the next legend.

Translated by Martin Wyness

The Virgin as Knight

Mary has been called a throne and God's pavilion,
An ark, a fort, a tower, house, well, tree,
*   garden, mirror,*
A sea, a star, the moon, the morning light, a hill:
How can she be all this? She is another world.

Angelus Silesius,
The Cherubinic Wanderer, Book II, 42

In addition to his original estates, Gebizo had acquired so many
new ones that Bertrade now ruled over a considerable earldom
and was famous in German lands for her wealth as well as her
beauty. Since she also exhibited great modesty and friendliness toward everyone, the jewel that was her person seemed to all noble-
men, whether enterprising or shy, bold or timorous, great or petty,
easy to win, and many a one, when he had once seen her, asked
himself why she was not already his wife. Nonetheless, more than
a year had passed and no one had yet been heard of who really
had cause for hope.

The Emperor had also heard of her and since he wished to see
such an important fief in the hands of the right man, he determined to visit the famous widow on one of his journeys and announced his purpose to her in a kind and friendly letter. The letter
he gave to a young knight called Zendelwald, who happened to

be riding just that way. Bertrade received him graciously and entertained him as she did everyone who came to her castle. With great respect, he inspected the splendid halls, the battlements and the gardens, and incidentally fell violently in love with the owner. But he did not on that account stay a single hour longer at the castle. When his mission was accomplished and he had seen everything, he briefly said farewell to the lady and rode away, the only one of all who had been here who had not thought of trying to win this prize for himself.

Zendelwald was a man indolent in deed and word. When his mind and heart had become set on something—which always took place with wholehearted passion—he could not make himself take the first step to bring about its realization, for the matter seemed to him settled when he was inwardly certain about it. Although he enjoyed conversation when it was not a question of achieving some end, he never said a word at the right moment, though that would have brought him luck. But his thoughts were not only ahead of his speech, they were also ahead of his hand, so that in battle he was often almost conquered by his foes because he hesitated to strike the final blow, since he saw his opponent already lying at his feet. For this reason, his mode of combat aroused wonderment at all the tournaments: at first he would scarcely bestir himself and then only in dire straits would he gain the victory by giving himself a vigorous jolt.

Deep in thought about the beautiful Bertrade, Zendelwald rode toward his own castle, which lay in a wooded mountain solitude. His only vassals were a few charcoal burners and woodcutters; therefore his mother always awaited his return with bitter impatience, wondering whether he would finally bring home some good fortune.

His mother was as active and determined as Zendelwald was easy going, though it hadn't done her much good, for she too had always brought her inborn traits to bear too vigorously and thus defeated her own purpose. In her youth she had tried to find a husband as quickly as possible and had on several occasions so eagerly overplayed her hand that in her impatience she finally made the worst possible choice in the person of a thoughtless, foolhardy young fellow who rapidly squandered his inheritance, met an early death and left her nothing but a long widowhood, poverty and a son who would not exert himself to take advantage of his opportunities.

The sole subsistence of this small family consisted in the milk of a few goats, wild berries and game. Zendelwald's mother was an accomplished hunter and shot with her crossbow as many doves and woodcocks as she liked. She also caught trout in the brooks and plastered the damaged spots on their little castle with lime and stone with her own hands. Now she had just come home with a hare she had shot and, looking out over the valley as she hung the carcass before the kitchen window, she saw her son come riding up the road. She lowered the drawbridge with much joy, for he had been away many months.

She immediately began to try to find out whether he had not caught at least the tail or a feather of some piece of good luck and brought it with him, something one could wisely hang on to, but when he related the experiences of his last expedition, which were as insignificant as usual, she angrily shook her head, and when he then finally mentioned his errand to the rich and charming Bertrade and praised her kindness and beauty, she called him a lazybones and a good-for-nothing because of his shameful retreat. When she saw, as she soon did, that Zendelwald was thinking of nothing but the distant noblewoman, she grew even more impatient because he had not the slightest notion of what to do with such a fine passion, his mooning infatuation constituting a hindrance rather than a stimulus to action.

So it was that Zendelwald had some rather hard days. His mother sulked and out of vexation repaired the tumbledown roof of the castle tower to distract herself, and her poor son trembled to see her climbing about up there. In her surly humor, she tossed down broken tiles and almost killed a horseman who was just coming through the gate to ask for a night's lodging.

At supper, however, the traveller succeeded in winning the friendliness of the austere lady by relating a number of good anecdotes and especially by telling her about the Emperor's visit to the great castle of the beautiful widow, which was now in progress. Here one gay time was following on the heels of another, he said, and the delightful noblewoman was constantly being besieged by the Emperor and his entourage to choose a husband from among the latter. She had resorted to the expedient of announcing a great tournament, promising her hand to the victor over all the others, firmly trusting that her protectress, the Holy Virgin, would intervene and guide the arm of the right man, the man most worthy of her, to victory.

"That would be an undertaking for you," said the stranger in conclusion, turning to Zendelwald, "a handsome young man like you ought to set his mind to that and win the best prize the world has to offer in these times of ours. People are also saying that the lady is hoping some unknown piece of luck will turn up in this way, some poor virtuous hero she can spoil to her heart's content, because these grand counts and vain suitors all go against her grain."

When the stranger had ridden away, the mother said, "Now I'll just bet it was Bertrade herself who sent that messenger to tempt you onto the right track, my dear Zendelwald! A blind man could see that. What else would such a character—who, by the way, drank up our last jug of wine—be doing riding around in the woods?"

At these words her son began to laugh heartily and then laughed harder and harder, partly because of the patent absurdity of these maternal pretensions, partly because they were so much to his liking. The mere idea that Bertrade could want him for a husband made him hold his sides with laughter. But his mother, who thought he was making fun of her, became angry and cried, "Listen to me! I'll give you my curse, if you don't obey me this instant and set out to gain the good fortune that's being offered to you. And don't come home a loser! If you do, I never want to see you again. But if you do come back anyway, I'll take my crossbow and go away myself and seek a grave where I'm unmolested by your stupidity!"

So Zendelwald had no choice. For the sake of peace, he heaved a sigh, inspected his weapons, and rode off in the direction of Bertrade's castle, commending himself to God, but unconvinced that he would actually reach his destination. Nonetheless, he stuck to the road fairly conscientiously and the nearer he came to his goal, the more distinctly did the idea take shape within him that he could really undertake this matter as well as the next man, and that when he had disposed of his rivals, it wouldn't cost him his head to venture a dance with the beautiful lady. Bit by bit, his adventurous undertaking began to take place in his imagination and turned out very well indeed. For days, as he rode through the summer-green land, he even held sweet converse with his beloved, inventing the loveliest things to say to her, so that she blushed with pride and joy. All this in his imagination.

Just as he was again inwardly picturing a joyous moment, he looked up and saw in reality on a line of blue hills the towers and battlements of Bertrade's castle shining forth in the morning light, the golden balustrades gleaming in the distance. This so alarmed him that all his dream work evaporated, leaving him with only a timid and irresolute heart.

Involuntarily, he reined in his horse and looked around, as the irresolute will, for some kind of refuge. At this moment he noticed a graceful little chapel, the very one that Bertrade had built to the Mother of God, the one in which she slept that famous sleep. He immediately decided to go in and collect his thoughts a bit before the altar, particularly since it was the day on which the tournament was being held.

The priest was just celebrating mass with only two or three poor people in attendance, so the knight was no small ornament to the congregation. When everything was over and the priest and the sexton had left, Zendelwald felt so much at home in this place of refuge that he comfortably went to sleep, forgetting both tournament and beloved, unless he dreamt of them.

Then the Virgin again descended from her altar, assumed his shape and donned his armor, mounted his horse and rode with closed visor, a bold Brunhilde, toward the castle in Zendelwald's stead.

After she had ridden a way, she saw lying beside the road a mound of grey debris and dry twigs. The attentive Virgin found this suspicious. She noticed besides that something like the end of a serpent's tail was peeking out from beneath this pile. Then she saw that it was the Devil, who, still in love, had also been sneaking about in the neighborhood of the castle and had quickly hidden from her in this rubbish heap. Pretending to pay no attention, she rode on past, but skillfully caused her mount to make a little sideward leap, so that it trod on the suspicious tail with a hind hoof.

Amused by this little adventure, she rode on full of good spirits right up to Bertrade's castle, arriving just when the two strongest contenders were left to decide the contest between them.

Slowly and nonchalantly, exactly like Zendelwald, she rode out onto the jousting field, seemingly undecided whether she wanted to enter the lists or not.

"There comes Zendelwald, late as usual," the people said, and the two strong knights asked, "What does *he* want from us? Let's finish him off in a hurry, then settle this matter between ourselves!"

One of these doughties called himself "Guhl the Swift." His favorite method of combat was to wheel his steed about like a whirlwind and try to confuse and conquer his opponents with a hundred tricks and dodges. It was with him that the supposed Zendelwald first had to do battle. He wore a pitch-black moustache whose ends stood out in the air horizontally so stiffly that two little silver bells attached to them could not bend them. The bells kept tinkling whenever Guhl moved his head. He called this the chime of terror for his enemies, the chime of delight for his lady. His shield gleamed, according to the way he turned it, now in one color, now in another, and he knew how to manipulate this alternation so rapidly that it blinded the eye. His helmet plume consisted of a tremendous rooster's tail.

The other sturdy knight called himself "Mouse the Numberless," by which he meant to signify that he was to be regarded as the equivalent of an untold army. As a sign of his might, he had let the hairs protruding from his nostrils grow to the length of about six inches and had braided them in two little pigtails that hung down over his mouth and were adorned at the ends with dainty red ribbons. Over his armor he wore a great loose cloak almost covering both him and his horse, artfully sewn together out of thousands of tiny mouse pelts. The outspread wings of a green hat, which served as the crest of his helmet, overshadowed his face and from beneath these wings he darted threatening looks from his slitty eyes.

The signal for battle with Guhl was now sounded. He rode forth toward the Virgin and began to prance about her in circles with ever-increasing rapidity, seeking to blind her with his shield and directing at her a hundred lance thrusts. Meanwhile she remained in the same spot in the middle of the field, seeming merely to ward off his attacks with her spear and shield and wheeling her horse with great dexterity on its hind legs so that she always faced the enemy. When Guhl noticed this, he suddenly rode away, then charged at her with lowered lance, attempting to knock her over.

Motionlessly, the Virgin awaited his charge. Man and horse seemed made of bronze, so firmly did they stand there. Not realizing that he was engaged in combat with a higher power, the poor chap ran against her spear, breaking his own like a straw, and before he knew it, it had flown out of the saddle and was lying on the ground. The Virgin immediately sprang from her horse, knelt on his chest, so that he could not budge beneath her tremendous strength, cut off with her dagger both mustachios with their little silver bells and fastened them to her baldric, while fanfares proclaimed her, or rather Zendelwald, the victor.

It was now the turn of Mouse the Numberless to join the dance. He charged in mightily, his cloak swaying behind him in the breeze like a grey cloud threatening disaster. But Virgin-Zendelwald, who now seemed to be warming to the battle, galloped toward him just as sturdily, easily knocking him out of the saddle at the first thrust, and then, while Mouse picked himself up and drew his sword, she sprang from her horse, in order to fight with him on foot.

He was soon stunned by the rapid blows that fell from her sword on his head and shoulders and, holding his cloak before him with his left hand, he hid behind it, awaiting a favorable opportunity to throw it over the head of his opponent. But the Virgin caught the tip of the cloak with the point of her sword and wrapped Mouse the Numberless from head to foot in his own garment with such elegant rapidity that in a short space he looked like a gigantic wasp cocooned by a spider and lay twitching on the ground.

The Virgin now threshed him with the flat of her sword with such agility that his cloak decomposed into its component parts and the air was darkened with flying mouse pelts—to the uproarious amusement of the spectators. During the process the knight himself gradually came to light and, after his conqueror had cut off his beribboned pigtails, limped away, a beaten man.

So it was that the Virgin as Zendelwald gained the field.

She raised her visor, strode up to the queen of the tournament, bent her knee and laid the trophies of victory at her feet. Then she rose and played the part of a Zendelwald such as Zendelwald himself was usually too bashful to be. Without too far compromising his modesty, she greeted Bertrade with a look whose effect on a woman's heart she well knew. In short, she knew how to conduct herself as a lover as well as a knight in such a way that Bertrade did not take back her promise but lent a willing ear to the urging of the Emperor, who was, after all, glad to see such a brave and noble man.

In festive procession the company now moved toward the linden garden with its high trees, where a banquet had been prepared. Bertrade sat between the Emperor and her Zendelwald, but it was good that the former was also provided with a lively neighbor, for the latter did not leave his prospective bride much time to talk to anyone else, so cleverly and tenderly did he entertain her. He must have told her some very lovely things, for she blushed happily again and again.

Serene bliss took possession of the whole company: in the high leafy arbors bird song vied with the musical instruments, a butterfly settled on the Emperor's golden crown, and from the beakers of wine there issued by special blessing a fragrance of violets and mignonette. But Bertrade above all felt so happy that, while Zendelwald was holding her hand, she remembered in her heart her protectress and offered up to her a fervent, quiet prayer of thanksgiving.

The Virgin Mary, who was of course sitting beside her in the form of Zendelwald, read this prayer in her heart and was so pleased at the pious gratitude of her protegée that she tenderly embraced her and planted a kiss on her lips, which understandably filled the lovely lady with heavenly bliss; for when heaven-dwellers once set about making fancy desserts, they turn out to be pretty sweet.

The Emperor and the rest of the company heartily congratulated Zendelwald, raised their cups and drank to the health of the beautiful couple.

In the meantime, the real Zendelwald had awakened from his untimely sleep and, seeing the sun so far down the sky, thought the tournament must be over. Although he was now safely shut of that business, he still felt very sad and downcast, for he now would have only too gladly married Lady Bertrade. Furth did not dare return to his mother. He therefore decided to begin an everlasting joyless wandering until death released him from his useless existence. But he wanted to see his beloved once more before he set out and impress her image upon his mind for the rest of his days, so that he would always know what he had missed.

He therefore proceeded on up to the castle. As he neared the throng, he heard everyone praising the good fortune of a poor knight named Zendelwald, who had won the prize, and full of embittered curiosity to learn who his lucky namesake might be, he dismounted and pushed through the crowd until he found a raised spot at the edge of the garden where he could overlook the whole festival.

From there, not far from the Emperor's gleaming crown, he caught sight of his beloved, dressed in magnificent finery, her face beaming with happiness, but head by head with her he also saw to his stunned amazement his own person, just as he lived and breathed. With a hypnotized stare, he saw his double embrace and kiss his devout fiancée; then he strode, unnoticed in the general rejoicing, straight through the ranks of the revelers until he stood, tortured by a strange jealousy, directly behind the couple.

At the same instant his double vanished from beside Bertrade, and she looked about for him with startled eyes. But when she saw Zendelwald standing behind her, she laughed with joy and said, "Where did you go? Come, stay right here beside me!"

So there he sat and, in order to put the supposed dream to the proof, he picked up the cup standing before him and emptied it at one draught. The wine passed the test and infused confidence into his veins. In a good mood, he turned to his smiling consort and looked into her eyes, whereupon she resumed the intimate conversation in which she had been interrupted. But Zendelwald didn't know what was happening to him when Bertrade said things he was sure he had already heard. Without thinking, he answered her several times in words that he too had already uttered somewhere or other, then after a while he realized that his predecessor must have had exactly the same conversation with her that he had conducted in his imagination on his ride to the castle. This conversation he now cautiously continued, curious to see how the game would end.

But did not end; on the contrary, it became ever more edify-

ing, and when the sun set, torches were lighted and the whole
company removed to the great castle hall to take their pleasure in
dancing. After the Emperor had had the first dance with the future
bride, Zendelwald took her in his arms and danced three or four
times around the hall until Bertrade, with flushed face, led him
aside by the hand into a quiet alcove bathed in moonlight. There
she threw herself on his bosom, stroked his blond beard and
thanked him for coming and for his affection.

Honest Zendelwald, however, now wanted to know whether he
was dreaming or waking and inquired closely into the true stat
of affairs, especially concerning his double. Bertrade did not know
what he meant, but one word led to another and Zendelwald said
this and that happened to me, and he told about his whole journey, his visit to the chapel, how he had fallen asleep there and
missed the tournament.

Then the matter became clear enough to Bertrade for her again
to see in it the hand of her gracious patroness. Now it was possible for her to regard the bold knight as nothing less than a gift of
heaven and she was thankful to be able to press this sturdy gift
right to her heart and to return in full measure the sweet kiss she
had received from heaven itself.

From this time on Zendelwald entirely renounced his indolence
and dreamy indecisiveness. He always spoke and acted at the right
moment, in the presence of his tender Bertrade as well as in society, and became a man of consequence in the realm, so that the
Emperor was as satisfied with him as was his spouse.

Zendelwald's mother appeared on horseback at the wedding, as
proud as though she had enjoyed good fortune all her life. She
managed the money and the estate and hunted to a ripe old age
in the extensive forests, while Bertrade would not forego the pleasure of having Zendelwald take her once a year to his lonely native castle, where she roosted with her lover in the grey tower as
tenderly as the wild doves in the surrounding trees. But on the
way she never forgot to step into the little chapel and offer a prayer
to the Virgin, who stood on her altar as still and holy as though
she had never descended from it.

Translated by Robert M. Browning

The Virgin and the Nun

Oh that I had wings like a dove!
For then would I fly away and be at rest.

Psalm 55:6

A cloister with a distant view over the countryside lay on a mountain and gleamed across the lands. Within, however, it was full of women, beautiful and not beautiful, who all served the Lord and his Virgin Mother according to a strict discipline.

The most beautiful of the nuns was called Beatrix and was the sexton of the cloister. Of splended figure, she performed her duties with a noble gait, ruled in the sacristy and rang the bell before dawn and at the rising of the evening star.

But between times she often gazed with damp eyes out into the glister of the bluish landscape; she saw the glint of arms, heard the huntsman's horn in the forest and the clear ringing shouts of men, and her breast was full of longing for the world.

When she could suppress her yearning no longer, she rose from her cot one moonlit night in June, put on strong new shoes and stepped before the altar, ready to begin her wanderings. "I have served you faithfully for many a year," she said to the Virgin Mary, "but now take back the keys, for I can no longer endure the longing in my heart!"

Then she laid her bunch of keys on the altar and left the cloister. She went down through the mountain solitude and walked until she reached a crossroads, where, undecided which turn to take, she sat down beside a spring walled with stone and provided with a bench for passersby. There she sat until the sun came up and she was dampened by the morning dew.

Then the sun rose above the treetops and its first beams playing through the woodland road struck a glorious knight riding along quite alone in full armor. The nun looked at him with her lovely eyes as hard as she could and missed not an inch of his manly figure, but she kept so still that the knight would not have seen her if the sound of the spring had not caught his ear and made him glance in that direction.

He immediately turned toward the spring, got off his horse and let it drink, meanwhile greeting the nun respectfully. He was a crusader wending his way homeward after a long absence and after having lost all his men. In spite of his respectful attitude, he never took his eyes off the beauteous Beatrix, who in turn never took her eyes off him, but gazed in continual amazement at this martial man; for he was a considerable piece of the world for which she had secretly yearned for such a long time. Then she suddenly lowered her gaze and felt ashamed.

Finally the knight asked her which way she was going and whether he could be of service to her. The loud clear ring of his voice startled her. She looked at him again and confessed that she had fled her cloister in order to see the world, but that she was already afraid and did not know which way to turn.

At this the knight gave a hearty laugh and offered to guide the lady to a good road, if she would entrust herself to his care. His castle, he added, was no more than a day's journey distant; there she could, if she liked, prepare herself in safety for the beautiful wide world.

Without replying, but also without resisting, she allowed herself to be lifted onto the horse. The knight swung himself into the saddle after her and, with the happy nun before him, trotted merrily on through forest and meadow.

The knight was delighted with the winsome little nun and the virgin also soon grew very fond of him. Before long she was listening to his words of love as eagerly as though she had never rung a cloister bell.

Under such circumstances they saw nothing of the countryside nor of the light that bathed it; and the nun, who had just been longing for the wide world, now closed her eyes before it and limited herself to the locality that could be carried on horseback.

Wonnebold, the knight, also hardly thought of his ancestral castle until its towers were gleaming before him in the moonlight. Here all was quiet without and even quieter within and nowhere was a light to be seen. Wonnebold's father and mother had died and all the retainers had left except for the ancient shrunken castellan, who after much knocking appeared with a lantern and almost fainted with joy when he saw the knight before the door he had finally managed to open.

But in spite of his years and his solitude the old man had kept the interior of the castle in a livable condition, so that the knight and his prospective bride could comfortably rest from their journey.

The next morning Wonnebold opened his mother's clothespresses. Beatrix dressed herself in the fine garments and adorned herself with the jewelry. The same day Wonnebold made the beautiful Beatrix his wife, so that she could now play an unrivaled role as a noble lady at hunt, festival and dance as well as in the cottages of the vassals and in the laird's pew at church.

The years passed with their vicissitudes and in twelve fertile autumns she gave her husband eight sons who grew up like young stags. When the oldest was eighteen, she rose one autumn night from beside her Wonnebold without his noticing it, carefuly laid her worldly finery back in the same clothespresses from which it had once been taken, closed them, and laid the keys at the side of her sleeping husband.

Then she went barefoot to the sleeping quarters of her sons and softly kissed one after the other; finally she returned to her husband's bed, kissed him too, then cut the long hair from her head, donned again the dark nun's habit she had carefully put away and secretly left the castle, walking through the windy autumn night and the fallen leaves towards the cloister from which she had once fled.

Ceaselessly she let the beads of her rosary slip through her fingers, thinking as she prayed about the life she had enjoyed. She walked on patiently until she stood again before the portal of the cloister. When she knocked, the aged portress opened the wicket and greeted her indifferently by name, as though she had hardly been away half an hour.

Beatrix went past her into the church, threw herself on her knees before the altar of the Holy Virgin, who began to speak, saying, "You stayed away a bit long, my daughter! I have fulfilled your duties as sexton the whole time, but now I'm glad you are back to take the keys again!" The image bent down and gave Beatrix the keys. She started in joyful fright at the great miracle. Then she at once set about her tasks, putting one thing and another in order, and when the bell rang for the midday meal, she went to the refectory.

Many of the nuns had grown old, others had died, new ones had arrived, and another abbess was sitting at the head of the table, but no one noticed what had happened to Beatrix, who sat down in her usual place, for Mary had filled her office in the nun's own form.

After some ten more years had passed, the nuns were to celebrate a great festival. They had agreed that each of them should offer the Mother of God the finest gift she could prepare. One embroidered a precious ecclesiastical banner, another an altar cloth, a third a vestment. One composed a Latin hymn and another set it to music, while a third copied and illuminated a prayer book. Those who could do nothing else sewed a new shirt for the Christ Child, and the Sister Cook fried him a plate of doughnuts.

Beatrix alone had prepared nothing, for she was rather tired from living and her thoughts clung more to the past than to the present.

When the festive day dawned and she had no consecrated gift to offer, the other nuns were surprised and blamed her for standing so humbly at one side when all those splendid things were laid before the altar in a solemn procession to the ringing of bells and the scent of rising incense in the flower-adorned church.

As the nuns now began to sing and make lovely music, a grey-haired horseman accompanied by eight young men beautiful as day, all armed and mounted on proud steeds and followed by eight squires, came riding by. It was Wonnebold with his sons, whom he was taking to join the imperial army.

Hearing high mass being celebrated in the house of God, he told his sons to dismount and entered the church with them to offer a prayer to the Holy Virgin. Everyone was astounded at the magnificant sight when the hale old man knelt with the eight youthful warriors, who looked like angels in armor. The nuns lost the place in their music and had to pause for a moment.

But Beatrix recognized all her children by her husband, and hastening toward them with a cry, she made herself known, publically revealed her secret and told of the great miracle she had experienced.

Now everyone had to admit that it was she who had this day offered the richest gift to the Virgin; that it was accepted, eight wreathes of young oakleaf, which were suddenly to be seen on the brows of the youths, placed there by the invisible hand of Heaven's Queen, bore witness.

Translated by Robert M. Browning

ACKNOWLEDGMENTS

We gratefully acknowledge permission to reprint material from the following publications:

Clothes Make the Man, from *Twelve German Novellas,* edited and translated by Harry Steinhauer. Copyright © 1977 by the University of California Press. Reprinted by permission of the University of California Press.
The Banner of the Upright Seven, from Gottfried Keller, *The Banner of the Upright Seven* and *Ursula,* translated by Bayard Quincy Morgan. Copyright © 1974 by Frederick Ungar Publishing Co., Inc. Reprinted by permission of the publisher.
Eugenia and *The Virgin and the Devil,* translated by Martin Wyness, appeared in *Legends and People,* Story Classics Division of the Rodale Press, special contents copyright © 1953 by J. I. Rodale.